Principles of Conducting Qualitative Research in Multicultural Settings

Ali Elhami
Unicaf University, Larnaca, Cyprus

Anita Roshan
Universidad Autónoma de Madrid, Spain

Harish Chandan
Independent Researcher, USA

A volume in the Advances in Library and
Information Science (ALIS) Book Series

Published in the United States of America by
    IGI Global
    Information Science Reference (an imprint of IGI Global)
    701 E. Chocolate Avenue
    Hershey PA, USA 17033
    Tel: 717-533-8845
    Fax: 717-533-8661
    E-mail: cust@igi-global.com
    Web site: http://www.igi-global.com

Library of Congress Cataloging-in-Publication Data

CIP Pending

Principles of Conducting Qualitative Research in Multicultural Settings
Ali Elhami, Anita Roshan, Harish Chandan
2024 Information Science Reference

ISBN: 979-8-3693-3306-8
eISBN: 979-8-3693-3307-5

British Cataloguing in Publication Data
A Cataloguing in Publication record for this book is available from the British Library.

The views expressed in this book are those of the authors, but not necessarily of the publisher.

For electronic access to this publication, please contact: eresources@igi-global.com.

Advances in Library and Information Science (ALIS) Book Series

Alfonso Ippolito
Sapienza University-Rome, Italy
Carlo Inglese
Sapienza University-Rome, Italy

ISSN:2326-4136
EISSN:2326-4144

Mission

The **Advances in Library and Information Science (ALIS) Book Series** is comprised of high quality, research-oriented publications on the continuing developments and trends affecting the public, school, and academic fields, as well as specialized libraries and librarians globally. These discussions on professional and organizational considerations in library and information resource development and management assist in showcasing the latest methodologies and tools in the field.

The **ALIS Book Series** aims to expand the body of library science literature by covering a wide range of topics affecting the profession and field at large. The series also seeks to provide readers with an essential resource for uncovering the latest research in library and information science management, development, and technologies.

Coverage

- Public Library Policy
- Collection Development
- Service Learning in Libraries
- Outsourcing of Library Services
- Free Online Resources
- Partnerships in Library Communities
- Human Side of Information Services
- Marketing Library Products and Services
- Open Access
- Conservation

IGI Global is currently accepting manuscripts for publication within this series. To submit a proposal for a volume in this series, please contact our Acquisition Editors at Acquisitions@igi-global.com or visit: http://www.igi-global.com/publish/.

Titles in this Series

For a list of additional titles in this series, please visit: www.igi-global.com/book-series

Foundational Theories and Practical Applications of Qualitative Research Methodology
Hesham Mohamed Elsherif (Independent Researcher, USA)
Information Science Reference • copyright 2024 • 474pp • H/C (ISBN: 9798369324141) • US $245.00 (our price)

Improving Library Systems with AI Applications, Approaches, and Bibliometric Insights
K.R. Senthilkumar (Sri Krishna Arts and Science College, India) and R. Jagajeevan (Sri Krishna Arts and Science College, India)
Information Science Reference • copyright 2024 • 326pp • H/C (ISBN: 9798369355930) • US $245.00 (our price)

Applications of Artificial Intelligence in Libraries
Iman Khamis (Northwestern University, Qatar)
Information Science Reference • copyright 2024 • 308pp • H/C (ISBN: 9798369315736) • US $240.00 (our price)

Examining Information Literacy in Academic Libraries
Sabelo Chizwina (North-West University, South Africa) and Mathew Moyo (North-West University, South Africa)
Information Science Reference • copyright 2024 • 313pp • H/C (ISBN: 9798369311431) • US $230.00 (our price)

AI-Assisted Library Reconstruction
K.R. Senthilkumar (Sri Krishna Arts and Science College, India)
Information Science Reference • copyright 2024 • 363pp • H/C (ISBN: 9798369327821) • US $235.00 (our price)

Challenges of Globalization and Inclusivity in Academic Research
Swati Chakraborty (GLA University, India & Concordia University, Canada)
Information Science Reference • copyright 2024 • 301pp • H/C (ISBN: 9798369313718) • US $225.00 (our price)

701 East Chocolate Avenue, Hershey, PA 17033, USA
Tel: 717-533-8845 x100 • Fax: 717-533-8661
E-Mail: cust@igi-global.com • www.igi-global.com

Table of Contents

Maha Mennani, Cadi Ayyad University, Morocco
Elhoussain Attak, Cadi Ayyad University, Morocco

Chapter 9
Kelly Burmeister Long, University of North Georgia, USA
Katherine Rose Adams, University of North Georgia, USA

Chapter 10
Mariam Sahraoui, Université Hassan 2, Morocco

Detailed Table of Contents

Chapter 1

    Anita Roshan, Universidad Autónoma de Madrid, Spain
    Ali Elhami, UNICAF University, Larnaca, Cyprus

This chapter is dedicated to discussing ethnographic research methods as a valuable tool for studying cultures and societies. The authors explore the theoretical foundations behind the use of ethnographic research in studying human behavior and the benefits it offers in gaining a comprehensive understanding of various social groups. In addition, they discuss the advantages and limitations of ethnography, as well as the ethical considerations that researchers must take into account when conducting ethnographic research. Since ethnographic research often emphasizes the importance of reflexivity, acknowledging the researcher's own biases and perspectives that may influence data collection and interpretation, the authors explore reflexivity as a crucial aspect of ethnographic research. By incorporating reflexivity, ethnographic research becomes more transparent and acknowledges the potential impact of the researcher on the data collected. Thus, the authors delve into the significance of reflexivity in ethnography and its implications for ensuring rigor and validity in research findings.

Chapter 2

    Casey Allison Esmeraldo, UNICAF University, South Africa

This chapter explores the application of grounded theory methodology in qualitative research, focusing on its role in unraveling cultural complexity. Grounded theory offers a systematic approach to understanding cultural phenomena by grounding theories in the data collected from diverse cultural contexts. The chapter begins by emphasizing the importance of cultural sensitivity and reflexivity, highlighting the need for researchers to acknowledge their own biases and engage with the perspectives of participants. It then discusses coding and analysis techniques across cultures, emphasizing the need to navigate cultural nuances and meanings. Strategies for ensuring trustworthiness and validity in cross-cultural research are examined. The chapter also explores the integration of diverse cultural perspectives in theory development, emphasizing the importance of co-constructing theories with participants. Overall, the chapter underscores the value of grounded theory and its role in fostering cross-cultural understanding in qualitative research.

Chapter 3

    Handan Akkaş, Ankara Science University, Turkey & Tilburg University, The Netherlands
    Cem Harun Meydan, Ankara Science University, Turkey

This chapter explores the complex field of application of qualitative sampling techniques in the context of multicultural settings, covering both probabilistic and non-probabilistic sampling approaches. It recognises the importance of capturing the diversity and distinctiveness of multicultural populations and describes the intricacies of sampling in culturally diverse settings. It also explores the different challenges and considerations that arise when applying each method in different ethnic, linguistic and cultural contexts. Moreover, it emphasises the importance of aligning sampling methods with research objectives, context-specific considerations, and ethical principles. By providing practical information and guidance, the chapter equips researchers with the necessary tools to effectively navigate the complexities of qualitative sampling in multicultural settings.

Chapter 4

> *Ali Elhami, UNICAF University, Larnaca, Cyprus*
> *Anita Roshan, Universidad Autónoma de Madrid, Spain*
> *Howard Giles, University of California, Santa Barbara, USA & The University of*
> *Queensland, Australia*

This chapter gives an overview of the various data collection methods in qualitative research. Then the authors concentrate on the communication accommodation theory (CAT) and its strategies. Additionally, they explore how utilizing CAT can enhance the quality and depth of information gathered through focus groups and interviews. According to this chapter, in order to build relationships, researchers need to modify their communication styles according to factors like the age, gender, or social status of interviewees, as this encourages informants to share more information and reduces the likelihood of concealing secrets. This approach, when conversing in native or foreign languages, helps researchers maintain a better understanding of participants' perspectives and insights. Furthermore, adapting communication styles can also help researchers navigate cultural nuances and sensitivities, leading to more meaningful and accurate data collection and uncovering deeper insights and perspectives that may have otherwise been overlooked.

Chapter 5

> *Isidro Miguel Martín Pérez, Universidad de La Laguna, Spain*
> *Sebastián Eustaquio Martín Pérez, Universidad Europea de Canarias, Spain*

The chapter highlights the relevance of qualitative methods, especially group discussions, in social research within multicultural contexts. It emphasizes selecting participants reflecting the study's cultural diversity and thorough preparation, including choosing a competent moderator and an accessible, inclusive venue. Steps for conducting these discussions are described, from creating the script to interpreting the discourse. During analysis, the focus is on understanding varied perspectives and intercultural interaction subtleties, recommending a systematic approach to ensure reliability and validity through careful data selection and category coding. Originating in the 1930s, group discussions have expanded beyond market research, distinguished by their flexibility and exploratory focus. Key phases include design, operation, data analysis, and reporting, with guidelines for participant selection and project preparation. The chapter concludes by highlighting the importance of these discussions in exploring perceptions and attitudes in multicultural settings.

Chapter 6

Cem Harun Meydan, Ankara Science University, Turkey
Handan Akkaş, Ankara Science University, Turkey

Triangulation is a methodological approach that involves using multiple methods or data sources to enhance the credibility and validity of research findings. This approach is useful in qualitative studies that aim to gain a deeper understanding of complex social phenomena and to understand the intricacies of multicultural environments. By embracing diverse perspectives, methods, and data sources, researchers can verify and validate their findings, leading to more comprehensive and reliable conclusions and can navigate cultural dynamics more effectively, leading to more nuanced and culturally sensitive findings. Beyond methodological considerations, triangulation allows researchers to capture diverse perspectives and enrich their analysis, playing a crucial role in qualitative research by enhancing the credibility, validity, and depth of research findings. Additionally, it is beneficial for mixed methods designs to provide a holistic understanding of research problems. Triangulation serves as a cornerstone for advancing knowledge and understanding in multicultural research contexts.

Chapter 7

Aissa Mosbah, Dhofar University, Oman

Social sciences (SS) researchers have produced far less qualitative than quantitative research. This is due to many factors including particularly the lack of straightforward and easy-to-implement guidelines that would help researchers in the process of ensuring research rigor through reliability, validity, and/ or other concepts. Nonetheless, the extant literature shows that most qualitative research measures on research rigor were developed in nursing, which is a natural science discipline, and that social science researchers often adopt these measures in their works. This chapter focuses on multiculturalism in business management discipline, as a rapidly growing field of the SS. While multiculturalism has become a key feature and a determinant of organizational success in today's rapidly globalized business environments, it may be a source of bias in qualitative research. Most importantly, the chapter develops a set of measures/ techniques that will aid qualitative social science researchers, and business researchers specifically, on how to ensure research rigor.

Chapter 8

Maha Mennani, Cadi Ayyad University, Morocco
Elhoussain Attak, Cadi Ayyad University, Morocco

Qualitative research methodology provides an effective way to explore participants' perceptions and unlock their experiences. In multicultural research settings, particularly in social sciences (e.g., sociology, psychology, theology, etc.), there is a strong tendency among qualitative researchers to collect the required data through interviews. This study employs qualitative research methodology, particularly lexicometric analysis via the IRaMuTeQ software, to analyze text data from semi-structured interviews. This software allows for detailed statistical analysis of the text corpus, including classic text analysis, specificity analysis, similarity analysis, and word cloud. In addition, this research aims to explore participants' perceptions and experiences through around twenty interviews, juxtaposing process and content in order to identify different themes. The IRaMuTeQ software helps to visualize lexicographic elements and ensure homogeneity between initial and resulting themes through correspondence factorial analysis.

This chapter explores prominent scholars' articulations of racial ideologies and frames used in discourse on race and racism. Focusing on qualitative research designs, the chapter aims to consolidate the insights from leading scholars into a consolidated conceptual framework for racial discourse. The conceptual framework draws on influential works, such as Helms' White identity statuses, to categorize racial ideologies, fostering a nuanced understanding of the complexities surrounding racial discourse and contributing to the ongoing efforts to understand societal views of race and racism. Then, this chapter discusses pertinent research designs that could be used in racial discourse analysis in deploying the conceptual framework of racial ideologies and frames.

The chapter delves into a qualitative analysis of research data focusing on the discourse exchanged during a sales transaction between a Moroccan intern and a native French client. The aim is to explore the linguistic and cultural dynamics inherent in intercultural business interactions, particularly in the context of sales operations. The analysis homes in on how the Moroccan intern navigates linguistic subtleties and cultural disparities while engaging with a French client. It scrutinizes verbal exchanges, language preferences, communication strategies, and cultural nuances to uncover pivotal factors that influence the success of such interactions. The research seeks to pinpoint the strengths and challenges encountered by the Moroccan intern when selling to a French-speaking clientele. The objective is to extract practical insights to augment the linguistic and intercultural competencies of interns enrolled in commerce and management programs, underscoring the significance of these skills in an increasingly globalized business landscape.

Foreword

Interaction between cultures is increasing due to digitalization, developments in communication and information technologies, and frequent migrations, which have impacted the twenty-first century. Among these factors, migration has come to the fore in recent years. Reasons such as wars, natural disasters, diseases, and political and economic crises cause people to migrate to other countries and establish new lives. While planned migrations can potentially increase the welfare level of countries, unplanned and mass migrations can produce undesirable and unforeseen results. As a matter of fact, various problems occur in societies whose social order is disrupted through migration and is subjected to unexpected cultural change. Some of these problems are related to residents, and some are related to immigrants. Scientific research should be carried out to detect, diagnose, and solve the problems arising from migration. While carrying out these studies, the experiences of both residents and immigrants must be understood very well.

It would be very appropriate to design and conduct qualitative research for this purpose because qualitative research is needed to conceptualize and deeply understand the phenomena that emerge for the first time in the social context. There are currently many reference books on qualitative research methods. However, these books generally address general conditions. Since *Principles of Conducting Qualitative Research in Multicultural Settings* focuses on multicultural contexts, unlike previous books, it can be a useful guide for those who want to conduct qualitative research studies to figure out the dynamics and mechanisms of migration-related issues. In this respect, I believe that *Principles of Conducting Qualitative Research in Multicultural Settings* meets an important need in qualitative research methods.

Ufuk Başar
Istanbul Ticaret University, Turkey

Preface

As editors of *Principles of Conducting Qualitative Research in Multicultural Settings*, we are honored to present this comprehensive reference book to students, researchers, practitioners, and professionals interested in delving into the intricacies of qualitative research within multicultural contexts.

Migration, a phenomenon deeply embedded in human history, has become increasingly prevalent in recent times due to globalization. Individuals from diverse backgrounds embark on journeys to new lands, seeking better opportunities, safety, and a brighter future for themselves and their families. However, the challenges they encounter in their host countries, ranging from racism to language barriers, often hinder their integration and well-being.

In this book, we explore the philosophical underpinnings of qualitative research methodologies, emphasizing the importance of understanding ontological and epistemological assumptions in shaping research design and data collection strategies. Whether adopting an interpretivist or positivist stance, researchers must navigate these theoretical frameworks to effectively capture the subjective experiences of individuals within multicultural settings.

Through qualitative research methods such as interviews, focus groups, participant observation, and visual documentation, scholars can uncover the nuanced narratives of immigrants and refugees, shedding light on their resilience, cultural identities, and adaptive strategies. However, conducting research in multicultural contexts requires sensitivity to gender dynamics, translation challenges, and the traumatic experiences of displaced populations.

This book addresses the fundamental principles of qualitative research design, data collection techniques, transcription, translation, and data analysis methodologies. It offers insights into the importance of triangulation and reflexivity in ensuring the validity and reliability of research findings. Moreover, it provides practical examples and case studies to illustrate the application of qualitative research in diverse fields such as anthropology, linguistics, sociology, psychology, and cultural studies.

We hope this book serves as a valuable resource for scholars embarking on research journeys in multicultural settings, enabling them to navigate the complexities of culture, language, and identity with diligence and empathy.

Chapter 1: Ethnographic Research Methods and the Role of Reflexivity in Qualitative Research

In this chapter, Roshan and Elhami delve into the intricate world of ethnographic research methods within multicultural settings. They offer a comprehensive discussion on the theoretical foundations of ethnography and its application in understanding various social groups. Furthermore, they examine the significance of reflexivity in ethnographic research, emphasizing the need for researchers to acknowledge their biases and perspectives that may influence data collection and interpretation. By shedding light on reflexivity's role in ensuring rigor and validity, this chapter provides valuable insights for researchers navigating the complexities of ethnographic studies.

Chapter 2: Grounded Theory: Unraveling Cultural Complexity in Qualitative Research

Esmeraldo guides readers through the application of grounded theory methodology in qualitative research, particularly its role in unraveling cultural complexities. This chapter emphasizes the importance of cultural sensitivity and reflexivity in engaging with diverse cultural contexts. It explores coding and analysis techniques across cultures and strategies for ensuring trustworthiness in research findings. By highlighting the integration of diverse cultural perspectives in theory development, this chapter underscores grounded theory's contribution to fostering cross-cultural understanding in qualitative research.

Chapter 3: Sampling Methods in Qualitative Research in Multicultural Settings

Akkas and Meydan provide a detailed exploration of qualitative sampling techniques within multicultural contexts. They navigate through the complexities of probabilistic and non-probabilistic sampling approaches, addressing challenges and considerations specific to diverse ethnic, linguistic, and cultural populations. This chapter equips researchers with practical guidance on aligning sampling methods with research objectives and ethical principles, empowering them to effectively navigate the intricacies of qualitative sampling in multicultural settings.

Chapter 4: Qualitative Research Data Collection Methods and the Significance of CAT in Cross-Cultural Interviewing

Elhami, Roshan, and Giles offer an overview of various data collection methods in qualitative research, with a specific focus on Communication Accommodation Theory (CAT). By exploring how CAT can enhance the quality of data gathered through interviews and focus groups, the chapter emphasizes the importance of adapting communication styles to cultural nuances. Through practical strategies, researchers can ensure meaningful and accurate data collection, uncovering deeper insights into participants' perspectives within multicultural settings.

Chapter 5: Group Discussions as a Methodology in Multicultural Settings

Martín Pérez and Martín Pérez highlight the relevance of group discussions in social research within multicultural contexts. They provide a step-by-step guide to conducting group discussions, emphasizing participant selection, moderator competence, and analysis techniques. By focusing on understanding varied perspectives and intercultural interaction subtleties, this chapter underscores the importance of group discussions in exploring perceptions and attitudes in multicultural settings.

Chapter 6: The Role of Triangulation in Qualitative Research: Converging Perspectives

Meydan and Akkas delve into the methodological approach of triangulation, emphasizing its significance in enhancing the credibility and validity of research findings within multicultural contexts. By embracing diverse perspectives, methods, and data sources, researchers can navigate cultural dynamics more effectively, leading to more nuanced and culturally sensitive findings. This chapter serves as a cornerstone for advancing knowledge and understanding in multicultural research settings.

Chapter 7: Ensuring Reliability and Validity in Qualitative Social Sciences Research

Mosbah addresses the challenges of ensuring research rigor in qualitative social sciences research within multicultural contexts, with a focus on business management. By developing measures and techniques to aid researchers in ensuring reliability and validity, this chapter offers valuable guidance for navigating biases and cultural nuances in research design and analysis.

Chapter 8: An Overview of Using IRAMUTEQ Software in Qualitative Analysis Designs

Maha and El Houssain introduce the IRaMuTeQ software as a tool for qualitative analysis in multicultural research settings. By employing lexicometric analysis, researchers can explore participants' perceptions and experiences, ensuring homogeneity between initial and resulting themes. This chapter provides practical insights into utilizing software tools for analyzing qualitative data in diverse cultural contexts.

Chapter 9: A Conceptual Framework of Racial Ideologies and Frames: Implications for Qualitative Research on Racial Discourse

Long and Adams explore racial ideologies and frames in discourse on race and racism, offering a conceptual framework for qualitative research. By consolidating insights from leading scholars, this chapter provides a nuanced understanding of societal views of race and racism, guiding researchers in deploying the conceptual framework in racial discourse analysis within multicultural settings.

Chapter 10: Qualitative Techniques in Action: Practical Example

This chapter delves into a qualitative analysis of research data focusing on the discourse exchanged during a sales transaction between a Moroccan intern and a native French client. The aim is to explore the linguistic and cultural dynamics inherent in intercultural business interactions, particularly in the context of sales operations. The analysis homes in on how the Moroccan intern navigates linguistic subtleties and cultural disparities while engaging with a French client. It scrutinizes verbal exchanges, language preferences, communication strategies, and cultural nuances to uncover pivotal factors that influence the success of such interactions. The research seeks to pinpoint the strengths and challenges encountered by the Moroccan intern when selling to a French-speaking clientele. The objective is to extract practical insights to augment the linguistic and intercultural competencies of interns enrolled in commerce and management programs, underscoring the significance of these skills in an increasingly globalized business landscape.

In concluding this preface to *Principles of Conducting Qualitative Research in Multicultural Settings*, we, as the editors, reflect on the profound significance of qualitative research within the context of global migration and cultural diversity. Our world is increasingly interconnected, with individuals from diverse backgrounds navigating new territories in search of better opportunities and safety. Yet, the challenges they face in their host countries, from discrimination to language barriers, underscore the importance of understanding and addressing the complexities of multicultural settings.

Throughout this book, we have embarked on a journey to explore the philosophical underpinnings, methodological approaches, and practical applications of qualitative research within multicultural contexts. From ethnographic research methods to grounded theory and sampling techniques, each chapter offers valuable insights and guidance for researchers seeking to unravel the intricacies of cultural diversity.

We have emphasized the importance of reflexivity, cultural sensitivity, and triangulation in ensuring the validity and reliability of research findings. By acknowledging researchers' biases, engaging with diverse perspectives, and employing multiple methods, researchers can navigate the nuances of multicultural environments with diligence and empathy.

Moreover, we have underscored the practical relevance of qualitative research in addressing real-world challenges, from understanding immigrants' experiences to exploring racial discourse. Through interviews, focus groups, and group discussions, researchers can uncover the nuanced narratives of marginalized populations, shedding light on their resilience, cultural identities, and adaptive strategies.

As editors, we hope that this comprehensive reference book serves as a valuable resource for students, researchers, practitioners, and professionals embarking on research journeys in multicultural settings. May it empower them to navigate the complexities of culture, language, and identity with sensitivity and rigor, ultimately contributing to a deeper understanding of the human experience in all its diversity.

Ali Elhami
Unicaf University, Larnaca, Cyprus

Anita Roshan
Universidad Autónoma de Madrid, Spain

Harish Chandan
Independent Researcher, USA

Introduction

CONDUCTING QUALITATIVE RESEARCH

A variety of approaches to conducting research are designed by philosophical assumptions about what makes up valid knowledge and show how researchers can attain it, together with an outline of what reality is and how it can be understood (Marsh & Furlong, 2002). In fact, philosophical assumptions are closely linked to the research design, strategy, and data collection tools that researchers use to advance research objectives (Saunders et al., 2009). To rephrase it, choosing the research methodologies depends on philosophical assumptions that are categorized as the ontology and epistemology of the essence of the research. Ontology deals with the study of existence or the instinct of reality (Lincoln et al., 2011), which is the understanding of the actuality and reality of what is being studied. Epistemology, on the other hand, is associated with imparting a framework for understanding possible knowledge and ensuring the researcher's adequacy and legitimacy (Guba & Lincoln, 2005).

Crotty (1998) implies that the terms theoretical perspective, epistemology, methods, and methodology delineate hierarchical levels of making decisions within the process of research design. Researchers initially follow a certain stance for the essence of knowledge (e.g., objectivism or subjectivism), which underlies the whole research process and controls the theoretical perspective, which is interpretivist or positivist (Denzin & Lincoln, 2005).

The interpretivist model is qualitative in essence and assumes that individuals experience reality in a subjective way and become involved in it, and researchers interpret the situation (Denzin & Lincoln, 2005). The positivist one, in contrast, assumes that the truth is verifiable and objective, so studies within the positivist paradigm seek quantification and measurement (Denzin & Lincoln, 2005). Interpretivism and positivism are philosophical assumptions that provide a better understanding and a structure for the research process. Based on the given background, the interpretivist model is explained in the following section, which is presented as the basic philosophical epistemology of this book.

Interpretiveness is a perspective that believes individual life stories and incidents matter so much that investigators, by providing an interpretation, provide value to those incidents (Suter et al., 2012). The participants of the qualitative studies, by sharing their life stories, develop their meaning subjectively and reflect their experiences relating to the objectives of the investigation. This clarification indicates that the participants impart subjective meanings to their stories that are directed into specific circumstances in accordance with the objectives of each research project. Suter et al. (2012) emphasize that in interpretive research, if a social phenomenon is addressed in a natural and cultural setting and from the individual's perspective, the purpose is to expand understanding and awareness. Practically, conducting qualitative research is one important way to gain a deeper understanding of the experiences and perspectives of immigrants facing these challenges. By conducting interviews or focus groups, and observation researchers can gather rich and nuanced data that can inform policies and interventions aimed at supporting immigrant populations (Barrett & Twycross, 2018; De Fina, 2019; Elhami & Khoshnevisan, 2022). Furthermore, qualitative research can also shed light on the resilience and strengths that immigrants possess, highlighting their ability to navigate and adapt to new environments despite the obstacles they face. In addition, conducting qualitative research in multicultural settings allows researchers to explore cultural beliefs, values, and practices, providing valuable insights into how culture influences individuals' experiences and perspectives. In addition, it shows how individuals negotiate and navigate their cultural identities in diverse settings. This approach also highlights the importance of context and the subjective nature of cultural experiences, emphasizing the need for researchers to engage in reflexivity throughout the research process. By employing qualitative research methods in multicultural settings, researchers can capture the richness and diversity of cultures, shedding light on the intricacies of human behaviour and social interactions. Additionally, these methods emphasize the importance of reflexivity and cultural sensitivity to ensure accurate interpretation and representation of participants' voices.

Qualitative Research Designs

In qualitative research, there are six most common research designs: *Phenomenological, (Auto)ethnographic, Grounded theory, Case study, Action research,* and *Historical studies.* Each design offers unique opportunities to delve into the complexities of multicultural settings and gain a deeper understanding of the experiences of immigrants.

- *Phenomenological studies* investigate human experiences by means of participant accounts. We refer to these encounters as lived experiences. Phenomenological research aims to characterize the significance that experiences have for each individual. Studies in fields with limited information are conducted using this kind of research (Donalek, 2004). Phenomenological research allows researchers to explore the subjective experiences of individuals in multicultural settings, shedding light on the unique perspectives of immigrants. By focusing on lived experiences, this approach helps to uncover the underlying meanings and implications of these encounters, contributing valuable insights to the field.

Respondents to phenomenological research are asked to characterize their experiences as they understand them. Although they might write about their experiences, interviews are typically used to gather information. In order to comprehend the lived experience from the subject's perspective, the researcher needs to consider their own feelings and beliefs. The procedure known as bracketing requires the researcher to first state what it is that they hope to learn, and then to consciously set these expectations aside. The only way to view the event through the eyes of the individual who has lived it is for the researcher to set aside her or his own theories about the phenomenon. Doing phenomenological can be challenging, as it requires the researcher to remain open-minded and unbiased throughout the data collection process. The study by Daly (2005) "Mothers living with suicidal adolescents: A phenomenological study of their experiences," is an example of this type of research, in which the researcher was able to truly understand and capture the unique experiences of mothers in this difficult situation. By setting aside preconceived notions and theories, the researcher was able to provide valuable insights into the lived experiences of these individuals. The researcher conducted unstructured interviews with six mothers of suicidal teenagers for this study. Six themes emerged: the inability to be a good mother, the eventual rejection, feeling isolated during the struggle, being helpless and helpless in the struggle, exercising caution when parenting, and maintaining an emotional distance. These themes shed light on the complex emotions and challenges faced by mothers of suicidal teenagers, highlighting the need for support and understanding in this vulnerable population. The findings from this study can inform interventions and support systems tailored to address the specific needs of these mothers, ultimately improving outcomes for both them and their children.

Another example of phenomenological research is "Cultural Structuring of Urok Practice: An Intercultural Communication of the Bago Tribe in Kalinga Province, Philippines," done by Manera and Vecaldo (2020), delves into how the cultural practices of the Bago Tribe influence their communication styles and interactions, shedding light on the importance of understanding cultural nuances in educational settings. By exploring these intercultural dynamics, pre-service teachers can gain valuable insights that will enhance their ability to create inclusive and culturally responsive learning environments for all students.

- *(Auto)Ethnography* (*see chapter 1*) involves immersing oneself in the culture or community being studied in order to gain a deep understanding of their beliefs, behaviours, and experiences. This approach can provide valuable insights into the social context surrounding integration in migrants and help identify potential areas for support. When doing an ethnographic study, the researcher usually resides among the subjects and absorbs their culture. Together with the locals, the researcher investigates their rituals and customs. This immersive approach allows for a deeper understanding of the community's way of life and values. By participating in daily activities and observing interactions, the researcher can gain valuable insights that may not be apparent through other research methods. Interviews, focus groups, and participant observation are the usual methods used to gather data. The difference between ethnography and phenomenology is that ethnography focuses on understanding a specific culture as a whole, while phenomenology delves into individual experiences and perceptions within that culture. Phenomenology seeks to uncover the meaning behind human experiences, while ethnography aims to provide a comprehensive understanding of a particular group's way of life. Hence, ethnography is more focused on the external behaviours and practices of a group and is a more holistic approach to studying cultures. Autoethnography, on the other hand, is a qualitative research method that examines and draws from the author's lived experience, provides a cultural interpretation of the researcher's autobiographical data, and links the researcher's insights to understanding oneself and how it relates to others (Adams et al., 2015; Chang, 2008; Poulos, 2021).

"Trajectories of Iranian migrants in Madrid" (Roshan, 2023) is an example of the ethnographic study, in which the researcher immerses herself in the Iranian community in Madrid to observe and document lived experiences and challenges of Iranians. She explored the trajectories, Socialization dynamics, Spanish language learning, application of English as a lingua franca, language barriers, and language investment of first-generation Iranian migrants. The data in this study was collected through participant observations, interviews, focus groups, and documents to provide a rich and detailed description of Iranian community in Spain. There are various examples in other societies where researchers have utilized similar methods to gain a deep understanding of different cultural groups (Ahmed, 2024; Gance-Cleveland, 2004; Rowe, 2024).

- *Grounded theory* (*see chapter 2*) was created by two sociologists named Glaser and Strauss (1967). Grounded theory includes the collection, analysis, and development of a theory based on facts. Grounded theory is particularly useful in exploring complex social phenomena and uncovering underlying patterns within a community. By using this method, researchers can generate new insights and theories that are grounded in the data collected from the community itself. Thus, instead of focusing on testing hypotheses, grounded theory is more interested in creating them. The resulting theory is self-correcting, meaning that it improves itself in response to new data to accommodate the interpretation of existing data. Williams and Irurita (2005) studied hospitalized patients' emotional comfort and sense of personal control using the grounded theory qualitative method. Forty patients were interviewed, and seventy-five hours were spent in the field. The researchers named "optimizing personal control to facilitate emotional comfort" as the fundamental psychological process. Patients' capacity to shape their surroundings was referred to as personal control, and emotional comfort was characterized as a relaxed state that had an impact on the patient's physical condition. One essential component of emotional comfort was discovered to be personal control.

In many other studies, scholars use grounded theory to explore various phenomena and develop theories based on data collected directly from participants, some of which are: Forouzanfar et al., 2024; Fife et al., 2023; Qadam et al., 2023)

- *Case study* is defined by Yin (2009) as "an empirical inquiry that investigates a contemporary phenomenon within its real-life context especially when the boundaries between the phenomenon and context are not clearly evident" (p. 18). As mentioned by Yin (2014) in case studies, participants are selected according to the purpose of the study, since in this approach researchers desire to discover meaning and individuals' experiences within the context. Merriam (2009) notes that the purpose of case studies is the provision of a holistic description, which enables researchers to look at an issue as a whole and in-depth (Sesek, 2007), and it clarifies individuals' understanding of the situation. Case studies in qualitative research and in multicultural settings allow researchers to explore complex phenomena within specific cultural contexts, providing rich and detailed insights that may not be easily captured through other research methods. This approach also allows for the examination of multiple perspectives and the consideration of various factors that influence the phenomenon under study. The data collection methods in case studies typically involve in-depth interviews, observations, and document analysis to gather comprehensive and detailed information. Additionally, the findings from case studies can be used to generate hypotheses for further research or to inform policy and practice in relevant fields. "Religion and higher education migrants' acculturation orientation" by Elhami and Roshan (2024) is an example of a case study, in which the authors conducted interviews with migrant students to explore how religion influences the acculturation process in higher education settings. The study provides valuable insights into the complex interplay between religion, culture, and education for migrants in a new country. Other examples of case studies are (Elhami, 2023; Şafak-Ayvazoğlu et al., 2021; Gallois et al., 2016).
- *Action research* looks for ways to enhance practice while also examining the results of such efforts (Streubert & Carpenter, 2002). Unlike with quantitative research studies, there is no attempt to generalize the study's findings. The application of solutions happens as a real-time component of the research process in action research. The solutions are being implemented without any delays. In the 1940s, action research gained popularity. Kurt Lewin (1946) had a significant impact on the development of action study. In essence, action research is learning by doing. In action research once an issue has been identified, it is addressed with the proper steps, evaluated for effectiveness, and repeated if the results are not satisfactory. Action research in multicultural setting focuses on addressing issues of diversity, equity, and inclusion. It involves collaboration with diverse stakeholders to create sustainable solutions that promote cultural understanding and respect. The difference of action research with other research designs

Action research is more common in settings such as educational settings, where teachers and administrators work together to improve classroom practices and student outcomes; or in organizational settings, where employees and managers collaborate to address workplace issues and improve overall performance. This type of research is characterized by its practical approach and emphasis on creating positive change within a specific context. This collaborative approach allows for real-time adjustments and continuous improvement based on feedback from those directly involved in the process.

- *Historical Studies* are essential for understanding the development of societies, cultures, and institutions over time. By examining the past, historians can provide valuable insights into current issues and trends. In addition to learning about historical events, historical research aims to connect these historical occurrences to the present and future.

Historical studies also help us recognize patterns and avoid repeating past mistakes. By understanding the context in which decisions were made in the past, we can make more informed choices for the future. This design can be used in multicultural settings to inform policy-making, improve critical thinking skills, and foster a deeper appreciation for the complexities of human experience. Ultimately, historical studies play a crucial role in shaping our understanding of the world around us and guiding us towards a more informed and enlightened future. Most comment data collection methods in historical studies include oral history interviews and documents. These methods allow historians to gather evidence and construct narratives that provide insights into the past and inform our understanding of the present. By critically examining historical events and their impact on society, we can gain valuable perspectives that can help us navigate the complexities of the modern world.

Key Steps For Conducting Qualitative Research

For conducting qualitative research, the first step is determining the research questions or objectives. This will guide the selection of appropriate data collection methods, such as interviews or observations, to gather in-depth insights and understanding. Research questions in qualitative research should focus on exploring the underlying reasons, motivations, and perspectives of individuals or groups, rather than simply seeking numerical data or statistical trends. By delving into the "why" and "how" of human behaviour, qualitative research can provide rich and detailed insights that quantitative data alone cannot capture. After forming research questions, sampling strategies (*see Chapter 3*) can be developed to ensure that the participants or data chosen are able to provide valuable information that aligns with the research objectives. Additionally, qualitative researchers must consider ethical considerations and ensure that participants' rights and confidentiality are protected throughout the research process. This can involve obtaining informed consent, maintaining anonymity, and securing data storage. By addressing these ethical concerns, researchers can build trust with participants and uphold the integrity of their study. After collecting the data (*see Chapter 4*), researchers can then begin the process of analysing and interpreting the information gathered. This step is crucial in order to draw meaningful conclusions and contribute to the existing body of knowledge in the field. Hence, in the following section, we will concentrate on the procedures required to analyse the collected data.

Steps For Analysing Data

There are four important steps for analysing the collected data. These steps include:

- *Familiarization* with the data, which means reviewing the data to gain an understanding of its content and structure, for example, if the data is collected through interviews, the researcher needs to listen to the interviews, transcribe them, (re)read them, translate them (if needed), and read the translated transcriptions. This process allows the researcher to become familiar with the data and get ready for the next step.
- *Categorizing and coding*, which is the next step. Categorizing and coding the information, based on the objectives of the study, involves organizing the data into meaningful categories and assigning codes to different pieces of information. This step helps in identifying patterns, themes, and relationships within the data, which are essential for drawing conclusions and making interpretations. For coding data, researchers can use various methods, for instance, using different colours to represent different categories or using numerical codes for easy reference. Overall, categorizing and coding data is a crucial step in the research process, as it helps in analysing and interpreting the information collected.
- *Identifying and organizing* is the next step, in which researchers review the data to ensure that the categories are correct and consistent. This step involves refining the categories and codes to accurately reflect the data. Researchers may also consult with colleagues or experts to validate their coding process and ensure reliability.
- *Interpreting the data* is the final step, in which researchers draw conclusions and make connections based on the categorized and coded data. This step involves analysing patterns, trends, and relationships within the data to answer research questions.

Selecting data analysis method in qualitative research requires careful consideration of the research questions, data type, and desired outcomes. Researchers must select appropriate techniques to effectively analyse and interpret the data. By carefully selecting the data analysis methods, researchers can enhance the credibility and trustworthiness of their findings. This will ultimately strengthen the overall impact of the research study and its implications for the field. The next section will outline various data analysis methods commonly used in qualitative research,

Data Analysis Methods

Data analysis in qualitative research involves the systematic examination and interpretation of non-numerical data such as text, images, or videos and voices to identify patterns, themes, and meanings. There are a few steps that must be taken before data analysis, such as data collection, transcription, coding, and analysis. Each step is crucial in ensuring the accuracy and reliability of the findings obtained from qualitative research. For a better understanding of data collection methods (see chapter 4), which a comprehensive overview of various techniques used in collecting qualitative data is provided. Transcription is the process of converting audio or video recordings into written text, allowing for easier analysis. Coding involves categorizing and labelling data to identify recurring themes or patterns within the information collected. These steps are essential in qualitative research to ensure a thorough and accurate analysis of the data obtained. There are five main data analysis techniques commonly used in qualitative research: *thematic analysis, content analysis, narrative analysis, discourse analysis, and conversation analysis.* Each technique offers a unique approach to interpreting qualitative data and can provide valuable insights into the research questions being explored. It is important for researchers to carefully consider which data analysis technique best aligns with their research objectives and the nature of their data.

- *Thematic analysis* involves identifying patterns or themes within the data. In thematic analysis, researchers categorize and code data to uncover recurring ideas or concepts that are relevant to the research topic. This technique allows for a deeper understanding of the underlying meanings and relationships present in the qualitative data (see, for example, studies in which researchers utilised Thematic analysis: Blackwell et al., 2024; Motaung, 2024; Razali, Sundana, & Ramli, 2024)
- *Content analysis* focuses on categorizing and interpreting the content of the data, such as words, phrases, or images. By examining the content of the data, researchers can gain insights into the prevalence of certain ideas or concepts within their dataset. This method is particularly useful for studying large amounts of textual or visual data in a systematic and structured way. The difference between thematic and content analysis lies in their approach to analysing qualitative data. Thematic analysis focuses on identifying patterns and themes that emerge from the data, while content analysis is more concerned with the specific details and elements within the data. Both methods have their own strengths and can be used in conjunction to provide a comprehensive analysis of qualitative data. (see, for example, studies in which researchers utilised Content analysis: Elhami & Roshan, 2024; Mapuya, 2024; Xu & Fang, 2024;).
- *Narrative analysis* focuses on storytelling and understanding the experiences of individuals. This approach allows researchers to explore complex social phenomena in a more holistic and nuanced way, providing rich and detailed insights into the lived experiences of participants. The difference between narrative and techniques lies in its emphasis on the personal stories and perspectives of individuals, allowing for a deeper understanding of how people make sense of their lives and experiences. By prioritizing the voices and narratives of participants, researchers can uncover deeper meanings and connections. The most common data collection for narrative analysis are interviews and observation, which allow researchers to directly engage with participants and observe their behaviours in real-life settings. Participants (see, for example, studies in which researchers utilised Narrative analysis: Codó, 2018; Elhami et al., 2024; Elhami & Roshan, 2023).
- *Discourse analysis* focuses on analysing language use and communication patterns, highlighting how individuals construct meaning through language and discourse. By examining the nuances of language, researchers can uncover power dynamics, social norms, and cultural influences that shape communication interactions. This method is particularly useful for understanding how language shapes identities and influences social relationships. Critical discourse analysis is a form of discourse analysis that goes beyond surface-level meanings to uncover underlying power structures and ideologies embedded within language. The goal of critical discourse analysis, an interdisciplinary approach, is to reveal hidden meanings and power dynamics in speech by viewing language as a type of social practice. It examines the institutional and social circumstances that conversation takes place in in addition to the text's structure. Hence the major difference discourse analysis and critical discourse analysis lies in the focus on power dynamics and ideologies within language. While discourse analysis primarily focuses on surface-level meanings and structures, critical discourse analysis delves deeper into the underlying societal influences that shape communication (see, for example, studies in which researchers utilised discourse or critical discourse analysis: Battista, 2022; Ndlangamandla et al., 2024; Padley, 2022; Raffone, 2022; Russo & Grasso, 2022)
- *Conversation analysis* involves studying the structure and dynamics of conversations. Researchers in conversation analysis often focus on turn-taking, interruptions, and repair sequences to understand how individuals co-construct meaning in interactions. By examining the intricacies of conversational patterns, scholars can gain insights into social hierarchies, power dynamics, and interpersonal

relationships. Conversation analysis is helpful because it provides a detailed understanding of how individuals communicate and interact in various social contexts. By analysing conversational patterns, researchers can uncover implicit norms, values, and beliefs that influence communication. To conduct conversation analysis, researchers typically transcribe and analyse recorded conversations, focusing on turn-taking, pauses, and non-verbal cues. Additionally, researchers may use software programs to assist in coding and categorizing different aspects of the conversation for further analysis (see, for example, studies in which researchers utilised Conversation analysis: Cashman, 2005; Falk & Kilpatrick, 2000; Kazemi & Salmani Nodoushan, 2018)

Each of these techniques offers a unique perspective on the data and can help researchers uncover different aspects of their research questions. Researchers should choose the analysis technique that best suits their research goals and objectives in order to effectively analyse and interpret their data.

CONCLUSION

This introduction presents important steps for conducting qualitative research. In each qualitative research project, researchers must be fully cognizant of the design they have selected according to the objectives of the study. It is critical that the researcher keep the study's objectives in mind during data collection, categorization, and analysis. By doing so, researchers can ensure that their findings are accurate and relevant to their research questions. Another important aspect to consider is choosing the most appropriate data analysis method based on the type of data collected and the research questions being addressed. Researchers should also consider potential biases and limitations in their study to ensure the validity and reliability of their findings.

In sum up, in qualitative research all steps are connected, and the researchers must be fully aware of all steps in order to produce high-quality results. It is essential for researchers to be cognizant and watchful throughout the entire research process to maintain the integrity of their study. By carefully considering each step and being mindful of potential pitfalls, researchers can enhance the rigor and credibility of their qualitative research findings. Additionally, seeking feedback from peers or experts in the field can provide valuable insights and help improve the overall quality of the study.

REFERENCES

Adams, T. E., Jones, S. H., & Ellis, C. (2015). *Autoethnography: Understanding qualitative research.* Oxford University Press.

Ahmed, A. O. A. (2024). A classroom ethnographic study on silence among EFL graduate students: A Case Study. *British Journal of Translation. Linguistics and Literature*, 4(1), 2–17. 10.54848/bjtll.v4i1.75

Barrett, D., & Twycross, A. (2018). Data collection in qualitative research. *Evidence-Based Nursing*, 21(3), 63–64. 10.1136/eb-2018-10293929858278

Battista, A. (2022). Donna Williams' Nobody nowhere and Somebody somewhere: A corpus-based discourse analysis of the author's language as a tool to negotiate one's relationship with the world and the self. *International Journal of Language Studies*, 16(4), 95–116.

Beiser, M., & Hou, F. (2001). Language acquisition, unemployment and depressive disorder among Southeast Asian refugees: A 10-year study. *Social Science & Medicine*, 53(10), 1321–1334. 10.1016/S0277-9536(00)00412-311676403

Blackwell, J., Allen-Collinson, J., Evans, A., & Henderson, H. (2024). How Person-Centred Is Cardiac Rehabilitation in England? Using Bourdieu to Explore Socio-Cultural Influences and Personalisation. *Qualitative Health Research*, 34(3), 239–251. 10.1177/104973232312102603793368

Candel, O. S. (2021). Acculturation stress among international students: A literature review. In *Teachers and students in multicultural environment. Romania*. Editura Universită ii Alexandru Ioan Cuza din Ia i.

Cashman, H. R. (2005). Identities at play: Language preference and group membership in bilingual talk in interaction. *Journal of Pragmatics*, 37(3), 301–315. 10.1016/j.pragma.2004.10.004

Chang, H. (2008). *Autoethnography as method.* Left Coast Press.

Codó, E. (2018). Lifestyle residents in Barcelona: A biographical perspective on linguistic repertoires, identity narrative and transnational mobility. *International Journal of the Sociology of Language*, 250(250), 11–34. 10.1515/ijsl-2017-0053

Crotty, M. J. (1998). *The foundations of social research: Meaning and perspective in the research process.* Sage Publications.

Daly, P. (2005). Mothers living with suicidal adolescents: A phenomenological study of their experiences. *Journal of Psychosocial Nursing and Mental Health Services*, 43(3), 22–28.15794529

De Fina, A. (2009). Narratives in interviews: The case of accounts. *Narrative Inquiry*, 19(2), 233–258. 10.1075/ni.19.2.03def

Denzin, N. K., & Lincoln, Y. S. (2005). Introduction: The Discipline and Practice of Qualitative Research. In Denzin, N. K., & Lincoln, Y. S. (Eds.), *Handbook of Qualitative Research* (3rd ed., pp. 1–32). Sage.

Donalek, J. G. (2004). Demystifying nursing research: Phenomenology as a qualitative research method. *Urologic Nursing*, 24, 516–517.15658739

Elhami, A. (2023). *A Study of Communicative Practices of Iranian Migrants in Madrid* [Unpublished Doctoral Dissertation]. Universidad Autónoma de Madrid.

Elhami, A., & Khoshnevisan, B. (2022). Conducting an Interview in qualitative research: The Modus Operandi. *Mextesol Journal*, 46(1), 1–7.

Elhami, A., & Roshan, A. (2023). A narrative study of Iranian females' acculturation orientation and Spanish learning experiences in Spain. In Chandan, H. (Ed.), *Strategies for cultural assimilation of immigrants and their children: Social, economic, and political considerations* (pp. 45–68). IGI Global. 10.4018/978-1-6684-4839-7.ch003

Elhami, A., & Roshan, A. (2024). Religion and higher education migrants' acculturation orientation. *Intercultural Education*, 35(3), 283–301. 10.1080/14675986.2024.2348428

Elhami, A., Roshan, A., Ghahraman, V., & Afrashi, A. (2024). Sociocultural adjustment by two international students: A critical look at multilingualism in Spain. *International Journal of Language Studies*, 18(3), 1–38.

Falk, I., & Kilpatrick, S. (2000). What is Social Capital? A Study of Interaction in a Rural Community (Version 1). *University of Tasmania*. https://hdl.handle.net/102.100.100/596469

Fife, S. T., Gossner, J. D., Theobald, A., Allen, E., Rivero, A., & Koehl, H. (2023). Couple healing from infidelity: A grounded theory study. *Journal of Social and Personal Relationships*, 40(12), 3882–3905. 10.1177/02654075231177874

Forouzanfar, A., Fatehizade, M., & Farahbakhsh, K. (2024). A Grounded Theory Study of Couple Caregiving: A Qualitative Study. *Journal of Counseling Research*, 22(88). Advance online publication. 10.18502/qjcr.v22i88.15452

Gallois, C., Weatherall, A., & Giles, H. (2016). CAT and talk in action. In Giles, H. (Ed.), *Communication accommodation theory: Negotiating personal relationships and social identities across contexts* (pp. 105–122). Cambridge University Press. 10.1017/CBO9781316226537.006

Gance-Cleveland, B. (2004). Qualitative evaluation of a school-based support group for adolescents with an addicted parent. *Nursing Research*, 53(6), 379–386. 10.1097/00006199-200411000-0000615586134

Glaser, B. G., & Strauss, A. C. (1967). *The discovery of grounded theory: Strategies for qualitative research*. Aldine.

Guba, E. G., & Lincoln, Y. S. (2005). Paradigmatic Controversies, Contradictions, and Emerging Confluences. In Denzin, N. K., & Lincoln, Y. S. (Eds.), *The Sage Handbook of Qualitative Research* (pp. 191–215). Sage.

Kazemi, A., & Salmani Nodoushan, M. A. (2018). A conversation analytic perspective on Quranic verses and chapters. *Studies in English Language and Education*, 5(1), 1–11. 10.24815/siele.v5i1.8620

Lewin, K. (1946). Action research and minority problems. *The Journal of Social Issues*, 2(4), 34–46. 10.1111/j.1540-4560.1946.tb02295.x

Lincoln, Y. S., Lynham, S. A., & Guba, E. G. (2011). Paradigmatic controversies, contradictions, and emerging confluences, revisited. In Denzin, L., & Lincoln, J. (Eds.), *The Sage Handbook of Qualitative Research* (pp. 97–128). Sage.

Manera, A. B., & Vecaldo, R. T. (2020). Cultural structuring of Urok practice: An intercultural communication of the Bago tribe in Kalinga province, Philippines. *International Journal of Psychosocial Rehabilitation*, 24(6), 13193–13217.

Mapuya, M. (2024). Exploring the contribution of decolonisation epistemologies: Promoting social justice in accounting education. *International Journal of Language Studies*, 18(1), 131–155. 10.5281/zenodo.10468331

Marsh, D., & Furlong, E. (2002). Ontology and Epistemology in Political Science. In David, M., & Gerry, S. (Eds.), *Theory and Methods in Political Science* (pp. 17–41). Palgrave. 10.1007/978-0-230-62889-2_2

Motaung, L. B. (2024). Translanguaging pedagogical practice in a tutorial programme at a South African university. *International Journal of Language Studies*, 18(1), 81–104. 10.5281/zenodo.10468213

Naghdi, A. (2010). Iranian Diaspora: With focus on Iranian Immigrants in Sweden. *Asian Social Science*, 6(11), 197–208. 10.5539/ass.v6n11p197

Ndlangamandla, S. C., Chaka, C., Shange, T., & Shandu-Phetla, T. (2024). COVID-19 crosslinguistic and multimodal public health communication strategies: Social justice or emergency political strategy? *International Journal of Language Studies*, 18(2), 7–34. 10.5281/zenodo.10475208

Padley, R. H. (2022). Shame, discrimination and disability: Unveiling narratives of obesity. *International Journal of Language Studies*, 16(4), 43–64.

Poulos, C. N. (2021). *Essentials of autoethnography*. American Psychological Association. 10.1037/0000222-000

Qadam, Z. S., Vafa, M. A., Hashemi, T., & Ali, A. P. (2023). Aging Enjoyment: A Grounded Theory Study. *Iranian Journal of Psychiatry*, 1–12.

Raffone, A. (2022). "Her leg didn't fully load in": A digitally-mediated social-semiotic critical discourse analysis of disability hate speech on TikTok. *International Journal of Language Studies*, 16(4), 17–42.

Razali, R., Sundana, L., & Ramli, R. (2024). Curriculum Development in Higher Education in Light of Culture and Religiosity: A Case Study in Aceh of Indonesia. *International Journal of Society. Culture & Language*, 12(1), 39–55. 10.22034/ijscl.2023.2010108.3144

Roshan, A. (2023). *Trajectories of Iranian migrants in Madrid* [Unpublished Doctoral Dissertation]. Universidad Autónoma de Madrid.

Rostamalizadeh, V., & Noubakht, R. (2020). Sustainable development and migration in Iranian frontier counties. *European Online Journal of Natural and Social Sciences*, 9(1), 135–152.

Rowe, E. (2024). Network ethnography in education: A literature review of network ethnography as a methodology and how it has been applied in critical policy studies. In Stacey, M., & Mockler, N. (Eds.), *Analysing education policy: Theory and method* (pp. 136–156). Routledge. 10.4324/9781003353379-13

Russo, K. E., & Grasso, A. (2022). Coping with dis/ableism in Twitter discourse: A corpus-based critical appraisal analysis of the Hidden Disabilities Sunflower Lanyard case. *International Journal of Language Studies*, 16(4), 65–94.

Şafak-Ayvazoğlu, A., Kunuroglu, F., & Yağmur, K. (2021) Psychological and socio-cultural adaptation of Syrian refugees in Turkey. *International Journal of Intercultural Relations, 80,* 99–111. https://doi.org/.2020.11.00310.1016/j.ijintrel

Saunders, M. L., Lewis, P., & Thornhill, A. (2009). *Research methods for business students.* Prentice, Hall.

Starck, A., Gutermann, J., Schouler-Ocak, M., Jesuthasan, J., Bongard, S., & Stangier, U. (2020). The relationship of acculturation, traumatic events and depression in female refugees. *Frontiers in Psychology, 11*, 906.

Streubert, H. J., & Carpenter, D. R. (2002). *Qualitative research in nursing: Advancing the humanistic imperative* (3rd ed.). Lippincott Williams & Wilkins.

Suter, E., Deutschlander, S., Mickelson, G., Nurani, Z., Lait, J., Harrison, L., & Grymonpre, R. (2012). Can IPC provide health human resources solutions? A knowledge synthesis. *Journal of Interprofessional Care*, 26(4), 261–268. 10.3109/13561820.2012.66301422390728

Wickrama, K. A., Beiser, M., & Kaspar, V. (2002). Assessing the longitudinal course of depression and economic integration of South-East Asian refugees: An application of latent growth curve analysis. *International Journal of Methods in Psychiatric Research*, 11(4), 154–168. 10.1002/mpr.13312459819

Williams, A. M., & Irurita, V. F. (2005). Enhancing the therapeutic potential of hospital environments by increasing the personal control and emotional comfort of hospitalized patients. *Applied Nursing Research*, 18(1), 22–28. 10.1016/j.apnr.2004.11.00115812732

Xu, Y., & Fang, F. (2024). Promoting educational equity: The implementation of translanguaging pedagogy in English language education. *International Journal of Language Studies*, 18(1), 53–80. 10.5281/zenodo.10468187

Chapter 1
Ethnographic Research Methods and the Role of Reflexivity in Qualitative Research

Anita Roshan
Universidad Autónoma de Madrid, Spain

Ali Elhami
http://orcid.org/0000-0002-8957-6000
UNICAF University, Larnaca, Cyprus

ABSTRACT

This chapter is dedicated to discussing ethnographic research methods as a valuable tool for studying cultures and societies. The authors explore the theoretical foundations behind the use of ethnographic research in studying human behavior and the benefits it offers in gaining a comprehensive understanding of various social groups. In addition, they discuss the advantages and limitations of ethnography, as well as the ethical considerations that researchers must take into account when conducting ethnographic research. Since ethnographic research often emphasizes the importance of reflexivity, acknowledging the researcher's own biases and perspectives that may influence data collection and interpretation, the authors explore reflexivity as a crucial aspect of ethnographic research. By incorporating reflexivity, ethnographic research becomes more transparent and acknowledges the potential impact of the researcher on the data collected. Thus, the authors delve into the significance of reflexivity in ethnography and its implications for ensuring rigor and validity in research findings.

INTRODUCTION

In qualitative research, researchers seek to understand the underlying motivations, attitudes, and behaviours of individuals through in-depth interviews, observations, and analysis of textual data. This approach allows for a deeper exploration of complex social phenomena that cannot be easily quantified or measured through quantitative methods. Qualitative research often involves smaller sample sizes compared to quantitative research, allowing for a more detailed and nuanced analysis of individual experiences and perspectives. Additionally, researchers may use various theoretical frameworks to guide

DOI: 10.4018/979-8-3693-3306-8.ch001

their analysis and interpretation of the data collected. These frameworks help researchers make sense of the data and provide a theoretical foundation for their findings. Overall, qualitative research provides rich and detailed insights into the human experience, shedding light on the complexities of social interactions and individual perspectives. One of the research methods in qualitative research is ethnography, which involves immersing oneself in a particular culture or community to observe and understand their behaviours and beliefs.

This chapter is dedicated to discussing ethnographic research methods as a valuable tool for studying cultures and societies. In ethnographic research, researchers often spend an extended period of time in the field, observing and participating in daily activities, conducting interviews, and collecting data through various methods such as participant observation and document analysis. This method allows for a deep understanding of the context and complexities of a particular group, providing rich insights into their culture and social dynamics. Thus, in this chapter, we will explore the theoretical foundations behind the use of ethnographic research in studying human behavior and the benefits it offers in gaining a comprehensive understanding of various social groups. In addition, we will discuss the advantages and limitations of ethnography, as well as provide some examples of ethnographic works to illustrate its application in different research settings. Furthermore, we will explore the ethical considerations that researchers must take into account when conducting ethnographic studies.

Since ethnographic research often emphasizes the importance of reflexivity, acknowledging the researcher's own biases and perspectives that may influence data collection and interpretation, we will explore reflexivity as a crucial aspect of ethnographic research. Reflexivity in ethnography refers to the researcher's awareness of their own biases, assumptions, and preconceptions that may influence the interpretation of data. This self-reflection allows researchers to critically analyze their role in the research process and acknowledge how their own background and experiences shape their understanding of the studied group. By incorporating reflexivity, ethnographic research becomes more transparent and acknowledges the potential impact of the researcher on the data collected. Thus, we will delve into the significance of reflexivity in ethnography and its implications for ensuring rigor and validity in research findings.

ETHNOGRAPHIC RESEARCH

Ethnography was developed by educational researchers in anthropology in the late 1960s, initiated by the studies of Malinowski (1922) and Boas (1962). Their research involved participation in small societies and systematic data collection over a long period to document these communities' belief systems and social life (Hammersly & Atkinson, 1995; Reeves et al., 2013). Ethnography was pivotal in the development of modern anthropology as it provided a deeper understanding of cultural practices and social structures. It is a research approach that emphasizes the importance of understanding cultures from an insider's perspective. Although the origin of ethnography dates back to Malinowski and Boas, it has since evolved to encompass a broader range of research methods and theoretical frameworks. Ethnography continues to be a valuable tool for studying and understanding diverse cultures in the current globalized world. Today, ethnography has become a widespread research method in different areas such as medicine, psychology, sociology, information systems, and education (Shagrir, 2017).

Ethnography has led to indispensable advancement in the field of social science -by drawing attention to the details of human interaction- which in many disciplines may not be considered (Blommaert & Jie, 2020). It allows researchers to understand the nuances of culture and behavior that quantitative methods may overlook, providing a more holistic understanding of society. It also enables researchers to uncover hidden power dynamics and inequalities that shape social interactions. On the other hand, to Reeves et al., (2013), ethnography enables researchers to overcome the limitations of relying solely on interview data. Through the collection of observations, interviews and documentary data, which are triangulated (i.e. compared and contrasted with one another) ethnographic research offers a qualitative approach with the potential to yield detailed and comprehensive accounts of different social phenomenon (actions, behaviour, interactions, beliefs) (Reeves, p. 1365).

Ethnography deals with describing and locating human behaviors, norms, values, thoughts, and customs in a natural setting (Shagrir, 2017). It provides the ethnographer the opportunity to participate and monitor the participants' real-life situations in order to understand the reasonable practices in their experiences (Sangasubana, 2011). It enables an understanding of the cultural context, life forms, and social dynamics that shape the participants' behaviors and beliefs. It allows for a deeper analysis of the reasons behind individuals' actions and beliefs, shedding light on the underlying motivations and societal influences that drive their behavior. On the other hand, Heller (2008) believes that ethnography allows the researcher to include an 'insider view' or 'emic view' of a particular group within a sociocultural situation and through immersion in the context of the study. In addition, ethnography is "open-ended, subject to self-correction during the process of inquiry itself" (Hymes, 1980, p. 92). Thus, ethnography is about entering the field and learning about a particular culture or society.

On this account, ethnographers pay attention to all the details during participant observations and describe the field via field notes. Ethnographers immerse themselves in the everyday lives of the people they are studying in order to gain a deep understanding of their culture and behaviors. This method allows them to see things from the perspective of the individuals within that society, which can provide valuable insights and context for their research. Immersion and personal engagement in the field enable the researcher to understand the subject and to explore predictable patterns (Angrosino, 2007; Duranti, 1997). Similarly, Hymes (1980) points out that ethnographic observations generate an in-depth and holistic understanding of the interlocutors' behaviors, values, beliefs, linguistic and life experiences in natural settings.

According to Blommaert and Jie (2020), ethnography goes beyond description, whereas it involves both epistemology and ontology perspectives- "the nature of knowledge and how we know it" (Heller, 2018, p.7) on the study of language and society. Ethnography also considers the power dynamics and social inequalities present in language use, highlighting the importance of understanding how these factors shape communication interactions. Ethnography can provide valuable insights into the ways in which language reflects and reinforces social structures. Through detailed observation and analysis, ethnography can reveal the underlying power dynamics at play in everyday communication interactions. By examining language use within specific cultural contexts, ethnography offers a deeper understanding of how social hierarchies and inequalities are perpetuated through communication. This holistic approach to studying language and society allows researchers to uncover the complex interplay between power dynamics, social structures, and linguistic practices. Ethnography is about learning and interpreting the anecdotes of those under study and "illuminate social processes and generate explanations of why people do and think the things they do" (Heller, 2008, p. 250).

However, ethnography like other research methods has its merits and demerits. The first benefit of ethnography is the possibility of involvement in the community of a particular group and observing verbal and non-verbal acts of individuals, which distinguished this from other methods (Duranti, 1997; Naidoo, 2012). It allows researchers to gain a deep understanding of cultural practices and behaviors in a natural setting. Thus, it is more likely to be particularly useful for studying the nuances of communication within a certain cultural context. Second, ethnography is longitudinal -although this characteristic is also considered as a drawback of ethnography (explained below)- which is an asset since "everyone present, researcher included, is likely either to let their guard down or to assume a more natural stance" (Wolcott, 1999, p.49). Thus, the researcher could obtain rich and detailed data in a naturally occurring situation during time and space. The researcher may have the opportunity to observe authentic behaviors and interactions. While minimizing the risk of participants altering their behavior due to the presence of an observer. Ultimately leading to more accurate and unbiased results in the study, which is crucial for drawing valid conclusions and making informed decisions. Third, ethnography can be done only by a researcher, in addition to not requiring expensive tools or equipment (Wolcott, 1999). This makes ethnography a cost-effective research method that is accessible to a wide range of researchers with varying levels of resources. Furthermore, it is exciting and adventurous as well as being a flexible method which enables the ethnographer to employ more than one method during the research (Reeves, Kuper & Hodges, 2008).

In contrast, ethnography is time-consuming, and the ethnographer might need to spend years on field observations (Singleton & Straits, 2005). Considerable time investment is required, not only in the site and after the data collection, but prior to the research to adjust the insights and attitude as well as to gain access to the field site. In the same vein, Blommaert and Jie (2020) note that ethnographers necessitate preparation and documentation and embracing ethnographic perspectives prior to the investigation. On the other hand, Iacono, Brown and Holtham (2009) criticize ethnographic research due to its deficiency of generalizability since it concentrates on a distinct subject or situation. However, Blommaert and Jie (2020) believe that generalization is achievable, although it depends on the theoretical claim that can be derived from the data. A further drawback is the difficulty of maintaining the balance between the researcher role as an observer and a participant (Singleton & Straits, 2005). Because once the researcher gets more familiar with the participants and setting, he/she "may be drawn into the lives of those people more as a participant than as an observer" (Sangasubana, 2011, p. 572). Moreover, Sangasubana (2011) identifies two other potential weaknesses of ethnography, including the prospect of bias from the researcher's side, and the necessity of considering the confidentiality of the participants and ethical issues.

After discussing the advantages and disadvantages of ethnographic research, it is worthwhile to look at different conceptualizations of ethnography -as a method, theory, or approach. For instance, Hammersley and Atkinson (1995) consider ethnography as a method of observation, since "it involves the ethnographer participating, overtly or covertly, in people's daily lives for an extended period of time, watching what happens, listening to what is said, asking questions - in fact collecting whatever data are available to throw light on the issues that are the focus of the research" (p. 1). To Smith (1987) ethnography is a strategy, "a commitment to an investigation and explication of how 'it' actually is, of how 'it' actually works, of actual practices and relations" (p. 160). On the other hand, Blommaert and Dong (2010) believe that "to Hymes, ethnography was a 'descriptive theory': an approach that was theoretical because it provided description in specific, methodologically and epistemologically grounded ways" (p.

8). Furthermore, Sabar-Ben Yehoshua (2016), and Shlasky and Alpert (2007) claim that ethnography is an approach combining methodology, data, data analysis, and researcher's interpretation.

In general, ethnography is a qualitative research method that involves immersion in a particular culture or social group. It is a qualitative research method established on personal understanding and systematic firsthand participant observations (Duranti, 1997). It involves a deep dive into understanding the nuances of social practices and interactions, providing a rich and detailed account of the studied phenomenon. It aims to provide a detailed and holistic view of the subject being studied through participant observation and interviews. Ethnography emphasizes the importance of context, reflexivity, and the researcher's role in shaping interpretations of the data collected.

EXAMPLES OF ETHNOGRAPHIC WORKS

Numerous studies have employed ethnography as a research method to comprehend various communities and cultures. These studies not only added to the existing body of knowledge but also provided valuable insights into the lives of people in different social contexts. The results of these studies have provided valuable insights into the social structures and practices of these groups. Additionally, they have highlighted the importance of understanding and respecting diverse perspectives.

The first instance of ethnographic work is the PhD dissertation of Roshan (2023), which focuses on exploring the socialization and lived experiences of Iranian migrants in Madrid. Her research represents as the first ethnographic research into the socialization of Iranian migrants in Madrid. She investigates the trajectories, language barriers, application of English as a lingua franca, Spanish language learning, language investment, and socialization dynamics of first-generation Iranian adults, with a particular emphasis on PhD students. She conducted her ethnographic fieldwork between January 2018 and February 2020 in two separate contexts, including a religious center and an educational institution. Besides using participant observations in both settings, she collected data through interviews, focus groups, and documents. Roshan's study explores how newcomers who arrive in Spain with certain linguistic backgrounds encounter challenges. Her research sought to investigate the impact of Englishization in higher education and neoliberal society by focusing on PhD students. She also examines the complexities of language investment and how participants questioned whether they should improve their Spanish or English.

Another example is the PhD dissertation of Augustyniak (2016), which focuses on portraying the voices of migrants' experiences learning Basque in the areas of ideology, attitudes, and positioning through an ethnographic perspective that is informed by the author's self-reflection on the site. Despite being Polish, she did not restrict her sample to exclusively immigrants from Poland. As a result, the criteria for choosing the participants in the study were focused on current or previous Basque language learners. She collected data through participant observations in migrant-targeted Basque language classes, documentation, and audio recordings of some activities outside the classroom.

Additionally, Caglitutuncigil's (2015) work on the language learning of Moroccan women in Madrid and Barcelona is a practical ethnographic work. A four-year critical ethnographic project by Caglitutuncigil is built on participant observations and interviews. She argues that learning the local language gives migrants both linguistic power and competence. Therefore, migrants invest in learning the legitimate language in language courses to develop their linguistic capital, which enables them to place in socio-economic advantage positions.

Also, Zachrison's dissertation (2014) goal is to understand how the context of adult migrants' ordinary routine, their attachments to their home countries, and their ethnic affiliations potentially determine their motivation and attitude toward learning and using Swedish as a second language in Sweden. Her study included classroom observation and interviews as data collecting methods. Her findings suggest that the majority of informants have experienced a lack of belonging both within and outside of the classroom when adopting the dominant language.

Finally, further examples of ethnographic research are the ethnographic studies on multilingual school contexts in Barcelona conducted by Corona (2017) and Llompart (2016). Corona's longitudinal study on multilingual interactions in the school and Latin American youth identity formation was commenced in 2005. Field notes, audio and video recordings, interviews, focus groups, and documents have all been used by him as data collection tools. On the other hand, Llompart's ethnographic thesis is grounded on the language socialization and trajectories of youth immigrants in a superdiverse high school in Barcelona and with the collaboration of action research.

Reflexivity and Autoethnography

Participant observations and the role of the researcher in creating knowledge in qualitative research are of paramount importance. In this way, the background, experiences, and position of the researcher in the study shape the knowledge that he/she generates. Albeit reflexivity received some criticism due to the researcher's potential bias, "the practice of incorporating the researcher perspective in the design and interpretation of data has now gained currency" (Patnaik, 2013, p. 98). As such, Thurairajah (2019) encourages reflexivity as a process expected in qualitative research, since it inevitably manipulates findings.

Reflexivity means "turning of the researcher lens back onto oneself to recognize and take responsibility for one's own situatedness within the research and the effect that it may have on the setting and people being studied, questions being asked, data being collected and its interpretation" (Berger, 2015, p. 220). It deals with placing ourselves in our research as a participant and "thinking about our experiences and questioning our ways of doing" (Haynes, 2012, p. 73).

On the other hand, Haynes (2012) claims the following:

> Reflexivity goes beyond simple reflection on the research process and outcomes, to incorporate multiple layers and levels of reflection within the research. These would include considering the complex relationships between the production of knowledge (epistemology), the processes of knowledge production (methodology), and the involvement and impact of the knowledge producer or researcher (ontology). Reflexivity enables the research processes and outcomes to be open to change and adaptive in response to these multiple layers of reflection. (p. 73)

Therefore, reflexivity is theoretically inevitable in contemporary sociolinguistics. As Pérez-Milans (2013) explains the vital role of epistemology and the researcher's field trajectories collide with "the spaces, social actors, and meaning making practices on which our analysis is based... in fact, sociolinguists are social actors who bring their own symbolic and material resources into the social space in which their data are collected" (p. 10). To Heller (2002), a certain degree of 'reflexivity' is needed for knowledge construction. That is to say, by the necessity to understand how research connects to the knowledge it creates and makes this process apparent while taking into consideration its social repercussions (Heller, 2002).

While reflexivity is fundamental in contemporary sociolinguistics, it is above all much more pronounced in ethnographic research because of "the involvement of the researcher in the society and culture of those being studied is particularly close" (Davies, 1999, p.4). Reflexivity in ethnographic research involves providing the ethnographer with a voice and establishing him/her as a contributor to the study. Thus, understanding the collected data and construction of knowledge are influenced by reflecting upon and writing about the situatedness of the ethnographer. Subsequently, "to achieve a reflexive stance the researcher needs to bend back upon herself to make herself as well as the other an object of study" (Chiseri-Strater, 1996, p.119).

Therefore, reflexivity is about the positionality of the researcher in the research process. To Berger (2015), reflexivity is "the process of a continual internal dialogue and critical self-evaluation of researcher positionality as well as active acknowledgment and explicit recognition that this position may affect the research process and outcome" (p. 220). Thus, by acknowledging the role of the researcher as being part of the research, the researcher takes "greater account of how they are influencing the research, and therefore be more cognizant about how they share the stories of others" (Thurairajah, 2019, p. 133).

Consequently, once a researcher/ethnographer approaches the field site, he/she is more likely to reflect on his/her position as a researcher as a vital piece of his/her practice in data collection and analysis. For instance, He/she may carefully consider to what extent his/her fieldwork observations would challenge his/her preconceived notions as well as to what extent his/her ideas and personality would prefigure the kind of questions that he/she might ask and the kind of practices that he/she may pay attention to. Thus, his/her fieldwork in the ethnographic research could carry out with the awareness that he/she as a social actor in the field as well as the social and emotional ties that he/she might have with the other individuals participating in the study were shaping the research and its outcomes.

Since in ethnographic research the positionality of the researcher is so crucial in the configuration of the study, it might be worthwhile to learn about autoethnographic work. This can provide valuable insights into how personal experiences and perspectives shape the research process. Additionally, autoethnographic work can also help researchers critically reflect on their own biases and assumptions. By engaging in autoethnographic work, researchers can better understand how their background, beliefs, and experiences influence their interpretations of the data and the conclusions they draw. This self-awareness can lead to more nuanced and reflexive research, ultimately enhancing the quality and validity of the study findings. Overall, incorporating autoethnographic methods into ethnographic research can lead to more impactful and transformative studies that truly capture the complexity of human experiences.

Autoethnography is a research and writing technique that seeks to explain and analyze personal experiences of the researchers and their interaction with individuals in the field in order to comprehend cultural experience (Ellis, Adams & Bochner, 2011; Reed-Danahay, 2017). It is an approach that enables the researcher to interrogate the community to that he/she belongs, given the centrality of his/her experience with that group. Likewise, Méndez (2013) claims that "autoethnography allows researchers to draw on their own experiences to understand a particular phenomenon or culture" (p. 280).

Furthermore, Reed-Danahay (2017) claims that autoethnography "provokes questions about the nature of ethnographic knowledge by troubling the persistent dichotomies of insider versus outsider, distance versus familiarity, objective observer versus participant, and individual versus culture" (p. 145). In contrast to establishing a dichotomy that favors the insider tale, she has argued that it is more constructive to conceptualize autoethnography as being at the confluence of insider and outsider views (Reed-Danahay, 2009, 2017). Thus, "autoethnography reflects a view of ethnography as both a reflexive and a collaborative enterprise, in which the life experiences of the anthropologist and their relationships with others 'in the field' should be interrogated and explored" (Reed-Danahay, 2017, p. 145).

On the other hand, similar to ethnography, with the ethnographer producing a "thick description" of a society or culture (Geertz, 1973, p.10), the researchers in autoethnography "seek to produce aesthetic and evocative thick descriptions of personal and interpersonal experience" (Ellis, et al., 2011, p. 277). To Atkinson, Coffey, and Delamont (2003),

> [Auto]ethnographers-as-authors frame their accounts with personal reflexive views of the self. Their ethnographic data are situated within their personal experience and sense making. They themselves form part of the representational processes in which they are engaging and are part of the story they are telling. (p. 62).

The idea of pairing ethnographic study with autoethnography allows researchers to not only observe and analyze a culture from an outsider's perspective but also to reflect on their own experiences within that culture. This dual approach can provide a more comprehensive understanding of the dynamics at play as well as shed light on the researcher's own biases and assumptions. By combining these two methods, researchers can create a richer, more nuanced depiction of the culture being studied. This approach also allows for a deeper connection to be formed between the researcher and the subjects of the study, as the researcher's own experiences and emotions become part of the narrative. Autoethnography can also help to humanize the research process, making it more relatable and accessible to a wider audience. In addition, by incorporating personal reflections into the analysis, researchers can offer a more authentic and holistic perspective on the culture under study.

The combination of ethnography and autoethnography is supported by several scholars (e.g., Wall, 2006; Siddique, 2011). If Wall (2006) suggests "the use of autoethnography alongside other well-known qualitative research methods" (p. 5), Siddique (2011) explicitly encourages combining ethnography and autoethnography in order to improve the quality of the study. She recommends the use of these two ethnographic methods together despite the discomfort and certain feeling of 'in-between-ness' that the combination may cause: "If auto-ethnography situates the researcher with the insider's perspective and ethnography is from the outsider's perspective, the researcher is caught 'in-between' these two approaches" (p. 310).

Ethical considerations in ethnographic research

Conducting qualitative research, especially when it deals with individuals as social actors, might pose ethical challenges for the researcher. Scholars who carry out studies with human beings should follow general principles related to ethical issues, which may vary by discipline, but which, at a minimum, should include the following: "voluntary participation and the right to withdraw, protection of research participants, assessment of potential benefits and risks to participants, obtaining informed consent and not doing harm" (Silverman, 2013, p.161).

Richards and Schwartz (2002) claim that in qualitative research informed consent, anonymity, and confidentiality (i.e., protecting the personal information of participants) need to be taken into account. To Orb, Eisenhauer and Wynaden (2001) informed consent is an essential issue of ethical consideration, and the researcher is responsible to inform participants of all the details related to the nature and objectives of the study, the role of the researcher(s) and participants, and to identify how the findings would be used or published. In addition, some researchers might anonymize the name of the participants by using pseudonyms, codes, or numbers to protect their identity.

Thus, in ethnographic research, the need to obtain informed consent from participants is essential to uphold ethical standards and protect the rights and privacy of individuals. This involves clearly explaining the purpose of the study, the potential risks and benefits, and the voluntary nature of participation. Additionally, researchers must ensure that participants understand their right to withdraw from the study at any time without consequences. Another important ethical consideration is the need to protect the confidentiality and anonymity of participants, particularly when sensitive or personal information is being shared. Researchers must take steps to securely store and protect data to prevent unauthorized access or disclosure.

CONCLUSION

This chapter has covered ethnographic research techniques as well as the benefits and drawbacks of using ethnography as a qualitative research methodology. The advantages and disadvantages of ethnography are important to consider when deciding on the most appropriate research approach for a particular study. It is essential to weigh the pros and cons of ethnography in order to effectively address research questions and gather meaningful data. By doing so, researchers can ensure that their methodology aligns with the goals and objectives of their study. We also provided examples of certain research studies that used ethnography as a means of gaining in-depth insights into different cultures and social phenomena.

Furthermore, since reflexivity has a crucial role in qualitative research, particularly ethnography, we emphasized the importance of researchers being self-aware and acknowledging their own biases and perspectives throughout the research process. This allows for a more comprehensive and unbiased interpretation of the collected data. Researchers must constantly reflect on their own positionality and its influence on the study. This is essential for maintaining the integrity and validity of the research findings.

Also, we explored autoethnography as a method for understanding the researcher's own experiences and perspectives. Autoethnography provides a unique and valuable perspective that can enhance the overall depth and richness of the research analysis. With the help of autoethnography, researchers can add personal accounts and reflections to their work, providing a more comprehensive understanding of the subject matter.

In this chapter, we finally discussed the significance of ethical considerations in ethnographic research. Greater care must be taken while conducting human subjects studies to guarantee the protection of participants' rights and well-being at all times. Informed consent is an essential issue of ethical consideration that should be obtained before conducting any research study involving human participants. This ensures that participants are fully aware of the risks and benefits of their involvement and can make an informed decision about whether or not to participate.

REFERENCES

Angrosino, M. (2007). *Doing ethnographic and observational Research*. SAGE Publications Ltd. 10.4135/9781849208932

Atkinson, P. A., Coffey, A., & Delamont, S. (2003). *Key themes in qualitative research: Continuities and change*. AltaMira Press.

Augustyniak, A. (2016). *'Basque for all?' Ideology and Identity in Migrants' Perceptions of Basque.* [Doctoral Dissertation]. University of Southampton, Southampton.

Berger, R. (2015). Now I see it, now I don't: Researcher's position and reflexivity in qualitative research. *Qualitative Research*, 15(2), 219–234. 10.1177/1468794112468475

Blommaert, J., & Dong, J. (2010). Language and movement in space. In Coupland, N. (Ed.), *The handbook of language and globalization* (pp. 366–385). Wiley-Black. 10.1002/9781444324068.ch16

Blommaert, J., & Jie, D. (2020). *Ethnographic fieldwork*. Multilingual Matters. 10.21832/BLOMMA7130h

Boas, F. (1962). *Anthropology and Modern Life*. The Norton Library.

Caglitutuncigil, T. (2015). Intersectionality in language trajectories: African women in Spain. *Applied Linguistics Review*, 6(2), 217–239. 10.1515/applirev-2015-0011

Chiseri-Strater, E. (1996). Turning In upon Ourselves: Positionality, Subjectivity, and Reflexivity in Case Study and Ethnographic Research. In P. Mortensen & G. Kirsch (Eds.), *Ethics and Representation in Qualitative Studies of Literacy* (pp. 115-133). New York: Stony Brook.

Corona, V. (2017). An ethnographic approach to the study of linguistic varieties used by young Latin Americans in Barcelona. In E. Moore & M. Dooly (Eds.), *Qualitative approaches to research on plurilingual education* (pp. 170-188). Research-publishing.net. 10.14705/rpnet.2017.emmd2016.627

Davies, Ch. A. (1999). *Reflexive Ethnography: a guide to researching selves and others*. Routledge.

Duranti, A. (1997). *Linguistic anthropology*. Cambridge University Press. 10.1017/CBO9780511810190

Ellis, C., Adams, T. E., & Bochner, A. P. (2011). Autoethnography: an overview. *Historical Social Research. Social Science Open Access Repository, 36*(4), 273-290. 10.12759/hsr.36.2011.4.273-290

Geertz, C. (1973). *The interpretation of cultures*. Basic Books.

Hammersley, M., & Atkinson, P. (1995). *Ethnography: principles in practice*. Routledge.

Heller, M. (2002). *Éléments d'une sociolinguiste critique*. Didier.

Heller, M. (2008). Language and the nation-state: Challenges to sociolinguistic theory and practice1. *Journal of Sociolinguistics*, 12(4), 504–524. 10.1111/j.1467-9841.2008.00373.x

Heller, M. (2018). Continuity and renewal. *Journal of Sociolinguistics*, 22(1), 3–4. 10.1111/josl.12267

Hymes, D. (1980). *language in education*. Centre for Applied Linguistics Haynes, K. (2012). Reflexivity in qualitative research. In G. Symon & C. Cassell (Eds.), *Qualitative Organizational Research: Core Methods and Current Challenges* (pp. 72-89). Sage.

Iacono, J., Brown, A., & Holtham, C. (2009). Research methods – a case example of participant observation. *Electronic Journal of Business Research Methods*, 7(1), 39–46.

Llompart, J. (2016). *Pràctiques plurilingües d'escolars d'un institut superdivers: de la recerca a l'acció educativa* [Doctoral tesis. Universidad Autónoma de Barcelona]. Retreived from https://www.tdx.cat/handle/10803/399835#page=1

Malinowski, B. (1922). Argonauts of the Western Pacific. George Routledge & Sons Ltd.

Méndez, M. (2013). Autoethnography as a research method: Advantages, limitations and criticisms. *Colombian Applied Linguistics Journal*, 15(2), 279–287. 10.14483/udistrital.jour.calj.2013.2.a09

Naidoo, L. (2012). *Ethnography: An Introduction to Definition and Method*. InTech. 10.5772/39248

Orb, A., Eisenhauer, L., & Wynaden, D. (2001). Ethics in Qualitative Research. *Journal of Nursing Scholarship*, 33(1), 93–96. 10.1111/j.1547-5069.2001.00093.x11253591

Patnaik, E. (2013). Reflexivity: Situating the researcher in qualitative research. *Humanities and Social Science Studies*, 2(1), 98–106.

Pérez-Milans, M. (2013). *Urban schools and English language education in late modern china: a critical sociolinguistic ethnography*. Routledge. 10.4324/9780203366189

Reed-Danahay, D. (2009). Anthropologists, education, and autoethnography. *Revista de Antropologia*, 38(1), 28–47. 10.1080/00938150802672931

Reed-Danahay, D. (2017). Bourdieu and Critical Autoethnography: Implications for Research, Writing, and Teaching. *International Journal of Multicultural Education*, 19(1), 144–154. 10.18251/ijme.v19i1.1368

Reeves, S., Kuper, A., & Hodges, B. D. (2008). Qualitative research methodologies: Ethnography. *Clinical Research*, 337(aug07 3), a1020. Advance online publication. 10.1136/bmj.a102018687725

Reeves, S., Peller, J., Goldman, J., & Kitto, S. (2013). Ethnography in qualitative educational research. *Medical Teacher*, 80(8), 1365–1379. 10.3109/0142159X.2013.80497723808715

Richards, H. M., & Schwartz, L. J. (2002). Ethics of qualitative research: Are there special issues for health services research? *Family Practice*, 19(2), 135–139. 10.1093/fampra/19.2.13511906977

Roshan, A. (2023). *Trajectories of Iranian migrants in Madrid* [Unpublished Doctoral Dissertation]. Universidad Autónoma de Madrid.

Sabar Ben-Yehoshua, N. (2016). *Traditions and Genres in Qualitative Research. Philosophies, Strategiesand Advanced Tools*. Mofet Institution.

Sangasubana, N. (2011). How to Conduct Ethnographic Research. *The Qualitative Report*, 16(2), 567–573. 10.46743/2160-3715/2011.1071

Shagrir, L. (2017). The Ethnographic Research. In *Journey to Ethnographic Research. SpringerBriefs in Education*. Springer. 10.1007/978-3-319-47112-9_2

Shlasky, S., & Alpert, B. (2007). *Ways of writing qualitative research: From dismantling the reality to structuring the text*. Mofet Institute.

Siddique, S. (2011). Being in-between: The relevance of ethnography and auto-ethnography for psychotherapy research. *Counselling & Psychotherapy Research*, 11(4), 310–316. 10.1080/14733145.2010.533779

Silverman, D. (2013). *Doing qualitative research* (4th ed.). SAGE.

Singleton, R. A. Jr, & Straits, B. C. (2005). *Approaches to Social Research* (4th ed.). Oxford University Press.

Smith, D. E. (1987). The everyday world as problematic: a feminist sociology. Northeastern University Press.

Thurairajah, K. (2019). Uncloaking the researcher: Boundaries in qualitative research. *Qualitative Sociology Review*, 15(1), 132–147. 10.18778/1733-8077.15.1.06

Wall, S. (2006). An autoethnography on learning about autoethnography. *International Journal of Qualitative Methods*, 5(2), 146–160. 10.1177/160940690600500205

Wolcott, H., F. (1999). *Ethnography: A way of seeing*. A Division of Rowman & Littlefield Publisher, Inc.

Zachrison, M. (2014). *Invisible voices: Understanding the Sociocultural Influences on Adult Migrants' Second Language Learning and Communicative Interaction* [Doctoral thesis, Linköpings University]. Retrieved from https://urn.kb.se/resolve?urn=urn:nbn:se:mau:diva-7388

ADDITIONAL READING

Blommaert, J. (2005). Bourdieu the ethnographer: The ethnographic grounding of habitus and voice. *The Translator*, 11(2), 219–236. 10.1080/13556509.2005.10799199

Blommaert, J. & Jie, D. (2010). *Ethnographic Fieldwork: A Beginner's Guide*. Bristol, Blue Ridge Summit: Multilingual Matters. 10.21832/9781847692962

Brewer, J. D. (2000). *Ethnography*. Open University Press.

Clifford, J. (1988). *The Predicament of Culture: Twentieth Century Ethnography, Literature and Art*. Harvard University Press.

Creswell, J. W. (2007). *Qualitative inquiry and research design – choosing among five approaches* (2nd ed.). Sage.

Fabian, J. (1995). Ethnographic misunderstanding and the perils of context. *American Anthropologist*, 97(1), 41–50. 10.1525/aa.1995.97.1.02a00080

Fetterman, D. M. (2010). *Ethnography: Step by step*. Sage.

Fook, J. (1999). Reflexivity as method. *Annual Review of Health Social Science*, 9(1), 11–20. 10.5172/hesr.1999.9.1.11

Hammersley, M. (1992). *What's wrong with Ethnography?* Routledge.

Hammersley, M., & Atkinson, P. (1991). *Ethnographic principles in practice*. Routledge.

Morrow, F., & Kettle, M. (2024). Putting the auto in ethnography: The embodied process of reflexivity on positionality. *Qualitative Social Work: Research and Practice*, 23(3), 554–565. 10.1177/14733250231196430

Murchison, J. (2010). *Ethnography Essentials: Designing, Conducting, and Presenting Your Research*. John Wiley & Sons.

Murchison, J. M. (2010). *Ethnography essentials: Designing, conducting, and presenting your research*. Jossey-Bass.

O'Reilly, K. (2005). *Ethnographic methods*. Routledge.

Pillow, W. (2003). Confession, catharsis, or cure? Rethinking the uses of reflexivity as methodological power in qualitative research. *International Journal of Qualitative Studies in Education : QSE*, 16(2), 175–196. 10.1080/0951839032000060635

Pillow, W. S. (2010). Dangerous reflexivity: rigour, responsibility and reflexivity in qualitative research. In Thomson, P., & Walker, M. (Eds.), *The Routledge Doctoral Student's Companion Getting to Grips with Research in Education and the Social Sciences* (pp. 270–282). Routledge.

Silverman, D. (2017). *Doing Qualitative Research* (5th ed.). Sage.

Spradley, J. (1979). *The ethnographic interview*. Holt, Rinehart and Winston.

Strudwick, R. M. (2020). Ethnographic research in healthcare – patients and service users as participants. *Disability and Rehabilitation*, 43(22), 3271–3275. 10.1080/09638288.2020.174169532202439

Wolcott, H. F. (1999). *Ethnography – a way of seeing*. Altimira Press.

KEY TERMS AND DEFINITIONS

Autoethnography: Is an approach to research and writing that seeks to describe and systematically analyze personal experience in order to understand cultural experience. This approach challenges canonical ways of doing research and representing others and treats research as a political, socially-just and socially-conscious act. A researcher uses tenets of autobiography and ethnography to do and write autoethnography. Thus, as a method, autoethnography is both process and product.

Ethical Considerations: In research are a set of principles that guide your research designs and practices. These principles include voluntary participation, informed consent, anonymity, confidentiality, potential for harm, and results communication. Scientists and researchers must always adhere to a certain code of conduct when collecting data from others. These considerations protect the rights of research participants, enhance research validity, and maintain scientific integrity.

Ethnographic Research: Ethnographic research is a qualitative research method involving the systematic study of people in their natural environment to understand their way of life, including how they see and interact with the world around them. The aim of an ethnography study is to produce a rich, comprehensive account of a social setting from the participants' point of view.

Participant Observation: Is a research method where the researcher immerses themself in a particular social setting or group, observing the behaviors, interactions, and practices of the participants. This can be a valuable method for any research project that seeks to understand the experiences of individuals or groups in a particular social context. In participant observation, the researcher is called a participant-observer, meaning that they participate in the group's activities while also observing the group's behavior and interactions. There is flexibility in the level of participation, ranging from non-participatory (the weakest) to complete participation (the strongest but most intensive.) The goal here is to gain a deep understanding of the group's culture, beliefs, and practices from an "insider" perspective.

Reflexivity: Reflexivity is the act of examining one's own assumption, belief, and judgement systems, and thinking carefully and critically about how these influence the research process. The practice of reflexivity confronts and questions who we are as researchers and how this guides our work.

Sociolinguistics: Is the study of the sociological aspects of language. The discipline examines how different social factors, such as ethnicity, gender, age, class, occupation, education, and geographical location can influence language use and maintain social roles within a community. In simple terms, sociolinguistics is interested in the social dimensions of language.

Chapter 2
Grounded Theory:
Unraveling Cultural Complexity in Qualitative Research

Casey Allison Esmeraldo
UNICAF University, South Africa

ABSTRACT

This chapter explores the application of grounded theory methodology in qualitative research, focusing on its role in unraveling cultural complexity. Grounded theory offers a systematic approach to understanding cultural phenomena by grounding theories in the data collected from diverse cultural contexts. The chapter begins by emphasizing the importance of cultural sensitivity and reflexivity, highlighting the need for researchers to acknowledge their own biases and engage with the perspectives of participants. It then discusses coding and analysis techniques across cultures, emphasizing the need to navigate cultural nuances and meanings. Strategies for ensuring trustworthiness and validity in cross-cultural research are examined. The chapter also explores the integration of diverse cultural perspectives in theory development, emphasizing the importance of co-constructing theories with participants. Overall, the chapter underscores the value of grounded theory and its role in fostering cross-cultural understanding in qualitative research.

INTRODUCTION

Qualitative research, particularly grounded theory methodology, holds a unique position in unraveling the difficulties of cultural complexity. Bergkamp (2010), defines qualitative research as "the emphasis on quality versus quantity of phenomena", researchers study phenomena and people in their natural environment and are concerned about the how, what, where, during research. Within the realms of cultural exploration, grounded theory provides a robust framework for understanding the dynamic interplay of beliefs, values, norms, and practices within diverse cultural contexts. Grounded theory is defined by Charmaz and Thornberg (2021) as "a systematic method of conducting research that shapes collecting data and provides explicit strategies for analyzing them." This chapter delves into the multifaceted application of grounded theory in qualitative research, emphasizing its role in uncovering the layers of cultural meaning, navigating cultural sensitivity and reflexivity, coding, and analysis techniques across cultures, ensuring trustworthiness and validity, integrating diverse cultural perspectives in theory development,

DOI: 10.4018/979-8-3693-3306-8.ch002

and responsibly communicating research findings. Cultural phenomena are inherently complex, shaped by historical, social, political, and economic factors that vary across geographical locations and societal groups. Grounded theory, with its emphasis on data-driven theory development, offers a systematic approach to dealing with this complexity by immersing researchers in the experiences lived by individuals and communities. By grounding theories in the realities of this field, grounded theory enables researchers to move beyond preconceived notions and delve into the nuances of cultural dynamics.

Central to the application of grounded theory in cultural research is the recognition of the importance of cultural sensitivity and reflexivity. Researchers should approach their work with humility, acknowledging their own cultural biases and assumptions, while remaining attuned to the perspectives of the individuals or communities under study. Reflexivity becomes a guiding principle, prompting researchers to continuously reflect on how their background, experiences, and positionality may influence every stage of the research process – from data collection to analysis and interpretation (Bergkamp, 2010). Coding and analysis, important components of grounded theory methodology, take on added significance in cross-cultural research. The process of identifying themes, patterns, and categories within the data requires a keen awareness of cultural nuances and meanings embedded within participants' narratives (Charmaz & Thornberg, 2021). Researchers must navigate the complexities of interpretation, translation, and cultural context, making use of open, axial, and selective coding techniques to capture the richness of cultural diversity. Ensuring trustworthiness and validity is paramount in grounded theory research, particularly when working across cultural boundaries. Establishing trust with participants, often from underrepresented or marginalized communities, necessitates building meaningful relationships based on mutual respect, transparency, and reciprocity (Engler, 2021). Strategies such as prolonged engagement, member checking, peer debriefing, and triangulation serve as pillars of methodological rigor, enhancing credibility and reliability of research findings. Moreover, grounded theory offers a unique opportunity to integrate diverse cultural perspectives in theory development, challenging monocultural narratives and fostering a more inclusive understanding of cultural phenomena (Nayar & Clair, 2020). By engaging with participants as co-researchers in the theory-building process, researchers can develop theories that authentically reflect the complexities of lived experiences within specific cultural contexts. And lastly, responsible communication of grounded theory findings requires researchers to navigate the delicate balance between academic rigor and cultural sensitivity. Presenting findings in a manner that respects the cultural context and perspectives of participants is essential for ethical research practice. By engaging with stakeholders from the involved cultures and employing culturally appropriate language and imagery, researchers can ensure that their findings are accurately represented and interpreted within cultural context.

Grounded theory methodology serves as a powerful tool for unraveling cultural complexity in qualitative research. By embracing cultural sensitivity, reflexivity, methodological rigor, and responsible communication, grounded theory enables researchers to develop theories that resonate with the richness and diversity of human experiences across cultures. As we continue to navigate an increasingly interconnected world, grounded theory remains indispensable for fostering cross-cultural understanding and advancing knowledge in the field of cultural research.

GROUNDED THEORY

Grounded theory is a qualitative research methodology introduced by sociologists Glaser and Strauss during the 1960s, who aimed to generate theories from data instead of testing preconceived hypotheses (Glaser & Strauss, 2017). This emphasizes the systematic gathering and analysis of data to construct theories grounded in empirical evidence, fostering a deeper understanding of complex social phenomena. The importance of grounded theory lies in its ability to uncover hidden patterns and relationships within data, providing insights to the underlying processes that shape human behavior and interactions.

There are several steps one may take when conducting grounded theory, from data collection to theory development:

1. Familiarization with literature – By reviewing existing literature relevant to your research topic to gain a better understanding of the context and to identify gaps in knowledge. However, it is important to not let the existing theories overly influence your approach as grounded theory aims to develop new theories from data.

2. Data collection – Employ a purposeful sampling strategy to select participants who can provide rich, diverse, and relevant data related to your research question. Data collection methods commonly used in grounded theory include interviews, observations, and document analysis. Conduct open-ended interviews or observations to gather rich qualitative data without imposing preconceived categories or hypotheses.

3. Coding – coding is an important tool in grounded theory as it helps uncover patterns, themes, and categories that may vary significantly and involves staying close to the data and avoiding premature abstraction or interpretation.

4. Focused coding – As patterns and themes emerge from the initial coding, begin to focus on the most significant concepts or categories by selectively coding data related to these central ideas. This involves clustering similar codes together and identifying relationships between them.

5. Theoretical sampling – use theoretical sampling to guide further data collection, selecting participants or sources of data that can provide insights into emerging theoretical concepts or gaps in understanding. This process helps refine and validate emerging theories through ongoing data collection and analysis.

6. Constant comparison – continuously comparing data within and across cases helps identify similarities, differences, and relationships between concepts. This involves moving back and forth between the collected data, coding, and analysis to refine theoretical concepts and develop theoretical explanations grounded in empirical evidence.

7. Theoretical Saturation – Continue data collection and analysis until theoretical saturation is reached, meaning no new concept or insights are emerging from the data. At this point the theoretical framework is sufficiently developed, and further data collection is unlikely to contribute significantly to theory development.

8. Validation – Validate the grounded theory through various means, such as member checking, peer debriefing, and triangulation. This helps ensure the credibility and trustworthiness of the theory being developed.

9. Theory development – Synthesize the emergent theoretical concepts into a coherent framework or model that explains the phenomena under investigation. This process involves articulating the relationship between concepts and identifying the core processes or mechanisms that drive these relationships.

10. Communicating Findings – Finally, communicating grounded theory findings in a clear and coherent manner, providing rich descriptions of data, the process of theory development, and the resulting theoretical framework. Present the theory in a way that is accessible to both academic audiences and practitioners, highlighting its relevance and implications for theory, practice, and policy.

Through these steps researchers can systematically conduct grounded theory research to develop rich and nuanced theoretical understandings of complex social phenomena grounded in empirical evidence. Within a multicultural context, grounded theory provides a powerful framework for exploring the dynamics of diverse cultural interactions and experiences. By employing an inductive approach, researchers can capture the rich complexity of cultural diversity, avoiding the imposition of pre-existing theoretical frameworks that may not adequately account for cultural nuances.

The most widely recognized types of grounded theory include classic grounded theory, constructive grounded theory, and situational analysis. Each type with its own approach to data collection, analysis, and theory development.

Classic grounded theory, as developed by Glaser and Strauss (2017), emphasizes the discovery of core theoretical concepts through constant comparison of data. This approach involves iterative coding data to identify categories and their properties, with a focus on generating a substantive theory that explains the underlying social processes. For example, in the study by Corbin and Strauss (2014), classic grounded theory was used to explore the process of "struggling to regain control" among individuals living with chronic illness, leading to the development of a theoretical framework that highlighted the dynamic interplay between illness management strategies and personal identity reconstruction.

Constructive grounded theory, proposed by Charmaz, takes a more interpretive stance, emphasizing the role of the researcher's reflexivity and engagement with participants' perspectives (Clarke & Charmaz, 2019). This approach recognizes the co-construction of knowledge between researcher and participant and encourages the exploration of multiple realities within the data. For instance, in a study by Clarke (2005), constructivist grounded theory was employed to investigate the experience of individuals living with HIV/Aids, revealing diverse coping strategies and meanings attached to illness within different cultural contexts.

Situational analysis, which was introduced by Clarke, uses a relational approach to analyze the interconnections between various elements of a social situation (Clarke & Charmaz, 2019). This method involves mapping out the social terrain through the identification of key actors, contexts, and processes, with a focus on understanding how these elements shape and are shaped by each other. For example, in the study done by Schatzki et al. (2001), situational analysis was employed to explore the dynamics of "telework" as a new form of work organization, revealing the complex interplay between technological affordances, organizational structures, and individual practices in shaping remote work experiences.

In a multicultural context, researchers may choose the type of grounded theory that aligns well with their perspectives, and the specific research questions and aims of their study. Regardless of the type of grounded theory chosen, it offers a systematic and rigorous approach to qualitative research that can illuminate the complexities of cultural diversity and inform more inclusive and culturally sensitive practices. Grounded theory offers a flexible and adaptive methodology that can accommodate the fluid and dynamic nature of multicultural contexts. It serves as a tool for researchers to generate theories that are deeply rooted in the lived experiences of individuals, thereby enhancing our understanding of cultural diversity, and ensuring a more inclusive and equitable social practice.

Limitations, Ethical Issues and Considerations of Grounded Theory

Grounded theory, despite its strengths, is not without its limitations, particularly when applied in multicultural settings. One significant limitation is the potential for researcher bias and subjectivity in the interpretation of data, especially when working across diverse cultural contexts. Researchers may inadvertently impose their own cultural assumptions or perspectives onto the analysis, leading to the misinterpretation or misrepresentation of participants' experiences. Additionally, the process of translation and interpretation in cross-cultural research pose challenges in maintaining the integrity and fidelity of participants' voices, as nuances in language and cultural meanings may be lost or distorted.

Ethical considerations also come into play when conducting grounded theory research in multicultural settings, including issues related to informed consent, confidentiality, and power dynamics. Researchers must navigate cultural norms and expectations regarding research participation and ensure that participants' rights and autonomy are respected throughout the research process. Furthermore, there is a risk of cultural appropriation if researchers fail to engage meaningfully with participants and communities, treating them as mere data rather than active partners in the research process. It is therefore essential for researchers to adopt a reflexive and culturally sensitive approach, engaging in ongoing dialogue and reflection to address these limitations and ensure the ethical conduct of grounded theory research in multicultural contexts.

Cultural Sensitivity and Reflexivity in Grounded Theory

Cultural Sensitivity is defined as the awareness, respect, and consideration of cultural differences and nuances, particularly in research and interactions with individuals or communities from diverse cultural backgrounds. Cultural sensitivity along with reflexivity - known as the process of critically examining one's own biases, assumptions, and positionality as a researcher, and how these factors may influence research design, data collection and interpretation - constitute fundamental principles in grounded theory research. Cultures are dynamic and multifaceted, shaped by historical legacies, socio-political dynamics, and individual experiences. Therefore, researchers engaging in grounded theory studies within diverse cultural contexts must navigate this complexity with humility, empathy, and a profound commitment to understanding. Cultural sensitivity demands an appreciation for the diversity of beliefs, values, and practices within any given cultural milieu (Oktay, 2012). It requires researchers to approach their work with openness and respect, recognizing the plurality that characterizes cultural identities (Engler, 2021). Moreover, cultural sensitivity necessitates a willingness to suspend judgement and actively listen to the voices of cultural insiders (Engler, 2021). This entails acknowledging and valuing their perspectives, experiences, and knowledge systems. At the heart of cultural sensitivity lies reflexivity – an ongoing process of self-awareness and critical introspection. Reflexivity prompts researchers to examine their own cultural presuppositions, biases, and positionalities (Bergkamp, 2010). It encourages them to reflect on how their background, experiences, and social identities may shape their perceptions and interactions with the research process (Bergkamp, 2010). By engaging in reflexivity, researchers can uncover hidden biases, challenge assumptions, and cultivate a deeper understanding of the cultural dynamics at play. Reflexivity is not a one-time exercise but an ongoing dialogue that unfolds throughout the research journey. It requires researchers to continually interrogate their assumptions, biases, and power dynamics, particularly in cross-cultural contexts where asymmetrical power relations may exist (Bergkamp, 2010).

This process of critical self-reflection enables researchers to navigate the complexities and ambiguities inherent in cross-cultural inquiry, ultimately enhancing the rigor and validity of their research.

Moreover, cultural sensitivity and reflexivity extend beyond individual researchers to encompass the entire research team. In collaborative endeavors, diverse perspectives and experiences enrich the research process, fostering a more nuanced understanding of cultural phenomena (Engler, 2021). Collaborative approaches also promote transparency, accountability, and ethical practice, as researchers collectively navigate the complexities of cultural dynamics. In grounded theory research, cultural sensitivity and reflexivity are integral to every stage of the research process – from conceptualization to data collection, analysis, and interpretation. During the initial stages of research design, researchers must carefully consider the cultural context in which their study will take place. This involves conducting a thorough review of relevant literature, engaging with cultural insiders, and establishing rapport and trust within the community (Bergkamp, 2010). As data collection commences, cultural sensitivity and reflexivity inform the researcher's approach to engaging with participants. This may involve employing culturally appropriate methods of data collection, such as interviews, focus groups, or participant observation, and adapting communication styles to resonate with the cultural norms and values of the participants (Timonen et al., 2018). Throughout the data collection process, researchers must remain attuned to the nuances of cultural expression, recognizing that meaning may vary across cultural contexts (Nayar & Clair, 2020). Once data has been collected, cultural sensitivity and reflexivity guide the process of data analysis. Researchers must approach the data with an open mind, allowing patterns, themes, and categories to emerge organically (Charmaz & Thornberg, 2021). This may involve employing open, axial, and selective coding techniques to identify salient themes within the data while remaining sensitive to cultural nuances and complexities (Oktay, 2012). Collaborative approaches to data analysis, involving cultural insiders in the interpretation of findings, can further enhance the validity and credibility of the research (Li, 2022).

In addition, researchers engaged in grounded theory studies within diverse cultural contexts may benefit from further valuable insights to navigate the complexities of their research endeavors effectively, such as:

1. **Cultural Humility:** Beyond mere sensitivity, researchers should strive for cultural humility – a stance characterized by curiosity, openness, and willingness to learn from cultural insiders. This involves recognizing the limitations of one's own cultural knowledge and embracing a lifelong commitment to cultural learning and self-improvement (Bergkamp, 2010).

2. **Intersectionality:** Acknowledging the intersecting layers of identity – such as race, ethnicity, sexuality, gender, class, and ability – is crucial in understanding how individuals navigate their cultural contexts (Engler, 2021). Researchers should consider how these intersecting identities shape participants' experiences and perspectives, ensuring a more nuanced analysis of cultural phenomena.

3. **Power Dynamics:** Cultural research often involves navigating power dynamics, both within and between cultural groups. Researchers must critically examine their own positionality and privilege relative to participants, recognizing how power imbalances may influence the research process and outcomes. Mitigating these power differentials requires actively listening to marginalized voices, amplifying their perspectives, and advocating for equitable representation and inclusion (Nayar & Clair, 2020).

4. **Ethical Considerations:** Cultural research raises unique ethical considerations, particularly regarding informed consent, confidentiality, and cultural representation (Engler, 2021). Researchers must ensure that participants fully understand the purpose and implications of the research, respecting their autonomy and right to withdraw at any time. Researchers should prioritize the protection of

participants' confidentiality and privacy, especially in sensitive cultural contexts (Engler, 2021). Additionally, researchers must approach cultural representation with care, avoiding harmful stereotypes or misrepresentations that may perpetuate cultural biases (Engler, 2021).

5. **Community Engagement:** Building strong relationships and partnerships with communities is essential for conducting culturally sensitive research (Engler, 2021). Researchers should involve community members in all stages of the research process, from study design to dissemination of findings (Engler, 2021). This participatory approach fosters trust, mutual respect, and collaboration, ultimately leading to more meaningful and impactful research outcomes.

By integrating these additional insights into their research practices, researchers can enhance the rigor, ethical integrity, and impact of their grounded theory studies within diverse cultural contexts.

Cultural sensitivity and reflexivity are essential principles in grounded theory research, particularly when exploring cultural phenomena. By approaching their work with humility, empathy, and a commitment to understanding, researchers can navigate the complexities of cultural diversity and contribute to the collective endeavor of knowledge production in an increasingly interconnected world. Through ongoing self-awareness and critical reflection, researchers can enhance the rigor, validity, and ethical integrity of their research, ultimately fostering mutual respect, understanding, and collaboration across cultural boundaries.

Ensuring Trustworthiness and Validity

* Trustworthiness: The dependability, credibility, and authenticity of research findings, often established through methods such as prolonged engagement, member checking, and triangulation to ensure the accuracy and reliability of the data.
* Validity: The extent to which a research study accurately measures and reflects the phenomenon it claims to investigate, often assessed through various methods such as internal consistency, external validity, and construct validity.

Grounded theory, as a qualitative research methodology, offers a systematic and rigorous approach to theory development based on the analysis of empirical data (Bergkamp, 2010). Bergkamp (2010) states that "building empirically grounded theory requires a reciprocal relationship between data and theory." Its application within diverse cultural contexts presents unique challenges and opportunities, particularly concerning the trustworthiness and validity of research findings. There are multifaceted strategies and considerations involved in ensuring the trustworthiness and validity in grounded theory research across cultures such as building trust with participants, employing methodological rigor, fostering reflexivity, attending to cultural context, transparently communicating findings, and identifying translational challenges and finding solutions.

1) Building Trust with Participants

Establishing trust with participants is foundational to the success of grounded theory research, particularly in cross-cultural settings where research practices may be unfamiliar or met with skepticism (Charmaz & Thornberg, 2021). Building rapport through transparent and respectful communication is essential for cultivating trust (Engler, 2021). Researchers must approach participants with humility, acknowledging their own cultural biases and demonstrating genuine interest in understanding participants' perspectives (Oktay, 2012). Prolonged engagement with participants, characterized by sustained interactions over an extended period, can facilitate the development of trust and rapport (Timonen et al., 2018). By investing time in building relationships with participants, researchers can create a safe and comfortable environment conducive to open and honest dialogue (Nayar & Clair, 2020). This may involve participating in community activities, attending cultural events, or even spending time getting to know participants in their natural environment (Bergkamp, 2010).

2) Methodological Rigor

Ensuring the credibility and reliability of grounded theory research requires adherence to rigorous methodological procedures (Charmaz & Thornberg, 2021; Timonen et al., 2018). One such procedure is member checking, whereby participants are invited to review and validate the research's interpretations of their experiences. Member checking serves as a form of validation, allowing participants to confirm the accuracy and authenticity of the researcher's interpretations (Engler, 2021). This process not only enhances the credibility of the findings but also empowers participants by giving them a voice in the research process.

Peer debriefing is another valuable strategy for enhancing the validity of grounded theory research. By seeking feedback from fellow researchers or cultural insiders, researchers can gain valuable insights and perspectives that may not have been apparent otherwise (Oktay, 2012). Peer debriefing sessions provide an opportunity to critically evaluate the research process, identify potential biases or blind spots, and refine the analysis accordingly.

Triangulation, the use of multiple data sources or methods to corroborate findings, is essential for ensuring the reliability of grounded theory research (Bergkamp, 2010). By triangulating data from different sources, such as interviews, observations, and documents, researchers can cross-validate their findings and minimize the risk of misinterpretation or distortion of data. Triangulation also enables researchers to capture the complexity and richness of participants' experiences from multiple perspectives, enhancing the comprehensiveness and depth of the analysis (Charmaz & Thornberg, 2021; Timonen et al., 2018).

3) Reflexivity

Transparently documenting reflexivity is essential for enhancing the transparency and credibility of grounded theory research. Researchers should explicitly discuss their own positionality, including their cultural background, personal experiences, and any preconceived notions or biases they may hold. By acknowledging their own subjectivity, researchers can invite critical reflection and dialogue, ultimately enriching the interpretation of findings (Bergkamp, 2010). By centering reflexivity in their research practice, researchers can strive to amplify the voices of participants, challenge dominant narratives, and promote social justice within the research process (Bergkamp, 2010). Reflexivity extends beyond individual self-reflection to encompass reflexivity within research teams and collaborative partnerships. By engaging in reflexive dialogue with colleagues, researchers can collectively interrogate their assumptions, perspectives, and interpretations, enriching the analysis and enhancing the validity of the research findings. Collaborative reflexivity fosters a culture of openness, humility, and intellectual rigor within the research team, ultimately strengthening the trustworthiness and validity of the research outcomes (Bergkamp, 2010).

4) Cultural Context

Attention to cultural context is paramount in grounded theory research with diverse cultural settings. Culture shapes individuals' beliefs, values, norms, and behaviors, influencing the way they perceive and interpret the world around them (Charmaz & Thornberg, 2021). Researchers must be sensitive to cultural nuances and meanings embedded within participants' narratives, recognizing that what may be considered normal or acceptable in one culture may be perceived differently in another (Engler, 2021). Language and translation pose significant challenges in cross-cultural research, particularly when working with participants who speak languages other than the research's own (Oktay, 2012). Researchers must ensure the accuracy and fidelity of translation by employing qualified translators or bilingual researchers and conducting back-translation checks to verify the consistency of translations (Timonen et al., 2018). Additionally, researchers should be attentive to the cultural connotations and nuances of language, avoiding literal translations that may not capture the full richness of participants' experiences (Bergkamp, 2010). Furthermore, researchers should provide detailed descriptions of the cultural context in which the research was conducted, including socio-political dynamics, historical influences, and power structures (Li, 2022). By contextualizing the findings within the broader cultural landscape, researchers can enhance the relevance and applicability of their findings to other cultural settings (Nayar & Clair, 2020).

5) Transparent Communication of Findings

Transparent communication of findings is essential for ensuring the credibility and validity of grounded theory research. Researchers should clearly articulate the limitations of their study, including any biases or constraints inherent in the research design or data collection methods (Engler, 2021). Additionally, researchers should acknowledge the potential for alternative interpretations of the data and invite dialogue with stakeholders from the involved culture to enrich the interpretation of findings (Nayar & Clair, 2020). Presenting findings in a manner that is accessible and meaningful to participants and stakeholders is essential for responsible communication (Charmaz & Thornberg, 2021). Researchers should avoid jargon or technical language that may be unfamiliar to participants and instead strive for clarity and simplicity in their presentations (Timonen et al., 2018). Researchers should consider the cultural sensitivity of their findings and ensure that they are communicated in a respectful and culturally appropriate manner (Bergkamp, 2010).

Translational Challenges and Solutions

Grounded theory research in multicultural settings often involves linguistic and translational challenges due to the diverse linguistic backgrounds of participants. Researchers must navigate these challenges with care to ensure that the integrity and validity of the research findings are maintained across cultural and linguistic boundaries (Engler, 2021). Utilizing qualified translators who are proficient in both the source and target languages and possess cultural competence is crucial in accurately conveying participants' perspectives (Oktay, 2012). Additionally, conducting back-translation checks and involving participants in the validation of translations can help mitigate translational discrepancies and ensure that the meanings conveyed in the research are consistent with participants' intended messages (Timonen et al., 2018). Cultural sensitivity in language use and terminology is paramount, as certain concepts may not have direct equivalents across cultures (Nayar & Clair, 2020). Researchers should adapt their language and communication styles to resonate with the cultural norms and values of the participants, promoting mutual understanding and respect (Bergkamp, 2010). By addressing translational challenges effectively, researchers can enhance the credibility and validity of their grounded theory research in multicultural settings, fostering meaningful cross-cultural dialogue and collaboration (Li, 2022).

By building trust with participants, employing rigorous methodological procedures, fostering reflexivity, attending to cultural context, and transparently communicating findings, researchers can enhance the credibility and validity of their research (Charmaz & Thornberg, 2021). Grounded theory offers a powerful framework for understanding the complexities of human experience across cultures, and by adhering to these principles, researchers can contribute to cross-cultural understanding and advance knowledge in the field of qualitative research (Engler, 2021).

Integrating Cultural Perspectives in Theory Development

Theory Development is the process of constructing, refining, and validating theoretical frameworks or explanations to understand and explain phenomena observed in research, often involving the integration of empirical evidence and conceptual insights. Grounded theory methodology is particularly well suited for theory development in multicultural settings due to its inherent flexibility and responsiveness to diverse cultural contexts. Grounded theory methodology offers a unique opportunity to integrate diverse cultural perspectives in theory development, transcending the limitations of monocultural frameworks and fostering a more inclusive understanding of cultural phenomena. Central to this endeavor is the recognition that culture shapes not only the ways in which individuals perceive and interpret the world but also the very fabric of social interactions, institutions, and collective identities (Nayar & Clair, 2020; Timonen et al., 2018). By engaging with participants as co-researchers in the theory-building process, grounded theory facilitates the exploration of cultural diversity while acknowledging the multifaceted nature of cultural phenomena.

Incorporating cultural perspectives into theory development begins with acknowledging the situatedness of knowledge and the multicity of truths inherent in diverse cultural contexts (Charmaz & Thornberg, 2021). Researchers should adopt an open and flexible mindset, recognizing that their own cultural background and worldview may differ significantly from those of the participants (Nayar & Clair, 2020). Through ongoing dialogue and reflexivity, researchers can navigate the complexities of cultural interpretation, challenging assumptions, and biases that may influence the research process (Timonen et al., 2018). Integrating cultural perspectives in theory development requires a collaborative and participatory approach that values the voices and experiences of marginalized or underrepresented communities (Engler, 2021). Researchers should actively seek input from participants, inviting them to co-construct theories that reflect their lived realities and cultural worldviews (Charmaz & Thornberg, 2021). This collaborative process not only enhances the validity and relevance of the research findings but also empowers participants as active agents in the production of knowledge (Nayar & Clair, 2020). A key aspect of integrating cultural perspectives in theory development is the recognition of cultural diversity within and across communities (Bergkamp, 2010). Researchers must be attuned to the multiplicity of identities, beliefs, and practices that exist within any given cultural context, avoiding the temptation to essentialize or homogenize cultural phenomena (Oktay, 2012). By embracing complexity and nuance, grounded theory allows for the exploration of divergent viewpoints and the identification of underlying patterns and themes that may transcend cultural boundaries (Charmaz & Thornberg, 2021). Moreover, integrating cultural perspectives in theory development necessitates a commitment to social justice and equity. Researchers must critically examine power dynamics and structural inequalities that shape the experiences of individuals and communities with specific cultural contexts (Engler, 2021). By centering the voices of marginalized or oppressed groups, grounded theory has the potential to uncover hidden power dynamics, challenge dominant narratives, and contribute to transformative social change.

Integrating cultural perspectives in theory development through grounded theory methodology is essential for advancing our understanding of cultural complexity and diversity. By embracing reflexivity, collaboration, and social justice, grounded theory enables researchers to develop theories that resonate with the lived experience of individuals and communities across cultures (Nayar & Clair, 2020; Timonen et al., 2018). As we continue navigating an increasingly globalized world, grounded theory remains a powerful tool for promoting cross-cultural dialogue, empathy, and mutual understanding. As researchers embark on the journey of integrating cultural perspectives into theory development, several key considerations emerge:

- It is essential to recognize the dynamic and fluid nature of culture (Bergkamp, 2010). Culture is not static but rather evolves over time in response to internal and external influences. Therefore, researchers must approach cultural analysis with a sense of humility and openness, acknowledging that their understanding of culture is always partial and situated within a particular historical and social context.
- Researchers must be mindful of the power dynamics inherent in cross-cultural research (Charmaz & Thornberg, 2021). The act of studying and representing another culture involves a degree of power imbalance, as researchers hold the authority to interpret and disseminate knowledge about the culture under study. To mitigate this imbalance, researchers should strive to engage in ethical and collaborative research practices that prioritize the voices and agency of the participants.
- Integrating cultural perspectives in theory development requires a nuanced understanding of language and communication (Li, 2022). Language not only serves as a medium for expressing cultural meanings but also shapes the ways in which individuals perceive and interpret the world around them. Therefore, researchers should pay careful attention to language use in data collection and analysis, recognizing that certain concepts may not have direct equivalents across cultural or linguistic boundaries.

In summary, integrating cultural perspectives into theory development is essential for producing nuanced and contextually sensitive understandings of cultural phenomena. Grounded theory methodology offers a valuable framework for conducting such research, allowing researchers to engage in iterative and collaborative processes of theory development that prioritizes the voices and experiences of the participants (Engler, 2021; Oktay, 2012). By embracing reflexivity, ethical practice, and a commitment to social justice, researchers can contribute to the development of theories that resonate with the complexity and diversity of human cultures.

Communicating Grounded Theory Findings Responsibly

Communication defined as the exchange of information, ideas, and findings between researchers, stakeholders, and participants, often involving various methods such as writing, presenting, and engaging in dialogue to disseminate research findings effectively and responsibly. Effectively communicating grounded theory findings in multicultural settings requires a thoughtful and nuanced approach that acknowledges the complexities of cross-cultural research. As researchers navigate the intricacies of diverse cultural contexts, they must prioritize transparency, reflexivity, and cultural sensitivity to ensure that their findings are accurately represented and interpreted (Engler, 2021). By engaging with stakeholders, using inclusive language, and fostering dialogue, researchers can navigate the challenges of communicating grounded theory findings responsibly and promote mutual understanding across cultural divides (Charmaz & Thornberg, 2021). Some practical steps on how to communicate grounded theory findings include:

1. **Establishing Trust and Transparency:** Building trust with participants in multicultural settings begins with transparent communication regarding objectives, methodologies, and potential implications (Engler, 2021). Researchers must articulate the purpose of the study clearly, ensuring participants understand how their contributions will be utilized in the research process and dissemination of findings. This transparency is especially important in multicultural settings where participants may come from diverse backgrounds and may have varying levels of familiarity with research practices. By fostering an environment of openness and honesty, researchers can cultivate trust and encourage active participation from individuals representing different cultural perspectives.

2. **Engaging in Reflexive Practice:** Engaging in reflexive practice is essential when communicating grounded theory findings in multicultural settings (Bergkamp, 2010). Researchers must continuously reflect on their own biases, assumptions, and positionality throughout the research process. In multicultural contexts, reflexivity takes on added significance as researchers navigate the complexities of cross-cultural interactions and interpretations (Bergkamp, 2010). Documenting reflexive insights in a journal or memo enables researchers to critically examine how their own cultural background and experiences may shape their interpretations of the data, ensuring that findings are presented in a nuanced and culturally sensitive manner.

3. **Using Inclusive and Empowering Language:** In multicultural settings, using inclusive and empowering language is important when communicating grounded theory findings (Engler, 2021). Researchers must avoid stereotypes, stigmatizing language, or other forms of linguistic bias that may perpetuate harmful narratives or marginalize certain cultural groups. Instead, researchers should use language that respects the agency and diversity of participants, allowing them to articulate their experiences in their own terms. This approach fosters a sense of empowerment among participants and ensures that their voices are accurately represented in the research findings.

4. **Involve Stakeholders in the Dissemination Process:** Involving stakeholders in the dissemination process helps ensure that research findings are culturally relevant and accurately interpreted (Nayar & Clair, 2020). Collaborating with community members, organizations, and other relevant stakeholders enables researchers to gain insights into the cultural nuances and perspectives that may influence the interpretation of findings. Seeking feedback from stakeholders on the presentation of findings can help researchers identify blind spots, clarify misunderstandings, and ensure that the research remains sensitive to the needs and priorities of the communities involved.

5. **Select Dissemination Mediums Appropriately:** Choosing appropriate dissemination mediums is essential when communicating grounded theory findings in multicultural settings (Oktay, 20). Researchers must consider the preferences, accessibility, and cultural norms of their target audience to effectively reach diverse communities.

6. **Provide Context and Interpretation:** Providing context and interpretation is essential when communicating grounded theory findings in multicultural settings (Li, 2022). Researchers must offer contextual information to help readers understand the cultural background and significance of the research findings. In multicultural contexts, this may involve explaining cultural norms, traditions,

and values that shape participants' experiences and perspectives. By providing cultural context, researchers can help readers interpret the findings accurately and appreciate the richness and complexity of cultural diversity represented in the research.

7. **Respect Participant Confidentiality and Privacy:** Respecting participant confidentiality and privacy is crucial when communicating grounded theory findings in multicultural settings (Timonen et al., 2018). Researchers must ensure that participant confidentiality is maintained throughout the dissemination process, especially when dealing with sensitive topics or vulnerable populations. In multicultural contexts, where participants may face additional risks due to cultural, social, or political factors, safeguarding participant privacy is paramount. Obtaining informed consent from participants regarding the use of their data in publications and presentations helps ensure that their rights and dignity are protected throughout the research process.

8. **Acknowledge Limitations and Ethical Considerations:** Acknowledging limitations and ethical considerations is essential when communicating grounded theory findings in multicultural settings (Engler, 2021). Researchers must be transparent about the limitations of the study, including any constraints or biases that may have influenced the research process or findings. In multicultural contexts, where researchers may encounter unique challenges related to language barriers, cultural differences, or power dynamics, acknowledging these limitations is crucial for promoting transparency and accountability. Reflecting on the ethical considerations involved in the research helps researchers navigate the complexities of cross-cultural research with integrity and sensitivity.

9. **Fostering Dialogue and Engagement:** in multicultural settings, fostering dialogue and engagement with stakeholders is key when communicating grounded theory findings (Charmaz & Thornberg, 2021). Researchers must create opportunities for meaningful interaction and collaboration with community members, organizations, and other relevant stakeholders. In multicultural contexts, where diverse perspectives and experiences abound, facilitating dialogue helps bridge cultural divides, promote mutual understanding, and build trust. Community forums, workshops, or other events provide platforms for stakeholders to participate in interpreting and applying the research findings, ensuring that the research remains relevant and responsive to the needs and priorities of multicultural communities.

10. **Reflect on Impact and Responsiveness:** Reflecting on the impact and responsiveness of the research is essential when communicating grounded theory findings in multicultural settings (Engler, 2021). Researchers must consider the potential implications of their research on participants, communities, and broader society. In multicultural contexts, where research findings may have far-reaching consequences for cultural identity, social cohesion, or policy development, reflecting on impact is crucial for promoting positive change and minimizing harm. By remaining responsive to feedback and critique from stakeholders, researchers adapt their communication strategies to address concerns and promote inclusivity and social justice in the research process (Engler, 2021).

Responsible communication of grounded theory findings in multicultural settings is essential for promoting equity, respect, and understanding in research practice. By following practical steps such as establishing trust, using inclusive language, and involving stakeholders, researchers can navigate the complexities of cross-cultural research with integrity and sensitivity (Engler, 2021). Through transparent and reflexive communication practices, researchers can foster meaningful dialogue, empower diverse communities, and contribute to positive social change. Ultimately, responsible communication is not just about disseminating research findings; it is about building bridges, fostering empathy, and promoting culture humility in the pursuit of knowledge.

CONCLUSION

Grounded theory methodology stands as an important tool of methodological rigor and flexibility for qualitative research, particularly in unraveling the intricacies of cultural complexity. Through this chapter, we have explored the multifaceted application of grounded theory, emphasizing its pivotal role in understanding cultural phenomena. Grounded theory not only provides a systematic framework for theory development but also offers a pathway to deeper insights into the lived experiences of individuals and communities within diverse cultural contexts. Grounded theory holds immense promise for advancing knowledge in the field of cultural research. As we navigate an increasingly interconnected and diverse world, grounded theory helps ensure cross-cultural understanding and promoting justice. By embracing cultural sensitivity, reflexivity, methodological rigor, and responsible communication, researchers can harness the power of grounded theory to illuminate the complexities of human experience and contribute to positive social change.

Cultural sensitivity and reflexivity emerge as foundational principles guiding grounded theory research across cultural boundaries. Acknowledging and interrogating one's own cultural biases while remaining open to the perspectives of participants are essential steps in conducting ethical and meaningful research. Moreover, the process of coding and analysis demands a nuanced understanding of cultural nuances and meanings embedded within the data, requiring researchers to navigate the complexities of translation, interpretation, and context. Reflexivity fosters a deeper understanding of how their positionality may impact data collection, analysis, and interpretation.

Grounded theory methodology provides a unique lens through which to explore the complexity of cultural phenomena. Its emphasis on theory development grounded in empirical data resonates particularly well with the intricacies of culture, which are often dynamic, multifaceted, and context dependent. By immersing themselves in the lived experiences of individuals and communities, grounded theory researchers can uncover the underlying patterns, meanings, and structures that shape cultural dynamics. Cultural meanings are often embedded within language, symbols, and behaviors, requiring researchers to engage in a process of interpretation that goes beyond surface-level observations.

Ensuring trustworthiness and validity in grounded theory research is paramount, particularly when working with marginalized or underrepresented communities. Strategies such as prolonged engagement, member checking, and triangulation serve as safeguards against bias and enhance the credibility of research findings. Furthermore, the integration of diverse cultural perspectives in theory development enriches our understanding of cultural phenomena, challenging monocultural narratives and promoting inclusivity. Ensuring trustworthiness and validity in grounded theory research is essential for maintaining the integrity of the findings. In cross-cultural research, building trust with participants is crucial, as it lays the foundation for meaningful data collection and interpretation.

Integrating diverse cultural perspectives in theory development is a key strength of grounded theory methodology. By engaging with participants as co-researchers in the theory-building process, researchers can develop theories that are more inclusive, representative, and contextually grounded. This collaborative approach fosters a deeper understanding of cultural phenomena, moving beyond simplistic or stereotypical representations to capture the complexities of lived experiences.

In the communication of grounded theory finding, researchers must tread carefully, balancing academic rigor with cultural sensitivity. By engaging with stakeholders from the studied culture and employing culturally appropriate language and imagery, researchers can ensure that their findings are accurately represented and interpreted within the cultural context. Responsible communication not only upholds ethical standards but also fosters mutual respect and understanding between researchers and participants. Researchers should be mindful of the power dynamics inherent in research relationships, striving to amplify the voices of marginalized groups while avoiding stereotypes or generalizations.

In conclusion, grounded theory methodology offers a powerful framework for unraveling cultural complexity in qualitative research. By embracing cultural sensitivity, reflexivity, methodological rigor, and responsible communication, researchers can develop theories the resonate with richness and diversity of human experiences across cultures. Grounded theory holds immense potential for fostering cross-cultural understanding, challenging dominant narratives, and contributing to positive social change in an increasingly interconnected world. As researchers continue to navigate the complexities of cultural research, grounded theory remains an indispensable tool for illuminating the intricacies of cultural dynamics and advancing knowledge in the field.

REFERENCES

Bergkamp, J. A. (2010). The paradox of emotionality & competence in multicultural competency training: A grounded theory. Academic Press.

Charmaz, K., & Thornberg, R. (2020). The pursuit of quality in grounded theory. *Qualitative Research in Psychology*, 18(3), 305–327. 10.1080/14780887.2020.1780357

Clarke, A. E. (2005). *Situational analysis: grounded theory after the postmodern turn*. Sage Publications. 10.4135/9781412985833

Clarke, A. E., & Charmaz, K. (2019). *Grounded theory and situational analysis*. Sage Publications.

Corbin, J., & Strauss, A. (2014). *Basics of qualitative research: Techniques and procedures for developing grounded theory*. Sage publications.

Engler, S., & Stausberg, M. (2021). *The Routledge Handbook of Research Methods in the Study of Religion*. Routledge. 10.4324/9781003222491

Glaser, B. G., & Strauss, A. L. (2017). The discovery of grounded theory. In *Routledge eBooks*. 10.4324/9780203793206

Li, J. (2022). Grounded theory-based model of the influence of digital communication on handicraft intangible cultural heritage. *Heritage Science*, 10(1), 126. Advance online publication. 10.1186/s40494-022-00760-z35968496

Nayar, S., & StClair, V. W. (2020). Multiple cultures – one process: Undertaking a cross cultural grounded theory study. *American Journal of Qualitative Research*, 4(3), 131–145. 10.29333/ajqr/9310

Oktay, J. S. (2012). *Grounded theory*. Pocket Guide to Social Work Re. 10.1093/acprof:oso/9780199753697.001.0001

Schatzki, T. R., Knorr-Cetina, K., & Von Savigny, E. (Eds.). (2001). *The practice turn in contemporary theory* (Vol. 44). Routledge.

Timonen, V., Foley, G., & Conlon, C. (2018). Challenges when using grounded theory. *International Journal of Qualitative Methods*, 17(1). Advance online publication. 10.1177/1609406918758086

ADDITIONAL READING

Barnes, D. M. (1996). An analysis of the grounded theory method and the concept of culture. *Qualitative Health Research*, 6(3), 429–441. 10.1177/104973239600600309

Birks, M., & Mills, J. (2015). Grounded theory: A Practical Guide. *Sage (Atlanta, Ga.)*.

Chiovitti, R. F., & Piran, N. (2003). Rigour and grounded theory research. *Journal of Advanced Nursing*, 44(4), 427–435. 10.1046/j.0309-2402.2003.02822.x14651715

Du Plessis, E., & Marais, P. (2015). A Grounded theory perspective on leadership in multicultural schools. *Journal of Asian and African Studies*, 52(5), 722–737. 10.1177/0021909615612122

Gentles, S. J., Jack, S. M., Nicholas, D. B., & McKibbon, K. A. (2014). Critical Approach to Reflexivity in Grounded Theory. *The Qualitative Report*, 19(44), 1–14. 10.46743/2160-3715/2014.1109

Hardy, M. A., & Bryman, A. (2004). *Handbook of Data Analysis*. SAGE. 10.4135/9781848608184

Khan, S. N. (2014). Qualitative research method: Grounded theory. *International Journal of Business and Management*, 9(11). Advance online publication. 10.5539/ijbm.v9n11p224

Lomborg, K., & Kirkevold, M. (2003). Truth and validity in grounded theory – a reconsidered realist interpretation of the criteria: fit, work, relevance and modifiability. *Nursing Philosophy, 4*(3), 189-200. 10.1046/j.1466-769X.2003.00139.x

Mills, J., Bonner, A., & Francis, K. L. (2006). The development of constructivist grounded theory. *International Journal of Qualitative Methods*, 5(1), 25–35. 10.1177/160940690600500103

Nayar, S. (2012). Grounded Theory: A research methodology for occupational science. *Journal of Occupational Science*, 19(1), 76–82. 10.1080/14427591.2011.581626

Oliveira, M. D. F. (2013). Multicultural environments and their challenges to crisis communication. International Journal of Business Communication, 50(3), 253–277. 10.1177/0021943613487070

Urquhart, C. (2022). Grounded theory for qualitative research: A Practical Guide. *Sage (Atlanta, Ga.)*.

KEY TERMS AND DEFINITIONS

Communication: The exchange of information, ideas, and findings between researchers, stakeholders, and participants, often involving various methods such as writing, presenting, and engaging in dialogue to disseminate research findings effectively and responsibly.

Cultural Perspectives: Varied viewpoints and interpretations that arise from individuals' cultural background, which includes their values, beliefs, customs, and social practices.

Cultural Sensitivity: The awareness, respect, and consideration of cultural differences and nuances, particularly in research and interactions with individuals or communities from diverse cultural backgrounds.

Reflexivity: The process of critically examining one's own biases, assumptions, and positionality as a researcher, and how these factors may influence research design, data collection and interpretation.

Theory Development: The process of constructing, refining, and validating theoretical frameworks or explanations to understand and explain phenomena observed in research, often involving the integration of empirical evidence and conceptual insights.

Trustworthiness: The dependability, credibility, and authenticity of research findings, often established through methods such as prolonged engagement, member checking, and triangulation to ensure the accuracy and reliability of the data.

Validity: The extent to which a research study accurately measures and reflects the phenomenon it claims to investigate, often assessed through various methods such as internal consistency, external validity, and construct validity.

Chapter 3
Sampling Methods in Qualitative Sampling in Multicultural Settings

Handan Akkaş
http://orcid.org/0000-0002-2082-0685
Ankara Science University, Turkey & Tilburg University, The Netherlands

Cem Harun Meydan
http://orcid.org/0000-0002-3604-1117
Ankara Science University, Turkey

ABSTRACT

This chapter explores the complex field of application of qualitative sampling techniques in the context of multicultural settings, covering both probabilistic and non-probabilistic sampling approaches. It recognises the importance of capturing the diversity and distinctiveness of multicultural populations and describes the intricacies of sampling in culturally diverse settings. It also explores the different challenges and considerations that arise when applying each method in different ethnic, linguistic and cultural contexts. Moreover, it emphasises the importance of aligning sampling methods with research objectives, context-specific considerations, and ethical principles. By providing practical information and guidance, the chapter equips researchers with the necessary tools to effectively navigate the complexities of qualitative sampling in multicultural settings.

INTRODUCTION

Qualitative research is becoming increasingly important in cross-cultural psychological studies (Tanggaard, 2014). Although it has its challenges, the use of qualitative approaches in multicultural research offers important advantages such as obtaining more diversity in participants' responses (Gómez & Kuronen, 2011). On the other hand, understanding the scope and rationale of the study is very important in the field of intercultural research. At this point, one of the issues to be considered is the cultural sampling process, which requires the deliberate selection of one or more populations for data collection. The second issue related to the conceptualization of culture-behavior links has been the sub-

DOI: 10.4018/979-8-3693-3306-8.ch003

ject of extensive debate about the appropriate technique to use in cross-cultural psychology, whether qualitative or quantitative (Demuth, 2013).

The participants in qualitative research are seen as competent persons who possess the ability to contemplate and articulate their experiences, values, beliefs, and views. Various qualitative methodologies have distinct sampling objectives with regards to participants. The process of selection is contingent upon the established sample criteria. According to predetermined inclusion and exclusion criteria, sampling criteria cover the specific characteristics of the sample population and their suitability for participation in the research (Patton, 2023).

QUALITATIVE AND QUANTITATIVE RESEARCH IN MULTICULTURAL SETTING

Qualitative methods are used to investigate and gain a comprehensive understanding of the factors that contribute to the successful or unsuccessful implementation of evidence-based practice and to identify strategies to facilitate implementation. On the other hand, quantitative methods are used to test and validate hypotheses derived from an established conceptual model and to gain a broad understanding of the determinants of successful implementation (Masiloane, 2008; Teddlie & Tashakkori, 2003).

The sampling tactics used in practical research for qualitative methods are typically less specific and less obvious than those used for quantitative approaches. Qualitative research differs from quantitative research in that it involves sampling a group with qualities that accurately represent a larger community rather than using random sampling. In qualitative research, non-probability sampling is used to selectively recruit populations for the purpose of investigating a particular topic or when the entire population is unknown or inaccessible. In a cultural setting, qualitative research sampling is examined using both probability and non-probability sampling methods (Berry et al., 2011).

As stated by Morse and Niehaus (2009), the aim of sampling procedures, whether quantitative or qualitative in nature, is to optimize both efficiency and validity. However, sampling should be compatible with the goals and assumptions involved in the use of both approaches. The primary aim of qualitative approaches is to achieve comprehensive knowledge, whereas quantitative methods are designed to achieve a broader understanding. Furthermore, in qualitative research, it is believed that samples are deliberately selected to obtain cases with rich information (Patton, 2002). Qualitative techniques prioritize saturation, which involves continuous sampling until no new significant information is obtained to gain a complete understanding (Brown, 2008). They prioritize the concept of generalizability, which requires ensuring that the information obtained reflects the wider population from which the sample was selected (Morse & Niehaus, 2009). Each technique has different expectations and criteria for determining the number of participants required to achieve its objectives. Additionally, quantitative methods use established formulae to avoid Type I and Type II errors, while qualitative methods often rely on precedent to determine the number of participants according to the type of analysis being conducted (Guest, Bunce & Johnson., 2006; Padgett, 2008).

As demonstrated by McArt and Brown (1990), when conducting cross-cultural research, it is important to consider three main concerns regarding recruitment and sampling. First and foremost, it underlines the importance of sample equivalence, which entails ensuring that the demographic characteristics of the sample are equivalent across the cultural contexts under investigation. This ensures that meaningful comparisons can be made between two different groups. The second concern is time equivalence; researchers should verify that the time required to collect data from both contexts is not excessively long. To overcome these concerns in qualitative research, it is recommended to use a sampling matrix that takes into account the specific needs of the research and the cultural norms of the setting (Padgett, 2008; Patton, 2002). Researchers should therefore consider these recruitment and sampling concerns and familiarize themselves with the various prerequisites before beginning their work.

Importance of Qualitative Sampling in Multicultural Settings

Qualitative sampling is essential in multicultural settings to fully represent the diverse array of human experiences, perspectives, and realities that occur within and between various ethnic groups. In contrast to quantitative research, qualitative research places greater importance on uncovering the intricacies and multifaceted nature of social phenomena via comprehensive investigation and contextual understanding, rather than prioritizing generalizability and statistical representativeness. According to Creswell and Clark (2017) and Mason (2002), qualitative sampling allows researchers to examine the impact of cultural dynamics on beliefs, actions, and relationships within multicultural environments. This approach is particularly useful when individuals and groups are involved in many cultural identities and contexts.

Researchers have unique challenges while conducting qualitative sampling in multicultural contexts, despite its importance. One of the fundamental challenges that has to be tackled is the imperative to retain cultural sensitivity and reflexivity throughout the sampling process. To reduce possible biases, researchers must have a conscious understanding of their own cultural biases, assumptions, and advantages, and actively engage in reflexivity (Patton, 2002). Furthermore, it is crucial to take into account that language barriers, cultural conventions, and power imbalances might influence participants' willingness to participate in research and influence their perspectives and experiences.

One more challenge is to ensure the inclusivity and inclusiveness of samples within multicultural environments. Given the wide range of cultural groups present, it is recommended that researchers utilize purposive sampling techniques that incorporate a vast array of perspectives, experiences, and voices. However, the endeavor of identifying and securing involvement from a diverse array of persons can present difficulties in terms of logistics and ethics, especially when engaging with marginalized or disadvantaged populations (Leedy & Ormrod, 2023; Robinson, 2014). To ensure the incorporation of diverse viewpoints in their research, scholars must confront obstacles pertaining to gatekeeping, trust establishment, and community engagement.

Despite these challenges, the use of qualitative sampling in multicultural settings offers several opportunities for scientific progress and societal impact. According to Ponterotto (2010), the implementation of culturally sensitive sampling methodologies can facilitate the improvement of collaboration, co-creation, and information exchange among diverse communities. Potential strategies for enhancing ethical and inclusive sampling methods in multicultural settings including the application of participatory methodologies, community-based research partnerships, and indigenous research approaches.

Furthermore, the advancements in digital technology and online platforms offer new opportunities for engaging diverse individuals and conducting research across various geographical and cultural settings. Virtual ethnography, online focus groups, and digital storytelling are innovative methods in cross-cultural research that successfully include participants and improve the portrayal of minority viewpoints. The utilization of qualitative sampling is of utmost importance in multicultural settings as it facilitates the thorough documentation of the complex, diverse, and profound human experiences that surpass cultural boundaries. The implementation of culturally sensitive and inclusive sampling procedures by researchers has the potential to promote equality, diversity, and inclusion in research, as well as contribute to the generation of comprehensive and socially advantageous information within heterogeneous communities (Berry et al., 2011; Creswell & Clark, 2017; Patton, 2023).

Sample Size in Qualitative Research

Critics have raised concerns over the insufficiency or absence of sufficient rationale for the sample sizes employed in qualitative research methodologies (Boddy, 2016; Marshall et al., 2013). Vasileiou et al., (2018) conducted a comprehensive literature analysis encompassing qualitative research employing in-depth interviews within health-related publications spanning a duration of 15 years. The findings of their study revealed that a significant proportion of the papers examined lacked a rationale for the determination of sample size. However, qualitative researchers argue that sample size is not a concern in qualitative research because it does not require establishing statistical generalizations (Onwuegbuzie & Leech, 2005).

Glaser and Strauss (1967) introduced the notion of saturation, which they referred to as 'theoretical saturation', within the framework of the grounded theory method. According to Hennink and Kaiser (2022), saturation is widely acknowledged as the predominant guiding factor for evaluating the sufficiency of purposive samples in qualitative research. Saturation is the stage in data gathering where no further difficulties or insights are found, and the data starts to repeat, rendering further data collecting superfluous and ensuring a sufficient sample size. Saturation has become a pivotal component in qualitative research, playing a significant role in enhancing the strength and credibility of data collection (O'Reilly & Parker, 2013). The level of saturation plays a pivotal role in determining the sufficiency of a sample for the phenomena being studied. Content validity is established when the data collected incorporates the entirety, comprehensiveness, and nuances of the issues being studied (Francis et al., 2010). Authors frequently highlight saturation as a means of ensuring qualitative rigor to reviewers and readers (Morse, 2015). While the concept of saturation is frequently mentioned as a justification for maintaining an adequate sample size (Guest et al., 2006), there exists a notable dearth of literature pertaining to the evaluation of saturation and the specific criteria employed to ascertain it in qualitative research.

According to Carlsen and Glenton (2011), a comprehensive analysis of 220 studies utilizing focus group deliberations revealed that 83% of these studies employed saturation as a rationale for sample size. However, these studies only offered a cursory account of the methods employed to achieve saturation, characterized by unsupported assertions of saturation and references to achieving saturation when utilizing a predetermined sample size. Marshall et al. (2013) conducted an analysis of 83 qualitative research and determined that none of them provided a definition for saturation.

In addition, several studies have been undertaken to investigate the quantity of people involved in qualitative research. According to Bernard (2000), ethnographic studies should include 30-60 interviews, while grounded theory research should include 20-30 interviews, as indicated by Charmaz (2006). For phenomenological investigations, Starks and Trinidad (2007) proposed a range of 6-10 interviews, however Francis et al. (2010) advocated for a minimum of 10 interviews. Creswell (2007) recommends a case study with 3-5 participants, a phenomenological study with 10 participants, and a grounded theory research with 15-20 people. On the other hand, Morse (1995) advises a sample size that varies from six participants for a phenomenological investigation to 30-50 participants for an ethnographic study. In certain instances, a substantial number of individuals may be engaged. In a study, Galvin (2015) introduced a statistical methodology for determining the optimal number of interviews needed to identify a certain topic, under the assumption of a random sample. Galvin's research revealed that, with a confidence level of 95%, a total of 14 interviews would be adequate for identifying themes that are shared by 20% of the population. In contrast, a larger sample size of 298 interviews would be necessary to identify themes that are shared by just 1% (six) of the population (Hagaman & Wutich, 2017).

In qualitative research, a reasonably similar sample size for saturation has been found across themes and methodology. These findings give good empirical recommendations on qualitative research sample sizes and may be utilized alongside study parameters to establish an acceptable sample size before data collection. For researchers, academic publications, journal reviewers, and ethical review boards, qualitative study sample sizes must be justified and reported more transparently. Further empirical study is needed to determine how saturation sample sizes depend on factors.

SAMPLING METHODS IN QUALITATIVE RESEARCH

Sampling involves a systematic procedure for selecting and including individuals from diverse cultural, ethnic, linguistic, or socioeconomic backgrounds (Patton, 2023). Qualitative sampling in multicultural settings typically aims to produce comprehensive and contextually informed data that accurately captures the multifaceted nature of cultural dynamics, identities, and interactions between different cultural groups. This approach seeks to intentionally include individuals from diverse cultural groups, subcultures, or communities and provides a basis for understanding, analyzing, and situating social phenomena within the broader framework of heterogeneous societies (Morse & Niehaus, 2009; Pelzang & Hutchinson, 2017). In this section, probability and non-probability sampling techniques in a multicultural context will be explained.

Non-Probability Sampling

Non-probability sampling is a valuable method when probability sampling is difficult to use and there is no viable alternative. The aim of non-probability sampling is to methodically select constituents who have first-hand knowledge of the phenomenon being studied and therefore know the phenomenon well, thus providing a comprehensive understanding of the phenomenon (Creswell et al., 2007).

Non-probability sampling does not use the random sampling technique, which ensures that every individual in a population has an equal chance of being selected for the research sample. The use of non-probability sampling methods is not suitable for extrapolating study findings to a wider target population. In contrast, non-probability sampling facilitates the identification of themes and patterns that contribute to the understanding of complex social, behavioral or cultural phenomena. Non-probability sampling enables research to draw conclusions about the individuals selected as sample subjects (Gokhale & Srivastava, 2017). Subjects in a sample may or may not represent a group other than their own. Non-probability sampling is associated with the potential for various levels of selection bias, and the presence of demographic similarities between the sample and the wider population does not always indicate the absence of bias within the sample. For example, individuals who willingly choose to take part in a research sample may have a purpose for their participation that is not common in the wider community (Liamputtong, 2006; Stratton, 2019).

According to Burns and Grove (2001), it is not possible to include all representative aspects of the population in the sample and the concept of randomness does not dictate the inclusion of items. However, the sample selected using non-probability sampling may contain potential biases and erroneous subjective findings of the researcher in the selection of the sample and thus the research data may be unrepresentative (Patton, 2005). Therefore, the findings obtained from this study lack generalizability.

Qualitative researchers should establish the purpose of the study before determining the individuals to be selected for the research and the sample selection method (Onwuegbuzie & Leech, 2004). To increase the applicability of the findings to a wider population, it is recommended that the researcher use a sampling technique that ensures both randomness and size (Creswell, 2002; Johnson & Christensen, 2004).

Various sampling methods are mentioned in the literature, but this section focuses on convenience, quota, snowball, theoretical, and purposive methods, which are often utilized non-probability sampling techniques:

Convenience Sampling

Convenience sampling is well recognized as a prevalent sampling approach. The term "voluntary sampling" or "random sampling" is also used to refer to this method (Mugenda & Mugenda, 2003). The selection of the sample is based on the researcher's preferred convenience. Typically, individuals are chosen based on their proximity, readiness, and willingness to engage in the research, and the process of sample selection can be repeated until the desired sample size is achieved (Young, 2015). The benefits of this technique are its speed, cost-effectiveness, and lack of need for a comprehensive list of all demographic characteristics. However, it is susceptible to selection bias and personal prejudice among respondents throughout the recruiting process (Yin, 2015). The measurement of sample error is not feasible when convenience sampling is employed. Nevertheless, the measurement and management of variability and bias pose challenges, potentially constraining researchers' capacity to extrapolate findings to a broader population (Creswell et al., 2007).

The utilization of convenience sampling in qualitative research may be effectively justified by establishing a sample group that is demographically and geographically localized. This approach restricts the scope of generalization to the local level, avoiding the formulation of abstract statements that lack contextualization (Robinson, 2014). As an illustration, if the convenience sample comprises psychology students from a particular university in Türkiye, modifying the sample population from "people in general" to "young adults studying at universities in Türkiye" would enhance the connection between the sample and the target population while reducing the potential for generalization and rendering it more logically defensible.

Purposeful sampling can yield crucial insights on pivotal cases. According to Patton (2002), convenience sampling is not purposeful or planned. Convenience sampling, in this context, is not a deliberate strategy, but rather a convenient method to enter the field (Morse, 2010). Patton (2005) asserts that qualitative sampling should be conducted in a deliberate and intentional manner, as it serves as a key indicator of qualitative excellence. This approach is predominantly employed in clinical research, wherein individuals who satisfy the predetermined inclusion criteria are selected for participation in the study.

Quota Sampling

Quota sampling is a non-probability sampling technique that involves selecting subjects based on their presence at a certain moment, rather than by random selection, similar to convenience sampling. When selecting a quota sample, if the population consists of a specific number of distinct ethnic groups, a proportional number of ethnic groups will be chosen based on the overall population size (Burns &

Grove, 2001). Quota sampling is a type of purposive sampling where researchers deliberately choose participants who possess specific qualities or quotas that accurately reflect the community under study. This method allows for the categorization of the population into subgroups that have comparable features in terms of the selected variables. These attributes may encompass age, gender, employment, diagnosis, ethnicity, and other relevant factors. The inclusion criteria guarantee the recruitment of individuals who possess or are likely to possess expertise in the study subject. As illustrated by Mugenda and Mugenda (2003), a researcher may opt to incorporate a certain religion or socioeconomic class inside the sample, thereby determining a quota for each group.

Quota sampling differs from traditional sampling methods by specifying a predetermined number of cases in various categories and the minimum number of instances needed for each category (Mason, 2002). Throughout the research, the numerical data in each location is closely observed to see if the quota has been met. An inherent constraint of this sampling technique is that only those who are available throughout the selection process have an opportunity to be chosen. Moreover, even efforts to replicate the population in specific facets may result in biases, since resemblance in the chosen facets does not ensure resemblance in other variables of significance (Cohen et al., 2002). Moreover, quota sampling distinguishes itself from purposive sampling by being more precise in determining the sizes and proportions of subsamples for each predetermined quota. As an illustration, in a research investigation pertaining to lung cancer associated with smoking, if the total count of patients admitted to the hospital amounts to 400, and the researcher opts to conduct interviews with 80 of them, the appropriate quota to be employed in the study is $Q = 80/400 = 1/5$. Within this particular framework, it is imperative for the researcher to conduct interviews with 16 patients from each subgroup that is defined by the specified characteristics (Gürbüz, 2018).

The objective of this sampling methodology is to establish sample groups that exhibit a proportional representation of the overall population. The researcher carefully considers maintaining the proportions of the population when choosing participants from the groups (Emmel, 2013). Quota sampling facilitates the examination of relationships among the chosen groups. Quota sampling has resemblance to stratified random sampling, however, with the distinction that subjects are not chosen by random selection, hence rendering the determination of potential sampling error unattainable. Furthermore, it is said that this method offers greater adaptability in determining the ultimate sample and is more convenient for recruitment compared to stratified and cell sampling (Robinson, 2014). Quota sampling is employed to guarantee the representation of individuals who are not adequately represented through convenience or purposive sampling methods. Due to the inability to ascertain sampling error, it is not feasible to draw conclusions about the whole research population. According to Morgan (2008), it is important for quota sample groups to be mutually exclusive and easily identifiable by the researcher.

Snowball SAMPLING

Snowball sampling, alternatively referred to as 'chain-referral' or 'networking' sampling, is a research technique in which the researcher starts collecting data from a limited number of individuals and then facilitates the connection of these individuals with acquaintances, family members, work colleagues or other significant others (Liamputtong, 2008). This approach involves a researcher referring a member of the population to other members, who in turn identify additional members until a sample of sufficient size is obtained (Babbie, 2020; Patton, 2002). The snowball technique appears to be a viable approach for cross-cultural research (Adamson and Donovan, 2002), similar to the responsive recruitment strategy

(Liamputtong, 2007). Nevertheless, the snowball approach is not without its limitations. One reason for this is that it often leads to "similar" individuals. According to Eide and Allen (2005), this phenomenon has the potential to limit diversity.

The use of this sampling method proves to be highly advantageous in identifying and recruiting "hidden populations" (Green & Thorogood, 2009) that are not easily accessible. Individuals who are typically concerned about confidentiality and consent may be more inclined to participate in a survey when they are guided by their social contacts. However, for the same reason, respondents often do not accurately reflect the population being surveyed.

Both snowball sampling and sequential sampling are effective procedures when the desired population is difficult to access. These groups are often observed in the upper echelons of society, such as senior executives and politicians, or in the lowest strata, such as drug users and homeless individuals. In such cases, the researcher assumes the role of a gatekeeper and directs the researcher to other members of the population who may express willingness to participate in the study (Neuman, 2006).

This sampling is typically not suitable for accurately representing the distribution of a variable in the population and does not enable the researcher to make generalizations from the sample to the population. Frequently, the researcher will have a keen interest in providing a comprehensive description of a particular sample (Mason, 2002).

Mani (2006) used snowball sampling for participant selection in her study with Indo-Canadians. Participants first suggested other people who might be interested in participating in the study. The snowball sampling approach was effective; however, it was observed that the people selected for the study exhibited similar levels of acculturation.

Theoretical Sampling

The concept of theoretical sampling is distinct from the purposive techniques stated earlier in that it occurs within the process of data collecting and analysis, subsequent to the sampling and early examination of some data (Coyne, 1997). The concept of theoretical sampling was first linked to grounded theory; however, its underlying concepts may be applied to several different research methodologies (Mason, 2002).

Although primarily employed in grounded theory investigations, this sampling method is also being increasingly utilized to gather data from people for theoretical purposes. The study starts with a homogeneous sample of limited size and thereafter progresses towards a heterogeneous sample of larger size in order to ascertain the similarities and differences among the chosen instances (Creswell et al., 2007). The process of sampling is conducted in a sequential manner and in combination with the analysis of the data. The data that has been previously analyzed serves as a guiding framework for the data collection process in the subsequent step. Initially, the researcher formulates the study goals and subsequently identifies a group, often a purposefully selected group, to engage in deliberation or conduct interviews pertaining to the research issue, employing predetermined criteria for such considerations. The aforementioned procedure entails the reconfiguration of the sample based on a revised set of criteria, hence altering the initial sampling technique that was previously selected (Robinson, 2014). After the initial session with the sample, the researcher examines and arranges the acquired information. Based on the results obtained in the initial session, the researcher chooses a second sample to analyze, assess, or conduct interviews on the findings from the initial session. The second sample has the potential to validate or disprove the conclusions made in the initial session. The research information is refined by comparing and combining the data from the second and first sessions. This refining process may involve presenting the refined information to a third sample or to the original subjects from the first session for confirmation (Patton, 2005). The process of theoretical sampling persists, wherein the researcher alternates between the stages of sampling, data gathering, and analysis, until the point at which data saturation is verified. The Delphi method is a frequently employed kind of theoretical sampling that offers a cost-effective and time-efficient technique to achieving a research goal. In contrast, theoretical sampling is predicated upon the researcher's exercise of judgment in identifying and selecting sample participants who possess knowledge or expertise pertaining to a certain study topic, while also demonstrating willingness and capability to participate. Similar to the method of purposive sampling, this approach introduces the possibility of sampling mistakes that are not quantifiable (Draucker et al., 2007).

Purposive (Purposeful) Sampling

Purposive sampling tactics refer to deliberate and non-randomised approaches used to ensure that certain types of cases from a given sampling population are included in the final sample of a project (Mason, 2002). It is based on the assumption that particular cases may have different and important perspectives on the concepts and issues under investigation, based on the researcher's pre-existing theoretical understanding of the topic under investigation (Patton, 2002; Robinson, 2014).

The concept of 'bias', typically seen as a limitation in analytical approaches, takes on a central role in qualitative sampling and thus becomes a valuable asset. The logic and effectiveness of purposive sampling lies in the deliberate selection of samples that contain rich material for comprehensive study. Information-rich cases are those that provide valuable insights into important topics of study and this is why purposive sampling is used (Cresswell & Clark, 2017; Kelly, 2010).

Rather than drawing empirical generalizations, analyzing cases with a wealth of information yields insightful knowledge. Purposive sampling is a method that prioritizes the selection of cases that contain rich information and shed light on the research questions at hand. For example, if the aim of an evaluation is to improve the effectiveness of a program in reaching people from low socio-economic backgrounds, a comprehensive study of a limited number of carefully selected poor families can provide valuable insights (Patton, 2023; Robinson, 2014).

On the other hand, with purposive sampling, the degree of variance is frequently not entirely known when the study first begins. To reduce this uncertainty, selecting a sample of informants with a wealth of information to cover this range assumes that the extent of variance is already known. To achieve saturation, it is generally recommended to use an iterative sampling and resampling strategy, as suggested by Miles and Huberman (1994). However, the determination of saturation in research can be based not only on an established theory or conceptual framework, but also on the data itself, as exemplified by the grounded theory method (Patton, 2002). In addition, it is expected that the individuals included in the sample have the necessary preparation and willingness to participate in the research, as well as the ability to effectively express their experiences and perspectives in a coherent, clear and thought-provoking manner (Bernard, 2002; Stratton, 2019).

Probability Sampling

Probability Sampling continues to be the predominant approach for the selection of extensive and representative samples, which is extensively employed in contemporary practice. This methodology allows for the statistical determination that every unit within the population possesses an equal likelihood of being chosen for inclusion in the sample, as well as the likelihood of the unit being picked from the population (Patton, 2023). For instance, let us consider a scenario where the population consists of 1000 responders. A sample of 100 units will be chosen from the population, with a probability of 10% for each unit to be included in the sample.

However, some prerequisites must be fulfilled before this approach can be used: Firstly, it is necessary to have a comprehensive inventory of the issues to be analyzed, to have a full understanding of all the characteristics of the population, to ensure the required sample size and to ensure that each element has an equal probability of being selected (Johnson & Christensen, 2004; Patton, 2023). When employing this approach for sample selection, it is imperative for the researcher to possess a comprehensive understanding of sample selection strategies. The method serves as a comprehensive representation of the whole target population and enables the drawing of inferences about such community, hence providing a significant level of representativeness (Pelzang & Hutchinson, 2017; Ponterotto, 2010). Nevertheless, the degree of dependability is contingent upon the true magnitude of the population and the magnitude of the sample. As the disparity between the two increases, the probability of preliminary results being incorrect also increases. A bigger sample size is associated with a lower variance. This methodology has the capability to compute the variables that contribute to sampling error in order to establish the credibility of the findings. The decision to include units from the population in the sample might be statistically predicted. The replication of the study and the validation of its findings by other researchers are feasible (Halkoaho et al., 2016; Neuman, 2000). The significance of researcher judgment in sample construction is small, hence enhancing the objectivity of the results. Probabilistic sampling is often regarded as the preferred approach in sampling methodology due to its potential to enhance the generalizability of study findings to the intended population. The aforementioned approach is characterized by its high cost, time-intensive nature, and inherent complexity, mostly due to the necessity of a substantial sample size and the dispersion of selected units throughout a wide geographical expanse (Sandelowski, 1995).

Prior to determining the individuals to be chosen for the investigation and the method of sample selection, qualitative researchers must establish the study's purpose (Onwuegbuzie and Leech, 2004). In order to expand the applicability of the findings to a broader population, it is advisable for the researcher to employ a sampling technique that ensures both randomness and size (Creswell, 2002; Johnson & Christensen, 2004).

Although many different sampling methods exist in the literature, in this section, simple random, stratified random, cluster random, systematic random, multistage random and maximum variation sampling methods are mentioned among the most commonly used probability sampling methods:

Simple Random Sampling

The selection of participants in this study ensures that every individual in the population has an equal chance of being chosen, and the selection of one individual does not impact the selection of another individual. Simple random sampling is a method in which every item within a population has an equal probability of being chosen for inclusion in a sample. This is achieved by assigning a numerical value to each item in the population list, which is then selected from a table of random numbers to be included in the sample (Kothari, 2004). The sampling process involves the selection of sample units by many approaches, including the lottery method, the skip method, and the grid method (Gokhale & Srivastava, 2017; Okoko et al., 2023):

The Lottery

This study utilizes a methodology that depends on the random selection of individual items or units from the population. Randomness is the state in which each item has an equal chance of being selected. This methodology assumes that each element within the population possesses an equivalent likelihood. In the context of a survey, a lottery can be employed to ensure that each participant is afforded an equitable opportunity of selection. This method entails creating a list of the target population and assigning a numerical identifier to each person. Afterwards, a specific number of papers is selected from the total number of papers thrown into the jar.

The Tippet's Table Method

The utilization of the Tippet Table Method is a prevalent approach in the field of random sampling, which enables the random selection of participants during the sampling process. This approach provides a practical solution, especially when the task requires choosing random samples from large populations.

A purpose-built table is utilized to randomly select samples from a designated population. The table consists of a collection of arbitrary numbers, typically spanning from 1 to 10,000. The researcher selects a random number that is appropriate for the population size and subsequently selects samples that correspond to this selected number.

For instance, a researcher may choose to select a sample size of 100 individuals from a population size of 1000 individuals. In this context, the participant selects a random number from the Tippet Table, which spans a range of 1 to 1000. For example, the number 437 is selected from the table. In this particular case, the sample comprises the 437th individual or object selected from the population. This procedure is repeated until the desired sample size is achieved.

Grid Method

The Grid Method is commonly used to sample from a population that is spread out over a large geographical area. In order to analyze the political viewpoints of voters within a specific state, it is imperative to take into account a significant sample size of voters. In this context, the collective votes from the entire state encompass the entirety of our universe. A representative sample is derived from the universe by constructing a cartographic representation of the state and demarcating squares on it. The squares illustrated on the map are numbered in a sequential manner. A lot of approach is employed to select multiple squares from the pool. The sample comprises the voters in that region who were chosen through the aforementioned lottery procedure. Therefore, it is possible to select a representative subset from a large population spanning a wide geographical area.

The method of Simple Random Sampling guarantees that each element has an equal likelihood of being chosen. This sampling approach is widely regarded as the most direct and uncomplicated to execute. The previously mentioned methodology could be utilized in combination with other probability sampling techniques. Prior knowledge of the population's actual composition is not necessary for the researcher; instead, they only need a minimal amount of information about the population. According to Benoot et al. (2016) and Sharma (2017), this approach requires limited population data, exhibits strong internal and external validity, and enables efficient data analysis. The employment of simple random sampling enables the identification of research participants who demonstrate a significant overlap with the entire target population. According to Masiloane (2008), the utilization of simple random selection allows for the mathematical calculation of the required sample size in order to achieve the desired level of precision in quantitative research outcomes. On the other hand, a disadvantage of simple random sampling is the time-consuming and sometimes impractical process of using random sampling in large populations, as it requires identifying and counting every individual in the population.

In comparison to alternative sampling methods, it results in a greater number of errors in the findings. When the researcher aims to divide the participants into subgroups or strata for the purpose of comparison, the use of this method is not viable. However, it has disadvantages such as its excessively high cost and the need for a sample frame. According to Acharya et al. (2013) and Stratton (2019), stratified samples of equal size demonstrate higher levels of accuracy and larger sampling errors in comparison to non-stratified samples.

Stratified Random Sampling

Stratified sampling is employed when the units that make up the population have diverse characteristics (gender, age, seniority, employment, etc.). Using the stratified sample approach, homogenous strata (subgroups-subuniverses) are created from the universe with varying features (Leedy & Ormrod, 2023). When a researcher wishes to choose a sample with a certain trait or attribute, they employ stratified sampling.

A population is divided into subpopulations using stratified random sampling, which is a sampling design wherein each subpopulation's members are relatively homogeneous with regard to one or more characteristics and relatively heterogeneous with regard to those characteristics when compared to members of all other subgroups. Next, using simple random or systematic sampling, a random sample is taken from each subpopulation. This ensures that a random number of elements proportionate to or representative of the elements in each stratum are chosen for the sample (Neuman, 2000). As even small subpopulations cannot be overlooked, stratifying the population and then selecting a sample from each stratum, according to De Vos (2001), improves the representativeness of the resulting sample.

The sample chosen by stratified sampling may reflect different demographic subgroups as well as distinctive tendencies within the target population. Consequently, it guarantees the representation of every group within the intended population. It is possible to assess and compare the traits of every stratum (Patton, 2002). Moreover, it lessens the variability brought on by systematic sampling. Its drawbacks include that the preparation of stratified lists is costly and need precise information on the distribution of each stratum. Because the statistical comparison is valid only if at least 20 individuals are present in each stratum, greater sample sizes are needed to get statistically significant findings compared to ordinary random sampling. For instance, based on their socioeconomic structure, nations, regions, or cities can be classified into three classes: the poor, middle class, and the rich. However, public opinion surveys can distinguish between two classes, such as rural and urban areas (Acharya et al., 2013; Sharma, 2017).

Compared to a basic random sample, stratified samples are probably a better representation of several factors (Babbie, 2020). It is crucial to choose research participants based on how well the group is represented in size; for instance, if women make up 70% of the population and men make up 30%, the sample should have a 7:3 female to male ratio. Stratified groups, where research participants are chosen at random, are very representative of the target population as a whole when implemented well. By enabling the sampling of a diverse population, stratified random sampling addresses a limitation of cluster random sampling.

Cluster Random Sampling

Cluster sampling is an important tool when the population is widely dispersed and it is impractical to select a representative sample from all elements. The sampling procedure involves selecting one element or topic at a time. However, this method can be time consuming and tedious when a large sample is required. Also, it may not always be possible for the researcher to have a complete list of all the elements in the universe. Therefore, the researcher prefers to select samples in groups or categories to overcome this problem (Patton, 2002). This method is called cluster sampling. Cluster sampling is a probability sampling procedure that determines the final sampling units by sampling from larger units. With this method, the researcher proceeds from larger sampling units to smaller ones. It is usually applied based on clusters or groups divided into geographical areas or regions. When cluster sampling is applied, it can be difficult to create a list of the components of the target population, especially if the population of interest is spread over a large geographical area (Burns and Grove, 2001). In the method, it is important to initially sample clusters that are as similar as possible. Within these clusters there are elements with different characteristics, which eventually form a population from which a sample is selected (Leedy & Ormrod, 2023).

Cluster random sampling is used to overcome the disadvantages of identifying all individuals in large populations and is commonly used in public health field assessment during disasters. Researchers randomly identify areas containing the target population of the study and select clusters or groups of people from these areas. Individuals within the randomly selected clusters are then considered potential study subjects (Johnson & Christensen, 2004). All individuals within a cluster can be part of the study sample, or simple random sampling can be used to select study subjects from clusters. Although cluster sampling is more feasible than simple random sampling in large populations, it is important that the clusters to be used are homogeneous with respect to the overall target population (Nauman, 2000).

Although cluster sampling is an efficient procedure, Collins (1999) notes that this leads to a further loss in representativeness, as sampling error can occur at each stage of listing. For example, populations with a large degree of heterogeneity (e.g. age, wealth or ethnicity) can produce results with undesirable selection bias unless clusters are well distributed, and a sufficient number of clusters are included in the sample.

Systematic Random Sampling

Systematic sampling is a commonly employed method when there is a comprehensive and current roster of sampling units. This method guarantees the systematic selection of sampling units and provides researchers with practicality in terms of time and resources. Nevertheless, it is crucial to consider the choice of the sampling interval and the potential introduction of bias, as a biased selection of the interval can impact the precision of the findings. Various methods can be employed to arrange items, such as numerically, alphabetically, demographically, or in alternative arrangements. The initial step in the sample selection process involves the random selection of the first sample, followed by the automatic selection of subsequent samples in a predetermined sequence. A systematic sampling technique involves the selection of individual items from a given population, with the sampling interval denoted as k. To determine the sampling interval, divide the population size by the sample size to be selected (Gokhale & Srivastava, 2017; Okoko et al., 2023):

So $k = N/n$, where k is an integer.

k = Sampling interval, Population size, Sample size. Sample selection procedure by systematic sampling

(i) If we want to select a sample of 100 employees from a company with 1000 employees, the sampling interval $k = N/n = 1000/100 = 10$.

Therefore, sampling interval = 10 means that one employee should be selected for every 10 employees.

(ii) The first sample is selected from the first 10 (sampling interval) samples by random selection procedures.

(iii) If the first random sample selected is 10, the other samples are automatically selected by increasing the value of the sampling interval (k = 10), i.e. 10, 20, 30, 40, 40, 50, 60, 70, 80, 90, 100, 110.

Example:

Suppose we need to select 25 people out of 5,000. The procedure is to number all 5,000 items from 1 to 5,000. The sampling interval is calculated as $k = N/n = 5000/25 = 200$.

The sampling interval = 200 therefore means that one sample must be selected for every 200 samples. The first sample is selected from the first 200 samples by random selection procedures. If the first random sample selected is 50, the remaining samples are automatically selected by increasing the value of the sampling interval (k = 200), i.e. 50, 250, 450, 650, 850, 1050, 1250, 1450, 1650, 1850, 2050, 2250, 2450, 2650, 2850, 3050, 3250, 3450, 3650, 3850, 4050, 4250, 4450, 4650, 4850.

Systematic sampling is often the preferred method when a complete and up-to-date list is available. The advantages of this method include simplicity, convenience, and the ability to represent the population more evenly. However, it should be noted that systematic sampling is not random sampling and may complicate the selection process if the sampling interval (k) is not an integer. Also, when using this method, attention should be paid to the presence of hidden periodic features that may affect the representativeness of sampling techniques. Systematic sampling is not considered as rigorous as random sampling strategies and it is important to determine the sample size correctly to ensure data validity.

Multi-stage Random Sampling

Multistage sampling is considered to be a very useful method as it involves more than one type of sampling. It is generally a preferred sampling technique when a complete list of all members of the population is not available and appropriate. One of its advantages is that it reduces costs compared to traditional cluster sampling. In the multi-stage sampling method, the same sampling method can be used at each stage or different sampling methods can be used (Acharya et al., 2013; Gokhale & Srivastava, 2017):

The process entails the iterative execution of two fundamental stages, namely listing and sampling. Usually, the cluster size is decreased at each stage, and finally subject sampling is conducted. The initial phase of sampling is referred to as the "Primary Sampling Unit" (PSU), followed by the "Secondary Sampling Unit" (SSU), and so forth, until the "Final" or "Ultimate" sampling units are attained.

In the first stage, the target group is clearly defined. In multi-country studies, this may involve selecting specific countries or regions that represent the diversity of your research interests. PSU: In the first stage, countries or large regions within countries are selected as primary sampling units PSUs. This stage involves deciding which countries or regions to include in the study based on factors such as relevance to our research question, diversity and feasibility.

SSU: Within each selected country or region, further sampling is conducted to select secondary sampling units (SSUs). The selection of SSUs should aim to capture diversity within each country or region.

TSU (if necessary): Depending on the complexity and scope of your survey, additional sampling stages may need to be carried out. For example, in selected cities or communities, specific groups or individuals may be further sampled to ensure diversity and representativeness.

Multistage sampling is a frequently used method in qualitative and quantitative research with large or diverse populations. The method is extremely convenient as it involves more than one stage of random sampling. Especially in qualitative research, it plays an important role in ensuring representativeness for multi-country samples. In cross-country studies with large sample sizes, more complex than simple random sampling methods may be needed (Ramanujan et., 2022).

For example, a company wants to measure employee satisfaction. Using a multi-stage sampling method, it selects representatives from different departments and positions. For example, random subgroups are identified from large departments and random employees are selected from each subgroup. In this way, a sample is obtained that represents both different departments and different positions within those departments.

Maximum Variation Sampling

Maximum Variation Sampling is a widely utilized purposive sample strategy (Sandelowski, 1995). In order to pick all or most of the individuals, groups, and diverse settings for the study, a wide range of people, groups, or locations are purposely chosen in order to capture distinct features within a community. Rather than attempting to select a representative sample of the total population, maximum variation sampling specifically chooses respondents who represent a wide range of variance in important characteristics across different countries or regions. By ensuring that the sample accurately represents the diversity present in the multi-country setting, this approach enables researchers to examine shared trends, original findings, and subtle cultural differences between various cultural contexts. This makes it possible to present various people's points of view that illustrate how complex the world is (Creswell, 2002).

High heterogeneity might be problematic in small samples since individual cases differ greatly from one another. In order to capture the essential elements and central, shared characteristics of a setting or phenomena, common patterns arising from tremendous variation are very valuable (Patton, 2015). This approach enables researchers to collect rich and comprehensive qualitative data that captures the complexity and diversity of the multi-country sample.

ETHICAL CONSIDERATIONS IN QUALITATIVE SAMPLING IN MULTICULTURAL SETTINGS

Researchers must take caution when using qualitative sampling approaches in multicultural contexts. This is due to the intricate dynamics that emerge from cultural diversity, disparities in power, and involvement of the community. Therefore, it is imperative to conduct a thorough assessment of ethical concerns. In order to prevent harm or misrepresentation, it is imperative for researchers to exhibit cultural sensitivity via the acknowledgment and respect of varied cultural values, the practice of reflexivity, and the avoidance of prejudices, biases, and assumptions (Marshall & Batten, 2004; Sanjari et al., 2014).

Furthermore, it is important to take into account the variations in language and cultural standards that exist within heterogeneous environments. The concept of informed consent has considerable importance in qualitative research, particularly within multicultural contexts characterized by language obstacles and cultural norms. The importance of researchers offering explicit and unambiguous information, promoting voluntary engagement, upholding participants' autonomy to withdraw from the study, and assuring comprehensive comprehension of the intended message is underscored by Halkoaho et al. (2016).

The preservation of participant confidentiality and anonymity has significant importance in multicultural environments, as it might amplify apprehensions over privacy and trust. Researchers place significant attention on the establishment of policies that emphasize the safeguarding of participants' identities and the secure management of sensitive data. Sanjari et al. (2014) put up a multitude of potential strategies aimed at enhancing data security. The used procedures encompass the utilization of pseudonyms, the elimination of identifying details from transcripts and publications, and the implementation of data storage techniques such as encryption and password safeguarding.

An in-depth understanding of the power dynamics that exist in cross-cultural research environments is essential for academics, particularly when engaging in collaborative efforts with marginalized or susceptible populations. The primary objective ought to be the cultivation of fair and impartial connections with participants, guided by the values of mutual involvement, esteem, and the promotion of trust. It may be considered crucial to include participatory methodologies, which entail the active engagement of community members in the study's planning and implementation, as well as the effective communication of research findings to participants in a way that is understandable and culturally appropriate (Ling et al., 2023).

In order to promote openness within the research process, it is imperative for researchers to provide a comprehensive account of their aims, techniques, and acknowledgment of any potential conflicts of interest. Moreover, it is imperative for individuals to demonstrate responsibility towards participants, communities, and other stakeholders by following ethical standards and principles of behavior. This entails aggressively soliciting perspectives and viewpoints from individuals within the community, and promptly and transparently resolving any apprehensions or complaints that may arise (Patton, 2023).

As a result, when performing qualitative sampling in multicultural situations, researchers are required to traverse intricate cultural, social, and ethical environments, hence emphasizing the significance of ethical considerations. In multicultural societies, researchers must adhere to values such as cultural sensitivity, informed consent, confidentiality, power sharing, beneficence, respect for local knowledge, and transparency to guarantee ethical and socially acceptable research. The aforementioned values are designed to maintain the dignity, rights, and overall welfare of individuals involved, while also making a good impact on society (Ponteratto, 2010; Woodland et al., 2021).

CONCLUSION

The analysis of qualitative sampling methods in multicultural settings reveals a multifaceted interplay of factors that need careful consideration and adaptability. Inside the present chapter, an examination has been conducted on the notions of probabilistic and non-probabilistic sampling techniques, wherein their respective merits and challenges in effectively capturing the intricacy and diversity observed inside multicultural groups have been acknowledged. When examining the intricacies of sampling in such circumstances, a number of noteworthy themes emerge that underscore the importance of contextual sensitivity, a rigorous technique, and ethical dedication (Marshall & Batten, 2004; Patton, 2023).

Qualitative researchers must prioritize the recognition and appreciation of the complex characteristics inherent in multicultural settings, as well as the diverse array of cultural identities, languages, and experiences that are present within these communities. Probability sampling methods, such as purposive sampling, offer a methodical approach to participant selection that effectively captures the diversity found in a community, while also ensuring sufficient representation of various cultural groups (Miles & Huberman, 1995; Padgett, 2008). The reliability and transferability of research findings can be improved by deliberately selecting participants according to predetermined criteria, so leading to a more thorough understanding of intercultural phenomena.

However, it should be noted that the rigid structures of probability sampling may not always be well-suited for the flexibility and vibrancy of multicultural settings. Non-probability sampling tactics, such as snowball and convenience sampling, offer alternative approaches to target ethnic groups who are challenging to access or stigmatized (Acharya et al., 2013). While probability sampling provides a higher level of statistical rigor in comparison to these methodologies, it nevertheless provides valuable insights into the lived experiences and perspectives of persons who may otherwise be marginalized from research endeavors. Moreover, non-probability sampling methods provide researchers the chance to build trust and rapport within communities, therefore fostering the collaborative relationships necessary for conducting ethical and culturally sensitive research.

In order to ensure that their methodologies adequately emphasize the perspectives and autonomy of individuals from various cultural origins, researchers must skillfully navigate the complex interplay of privilege, representation, and voice. It is critical to actively engage in reflective practices to address the risk of reductionist or essentialist portrayals of heterogeneous communities. These activities entail acknowledging and embracing one's own biases and viewpoints. Furthermore, it is imperative for researchers to embrace a reciprocal and empowering methodology when engaging in the process of sampling. This involves the acknowledgment and appreciation of the important contributions made by participants, as well as the endeavor to collect study findings that possess importance and relevance within their own cultural contexts.

In conclusion, the establishment of inclusive study environments that demonstrate respect for the perspectives and experiences of participants from various cultural backgrounds can be achieved by researchers via the recognition and acceptance of the complexities associated with diversity, as well as the utilization of ethical and culturally sensitive methodologies. As we navigate the complexities of multicultural research, it is crucial to prioritize the promotion of equity, justice and empowerment in our research methodology and communities.

REFERENCES

Acharya, A. S., Prakash, A., Saxena, P., & Nigam, A. (2013). Sampling: Why and how of it. *Indian Journal of Medical Specialties*, 4(2), 330–333. 10.7713/ijms.2013.0032

Adamson, J., & Donovan, J. L. (2002). Research in black and white. *Qualitative Health Research*, 12(6), 816–825. 10.1177/104323020120060081210972

Babbie, E. R. (2020). *The Practice of Social Research*. Cengage AU.

Benoot, C., Hannes, K., & Bilsen, J. (2016). The use of purposeful sampling in a qualitative evidence synthesis: A worked example on sexual adjustment to a cancer trajectory. *BMC Medical Research Methodology*, 16(1), 1–12. 10.1186/s12874-016-0114-626891718

Bernard, H. R. (2000). *Research Methods in Anthropology: Qualitative and Quantitative Approaches*. AltaMira.

Bernard, H. R. (2002). *Research Methods in Anthropology: Qualitative and Quantitative Methods* (3rd ed.). AltaMira Press.

Berry, J. W., Breugelmans, S. M., & Poortinga, Y. H. (2011). *Cross-Cultural Psychology*. Cambridge University Press. 10.1017/CBO9780511974274

Boddy, C. R. (2016). Sample size for qualitative research. *Qualitative Market Research*, 19(4), 426–432. 10.1108/QMR-06-2016-0053

Bowen, G. A. (2008). Naturalistic inquiry and the saturation concept: A research note. *Qualitative Research*, 8(1), 137–152. 10.1177/1468794107085301

Burns, N., & Grove, S. K. (2001). Introduction to qualitative research. *The Practice of Nursing Research. Conduct, Critique and Utilization*, 67-68.

Carlsen, B., & Glenton, C. (2011). What about N? A methodological study of sample-size reporting in focus group studies. *BMC Medical Research Methodology*, 11(1), 1–10. 10.1186/1471-2288-11-2621396104

Charmaz, K. (2006). *Constructing Grounded Theory*. Sage.

Cohen, L., Manion, L., & Morrison, K. (2002). *Research Methods in Education*. Routledge. 10.4324/9780203224342

Collins, A. (1999). The changing infrastructure of education research. In Lagemann, E., & Shulman, L. (Eds.), *Issues in Education Research* (pp. 289–298). Jossey-Bass.

Coyne, I. T. (1997). Sampling in qualitative research. Purposeful and theoretical sampling; merging or clear boundaries? *Journal of Advanced Nursing*, 26(3), 623–630. 10.1046/j.1365-2648.1997.t01-25-00999.x9378886

Creswell, J. W. (2002). *Educational Research: Planning, Conducting, and Evaluating Quantitative and Qualitative Research*. Pearson Education.

Creswell, J. W. (2007). *Qualitative Inquiry and Research Design: Choosing Among Five Approaches* (2nd ed.). Sage.

Creswell, J. W., & Clark, V. L. P. (2017). *Designing and Conducting Mixed Methods Research*. Sage publications.

Creswell, J. W., Hanson, W. E., Clark Plano, V. L., & Morales, A. (2007). Qualitative research designs: Selection and implementation. *The Counseling Psychologist*, 35(2), 236–264. 10.1177/0011000006287390

De Vos, A. S. (2001). *Research at Grass Roots: A Primer for The Caring Professions*. Van Schaik.

Demuth, C. (2013). Ensuring Rigor in Qualitative Research Within the Field of Cross-. *Culture and Psychology*.

Draucker, C. B., Martsolf, D. S., Ross, R., & Rusk, T. B. (2007). Theoretical sampling and category development in grounded theory. *Qualitative Health Research*, 17(8), 1137–1148. 10.1177/10497323 0730845017928484

Eide, P., & Allen, C. B. (2005). Recruiting transcultural qualitative research participants: A conceptual model. *International Journal of Qualitative Methods*, 4(2), 44–56. 10.1177/160940690500400204

Emmel, N. (2013). *Sampling and Choosing Cases in Qualitative Research: A Realist Approach*. Sage. 10.4135/9781473913882

Galvin, R. (2015). How many interviews are enough? Do qualitative interviews in building energy consumption research produce reliable knowledge? *Journal of Building Engineering*, 1, 2–12. 10.1016/j.jobe.2014.12.001

Glaser, B. G., & Strauss, A. L. (1967). *The Discovery of Grounded Theory: Strategies for Qualitative Research*. Aldine de Gruyter.

Gokhale, S. J., & Srivastava, N. (2017). *UNIT 2 Research Design and Sampling*. https://egyankosh.ac.in/bitstream/123456789/4114/1/MWG-005B3E-U2.pdf

Gómez, M. V., & Kuronen, M. (2011). Comparing local strategies and practices: Recollections from two qualitative cross-national research projects. *Qualitative Research*, 11(6), 683–697. 10.1177/1468794111413366

Green, J., & Thorogood, N. (2009). *Qualitative Methods for Health Research* (2nd ed.). Sage Publications.

Guest, G., Bunce, A., & Johnson, L. (2006). How many interviews are enough? An experiment with data saturation and variability. *Field Methods*, 18(1), 59–82. 10.1177/1525822X05279903

Gürbüz, B. (2018). *Statistics (Population and Sample)* [İstatistik (Evren ve Örneklem)]. Ankara University Open Class Sources.

Hagaman, A. K., & Wutich, A. (2017). How many interviews are enough to identify metathemes in multisited and cross-cultural research? Another perspective on Guest, Bunce, and Johnson's (2006) landmark study. *Field Methods*, 29(1), 23–41. 10.1177/1525822X16640447

Halkoaho, A., Pietilä, A. M., Ebbesen, M., Karki, S., & Kangasniemi, M. (2016). Cultural aspects related to informed consent in health research: A systematic review. *Nursing Ethics*, 23(6), 698–712. 10.1177/0969733015579312225904548

Hennink, M., & Kaiser, B. N. (2022). Sample sizes for saturation in qualitative research: A systematic review of empirical tests. *Social Science & Medicine,* 292-302.

Johnson, R. B., & Christensen, L. B. (2004). *Educational Research: Quantitative, Qualitative, and Mixed Approaches.* Allyn and Bacon. 10.3102/0013189X033007014

Kelly, M. (2010). The role of theory in qualitative health research. *Family Practice*, 27(3), 285–290. 10.1093/fampra/cmp07719875746

Kothari, C. R. (2004). *Research Methodology: Methods and Techniques.* New Age International.

Leedy, P. D., & Ormrod, J. E. (2023). *Practical Research: Planning and Design.* Pearson.

Liamputtong, P. (2007). *Researching The Vulnerable: A Guide to Sensitive Research Methods.* Sage Publications. 10.4135/9781849209861

Liamputtong, P. (2008). Doing research in a cross-cultural context: Methodological and ethical challenges. *Doing Cross-Cultural Research: Ethical and Methodological Perspectives*, 3-20.

Lie-A-Ling, H. J. M., Zuurbier, P. H., Roopnarine, J. L., & Lindauer, L. R. (2023). Cultural Sensitivity: Guidelines for Qualitative Research. *Pedagogische Studiën*, 100(2), 248–260. 10.59302/ps.v100i2.14225

Mani, P. S. (2006). Methodological dilemmas experienced in researching Indo-Canadian Young Adults' decision-making process to study the sciences. *International Journal of Qualitative Methods*, 5(2), 55–72. 10.1177/160940690600500209

Marshall, A., & Batten, S. (2004). Researching across cultures: Issues of ethics and power. In *Forum Qualitative Sozialforschung. Forum Qualitative Social Research*, 5(3). Advance online publication. 10.17169/fqs-5.3.572

Marshall, B., Cardon, P., Poddar, A., & Fontenot, R. (2013). Does sample size matter in qualitative research? *A Review of Qualitative Interviews in IS Research.Journal of Computer Information Systems*, 54(1), 11–22. 10.1080/08874417.2013.11645667

Masiloane, E. T. (2008). *A comparison of qualitative and quantitative research: similarities and differences* (Doctoral dissertation, University of the Free State, Bloemfontein).

Mason, J. (2002). *Qualitative Researching. Sage Publications.*

McArt, E. W., & Brown, J. K. (1990). The challenge of research on international populations: Theoretical and methodological issues. *Oncology Nursing Forum*, 17(2), 283–286.2315194

Miles, M. B., & Huberman, A. M. (1994). *Qualitative Data Analysis: An Expanded Sourcebook.* Sage.

Morgan, D. L. (2008). Snowball sampling. In Given, L. M. (Ed.), *The Sage encyclopedia of qualitative research methods* (pp. 816–817). SAGE Publications, Inc. 10.4135/9781412963909

Morse, J. M. (1995). The significance of saturation. *Qualitative Health Research*, 5(2), 147–149. 10.1177/104973239500500201

Morse, J. M. (2010). How different is qualitative health research from qualitative research? Do we have a subdiscipline? *Qualitative Health Research*, 20(11), 1459–1464. 10.1177/104973231037911620693515

Morse, J. M., & Niehaus, L. (2009). *Mixed Method Design: Principles and Procedures.* Left Coast Press.

Mugenda, O. M., & Mugenda, A. G. (2003). *Research methods: Quantitative & Qualitative Approaches.* Acts press.

Neuman, W. L. (2000). *Social Research Methods Qualitative and Quantitative Approaches* (4th ed.). Allyn & Bacon.

Neuman, W. L. (2006). Social Research Methods: Qualitative and Quantitative Approaches. 6th Edition, Pearson International Edition.

Okoko, J. M., Tunison, S., & Walker, K. D. (Eds.). (2023). *Varieties of Qualitative Research Methods: Selected Contextual Perspectives.* Springer Nature. 10.1007/978-3-031-04394-9

Onwuegbuzie, A. J., & Leech, N. L. (2004). Enhancing the interpretation of "significant" findings: The role of mixed methods research. *The Qualitative Report*, 9(4), 770–792.

Onwuegbuzie, A. J., & Leech, N. L. (2005). The role of sampling in qualitative research. *Academic Exchange Quarterly*, 9(3), 280.

Padgett, D. (2008). Qualitative Methods in Social Work Research (2nd ed.). Sage Publications.

Patton, M. (2015). *Qualitative Research and Evaluation Methods* (4th ed.). Sage Publications.

Patton, M. Q. (2002). Two decades of developments in qualitative inquiry: A personal, experiential perspective. *Qualitative Social Work: Research and Practice*, 1(3), 261–283. 10.1177/1473325002001003636

Patton, M. Q. (2023). *Qualitative Research & Evaluation Methods: Integrating Theory and Practice.* Sage Publications.

Pelzang, R., & Hutchinson, A. M. (2017). Establishing cultural integrity in qualitative research: Reflections from a cross-cultural study. *International Journal of Qualitative Methods*, 17(1). Advance online publication. 10.1177/1609406917749702

Ponterotto, J. G. (2010). Qualitative research in multicultural psychology: Philosophical underpinnings, popular approaches, and ethical considerations. *Cultural Diversity & Ethnic Minority Psychology*, 16(4), 581–589. 10.1037/a0012051058824

Ramanujan, P., Bhattacharjea, S., & Alcott, B. (2022). A Multi-Stage Approach to Qualitative Sampling within a Mixed Methods Evaluation: Some Reflections on Purpose and Process. *The Canadian Journal of Program Evaluation*, 36(3), 355–364. 10.3138/cjpe.71237

Robinson, O. C. (2014). Sampling in interview-based qualitative research: A theoretical and practical guide. *Qualitative Research in Psychology*, 11(1), 25–41. 10.1080/14780887.2013.801543

Sandelowski, M. (1995). Sample size in qualitative research. *Research in Nursing & Health*, 18(2), 179–183. 10.1002/nur.4770180211 7899572

Sanjari, M., Bahramnezhad, F., Fomani, F. K., Shoghi, M., & Cheraghi, M. A. (2014). Ethical challenges of researchers in qualitative studies: The necessity to develop a specific guideline. *Journal of Medical Ethics and History of Medicine*, 7.25512833

Sharma, G. (2017). Pros and cons of different sampling techniques. *International Journal of Applied Research*, 3(7), 749–752.

Stratton, S. J. (2019). Data sampling strategies for disaster and emergency health research. *Prehospital and Disaster Medicine*, 34(3), 227–229. 10.1017/S1049023X1900441231204646

Tanggaard, L. (2014). Ethnographic Fieldwork in Psychology: Lost and Found? *Qualitative Inquiry*, 20(2), 167–174. 10.1177/1077800413510876

Tashakkori, A., & Teddlie, C. (2003). *Handbook of Mixed Methods in Social and Behavioral Research*. Sage.

Vasileiou, K., Barnett, J., Thorpe, S., & Young, T. (2018). Characterizing and justifying sample size sufficiency in interview-based studies: Systematic analysis of qualitative health research over a 15-year period. *BMC Medical Research Methodology*, 18(1), 1–18. 10.1186/s12874-018-0594-730463515

Woodland, L., Blignault, I., O'Callaghan, C., & Harris-Roxas, B. (2021). A framework for preferred practices in conducting culturally competent health research in a multicultural society. *Health Research Policy and Systems*, 19(1), 1–11. 10.1186/s12961-020-00657-y33602261

Yin, R. K. (2015). *Qualitative Research from Start to Finish*. Guilford Publications.

Young, T. J. (2015). Questionnaires and surveys. *Research Methods in Intercultural Communication: A Practical Guide*, 163-180. .10.1002/9781119166283.ch11

ADDITIONAL READING

Bazeley, P. (2020). *Qualitative Data Analysis: Practical Strategies*. SAGE Publications.

Court, D., Abbas, R., Riecken, T., Seymour, J., & Le Tran, M. A. (2018). What is Culture? In *Qualitative Research and Intercultural Understanding: Conducting Qualitative Research in Multicultural Settings* (pp. 14-22). Routledge.

Etikan, I., Musa, S. A., & Alkassim, R. S. (2016). Comparison of convenience sampling and purposive sampling. *American Journal of Theoretical and Applied Statistics*, 5(1), 1–4. 10.11648/j.ajtas.20160501.11

Flick, U. (2018). *An Introduction to Qualitative Research* (6th ed.). SAGE Publications.

Hox, J. J., Moerbeek, M., & van de Schoot, R. (2017). *Multilevel analysis: Techniques and applications* (3rd ed.). Routledge., 10.4324/9781315650982

Marshall, C., & Rossman, G. B. (2016). *Designing Qualitative Research* (6th ed.). SAGE Publications.

Merriam, S. B., & Tisdell, E. J. (2015). *Qualitative Research: A Guide to Design and Implementation* (4th ed.). Jossey-Bass.

Mills, J., & Birks, M. (2014). Qualitative methodology: A practical guide. 10.4135/9781473920163

Moser, A., & Korstjens, I. (2018). Practical guidance to qualitative research. Part 3: Sampling, data collection and analysis. *The European Journal of General Practice*, 23(1), 9–18. 10.1080/13814788.2017.137509129199486

KEY TERMS AND DEFINITIONS

Multilevel Research: Multilevel research involves studying phenomena that operate across multiple levels of analysis, such as individuals within groups or organizations. This approach is used to understand how relationships and interactions at one level (e.g., individual behavior) are influenced by factors at another level (e.g., organizational structure). It is common in fields like education, healthcare, and organizational studies, where data are often hierarchically structured (e.g., students within schools).

Non-Probability Sampling: Non-probability sampling is a method where samples are selected based on subjective judgment rather than random selection. Examples include convenience sampling, quota sampling, and purposive sampling. This approach is often used when it is impractical to conduct random sampling, but it can introduce bias and limit the generalizability of the results.

Probability Sampling: Probability sampling is a technique where each member of the population has a known, non-zero chance of being selected. This includes methods like simple random sampling, stratified sampling, and cluster sampling. Probability sampling is essential for producing representative samples and allows researchers to make valid inferences about the entire population.

Qualitative Sampling: Qualitative sampling involves deliberately selecting participants or cases that can provide deep, rich, and relevant information about the research topic. It is typically purposive, aiming to include individuals who have specific experiences or characteristics of interest. This method focuses on depth rather than breadth, often seeking to explore complex phenomena in detail rather than to generalize findings to a larger population. Qualitative sampling is crucial in studies where understanding the context and meaning of human behavior and experiences is paramount.

Chapter 4
Looking at Qualitative Research Data Collection Methods and the Significance of CAT in Cross–Cultural Interviewing

Ali Elhami
http://orcid.org/0000-0002-8957-6000
UNICAF University, Larnaca, Cyprus

Anita Roshan
Universidad Autónoma de Madrid, Spain

Howard Giles
http://orcid.org/0000-0001-8673-271X
University of California, Santa Barbara, USA & The University of Queensland, Australia

ABSTRACT

This chapter gives an overview of the various data collection methods in qualitative research. Then the authors concentrate on the communication accommodation theory (CAT) and its strategies. Additionally, they explore how utilizing CAT can enhance the quality and depth of information gathered through focus groups and interviews. According to this chapter, in order to build relationships, researchers need to modify their communication styles according to factors like the age, gender, or social status of interviewees, as this encourages informants to share more information and reduces the likelihood of concealing secrets. This approach, when conversing in native or foreign languages, helps researchers maintain a better understanding of participants' perspectives and insights. Furthermore, adapting communication styles can also help researchers navigate cultural nuances and sensitivities, leading to more meaningful and accurate data collection and uncovering deeper insights and perspectives that may have otherwise been overlooked.

DOI: 10.4018/979-8-3693-3306-8.ch004

INTRODUCTION

Qualitative research is a method used to explore and understand people's beliefs, experiences, attitudes, and behaviours. In qualitative research, phenomenological, ethnographic, grounded theory, and case study, are more commonly used designs in the social sciences and humanities. Each design offers a unique approach to gathering and analysing data to uncover rich insights into the human experience. Phenomenological is focused on understanding the essence of a particular phenomenon as experienced by individuals (Bicay et al., 2024; Kartini et al., 2024). Ethnographic research involves immersing oneself in a specific culture to gain a deep understanding of their beliefs and practices (see Ahmed, 2024; Roshan, 2023; Rowe, 2024). Grounded theory, on the other hand, aims to develop theories grounded in data collected from observations and interviews (Sun & Zhao, 2024; Weda & Lemmer, 2024). Case study research involves an in-depth examination of a specific individual, group, or event to understand its unique characteristics and complexities (Elhami, 2023; Elhami & Roshan, 2024a; Şafak-Ayvazoğlu et al., 2021) and for communication accommodation theory (CAT) (Bernhold & Giles, 2019; Gallois et al., 2016).

Each design offers a valuable perspective for researchers seeking to understand the complexities of human behaviour and beliefs. Each design in qualitative research needs to be carefully considered based on the research questions and goals of the study in order to determine the most appropriate method(s) for data collection. Regardless of the research project's design, selecting the most suitable data collection methods is crucial to guaranteeing that participant stories and experiences are accurately recorded and analysed. Data collection methods can include surveys, interviews, observations, and document analysis, among others, each offering unique advantages and limitations depending on the research context. Researchers must carefully evaluate these options to ensure that the chosen methods align with the study's objectives and provide meaningful insights into the phenomena under investigation. In this chapter, we review various data collection methods commonly used in qualitative research and discuss their strengths and weaknesses in multicultural settings. Additionally, we explore how researchers can combine multiple data collection methods to enhance the depth and validity of their findings.

For data collection, specifically interviews and focus groups, researchers need to know communicative strategies that can help facilitate open and honest discussions with participants from diverse cultural backgrounds. Hence, in the second section of this chapter, we discuss the importance of communication accommodation theory and its strategies for effective (cross-cultural) communication during interviews and focus groups, through which researchers will be able to gather rich and nuanced data from participants. By understanding how to adapt communication styles to fit the cultural norms and demographic characteristics (e.g., age, gender, career) of participants, researchers can create a more inclusive and productive research environment that fosters meaningful dialogue and insights, leading to richer data collection and more robust findings.

Observation

The act of observation involves carefully observing and documenting events, actions, and artifacts in the social situation that has been selected for the study. Field notes, which are thorough, objective, and concrete accounts of what has been observed, is a common name for the observational record. For studies that only rely on observation, it suffices for the researcher to be in the environment as an inconspicuous observer without making any extra effort or playing a specific role. Classroom, cultural, and language studies are types of observations that are frequently used in research, where the researcher records and explains complicated behaviours and interactions from which it is only possible to infer meaning in the absence of other information see, for example studies in which researchers utilized observation (Elhami, 2020a; Papadopoulos & Shin 2021; Roshan, 2023)

The researcher often enters the environment in the early stages of a qualitative investigation with broad areas of interest but without fixed categories or rigid observational checklists. In this way, the researcher can learn about recurring relationships and behaviour patterns. Checklists become more relevant and context-sensitive once these patterns have been found and documented through early analysis of field notes. Later in the study, focused observation is employed, typically to determine, for instance, whether analytic themes can account for relationships and behaviour across a lengthy period of time or in a range of contexts.

In almost all qualitative research, observation is a key and crucial method. Complex interactions in real-world social settings are discovered using this method. Even while conducting in-depth interviews, the researcher must often pay close attention to the interviewee's nonverbal cues and emotional state in addition to their speech. Observation allows researchers to capture nuances and subtleties that may not be conveyed through verbal communication alone. By observing nonverbal cues and emotional states, researchers can gain a deeper understanding of the interviewee's thoughts, feelings, and experiences. This holistic approach enhances the richness and validity of the qualitative data collected.

Field notes are valuable, the researcher should have clear, organized, and managed note-taking techniques. These techniques help ensure that important information is not missed or forgotten during data collection. Additionally, well-maintained field notes can be used as a reference for future analysis and interpretation of the research findings. Besides field notes, observers' comments can be a very beneficial source of analytical insights and hints that help narrow the scope of data collection and focus on key areas of interest. Observers' comments is defined as the subjective observations and interpretations made by individuals who are not directly involved in the research process but are able to offer valuable insights based on their unique perspectives and experiences. These comments can offer a different viewpoint that complements the researcher's own observations and enriches the overall analysis of the data collected. Observers' comments can provide a fresh perspective and highlight patterns or trends that may have been overlooked by the researcher. By incorporating these insights into the data collection process, researchers can enhance the depth and accuracy of their findings, ultimately leading to more robust and meaningful conclusions. They might also offer crucial inquiries for interviews.

Participant observation is both a general approach to inquiry and a method for acquiring data, was originally developed from sociological and anthropological studies (Kawulich, 2005) and is a necessary component of all qualitative investigations, to some extent. Participant observation, as the name implies, necessitates direct participation in the social environment under investigation. The researcher can see, hear, and start to perceive reality like the participants when they are fully immersed in the environment. The researcher should ideally immerse themselves in the environment for a significant length of time to get to know the local culture. The researcher has the chance to gain knowledge directly from his experience through this immersion. Personal reflections are essential to developing an understanding of an ethnic community because they give the researcher fresh perspectives and chances to familiarize themselves with the unfamiliar (Glesne, 1999).

In general, for researchers conducting ethnographic studies, immersing themselves in the environment is crucial for gaining a deep understanding of the culture and community they are studying. This immersion allows for a more authentic and comprehensive exploration of the social dynamics and practices within the community, ultimately leading to richer and more insightful research findings. By actively participating in the daily activities and interactions of the community members, researchers can gain firsthand experience that goes beyond what can be observed from a distance. This level of engagement also helps to build trust and rapport with the individuals being studied, leading to more open and honest responses during interviews and observations.

Materials and Documents

Data on the context's past and present are acquired for some qualitative investigation. Even though this may not constitute a significant portion of data gathering, the researcher nonetheless gets demographic information and provides geographic and historical details by suggesting a specific location. Researchers get data when they peruse current newspaper articles or get information from a website (see, for example, studies in which researchers utilised materials and documents: Ghahraman et al., 2023; Hernandez, 2023; Salmani Nodoushan, 2023). Whether they consider this to be data collection or not, they must exercise discretion. This discretion is crucial, as the reliability and accuracy of the information obtained from newspapers or websites may vary. Additionally, researchers should be mindful of potential biases or limitations in the data they gather from these sources, ensuring that it aligns with their research objectives and overall methodology.

Part of understanding the background and significance of a particular area comes from reading documents. In addition to participant observation, and interviewing, researchers also collect and analyse documents generated during routine activities or created especially for the project at hand. In fact, it can be said that reviewing documents and observation, can also help researchers ask better questions while conducting interviews. An inconspicuous method that is rich in presenting the values and beliefs of participants in the situation is document review. Meeting minutes, letters, notifications, official policy statements, correspondence, and other documents can all be helpful in understanding the environment or organization being examined. Research publications are also quite instructive.

In general, document review provides a comprehensive view of the context in which research is being conducted, offering valuable insights that may not be obtained through other methods alone. Additionally, analysing research publications can provide a broader perspective on the existing knowledge and gaps in the field, guiding researchers towards more informed inquiries during interviews. By combining document review with other research methods, researchers can gain a more holistic understanding of the subject matter. This approach can lead to more thorough and insightful findings that contribute to the overall body of knowledge in the field.

A specialized analytical technique called content analysis is frequently required while using documents. Historically, content analysis was seen as a method of quantitatively describing the content of various types of communication that was neutral, objective, and impartial. However, as it has developed, it is now seen more favourably as a way of characterizing and understanding the artifacts of a culture or social group.

Focus Groups

Focus groups are similar to interviews and have all characteristics of interviews (see the interview section), but they are conducted in groups and are mostly used by social science researchers (for example studies in which researchers utilised focus groups) (Coyne et al, 2016; Cuesta et al, 2016; Gillham et al, 2018; Goel & Penman, 2015; Papadopoulos, 2021; Papadopoulos, 2022; Willis et al. 2018; Roshan, 2023). The groups are typically made up of 3 to 10 individuals who may not know one another and who were chosen because they have particular traits that are pertinent to the objectives of the study. In order to promote conversation and the expression of different perspectives and points of view, the interviewer fosters a supportive environment by asking specific questions. In order to uncover trends in the impressions and opinions given, the researcher may conduct these focus groups with various people at various times. These tendencies will be exposed through rigorous, methodical analysis (Krueger, 1988).

This method makes the assumption that a person's attitudes and views are not formed in isolation and that people frequently need to hear other people's perspectives and understandings before forming their own. Focus-groups have the advantage of being socially oriented, analysing participants in a setting that is more relaxed than one-on-one interviews and more realistic than artificial experimental situations. In focus groups, the interviewer can observe interactions between participants and gain insights into how individuals influence each other's opinions. Additionally, focus groups allow for a deeper exploration of topics as participants can build upon each other's responses, leading to a more comprehensive understanding of the subject matter. However, it has some disadvantages as well. For instance, compared to individual interviews in focus groups, the interviewer frequently has less control over group interviews, time can be wasted while discussing pointless or unrelated matters, transcribing, translating, and analysing is more difficult than interviews, and the arrangement of time and place of the interview is much more difficult than when it is happening with only one participant. Additionally, group dynamics can sometimes lead to certain participants dominating the conversation, while others may not feel comfortable sharing their thoughts. This can result in valuable insights being overlooked or not fully explored. Despite these challenges, group interviews can still be a valuable research tool when managed effectively. Group interviews can also provide a richer understanding of complex topics through the interaction and exchange of ideas among participants. Additionally, they can offer a more diverse range of perspectives and experiences compared to individual interviews, leading to a more comprehensive analysis of the research topic.

Interviews

Many social science professionals believe that using interviews as a method of data collection is essential while doing qualitative research (Barrett & Twycross, 2018; De Fina, 2019; De Fina & Perrino, 2011; Denzin & Lincoln, 2005a/b; Fuller, 2000; Mishler, 1986). There are many qualitative studies to have utilized interviews as a way to gather rich, in-depth information from participants (see, for example, studies in which researchers utilised focus groups: Aboderin, 2007; Adhikari & Melia 2015; Berdes & Echert. 2001; Christensen, 2017; Codó, 2018; Coyne et al., 2016; Elhami & Roshan, 2023; Elhami et al., 2024; Et-Bozkurt & Yağmur, 2022; Ham, 2019; Kotera et al. 2022; Kumar et al, 2022; Lightman, 2021; Munkejord, 2017; Novek, 2013; Nursalam et al., 2020; Papadopoulos, 2020; Remennick, 2001; Saraswati, 2017; Shutes, 2012; Van Riemsdijk 2010;) These studies have demonstrated the value of interviews in capturing the perspectives and experiences of participants in a detailed and nuanced manner. Researchers continue to utilize interviews as a powerful tool for qualitative data collection in various fields of study. To acquire useful data, researchers must be able to choose the best interview method type and also be skilled in conducting interviews effectively, including building rapport with participants and asking open-ended questions to elicit rich responses. In this chapter, we provide a brief description of potential qualitative research interview types, which are classified as structured, unstructured, and semi-structured (Neergaard & Leitch, 2015; Nicholls, 2009).

In-depth, loosely or semi-structured interviewing is what Mason (2002) defines as "qualitative interviewing." This kind of interview calls for a variety of open-ended related questions pertaining to the study's objectives (Hancock et al., 2007), including follow-up inquiries to elucidate the respondents' speech and the concepts they presented (Elhami & Khoshnevisan, 2022). Compared to written surveys, semi-structured interviews are more like casual discussions (Duranti, 2011).

Open-ended questioning is applied by the researcher in semi-structured interviews to discuss specific topics in more depth (Hancock et al., 2007). With the aid of personal thoughts, feelings, and beliefs, and less self-censorship, the interviewer is better able to elicit pertinent information from the interviewee(s) in depth when using open-ended questions (Brinkman & Kvale, 2005). According to Mason (2002) qualitative interviews involve a tremendous deal of preparation. As the name suggests, a semi-structured interview requires careful planning and preparation. The interviewer ought to have broad inquiries about their study or a topical guideline (Hancock et al., 2007). General inquiries don't probe the interviewee's comprehension; instead, they serve to ease tension and briefly touch on the subject in order to get the interviewee ready for tougher inquiries. In addition, the interviewer creates follow-up inquiries depending on the interviewee's responses or discourse(s). According to Neergaard and Leitch (2015), semi-structured interviews are quite flexible, and the majority of the questions are developed as the interview is going on.

The other interview formats are unstructured and structured. Unplanned discussions could be considered the equivalent of unstructured interviews, in which the interviewer undertakes the interview with no preparation. There are some drawbacks to this interview format. For instance, it can be exceedingly challenging to guarantee that the talk will yield the data required for the study, and typically a second or third interview will also be required. To collect the needed data, researchers must guide the dialogue to a specific point. As a result, gathering data using unstructured interviews in qualitative studies would be exceedingly challenging and would prevent the researcher from obtaining the information they are looking for.

A structured interview is fully prepared, in comparison to an unstructured interview; however, it is not a questionnaire (Gillham, 2005). During conducting a structured interview, relevant questions pertaining to the study's objectives are written out beforehand and posed during the interview (see, for example study in which researchers utilised structured interview: Salmani Nodoushan, 2021). This allows for consistency in data collection and ensures that all participants are asked the same questions. Additionally, structured interviews provide a more efficient way to analyse and compare responses across participants. However, there are a number of drawbacks to this type, which are discussed in the paragraphs that follow.

Because a structured interview is entirely predicated on a predetermined set of questions in order to gather data, the interviewer is prevented from formulating innovative follow-up questions. Additionally, because of a limitation of time, interviewers may stop an applicant during a scheduled interview. As a result, the structure of the questions, the formality of the setting, and interruptions may prevent interviewers from sharing their actual thoughts and feelings. Given the aforementioned discussion, qualitative researchers rarely use structured interviews as a method of data collection (Nicholls, 2009). While this interview format is simple to conduct and analyse, it could limit the participant's ability to completely reveal themselves (Barrett & Twycross, 2018).

Because of this, it limits naturalness and causes restrictive limitations placed both on the researcher and on their own study subject (Muylaert et al., 2014), which may impede the investigators from obtaining relevant data for their investigation.

Important Tips for Conducting Semi-Structured Interviews

If the researcher ignores the following factors, a successful qualitative interview will fall short of its purpose in data collection:

To be natural: Qualitative interviews should be natural, much like ordinary conversations. Participants can openly discuss their experiences and thoughts when things are left natural. This approach allows for a deeper understanding of the participants' perspectives and provides rich, detailed insights that may not be captured through structured or standardized interviews. By creating a comfortable and relaxed atmosphere, qualitative interviews encourage participants to express themselves freely, leading to more authentic and valuable data.

Note taking: Since one of an interviewer's responsibilities is to listen well, adding material like data to the notebook could divert the researcher. As a result, it is advised to invite a second person to act as a note-taker during the interviews (Neergaard & Leitch, 2015). The person taking the notes should be competent about both notetaking and interviewing, as well as the study's objectives. This will ensure that all important information is accurately captured, while the interviewer can focus solely on engaging with the participant. Additionally, having a dedicated note-taker allows for more in-depth analysis of the data collected post-interview.

Having the objectives in mind: The third tip for conducting a qualitative interview is to keep the study's objectives in mind. This will make it easier for the research team to formulate pertinent follow-up questions during the interview, if needed. When the investigator is not sufficiently prepared for the interview, they are unable to ask follow-up questions during the interview. Thus, being well-prepared enables the researcher to conduct a successful interview. Additionally, having a clear understanding of the study's objectives helps the researcher stay focused and on track during the interview. This ensures that the questions asked are relevant and aligned with the research goals, leading to more meaningful insights from the participants. Ultimately, a well-prepared interviewer can effectively navigate through the interview process and gather valuable data for analysis.

Voice recording: For data analysis in almost all qualitative investigations, a transcription of the interview is required. However, the interviewee(s) must give permission for the researchers to record their voice. Voice recording is one of the several simultaneous tasks that a modern mobile phone can perform. To prevent notifications and ringtones from interfering with the discussion, it is imperative to switch the phone to flight mode. This will ensure that the interview is conducted smoothly and without interruptions. Additionally, having a backup recording device on hand is recommended in case of technical difficulties with the phone.

Language of the interview: Another crucial factor that researchers must take into consideration is the interview language. The interviewees' native tongue is the suggested language (Elhami & Khoshnevisan, 2022; Jovchelovich & Bauer, 2002). Participants can be more thorough when asked to respond in their mother tongue, which results in high-quality data. Conducting the interview in the interviewee's native language can also help establish rapport and trust, leading to more candid responses. It is important to ensure that the interviewer is fluent in the language of the interview in order to accurately understand and interpret responses. Additionally, providing interpretation services if needed can help bridge any language barriers and ensure effective communication during the interview process.

According to the language in the interviews, De Fina (2019) suggests that "ignoring the possibility of speech accommodation or negotiation may result in serious misclassifications of respondents' speech" (p. 3). Hence, in the following section we focus on speech/communication accommodation theory and its relation to the qualitative interviews.

Communication Accommodation Theory

The 1970s saw the initial presentation of communication accommodation theory (CAT) as speech accommodation theory (SAT) (for recent reviews of the 50 years of CAT research, both qualitative and quantitative, see Giles et al., 2023; in press). Giles (1973) suggested that when people converse with one another, they alter their accent to sound more like their interlocutors. Some years later, Giles and Smith (1979) note that in addition to accent, speakers also alter their speech tempo, pauses, sentence length, and pronunciation. People, however, make adjustments to their speech in an effort to fit in or be understood by others. According to Bandura (1986), socialization and imitation may be two factors in adjustment. Similarly, people alter their speech rate, volume, pitch, syntax, lexical choices, pitch, and topic in order to be similar or distinct to each other's, as well as to facilitate or hamper social interaction and relations (Gasiorek, 2016; Gallois et al., 2005). According to this hypothesis, communication features eventually replaced the focus speech acts (Giles, et al, 1991).

Accordingly, Gasiorek (2016) defines communication with commendable succinctness and clarity as a social tool; to make a favourable impression (Gallois et al., 2005; Bulatov, 2009), or a deleterious impression, to influence others, to lessen the social distance (Bulatov, 2009), and to achieve their social goals (Stupka, 2011; Pitts & Harwood, 2015). People consciously or unconsciously adapt their communication to each other while conversing (Gasiorek, 2016). For instance, when speaking to older people, we should speak louder, and parents should use simpler grammatical and vocabulary structures when speaking to their children. These adaptations in communication can help bridge social gaps and facilitate smoother interactions. By adjusting our communication styles, we can better connect with others and achieve our desired outcomes in social interactions. This adjustment is made again and again in various contexts, such as when immigrants relocate to a new culture and attempt to adapt their communication to the target society, or even when native speakers of the target society attempt to accommodate the immigrants' communication (see, for example, Petrou & Dragojevic, 2024). This can also help newcomers feel more included and integrated into their new community, foster a sense of belonging and acceptance, and encourage them to learn about the customs and norms of their new environment (Elhami, 2020b, 2020c; Elhami & Roshan, 2024b). Ultimately, effective communication plays a crucial role in building relationships and creating a harmonious social environment for everyone involved. Additionally, adapting communication styles (including nonverbal, dress styles and appearance) can lead to increased understanding, rapport, and empathy between individuals from different backgrounds, ultimately often promoting harmony and cooperation within diverse communities.

Four elements of communication accommodation have been taken into consideration in a related study of CAT (Giles et al., 2007). Gasiorek and Giles (2012) elaborated on these four principles as follows: First, when they attempt to present a positive face and emotion, or even when they search for a shared social identity; second, when they seek the satisfaction and comprehension of the interlocutor(s); thus, in the first and second, people will accommodate; however, in the third, in which they attempt to express their dissatisfaction or dishonour toward the interlocutor(s); and in the fourth, in which they strive to convey their unfavourable intention toward the interlocutor(s), they won't accommodate.

Adjustment Strategies

Different tactics are used by people to adapt to different interlocutors and those tactics speak to their objectives and requirements (Giles et al., 1991; Giles et al., 2023). The classic and initial CAT strategies cam in offers three forms of convergence, maintenance, and divergence.

Before moving on, it is important to underscore there are two functions of adjustment, namely affective and cognitive (Giles et al., 1979). The former is connected to identity and social distance; in this context, Elhami (2020b) suggests that accommodation between ingroup members and outgroup members results in an increase or decrease in social distance. In fact, speakers modify their communication style when they want to join the speaker(s) and need to bridge a social gap (Gallois et al., 2005). People tend to assimilate or even emphasize differences in order to appear more similar and likeable due to emotive function, which heightens their sense of identities (Gallois, et al., 2005).

Giles and Gasiorek (2013) note that, in relation to affective function, "a number of more specific social effects of accommodation have been put forward, among them identifying or appearing similar to others, maintaining face, maintaining a relationship, and maintaining interpersonal control as it relates to power or status differentials" (p. 5). The latter, however, is related to communication understanding, which may be either favorable to promote closeness (convergence) or unfavorable to increase differences (divergence) (Gallois, et al., 2005). Palomares et al. (2016) note that understanding between ingroups and outgroups is possible through accommodation. For example, way to increase or decrease comprehension are by speaking more slowly or more quickly.

A larger perspective shows that there are several so-called discourse management strategies that correspond to the affective and cognitive social functions outlined above (Coupland & Giles, 1988; Dragojevic et al., 2016a). First, people pay attention to the interlocutors' productive language and adapt (converge or diverge) verbally and nonverbally to it (Dragojevic et al., 2016a; Elhami, 2020b; Elhami & Roshan, 2021; Giles & Gasiorek, 2013; McGlone & Giles, 2011). In contrast, another tactic is related to the interlocutors' comprehensive ability, in which people shorten their speech, use relatively simple vocabulary, or even speak louder. In the third category, which is need-related, the topic is chosen with the interlocutors' needs and interests in mind. The fourth, to remind them of their relative standing with the interlocutor when the focus is on role relationships when interacting. (Dragojevic, et al., 2016b). The fifth is that people employ emotional expressions when other people's feelings are significant in order to make conversation comfortable and secure (Hewett et al., 2015). Discussing these five tactics, Bilous and Krauss (1988) and Dragojevic et al. (2016b) note that speakers can employ many methods simultaneously. A notable example of adopting two tactics simultaneously is when people utilize simpler vocabulary and grammatical norms for better understanding yet, at the same time, remind others of their respective social position (Dragojevic et al. 2016b).

Convergence is defined as an attempt by communicators to lessen differences (Giles & Smith, 1979) and to be more like the behavior of their interlocutors (Giles, et al., 1991; Gallois, et al., 2005; Dragojevic et al., 2016b); and to be likeable to the communicator (Gallois, et al, 2005). In this regard, Giles (1980) introduced speech complementarity, which explains how speakers complement one another's speech. This is demonstrated and made clear in romantic heterosexual partnerships in some countries, where men might highlight their more rugged vocal traits, while their female partners can stress their more feminine traits. Recently, there has been a renewed focus on empirical research on this so-called speech complementarity approach (e.g., Giles, 1980; Guydish & Fox Tree, 2021). Another example for convergence would be younger people, when they speak louder or use more examples while communicating with older people in order to bridge the generation gap and establish a connection based on mutual understanding and respect. This, arguably over-accommodative communication style reflects the importance of social norms and values in effective interpersonal interactions but can also be interpreted by the recipient as demeaning.

Divergence, on the other hand, accentuates and highlights social contrasts and raises the distinctions between interlocutors (Gallois, et al., 2005), this as above, is in contrast to convergence which is an adjustment for enabling and revealing greater similarities between communicators (Bulatov, 2009). Contrarily, those who diverge seek to stand out from the crowd and work to imprint their own distinctive social identity on others around them (Berger & Heath, 2008). In essence, divergence serves as a way to assert individuality and uniqueness in communication interactions. It can often be a deliberate strategy used to socially differentiate from others in a conversation.

Maintenance, which can be kindred to divergence (Gallois et al., 2005) evolved to mean continuing to communicate at one level, but refusing to adapt to others (Bourhis, 1979; Dragojevic, 2016b). According to Giles and Gasiorek (2013), maintenance is defined as "the absence of accommodation adjustment by individuals, that is, maintaining their 'default' way of communicating without taking into account the characteristics of their fellow interactants" (p. 6).

The emphasis in this section is on the strategies people use—consciously or unconsciously—to take advantage of various communication styles. Ten strategies for modifying communication are discussed by Gasiorek (2016) are: code-switching, response matching, audience design, grounding, receipt design, linguistic style matching, mimicry, constructivism, interaction adaptation theory, and discrepancy arousal theory (Gasiorek, 2016). These strategies can be applied in various interpersonal interactions to enhance communication effectiveness and build rapport with others. By understanding and utilizing these strategies, individuals can adapt their communication style to better connect with different types of people. Approximation, emotional expression, interpretability, interpersonal control, and discourse management are the five methods that CAT offered as its classification to help with constructive conversation (see Coupland et al., 1988; Giles et al., 2015). Approximate techniques are ways of making one's language and communication patterns (e.g., accent, tempo, and voice level) more or less similar to those of another. Emotional expression tactics centre on meeting the acknowledged emotional and interpersonal needs of others. In order to promote mutual comprehension among speakers, interpretability tactics include minimizing jargon and accommodating others expressed or perceived abilities. "Interpersonal control strategies" refers to the ways in which individuals adjust their communication based on role relationships, position, and relative power. Discourse management strategies involve adapting communication to meet the explicit or perceived conversational expectations of the other interlocutor. Examples of these strategies include subject redirection, open-ended questioning, and active listening.

CONCLUSION

One of the most crucial aspects of any study is data collection, and understanding the CAT may enable researchers to conduct qualitative interviews and focus groups that yield more accurate data. In certain ways, it is critical to be familiar with the CAT when conducting interviews and focus group. For instance, it may be necessary for researchers to interview subjects in a language other than their own. In this case, it is important for researchers to adjust their language use to the interviewee's degree of language proficiency and to match the difficulty of words and phrases. This can help ensure that the interviewee fully understands the questions being asked and can provide more accurate responses. Additionally, being aware of cultural differences and nuances in communication can also improve the quality of data collected during interviews and focus groups.

In line with CAT of course, speakers modify their communication styles with participants based on their listeners' ages, genders, social statuses or other social identities (for a review of the dynamics of intergroup accommodation, see Giles, 2012, Giles & Harwood, 2018; Keblusek et al., 2017). These and other social groups' identities likely have very different perceived group vitalities associated with them, including the numbers of these groups, together with the levels of institutional support they receive (for recent, but different, reviews of group vitality theory, see Bourhis et al., 2019; Smith et al., 2018). Hence, interviewers and/or group focused discussion leader will need to adapt their communicative approaches according to their participants' social group memberships and relative vitalities to ensure effective communication and understanding. For instance, when interviewing a person from a more socially elite group, it may be necessary to use more formal language and show respect for their status or, when interviewing young children, it may be beneficial to use simpler language and ask questions in a more engaging and playful manner to keep their attention and encourage honest responses. To demonstrate a better connection with teenage interviewees, the interviewer needs to show genuine interest in their interests and use language that is relatable to their age group. By adapting communication styles based on the interviewee's characteristics, the interviewer can create a more comfortable and effective interview environment. Online interviewing has become increasingly popular in recent years, requiring interviewers to also consider factors such as internet connection and video conferencing etiquette. For conducting online interviews, the interviewers should also familiarize themselves with the technology and platforms being used to ensure a smooth and professional interaction (see Giles et al., 2023 and CAT Stage 7). Additionally, regarding communication strategies, the researcher should likely speak louder during online interviews or when interviewing an older individual who is perceived to have issues of diminished cognitive capacities and depending on the circumstances and surroundings. This can help ensure that the message is clearly understood and received by the interviewee and, as a result, the data collected is likely found to be more accurate and reliable.

Therefore, being aware of CAT and its strategies (e.g., approximation, interpretability, emotional expression, and interpersonal control) increases the quality of qualitative interviewing, which makes informants divulge more information, and exploring their experiences aids in revealing insights and deeper analysis.

REFERENCES

Aboderin, I. (2007). Contexts, motives and experiences of Nigerian overseas nurses: Understanding links to globalization. *Journal of Clinical Nursing*, 16(12), 2237–2245. 10.1111/j.1365-2702.2007.01999.x18036114

Adhikari, R., & Melia, K. M. (2015). The (mis)management of migrant nurses in the UK: A sociological study. *Journal of Nursing Management*, 23(3), 359–367. 10.1111/jonm.1214124033826

Ahmed, A. O. A. (2024). A classroom ethnographic study on silence among EFL graduate students: A Case Study. *British Journal of Translation. Linguistics and Literature*, 4(1), 2–17. 10.54848/bjtll.v4i1.75

Bandura, A. (1986). *Social foundations of thought and action: A social cognitive theory*. Prentice-Hall, Inc.

Barrett, D., & Twycross, A. (2018). Data collection in qualitative research. *Evidence-Based Nursing*, 21(3), 63–64. 10.1136/eb-2018-10293929858278

Berdes, C., & Eckert, J. M. (2001). Race relations and caregiving relationships: A Qualitative Examination of Perspectives from Residents and Nurse's Aides in Three Nursing Homes. *Research on Aging*, 23(1), 109–126. 10.1177/0164027501231006

Berger, J., & Heath, C. (2008). Who drives divergence? Identity signalling, out-group similarity, and the abandonment of cultural tastes. *Journal of Personality and Social Psychology*, 95(3), 593–607. 10.1037/0022-3514.95.3.59318729697

Bernhold, Q., & Giles, H. (2019). Communication Accommodation Theory as a lens to examine painful self-disclosures in grandparent-grandchild relationships. In Avtgis, T., Rancer, A., MacGeorge, E., & Liberman, C. (Eds.), *Casing communication theory* (pp. 31–48). Kendall Hunt.

Bicay, E. G., Cambalon, A. J., Gulada, Q. M., & Monteza, A. (2024). Tagakaulo in trade: A phenomenological exploration on the journey of language preservation. *International Journal of Innovative Research in Multidisciplinary Education.*, 3(4), 607–620. 10.58806/ijirme.2024.v3i4n16

Bilous, F. R., & Krauss, R. M. (1988). Dominance and accommodation in the conversational behaviours of same- and mixed-gender dyads. *Language & Communication*, 8(3), 183–194. 10.1016/0271-5309(88)90016-X

Bourhis, R. Y. (1979). Language in ethnic interaction: A social psychological approach. In Giles, H., & St. Jacques, B. (Eds.), *Language and ethnic relations* (pp. 117–141). Pergamon.

Bourhis, R. Y., Sachdev, I., Ehala, M., & Giles, H. (2019). Forty years of group vitality research. *Journal of Language and Social Psychology*, 38, 408–421. 10.1177/0261927X19868974

Brinkmann, S., & Kvale, S. (2005). Interviews: Learning the craft of qualitative research interviewing. *Sage (Atlanta, Ga.)*.

Bulatov, D. (2009). The effect of fundamental frequency on phonetic convergence. *UC Berkeley Phonology Lab Annual Report*, 404-434. 10.5070/P72W68F1C6

Christensen, K. (2017). Life trajectories of migrant care workers in the long—Term care sectors in Norway and the UK. *Social Policy and Society*, 16(4), 635–644. 10.1017/S1474746417000252

Codó, E. (2018). Lifestyle residents in Barcelona: A biographical perspective on linguistic repertoires, identity narrative and transnational mobility. *International Journal of the Sociology of Language*, 250(250), 11–34. 10.1515/ijsl-2017-0053

Coupland, N., & Giles, H. (1988). Communication accommodation: Recent advances. *Language & Communication*, 8, 3–4. https://digilib.ars.ac.id/index.php?p=fstream-pdf&fid=13684&bid=6370

Coyne, E., Rands, H., Gurung, S., & Kellett, U. (2016). I-Kiribati nursing graduates experience of transition from university to residential aged care facilities in Australia. *Nurse Education Today*, 36, 463–467. 10.1016/j.nedt.2015.10.02026549264

Cuesta, M., Rämgård, M., & Ramgard, M. (2016). Intersectional perspective in elderly care. *International Journal of Qualitative Studies on Health and Well-being*, 11(1), 30544. 10.3402/qhw.v11.3054427167554

De Fina, A. (2019). The interview as an interactional event. In Patrick, P. L., Schmid, M. S., & Zwaan, K. (Eds.), *Language analysis for the determination of origin: Current perspectives and new directions* (pp. 21–40). Springer. 10.1007/978-3-319-79003-9_2

De Fina, A., & Perrino, S. (2011). Introduction: Interviews vs. 'natural' contexts: A false dilemma. *Language in Society*, 40(1), 1–11. 10.1017/S0047404510000849

Denzin, N. K., & Lincoln, Y. S. (2005a). *The Sage handbook of qualitative research* (3rd ed.). Sage.

Denzin, N. K., & Lincoln, Y. S. (2005b). Introduction: The discipline and practice of qualitative research. In Denzin, N. K., & Lincoln, Y. S. (Eds.), *The Sage handbook of qualitative research* (pp. 1–32). Sage.

Dragojevic, M., Gasiorek, J., & Giles, H. (2016a). Communication accommodation theory. In Berger, C. R., & Roloff, M. (Eds.), *The international encyclopedia of interpersonal communication* (pp. 176–196). Wiley Blackwell.

Dragojevic, M., Gasiorek, J., & Giles, H. (2016b). Accommodative strategies as core of the theory. In Giles, H. (Ed.), *Communication accommodation theory: Negotiating personal and social identities across contexts* (pp. 36–59). Cambridge University Press. 10.1017/CBO9781316226537.003

Duranti, A. (2011). Linguistic anthropology: The study of language as a non-neutral medium. In Mesthrie, R. (Ed.), *The Cambridge handbook of sociolinguistics* (pp. 28–46). Cambridge University Press. 10.1017/CBO9780511997068.006

Elhami, A. (2020a). A Socio-pragmatic perspective of Spanish and Persian greeting. *Theory and Practice in Language Studies*, 10(9), 1009–1014. 10.17507/tpls.1009.01

Elhami, A. (2020b). Communication Accommodation Theory: A brief review of the literature. *Journal of Advances in Education and Philosophy.*, 4(5), 192–200. 10.36348/jaep.2020.v04i05.002

Elhami, A. (2020c). Acculturation Strategies: The Study of Bi-Dimensional and Uni-Dimensional of Filipino Immigrants in Madrid. *International Journal of Social Science Research*, 8(2), 1–15. 10.5296/ijssr.v8i2.16428

Elhami, A. (2023). *A Study of Communicative Practices of Iranian Migrants in Madrid* [Unpublished Doctoral Dissertation]. Universidad Autónoma de Madrid.

Elhami, A., & Khoshnevisan, B. (2022). Conducting an interview in qualitative research: The Modus Operandi. *Mextesol Journal*, 46(1), 1–7.

Elhami, A., & Roshan, A. (2021). Communication Accommodation Theory in Covid-19 Pandemic. *Academia Letters.Article*, 1641. Advance online publication. 10.20935/AL1641

Elhami, A., & Roshan, A. (2023). A narrative study of Iranian females' acculturation orientation and Spanish learning experiences in Spain. In Chandan, H. (Ed.), *Strategies for cultural assimilation of immigrants and their children: Social, economic, and political considerations* (pp. 45–68). IGI Global. 10.4018/978-1-6684-4839-7.ch003

Elhami, A., & Roshan, A. (2024a). Religion and higher education migrants' acculturation orientation. *Intercultural Education*, 35(3), 283–301. 10.1080/14675986.2024.2348428

Elhami, A., & Roshan, A. (2024b). The history of acculturation: A review article. Social Sciences. *Humanities and Education Journal*, 5(1), 180–196.

Elhami, A., Roshan, A., Ghahraman, V., & Afrashi, A. (2024). Sociocultural adjustment by two international students: A critical look at multilingualism in Spain. *International Journal of Language Studies*, 18(3), 1–38.

Et-Bozkurt, T., & Yağmur, K. (2022). Family language policy among second- and third-generation Turkish parents in Melbourne, Australia. *Journal of Multilingual and Multicultural Development*, 43(9), 821–832. 10.1080/01434632.2022.2044832

Fuller, J. M. (2000). Changing perspectives on data: Interviews as situated speech. *American Speech*, 75(4), 388–390. 10.1215/00031283-75-4-388

Gallois, C., Ogay, T., & Giles, H. (2005). Communication accommodation theory: A look back and a look ahead. In Gudykunst, W. B. (Ed.), *Theorizing about intercultural communication* (pp. 121–148). Sage.

Gallois, C., Weatherall, A., & Giles, H. (2016). CAT and talk in action. In Giles, H. (Ed.), *Communication accommodation theory: Negotiating personal relationships and social identities across contexts* (pp. 105–122). Cambridge University Press. 10.1017/CBO9781316226537.006

Gasiorek, J. (2016). Theoretical perspectives on interpersonal adjustments in language and communication. In Giles, H. (Ed.), *Communication accommodation theory: Negotiating personal and social identities across contexts* (pp. 13–35). Cambridge University Press. 10.1017/CBO9781316226537.002

Gasiorek, J., & Giles, H. (2012). Effects of inferred motive on evaluations of nonaccommodative communication. *Human Communication Research*, 38(3), 309–331. 10.1111/j.1468-2958.2012.01426.x

Ghahraman, V., Karlsson, M., Kazemi, A., Saeedi, S., & Elhami, A. (2023). On the functions of hedging in research articles (RAs): A study on RA discussions. *International Journal of Language Studies*, 17(1), 165–187. 10.5281/zenodo.7513381

Giles, H. (1973). Accent mobility: A model and some data. *Anthropological Linguistics*, 15(2), 87–109.

Giles, H. (1980). Accommodation theory: Some new directions. In de Silva, S. (Ed.), *Aspects of linguistic behavior* (pp. 105–136). York University Press.

Giles, H. (Ed.). (2012). *The handbook of intergroup communication*. Routledge. 10.4324/9780203148624

Giles, H., Clementson, D., & Markowitz, D. (in press). CAT-aloguing the past, present and future. In Giles, H., Markowitz, D., & Clementson, D. (Eds.), *New directions for, and panaceas arising from, Communication Accommodation Theory*. Peter Lang.

Giles, H., Coupland, J., & Coupland, N. (1991). Accommodation theory: Communication, context, and consequence. In Giles, H., Coupland, J., & Coupland, N. (Eds.), *Contexts of accommodation: Developments in applied sociolinguistics* (pp. 1–68)., 10.1017/CBO9780511663673.001

Giles, H., Edwards, A. L., & Walther, J. B. (2023). Communication Accommodation Theory: Past accomplishments, current trends, and future prospects. *Language Sciences*, 99, 101571. 10.1016/j.langsci.2023.101571

Giles, H., & Gasiorek, J. (2013). Parameters of non-accommodation: Refining and elaborating communication accommodation theory. In Forgas, J., Vincze, O., & László, J. (Eds.), *Social cognition and communication* (pp. 155–172). Psychology Press.

Giles, H., & Harwood, J. (Eds.). (2018). *The Oxford encyclopedia of intergroup communication* (Vol. 1–2). Oxford University Press.

Giles, H., Scherer, K. R., & Taylor, D. M. (1979). Speech markers in social interaction. In Scherer, K. R., & Giles, H. (Eds.), *Social markers in speech*. Cambridge University Press.

Giles, H., & Smith, P. M. (1979). Accommodation theory: Optimum levels of convergence. In Giles, H., & St. Clair, R. N. (Eds.), *Language and social psychology* (pp. 45–65). Blackwell.

Giles, H., Willemyns, M., Gallois, C., & Anderson, M. C. (2007). Accommodating a new frontier: The context of law enforcement. In Fiedler, K. (Ed.), *Social communication* (pp. 129–162). Psychology Press.

Gillham, B. (2005). *Research Interviewing: The range of techniques: A practical guide*. McGraw-Hill Education.

Gillham, D., De Bellis, A., Xiao, L., Willis, E., Harrington, A., Morey, W., & Jeffers, L. (2018). Using research evidence to inform staff learning needs in cross-cultural communication in aged care homes. *Nurse Education Today*, 63, 18–23. 10.1016/j.nedt.2018.01.00729407255

Glesne, C. (1999). *Becoming qualitative researchers: An introduction* (2nd ed.). Longman.

Goel, K., & Penman, J. (2015). Employment experiences of immigrant workers in aged care in regional *South Australia. Rural and Remote Health*, 15(1), 1–14. 10.22605/RRH269325798891

Guydish, A. J., & Fox Tree, J. E. (2021). Good conversations: Grounding, convergence, and richness. *New Ideas in Psychology*, 63, 100877. 10.1016/j.newideapsych.2021.100877

Ham, A. (2019). Social processes affecting the workforce integration of first-generation immigrant health care professionals in aging citizens in The Netherlands. *Journal of Transcultural Nursing*, 31(5), 460–467. 10.1177/104365961987519631530232

Hancock, B., Windridge, K., & Ockleford, E. (2007). An introduction to qualitative research. *Sage (Atlanta, Ga.)*.

Hernandez, H. P. (2023). Nouns as nominal premodifiers in disciplinary research articles written by Filipino research writers: A cross-investigation. *International Journal of Language Studies*, 17(1), 31–52. 10.5281/zenodo.7513342

Hewett, D. G., Watson, B. M., & Gallois, C. (2015). Communication between hospital doctors: Underaccommodation and interpretability. *Language & Communication*, 41, 71–83. 10.1016/j.langcom.2014.10.007

Jovchelovich, S., & Bauer, M. W. (2002). Entrevista Narrativa [Narrative Interview]. In Bauer, M. W., & Gaskell, G. (Eds.), *Pesquisa qualitativa com texto, imagem e som: Um manual prático* (pp. 90–113). Vozes. https://www.redalyc.org/pdf/3610/361035360027_2.pdf

Kartini, K., Anwar, M., & Muliastuti, L. (2024). A Map of students' language impoliteness: A phenomenological study. *Journal of Languages and Language Teaching*, 12(2), 996–1006. 10.33394/jollt.v12i2.8864

Kawulich, B. (2005). Participant observation as a data collection method. *FORUM: Qualitative Social Research, 6*, Article 43. Retrieved from: http://nbn-resolving.de/urn:nbn:de:0114-fqs0502430

Keblusek, L., Giles, H., & Maass, A. (2017). Communication and group life: How language and symbols shape intergroup relations. *Group Processes & Intergroup Relations*, 20(5), 632–643. 10.1177/1368430217708864

Kotera, Y., Ozaki, A., Miyatake, H., Tsunetoshi, C., Nishikawa, Y., Kosaka, M., & Tanimoto, T. (2022). Qualitative Investigation into the mental health of healthcare workers in Japan during the COVID-19 pandemic. *International Journal of Environmental Research and Public Health*, 19(1), 1–14. 10.3390/ijerph1901056835010828

Krueger, R. A. (1988). Focus Groups. A Practical Guide for Applied Research. *Sage (Atlanta, Ga.)*.

Kumar, B. N., James, R., Hargreaves, S., Bozorgmehr, K., Mosca, D., Hosseinalipour, S.-M., . . . Severoni, S. (2022). Meeting the health needs of displaced people fleeing Ukraine: Drawing on existing technical guidance and evidence. *The Lancet Regional Health-Europe, 17*, 1-6. https://doi.org/.lanepe.2022.10040310.1016/j

Lightman, N. (2022). Caring during the COVID-19 crisis: Intersectional exclusion of immigrant women health care aides in Canadian long-term care. *Health & Social Care in the Community*, 30(4), 1343–1351. 10.1111/hsc.1354134396607

Mason, J. (2002). *Qualitative researching* (2nd ed.). Sage. Retrieved from http://www.sxf.uevora.pt/wp-content/uploads/2013/03/Mason_2002.pdf

McGlone, M. S., & Giles, H. (2011). Language and interpersonal communication. In Knapp, M. L., & Daly, J. A. (Eds.), *The SAGE handbook of interpersonal communication* (4th ed., pp. 201–237). Sage. https://ci.uky.edu/grad/sites/default/files/mdragojevic_cv_9-2016.pdf

Mishler, E. G. (1986). *Research interviewing: Context and narrative*. Harvard University Press. 10.4159/9780674041141

Munkejord, M. C. (2017). 'I work with my heart': Experiences of migrant care workers in a Northern, rural context. *Journal of Population Ageing*, 10(3), 229–246. 10.1007/s12062-016-9157-z

Muylaert, C. J., Sarubbi, V.Jr, Gallo, P. R., Neto, M. L. R., & Reis, A. O. A. (2014). Narrative interviews: An important resource in qualitative research. *Revista da Escola de Enfermagem da USP*, 48(2), 184–189. 10.1590/S0080-623420140000080002725830754

Neergaard, H., & Leitch, C. M. (2015). *Handbook of qualitative research techniques and analysis in entrepreneurship*. Edward Elgar. 10.4337/9781849809870

Nicholls, D. (2009). Qualitative research: Part three: Methods. *International Journal of Therapy and Rehabilitation*, 16(12), 638–647. 10.12968/ijtr.2009.16.12.45433

Novek, S. (2013). Filipino health care aides and the nursing home labour market in Winnipeg. *Canadian Journal on Aging*, 32(4), 405–416. 10.1017/S071498081300038X24063532

Nursalam, N., Chen, C. M., Efendi, F., Has, E. M. M., Hidayati, L., & Hadisuyatmana, S. (2020). The lived experiences of Indonesian nurses who worked as care workers in Taiwan. *The Journal of Nursing Research*, 28(2), 1–7. 10.1097/jnr.0000000000000035531714449

Palomares, N. A., Giles, H., Soliz, J., & Gallois, C. (2016). Intergroup accommodation, social categories, and identities. In Giles, H. (Ed.), *Communication accommodation theory. Negotiating personal relationships and social identities across contexts* (pp. 123–151). Cambridge University Press. 10.1017/CBO9781316226537.007

Papadopoulos, I. (2020). *From translanguaging pedagogy to classroom pedagogy: Supporting literacy, communication and cooperative creativity*. Disigma Publications.

Papadopoulos, I. (2021). Translanguaging as a pedagogical practice in primary education: Approaching, managing and teaching diverse classrooms. In I. Papadopoulos. & M. Papadopoulos (Eds.), *Applied linguistics research and good practices for multilingual and multicultural classrooms.* (pp. 147-168). NOVA Science Publisher.

Papadopoulos, I. (2022). Translanguaging as a pedagogical practice for successful inclusion in linguistically and culturally diverse classrooms. In E, Meletiadou (Ed.), *Handbook of research on policies and practices for assessing inclusive teaching and learning* (pp. 422-448). IGI Global. 10.4018/978-1-7998-8579-5.ch019

Papadopoulos, I., & Shin, J. K. (2021). Developing young foreign language learners' persuasive strategies through intercultural folktales. *Research Papers in Language Teaching and Learning*, 1(1), 185–202.

Petrou, M., & Dragojevic, M. (2024). "Where are you from?" Language attitudes and (non)accommodation during native–nonnative speaker interactions in Germany. *Journal of Language and Social Psychology*, 43(3), 353–375. 10.1177/0261927X231222447

Pitts, M. J., & Harwood, J. (2015). Communication accommodation competence: The nature and nurture of accommodative resources across the lifespan. *Language & Communication*, 41, 89–99. 10.1016/j.langcom.2014.10.002

Remennick, L. I. (2001). 'All my life is one big nursing home': Russian immigrant women in Israel speak about double caregiver stress. *Women's Studies International Forum*, 24(6), 685–700. 10.1016/S0277-5395(01)00205-9

Roshan, A. (2023). *Trajectories of Iranian migrants in Madrid* [Unpublished Doctoral Dissertation]. Universidad Autónoma de Madrid.

Rowe, E. (2024). Network ethnography in education: A literature review of network ethnography as a methodology and how it has been applied in critical policy studies. In Stacey, M., & Mockler, N. (Eds.), *Analysing education policy: Theory and method* (pp. 136–156). Deakin University. 10.4324/9781003353379-13

Şafak-Ayvazoğlu, A., Kunuroglu, F., & Yağmur, K. (2021) Psychological and socio-cultural adaptation of Syrian refugees in Turkey. *International Journal of Intercultural Relations, 80,* 99–111. https://doi.org/.2020.11.00310.1016/j.ijintrel

Salmani Nodoushan, M. A. (2021). Demanding versus asking in Persian: Requestives as acts of verbal harassment. *International Journal of Language Studies*, 15(1), 27–46. 10.5281/zenodo.7514622

Salmani Nodoushan, M. A. (2023). Native experts and reputable journals as points of reference: A study on research-article discussions. *Studies in English Language and Education*, 10(2), 562–574. 10.24815/siele.v10i2.29282

Saraswati, L. A. (2017). The gender politics of human waste and human-as-waste: Indonesian migrant workers and elderly care in Japan. *Gender, Work and Organization*, 24(6), 594–609. 10.1111/gwao.12183

Shutes, I. (2012). The employment of migrant workers in long-term care: Dynamics of choice and control. *Journal of Social Policy*, 41(1), 43–59. 10.1017/S0047279411000596

Smith, B., Ehala, M., & Giles, H. (2018). Vitality theory. In H. Giles & J. Harwood (Eds.), *The Oxford encyclopedia of intergroup communication* (pp. 485-500). New York, NY: Oxford University Press.

Stupka, R. (2011). Communication accommodation in mixed gender dyads. *Oshkosh Scholar*, 6, 64–78.

Sun, G., & Zhao, L. (2024). The construction of competency training mechanism model for tourism undergraduates based on grounded theory. *PLoS One*, 19(2), e0296683. 10.1371/journal.pone.029668338422000

Van Riemsdijk, M. (2010). Neoliberal reforms in elder care in Norway: Roles of the state, Norwegian employers, and polish nurses. *Geoforum*, 41(6), 930–939. 10.1016/j.geoforum.2010.06.008

Weda, Z. L., & Lemmer, E. M. (2024). Managing status: A grounded theory of teacher migration from Zimbabwe to south Africa. *Mediterranean Journal of Social Sciences*, 5(7), 416–425. 10.5901/mjss.2014.v5n7p416

Willis, E., Xiao, L. D., Morey, W., Jeffers, L., Harrington, A., Gillham, D., & De Bellis, A. (2018). New migrants in residential aged care: Managing diversity in not-for- profit organizations. *Journal of International Migration and Integration*, 19(3), 683–700. 10.1007/s12134-018-0564-2

ADDITIONAL READING

Bourhis, R. Y., Giles, H., Leyens, J. P., & Tajfel, H. (1979). Psycholinguistic distinctiveness: Language divergence in Belgium. In Giles, H., & St. Clair, R. N. (Eds.), *Language and Social Psychology* (pp. 158–185). Blackwell.

Brinkmann, S. (2007). Could interviews be epistemic? An alternative to qualitative opinion polling. *Qualitative Inquiry*, 13(8), 1116–1138. 10.1177/1077800407308222

Brinkmann, S., & Kvale, S. (2015). *Interviews: Learning the craft of qualitative research interviewing* (3rd ed.). Sage.

Castillo-Montoya, M. (2016). Preparing for interview research: The interview protocol refinement framework. *The Qualitative Report*, 21(5), 811–831. 10.46743/2160-3715/2016.2337

Chenail, R. J. (2011). Interviewing the investigator: Strategies for addressing instrumentation and re-searcher bias concerns in qualitative research. *The Qualitative Report*, 16(1), 255–262.

Coupland, N., Giles, H., & Wiemann, J. M. (Eds.). (1991). *"Miscommunication" and Problematic Talk*. Sage.

deMarrais, K. (2004). Qualitative interview studies: Learning through experience. In deMarrais, K., & Lapan, S. D. (Eds.), *Foundations for research* (pp. 51–68). Erlbaum.

DiCicco-Bloom, B., & Crabtree, B. F. (2006). The qualitative research interview. *Medical Education*, 40(4), 314–321. 10.1111/j.1365-2929.2006.02418.x16573666

Giles, H. (1978). Linguistic differentiation between ethnic groups. In Tajfel, H. (Ed.), *Differentiation between Social Groups: Studies in the Social Psychology of Intergroup Relations* (pp. 361–393). Academic Press.

Giles, H. (Ed.). (2016). *Communication Accommodation Theory: Negotiating Personal Relationships and Social Identities Across Contexts*. Cambridge University Press.

Giles, H., & Maass, A. (Eds.). (2016). *Advances in Intergroup Communication*. Peter Lang. 10.3726/b10467

Jacob, S. A., & Ferguson, S. P. (2012). Writing interview protocols and conducting interviews: Tips for students new to the field of qualitative research. *The Qualitative Report*, 17(42), 1–10.

Maguire, E. R., Hill, S. L., & Giles, H. (2023). Caught in the middle: Accommodative dilemmas in police-community relations. *Psychology, Public Policy, and Law*, 29(4), 486–496. 10.1037/law0000399

Pitts, M., & Giles, H. (2008). Social psychology and personal relationships: Accommodation and relational influence across time and contexts. In Ventola, E., & Antos, G. (Eds.), *The handbook of interpersonal communication* (pp. 15–31). Mouton de Gruyter. 10.1515/9783110211399.1.15

Robinson, W. P., & Giles, H. (Eds.). (2001). *The New Handbook of Language and Social Psychology*. Wiley.

Sachdev, I., Giles, H., & Pauwels, A. (2012). Accommodating multilinguality. In Bhatia, T. K., & Ritchie, W. C. (Eds.), *The Handbook of Bilingualism and Multilingualism* (pp. 391–416). Blackwell. 10.1002/9781118332382.ch16

Soliz, J., & Giles, H. (2014). Relational and identity processes in communication: A contextual and meta-analytical review of Communication Accommodation Theory. *Annals of the International Communication Association*, 38(1), 107–144. 10.1080/23808985.2014.11679160

Tracy, S. J. (2013). *Qualitative research methods: Collecting evidence, crafting analysis, communicating impact*. Wiley-Blackwell.

Turner, D. W.III. (2010). Qualitative interview design: A practical guide for novice investigators. *The Qualitative Report*, 15(3), 754–760.

KEY TERMS AND DEFINITIONS

Approximation Strategy: Is making one's language and communication patterns—such as speech volume, tempo, and accent—more or less similar to another.

Case Study: Is one of the most popular qualitative designs that are used to investigate an individual, a group, a community, or an organization.

Communication Accommodation Theory (CAT): Is a theory of communication, developed by Howard Giles, that explains how people adjust their communication styles to accommodate or adapt to others.

Discourse Management: Strategies, such as active listening, open-ended questioning, and topic redirection, relate to modifying communication to accommodate the other interlocutor's expressed or perceived conversational demands.

Emotional Expression: Emotional expression strategies center on meeting the acknowledged emotional and interpersonal needs of others.

Ethnography: Is the study of a particular group within a culture. By using this study style, researchers will fully immerse themselves in the culture they are studying. Participants in that culture are directly observed, and interactions with them are used to collect the qualitative data.

Field Notes: Are often taken during participant observation to record observations, reflections, and any non-verbal cues that may be important for analysis.

Focus Group: Is a data collection method in qualitative research that involves a small group of participants discussing a specific topic or product. The goal is to gather in-depth insights and opinions from diverse perspectives to inform decision-making processes.

Grounded Theory: Is a design used in qualitative research, that enables researchers to develop a theory that explains a specific phenomenon.

Historical Study: Is an excellent choice for studies that require a thorough examination of the past, including people, events, and documents.

Interpersonal Control: Describes how people modify their communication depending on status, relative power, and role relationships.

Interpretability Strategies: Embrace avoiding jargon and accommodating others expressed or perceived abilities in order to facilitate mutual understanding among speakers.

Material and Documents: Are a data collection method that allows researchers to gather information from various sources, such as surveys, images, the internet, and magazines. This method provides researchers with a wide range of information that can be analyzed to draw conclusions and make informed decisions.

Participants Observation: Participants Observation is a valuable data collection method that allows researchers to observe participants in their natural environment. This method can provide a more holistic understanding of behaviors and interactions.

Phenomenology: Is a broad field of study. Under this research paradigm, the investigator seeks data that clarifies people's experiences with and perceptions of a phenomenon.

Qualitative Interview: Is a valuable method for exploring complex topics and capturing rich, detailed data. It can also help researchers uncover unexpected findings and perspectives that may not have emerged through other data collection techniques.

Chapter 5
Group Discussions as a Methodology in Multicultural Settings

Isidro Miguel Martín Pérez
Universidad de La Laguna, Spain

Sebastián Eustaquio Martín Pérez
Universidad Europea de Canarias, Spain

ABSTRACT

The chapter highlights the relevance of qualitative methods, especially group discussions, in social research within multicultural contexts. It emphasizes selecting participants reflecting the study's cultural diversity and thorough preparation, including choosing a competent moderator and an accessible, inclusive venue. Steps for conducting these discussions are described, from creating the script to interpreting the discourse. During analysis, the focus is on understanding varied perspectives and intercultural interaction subtleties, recommending a systematic approach to ensure reliability and validity through careful data selection and category coding. Originating in the 1930s, group discussions have expanded beyond market research, distinguished by their flexibility and exploratory focus. Key phases include design, operation, data analysis, and reporting, with guidelines for participant selection and project preparation. The chapter concludes by highlighting the importance of these discussions in exploring perceptions and attitudes in multicultural settings.

INTRODUCTION

This chapter argues the relevance of qualitative methods, which employ natural language, to quickly access the life world of individuals. It focuses on the value of *Group Discussions* as a key qualitative tool, especially in social research involving multicultural settings. The chapter starts by highlighting the need to carefully select participants who reflect the cultural diversity of the study context. It also under-

DOI: 10.4018/979-8-3693-3306-8.ch005

scores the importance of thorough preparation, including choosing a capable moderator and addressing logistical details like selecting and inclusive an accessible meeting place.

Moving onto implementation phase, the chapter outlines the essential steps for successfully conducting *Group Discussions*. It covers everything from creating the discussion script to interpreting the discourse. During the analysis phase, the chapter emphasizes understanding the varied perspectives within the group and the nuances of intercultural interaction. It underlines the need for a systematic a verifiable approach to ensure the reliability and validity of the findings, which involves cautious data selection, information segmentation and coding of relevant categories to identify emerging themes.

Furthermore, the chapter stresses the importance of clearly communicating research findings through well-structured reports. By following these details practices, researchers can deepen the understanding and gain valuable insights in multicultural research environments. This comprehensive framework supply scientists to effectively design, conduct and analyse *Group Discussions*, thereby contributing significant knowledge to the field of social research in diverse cultural contexts.

HISTORY OF GROUP DISCUSSIONS

In the late 1930s, social scientists began exploring the relevance of non-directive individual interviews as a refined source of information, aiming to address the limitations of traditional interview methods (Ortega, 2005). This shift was driven by the recognition that traditional individual interviews, employing predetermined questionnaires with closed-ended response choices, often restricted respondents' answers and risked introducing inadvertent interviewer bias or omission. Non-directive procedures emerged as a promising alternative, starting from minimal initial assumptions and placing considerable emphasis on connecting with the interviewee's reality (Krueger, 1991).

Concurrently, psychologists and social scientists in this era found particular appeal in the non-directive approach (Krueger, 1991). Key procedures that would later become common practice in *Group Discussions* were introduced in the seminal work "*The Focused Interview*" (1956) by Robert K. Merton, Marjorie Fiske, and Patricia L. Kendall. By the late 1930s, *Group Discussions* were predominantly employed in market research settings, proving valuable for understanding consumer behavior and preferences (Krueger, 1991).

Over time, their utility expanded beyond advertising, gaining popularity among researchers in diverse fields such as social sciences, evaluation, planning, and education (Ortega, 2005). Currently, *Group Discussions* are acknowledged as pivotal instruments for gaining insights into perceptions, emotions, and attitudes within multicultural settings. They play a significant role in educational, medical, and social intervention initiatives, where accountability and impact assessment hold paramount importance (Krueger, 1991).

DEFINITION OF GROUP DISCUSSIONS

To begin, let us clarify Focus Groups, *Group Discussions*, and Group Interviews. Broadly, Focus Groups are more common in English-speaking contexts, while *Group Discussions* are often used in Spanish-speaking countries. These methodologies diverge in terms of in their degree of structure and focus. *Group Discussions* are flexible and exhibit exploratory characteristics, observing and understanding group dynamics, while Focus Groups are characterized by greater organization and directionality (Sanjuán-Núñez, 2019).

Group Discussions, a qualitative research modality, involve eliciting discursive content from multiple meetings, serving as a mechanism to collectivelly gather data from individuals sharing common experiences; they are delineated from Focus Groups by their broader scope and participant dynamics (Payne & Payne, 2004; Sanjuán-Núñez, 2019).

It is imperative to note that what we seek with the Focus Groups is not inference but understanding. The aim is not to abstract general data representative of the entire population, but rather to delve into the myriad of individual opinions coexisting within it. The focus is on capturing the perceptions of members regarding a given situation (Krueger, 1991).

This material serves as the foundation for identifying collective representations, imaginary, and underlying group structures pertinent to a specific topic or issue (Montañez-Serrano, 2010). These discussions are usually planned meetings comprising a predetermined number of participants, typically seven to ten participants. Although this number can fluctuate from four to twelve, with participants exhibiting homogeneity (Ortega, 2005). The group size is influenced by two factors: it should be small enough to afford each participant the opportunity to contribute to discussions, yet large enough to encapsulate diverse perspectives (Krueger, 1991).

When the group exceeds twelve participants, fragmentation tendency may emerge, prompting participants to engage in peripheral conversations with nearby peers (Ortega, 2005). Smaller groups, comprised of four to six participants, offer enhanced opportunities for idea generation, albeit potentially limited in their diversity of perspectives. These smaller units, known as mini focus groups, confer logistical advantages, given their ease of accommodation in spatially constrained settings such as restaurants or private residences (Krueger, 1991).

Participants engage in an open and inhibited exchange of ideas on the topics under consideration, guided by an expert moderator (Porto & Ruiz, 2014). This technique facilitates the acquisition of insightful information pertaining to the rationale behind participants' thoughts and feelings.

From a theoretical perspective, group discussions serve as a valuable tool for examining the acceptance and construction of ideological discourses within a social context. Drawing on Goffman's concepts of symbolic interactionism, particularly the notions of "*front stage and back stage behavior*" this research methodology offers insights into how participants present themselves and manage impressions during discussions (Goffman, 1967). Moreover, an understanding of discourse analysis and power dynamics informs methodologies for investigating how language and knowledge shape group discussions (Foucault, 1969). This approach facilitates an exploration of how societal influences shape the interpretation and decoding of messages, as elucidated in Clifford Geertz's concept of "*Thick Description*" (Geertz, 2011). Similarly, in considering how culture and socioeconomic factors sculpt social behaviour, Pierre Bourdieu (1993) positioned group discussions as examples of methodologies that allow for the exploration of how participants' social positions and cultural capital influence their roles and interactions within such contexts.

In contrast to some authors, which emphasize the meeting aspect of *Group Discussions* over the group itself (Callejo, 2001), these discussions inherently foster dialogue, resulting in the generation of meaningful discourse. Moreover, *Group Discussions* can be seamlessly integrated with quantitative methods in various configurations, including precedent, parallel, posterior, and independent utilization. This amalgamation facilitates a comprehensive exploration of topics by merging qualitative insights with quantitative data analysis techniques.

Advantages of Group Discussions

Group Discussions represent a multifaceted research approach, serving as a platform for the efficient collection of diverse perspectives while fostering participant interaction. Positioned within a clear social framework, they immerse individuals in authentic, real-life contexts influenced by the input and decisions of others (Krueger, 1991).

Furthermore, their open-ended structure allows moderators to deviate from predefined scripts, enhancing flexibility. Notably, *Group Discussions* exhibit high subjective validity and offer a cost-effective research method, rendering them an appealing choice for investigators. Additionally, they afford researchers expedited access to findings and facilitate the broadening of sample scope (Krueger, 1991).

Regarding the main advantages of a *Group Discussions,* we gather the following characteristics explained in Table 1. *Advantages of a Group Discussions.*

Table 1. Advantages of Group Discussions

Advantages	Explanation
1. Gathering diverse perspectives efficiently and economically.	● *Group Discussions* allow for the collection of diverse viewpoints from multiple participants in a single session. ● This saves time and resources compared to conducting individual interviews separately. ● The exchange of perspectives in a group setting often leads to richer insights and varied opinions on the topic.
2. Compatible with both quantitative and qualitative methods.	● *Group Discussions* can be used in research employing both quantitative and qualitative methodologies. ● Structured discussions can gather quantitative data on specific variables or behaviours through standardized questions. ● Open-ended discussions enable qualitative exploration of participants' experiences, attitudes, and beliefs, providing rich qualitative data.
3. Adaptable to various fields and settings.	● *Group Discussions* are versatile and can be adapted to suit various research fields and settings. ● They are utilized in academia, market research, community development, and organizational contexts to address specific research questions or objectives.
4. Encourages group interaction and expression.	● *Group Discussions* foster an environment of interaction and collaboration among participants. ● Active participation and exchange of ideas allow individuals to build upon each other's contributions, leading to deeper insights. ● Participants are encouraged to express their opinions and experiences, contributing to a richer data set.
5. Enhances understanding of group dynamics and shared meanings.	● Observing group dynamics during discussions provides insights into how individuals interact and influence each other within a social context. ● Analysis of communication patterns, power dynamics, and group norms leads to a better understanding of shared meanings and social processes. ● This understanding adds depth to the interpretation of research findings and facilitates the development of targeted interventions or strategies.

Disadvantages of Group Discussions

Group Discussions pose challenges for researchers despite their potential benefits. While they provide a platform for gathering diverse perspectives and stimulating participant interactions, researchers face diminished control over individual interviews within this context (Ortega, 2005). Moreover, the intricate social dynamics generated by group interaction heighten the complexity of data analysis, necessitating careful interpretation of comments within this social framework. Furthermore, effective management of group dynamics and facilitation of productive discussions demand skilled and adequately trained interviewers (Krueger, 1991).

Additionally, the inherent variability between groups presents a challenge, as each group may manifest unique characteristics and dynamics. Moreover, logistical obstacles, such as recruiting an adequate number of participants and securing appropriate meeting venues, further complicate this process (Ortega, 2005). Consequently, while *Group Discussions* offer valuable insights, meticulous planning and execution are essential to surmount their inherent limitations and ensure the validity and reliability of research outcomes. When considering the disadvantages of *Group Discussions*, we compile the following attributes as outlined in Table 2. *Disadvantages of Group Discussions*.

Table 2. Disadvantages of Group Discussions

Disadvantages	Explanation
1. Difficulty in balancing participant homogeneity and heterogeneity.	● Researchers may struggle to ensure a mix of participants with diverse backgrounds and perspectives while also maintaining cohesion within the group.
2. Artificial settings may compromise response authenticity.	● Participants may alter their responses or behavior in a structured setting, leading to less authentic or genuine feedback.
3. Moderator and peer influence can skew opinions.	● The influence of the moderator and other group members can inadvertently shape participants' opinions, potentially leading to biased outcomes.
4. Risk of intense participant reactivity.	● Emotions or conflicts within the group may escalate, hindering productive discussion and leading to defensive or reactive responses.
5. Tendency towards group identity over moderator influence.	● Participants may align with the group's consensus rather than expressing individual opinions, diminishing the impact of the moderator's facilitation
6. Challenges in gathering a sufficient number of participants.	● Recruiting and assembling a diverse and representative group of participants can be logistically challenging, especially in niche or hard-to-reach populations.
7. Requirement for accessible meeting locations.	● Securing suitable meeting locations that accommodate participants' needs and preferences can be challenging, potentially limiting participation.
8. Inherent biases in group dynamics.	● Pre-existing group dynamics, hierarchies, or power structures may influence the direction and outcomes of the discussion, introducing biases into the data.
9. Limited researcher control compared to individual interviews.	● Researchers have less control over the flow and dynamics of *Group Discussions* compared to individual interviews, potentially impacting data quality.
10. Complex data analysis and preparation.	● Analyzing and synthesizing data from *Group Discussions* can be complex and time-consuming due to the volume and variability of responses.
11. Moderator training necessities.	● Effective moderation requires specialized training to manage group dynamics, facilitate productive discussion, and mitigate biases, adding to the overall resource investment
12. Uncertainty in achieving actionable outcomes like socio-analysis	● The multifaceted nature of group dynamics and interactions may pose challenges in translating discussion outcomes into actionable insights or socioanalytical conclusions.

Phases for the Development of Group Discussions

In each group, it is essential to initially establish specific elements and then adjust them as the research progresses. These elements include alignment with the design, sampling, functionality, data analysis, and report elaboration (Tümen-Akyıldız & Ahmed, 2021). More details are described in Table 3. *Phases for the development of Group Discussions.*

Table 3. Phases for the Development of Group Discussions

Phase	Description
Designing	● Determination of initial objectives ● Sampling ● Preparation of preliminary and cost estimation
Functioning	● Starting ● Presentation of the topic ● Group Closure
Data analysis	● Information segmentation ● Categorization ● Encoding
Report	● Reporting

Design of Group Discussions

Determination of Initial Objectives

Integral to the initial stages of the design process is the imperative of fostering consensus among relevant stakeholders regarding the fundamental nature of the identified problem and the requisite types of data essential for its comprehensive exploration and resolution (Ortega, 2005). Following the establishment of a collective understanding of the problem landscape, the researcher proceeds to deliberate on the selection of research procedures deemed most suitable and effective for addressing the identified research questions and objectives (Krueger, 1991).

The inception of designing *Group Discussions* within a multicultural context involves a deliberate consideration of the underlying rationale propelling the research endeavour. This initial phase aims to elucidate the core motivations and objectives guiding the study forward (Ortega, 2005). Afterward, the researcher crafts a detailed description of the prevailing issues and the specific objectives intended to be accomplished through the study, ensuring meticulous composition with a focus on precision and clarity in written form (Krueger, 1991).

Selection the best questions to answer specific objectives within a *Group Discussions* in multicultural settings involves several key considerations. On the one hand, open-ended questions offer the advantage of eliciting participants' genuine thoughts and perspectives, allowing them the freedom to determine the direction of their responses. Their responses often stimulate the appearance of new ideas or associations among others participants which are essential for exploring the full spectrum of opinions, thoughts or attitudes (Krueger, 1991).

However, as discussions progress, it may be advantageous for the moderator to transition from these types of questions to closed-ended questions to focus more on specific responses. Limiting the scope and number of questions (Krueger, 1991) can assist the moderator in regaining control in situations where the discussion deviates from the intended path or when specific data needs to be collected (Ortega, 2005).

Closed-ended questions, particularly those requiring a simple yes or no response, often fail to stimulate the desired *Group Discussions*. Instead, they may be used strategically by the moderator to guide the discussion or elicit specific information as needed (Krueger, 1991). Overall, the goal of posing questions within a *Group Discussions* is to provide structure while allowing for comprehensive exploration of relevant research topics (Montañez-Serrano, 2010).

> *[...] The script, previously prepared by the researchers M.D.B, R.M.R, and S.V., consisted of a set of open-ended questions aimed at exploring the thematic units: 1) knowledge about Fibromyalgia, 2) experiences with the syndrome, 3) coping strategies, 4) expectations regarding the healthcare system, and 5) expectations regarding healthcare professionals. [...] (Martín-Pérez, 2023, p.10)*

Sampling

In crafting a study, researchers must carefully define their objectives, identifying individuals capable of providing valuable insights and information. The selection criteria, as noted by Montañez-Serrano (2010), are contingent upon the research problem, objectives, and the target population under scrutiny. This mandates a thoughtful evaluation of the socioeconomic and cultural attributes sought in potential participants.

Krueger (1991) emphasizes the critical nature of determining who to study, as it directly influences the relevance and applicability of the findings obtained in the study. Meanwhile, Montañez-Serrano (2010) emphasizes that the representativeness of the sample of participants in *Group Discussions* has a meaning more related to the social structure rather than statistical one. Participants frequently articulate perspectives that mirror their affiliations with social groups, underscoring the importance of conducting a thorough examination of group composition and, when applicable, striving for a certain level of homogeneity within the group (Porto & Ruiz, 2014).

Furthermore, apart from possessing specific shared characteristics relevant to the topic at hand, it is imperative to ensure that they are not familiar with each other. In studies conducted in multicultural settings, it is important that researchers include people from diverse cultural backgrounds, ethnicities, religions, and linguistic communities to capture the richness and complexity of the study context. For example, if the research aims to investigate the impact of a new educational program in unaccompanied foreign minors, participants may include educators, students, legal guardians, and administrators directly involved in the educational system.

When constructing the sample for *Group Discussions*, researchers should also heed both the discussion objectives and traditional classification criteria for individuals, as highlighted by Krueger (1991). Montañez-Serrano (2010) outlines five overarching axes for sample structuring, encompassing social class, age, gender, ethnicity, and habitat. This necessitates accounting for factors such as gender, age, ethnicity, socioeconomic status, immigration status, habitat, ideology, and sexual orientation (Porto & Ruiz, 2014).

When engaging children in *Group Discussions* settings, it is crucial to employ straightforward language and engaging activities, ensuring their comfort in self-expression. Facilitators should cultivate kindness and understanding, recognizing and incentivizing participation to sustain interest. These strategies foster effective and meaningful elicitation of their viewpoints (Krueger & Casey, 2015).

Gender discrepancies exert considerable influence on the dynamics of focus group discussions, irrespective of their composition—solely men, solely women, or mixed-gender (Kimmel & Aronson, 2018). In single-gender scenarios, individuals may find it simpler to articulate gender-specific perspectives, while mixed-gender settings may introduce power dynamics impacting participation and recognition of diverse viewpoints.

Sample selection prioritizes replicable participant relationships during sessions rather than individual demographics, as underscored by Montañez-Serrano (2010). This approach accentuates relational dynamics among participants over individual traits. Considering these intersecting identities enables researchers to ensure their study reflects the full diversity spectrum within the population.

Regarding the optimal size for a group discussion typically falls within a range of four to twelve participants.

[...] This study included 12 women, aged between 33.0 and 74.0 years, with a mean age of 62.2 years (SD = 11.6) [...] (Martín-Pérez, 2023, p.12)

It is widely agreed that groups exceeding twelve participants are not conducive to productive discussions. In such larger groups, subgroups often form, limiting individual opportunities to contribute effectively. On the other hand, smaller mini-groups, comprising three to five people, may offer less information but encourage greater participation from each member (Montañez-Serrano, 2010).

Once the population characteristics and selection criteria are established, researchers may explore existing groups within the community that meet these criteria (Krueger, 1991).

[...] Patients were identified and recruited at the headquarters of the Fibromyalgia and Chronic Fatigue Association of Tenerife (AFITEN) through intentional non-probabilistic sampling according to the following inclusion criteria: 1) female users of the association, 2) over 18 years old, 3) diagnosed with FM, 4) without therapeutic, familial, and/or friendship ties with the research staff, 5) fluent in Spanish, and 6) who provided written consent to participate. On the other hand, the following exclusion criteria were used: 1) not suffering from potentially life-threatening illnesses and 2) not presenting severe alterations in cognitive and/or auditory function that would hinder understanding of the information provided by the researchers. [...] (Martín-Pérez, 2023, p.9-10)

Otherwise, we could also illustrate the composition of the *Group Discussions* using this example:

[...] Non-probability convenience sampling was carried out to recruit low-income women with FMS in a sub-urban and peri-urban areas of Tenerife (Spain). Upon receiving the signed Informed Consent, the researcher A.A.S. proceeded with a clinical interview to determine whether the candidate met the study's inclusion criteria that were: (1) female, (2) over 18 years of age, (3) with medical diagnosis of FMS, (4) and being registered in the Fibromyalgia and Chronic Fatigue Association of Tenerife (AFITEN), (5) being categorized as low-income by a Social Worker, (6) living in the conurbation of Santa Cruz de Tenerife and San Cristóbal de La Laguna, municipalities located in the island

of Tenerife (Canary Islands, Spain), (7) having not visual or hearing disability or neurological or psychiatric disorder that would interfere their ability to understand or speak Spanish, and (8) giving the consent to participate in the study [...] (Martín-Pérez, 2023, p.3)

Once the group structures are established, it becomes essential to incorporate a degree of inclusive heterogeneity to encourage debate and reflect diversity within the composition (Porto & Ruiz, 2014). Group discussions are typically marked by homogeneity while ensuring adequate heterogeneity to facilitate a divergence of opinions (Ortega, 2005). For example, in a study conducted by Martín-Pérez (2023), participants consisted of women residing in Tenerife and migrants from various social strata, primarily hailing from the Caribbean and South America, all proficient in Spanish.

[...] Likewise, it was ensured that the participants had a fluent command of the Spanish language [...] (Martín-Pérez, 2023, p.10)

The multicultural environment, featuring a range of nationalities such as Spain, Cuba, and Venezuela, plays a pivotal role in cultivating dynamic discussions within group settings. Within Latin American cultural contexts, the coexistence of diverse identities influenced by varied migration patterns is evident (García-Canclini, 2005). Migrants undergo processes of displacement and adaptation, navigating the complexities of deculturation and acculturation in pursuit of synthesis through transculturation (Ortiz, 1999), leading to the emergence of novel cultural phenomena. García-Canclini (2005) observes that interculturality is increasingly manifested through media communication, supplementing traditional migratory movements.

Once groups are formed, the next step involves reaching out to potential participants and extending personalized invitations to gatherings at suitable venues (Montañez, 2010). Common procedures include reviewing censuses, contacting associations, seeking referrals, and conducting random telephone searches (Ortega, 2005). The facilitator responsible for guiding the discussion sends these personalized invitations, emphasizing confidentiality regarding the meeting's agenda and ensuring participants are unfamiliar with each other. They simply inform invitees of an informal exchange of ideas within their expertise, aimed at gathering valuable insights (Montañez-Serrano, 2010).

Upon acceptance, participants are reminded a day in advance of meeting details, including date, time, location and directions, dress code, along with an estimated duration to facilitate planning and avoid early departures. For example, in research that focuses on individuals' coping mechanisms for a specific painful condition and cultural patterns, participants may be selected based on diagnosis, symptom severity, treatment history, or other relevant factors (LeBreton, 1999).

Preparation of the Preliminary Project and Cost Estimation

The formulation of the project proposal and cost estimation for a *Group Discussions* entails specific considerations to account for the diverse perspectives and contexts involved. Firstly, it is crucial to recognize the complexity of multicultural settings and the various cultural backgrounds represented within the group (Callejo, 2001; Krueger,1991).

In developing the project proposal, researchers must consider the unique cultural dynamics and communication styles present in multicultural contexts. This includes acknowledging potential language barriers, cultural norms, and power dynamics that may influence group interactions. Additionally, researchers should outline a comprehensive plan for facilitating inclusive and respectful dialogue among participants from different cultural backgrounds (Callejo, 2001).

Furthermore, estimating the costs associated with conducting them requires careful consideration of various factors. This includes budgeting for translation services, cultural sensitivity training for moderators, and resources for accommodating diverse dietary preferences or accessibility needs. Additionally, researchers should account for potential travel expenses or incentives for participants from marginalized or underrepresented communities to ensure equitable participation (Callejo, 2001).

Functioning of Group Discussion

During this phase, the group consolidates its cohesion, commencing discussions under the moderator's guidance. As the topic is introduced, it becomes the focal point of collective exploration, with participants contributing references and establishing the discourse framework (Porto & Ruiz, 2014). This organic approach allows for the natural evolution of group dynamics, fostering active engagement in shaping the shared conversation.

The resultant guide should encompass all pertinent themes and subtopics, along with potential discussion prompts to enhance participation as necessary. The objective is to strike a balance between granting the group autonomy and addressing essential research themes (Montañez-Serrano, 2010).

Another crucial consideration in *Group Discussions* is understanding the session's functioning process. Group dynamics typically progress through four phases: 1) starting, 2) introduction of the topic, 3) facilitation, and 4) closure.

Starting

In the realm of applied research within exploratory objectives, the aim is to delve into the intricacies of particular phenomena within their contextual framework (Porto & Ruiz, 2014). These endeavors often involve meetings held in formal interview settings, albeit entirely artificial, where communication patterns similar to those found in natural group dynamics are observed.

Venue Selection

A critical aspect of organizing a successful *Group Discussions* lies in the careful selection and preparation of the meeting venue. The choice of venue plays a pivotal role in shaping the atmosphere and facilitating meaningful interactions among participants (Montañez-Serrano, 2010; Porto & Ruiz, 2014). It is crucial to choose a meeting place that does not carry symbolic weight capable of influencing discourse, thus preventing participant inhibition or exaggeration.

In this sense, it is recommendable a neutral space, free form external distractions (Krueger, 1991), and equipped with essential amenities such as seating arrangements and refreshments like water and non-alcoholic beverages. Additionally, ensuring that the space boasts excellent acoustics, adequate lighting, and comfortable furniture is vital for ensuring the comfort and engagement of all participants. Specifically, employing an oval table is recommended as it facilitates visual and auditory interaction among collaborators (Montañez-Serrano, 2010).

Moderation and Facilitation

Moderation strategies can vary depending on the role assumed by the group facilitator. Encouraging open dialogue among group members facilitates the exploration of how meaning is constructed in their interactions, prioritizing process-oriented logic over strict adherence to a predetermined script (Krueger, 1991). Minimizing moderator intervention during sessions enhances the depth and richness of the data collected for subsequent analysis. Moreover, moderators' ability to foster group participation and, notably, actively listen, is pivotal for the success of *Group Discussions* (Porto & Ruiz, 2014).

Additionally, moderators must adeptly manage group dynamics, intervening as needed to address stagnation or a lack of direction. In this regard, and considering their performance in multicultural contexts, it is imperative to select facilitators with a robust understanding of the study topic that promotes effective group dynamics. Furthermore, establishing rapport with participants can be facilitated through attire and behavior that are socially accepted by the group, such as incorporating specific slang or introducing controlled humor expressions (Krueger, 1991).

Through expert redirection and facilitation techniques, the moderator must guide the discourse and encourage collaborative engagement to achieve the desired results (Montañez-Serrano, 2010). It is advisable to have an assistant who takes care of logistical issues such as note taking and environmental management (Krueger, 1991).

Challenges may arise from self-appointed "experts" or dominant individuals within the group, potentially stifling open dialogue (Krueger, 1991). Similarly, dominant individuals may assert themselves as authorities (Krueger, 1991), while more reticent participants may require encouragement to contribute meaningfully to the discussion (Krueger, 1991). The moderator's skill in managing these dynamics and promoting inclusivity is crucial for ensuring productive discussions.

Participants who pose challenges can disrupt the group's dynamics, necessitating careful management. To maintain consistency, it is preferable for participants to commence and conclude sessions simultaneously. Additionally, it is important not to offer explicit compensation for participation. Instead, establishing a system of reciprocity or indebtedness is recommended. If participants lack personal connections within the research group, their voluntary contribution of time is presumed, often motivated by altruism. Conversely, pre-existing relationships create stronger bonds than monetary incentives, indicating alternative motivating factors for voluntary participation (Porto & Ruiz, 2014).

During the implementation of *Group Discussions,* efforts are made to identify trends and consistencies in opinions (Ortega, 2005). The conclusion of these discussions typically occurs when discursive saturation is reached, signifying that data collection has maximized and no further themes or perspectives pertinent to the study are discovered. It is important to note that the aim of this technique is not to obtain a sample representative of the entire population under study or to generalize findings. Instead, the focus is on strategically selecting samples to achieve saturation and effectively conclude the study (Krueger, 1991).

It is essential to carefully manage the duration of *Group Discussions* sessions, ensuring they do not exceed ninety minutes. This timeframe is chosen to accommodate participants' leisure and free time segments effectively. Porto and Ruiz (2014) emphasize the importance of communicating this duration at the outset of the session to set clear expectations and allow participants to plan accordingly. Adhering to this time constraint is crucial as it respects the participants' schedules while maximizing the efficiency and effectiveness of the discussion.

The initiation of *Group Discussions* typically follows a structured framework as recommended, comprising several key components. Upon participants' arrival at the meeting venue, it is essential for the moderator or their assistant to extend greetings and ensure a welcoming atmosphere, fostering a sense of comfort among attendees (Ortega, 2005). A brief period of informal conversation is maintained, consciously steering clear of any topics related to the research at hand. This introductory phase, lasting between five to ten minutes, serves to establish rapport and ease participants into the discussion (Krueger, 1991). Meanwhile, the moderator tactfully manages the dynamics of the group, diplomatically redirecting the attention of dominant members to allow space for others to contribute. As participants enter the designated meeting room, they are met with a setup consisting of an oval table surrounded by chairs, visible audiovisual equipment, and the presence of the moderator and their assistants.

Compliance with suitable attire and language is expected throughout the session. Group formation commences as each participant takes their seat around the table, signaling the start of proceedings. The moderator initiates the session by extending gratitude to attendees for their presence and providing an overview of the session's logistics, including the use of audiovisual recording devices and the importance of respecting diverse viewpoints (Krueger, 1991). The utilization of audiovisual aids is essential for fostering productive discussions, as they often assist in presenting initial discursive stimuli to stimulate debate among participants (Montañez-Serrano, 2010).

In the context of recording *Group Discussions*, two methods are commonly employed: the use of recording devices and the taking of notes by the moderator or their assistant (Krueger, 1991). The latter method is particularly vital for capturing nuanced insights and interactions during the discussion. It is emphasized that the entire conversation will be recorded, with participants being briefed on the rationale behind this practice. This comprehensive approach ensures that valuable insights and contributions are accurately documented for further analysis and review.

When participants arrive at the meeting place, the moderator or assistant greets them and ensures their comfort, engaging in a brief, casual conversation. All discussions consciously avoid research-related topics and this informal exchange should last between five to ten minutes. The moderator may discreetly redirect the attention of dominant members, encouraging others to speak. Once settled around the worktable, the moderator extends gratitude for attendance, outlines the use of audiovisual recording devices, sets the time frame, and underscores the importance of respecting all opinions. *Group Discussions* sessions are typically recorded using both audio recording and note-taking, with the latter being deemed essential (Krueger, 1991; Montañez-Serrano, 2010).

The entire conversation will be recorded, and the reason for this must be explained.

> *[...] By accepting the Informed Consent, individuals agree to be interviewed and have their testimonials recorded in audio [...]* (Martín-Pérez,2023,p.10).

If the recorder is not visible to the interviewee, they may forget they are being recorded. While the recording provides a more comprehensive record than notes, it does not capture the nonverbal and physical aspects of the situation (Hammersley & Atkinson, 1994)

It should be clarified that if anyone wishes for the recording to be interrupted or deleted at any time, their request will be promptly fulfilled (Montañez-Serrano, 2010; Sanjuán-Núñez, 2019) Participants should be informed that the anonymity of all contributors is guaranteed.

[…] They also agreed that their data would be included in an anonymized database for research purposes [...] (Martín-Pérez, 2023, p.3)

Following any clarifications, the moderator introduces the debate topic.

Presentation of the topic

It is important to highlight that the debate proposal does not rigidly define the discussion framework. Occasionally, instead of providing a discursive prompt, an advertisement or other miscellaneous content is displayed on a screen to initiate the discussion.

[…] The discussion group leader conducted the session following the script and interspersing, before each thematic unit, various slideshow images and videos that served as materials for the projective exercises aimed at stimulating discussion among the participants [...] (Martín-Pérez, 2023, p.10)

After viewing the images, participants engage in discussions to exchange their interpretations. The moderator maintains silence to allow any participant to speak, focusing on analyzing the setting - the characters and their relationships - and the scene, the actions within the depicted "play," aiming to comprehend the story portrayed within the group (Porto & Ruiz, 2014). When we delve into these gestures, we also reveal their cultural backgrounds and how they unfold in cross-cultural communication (Rodriguez, 2011). However, when examining the participants and their relationships, it is important to consider that cross-cultural communication depends on aspects such as their personalities, backgrounds, motivations, and conflicts (Huer, 2003). Additionally, we must mention that although the environment may seem neutral, the location where the discussion group is held conditions the actions and interactions of the participants, as each place acquires different meanings for each culture, influencing how participants behave and relate to each other (Schultz, 2012).

It is crucial to establish the context of a question through introductory remarks by the interviewer, as well as through the initial questions directed to the group. The interviewer guides individuals from the immediate interview situation to the original action. Occasionally, introducing a short written questionnaire at the beginning of the interview can effectively focus attention on the topic under discussion (Ortega, 2005). Questions should be arranged in a sequence that appears logical to the participants, even if it does not necessarily seem so to the researcher. These casually originated questions can be fruitful. It is best to reserve the last five to ten minutes of discussion for such questions (Krueger, 1991).

Group Closure

The standard protocol usually entails thanking participants for their contributions. It's worth noting that expressions of gratitude differ across cultures and can vary among individuals within the same society (Gudykunst & Ting-Toomey, 1988). In multicultural discussion groups, it's advisable to be mindful of diverse farewell customs, as adjusting our expressions of gratitude and farewell can enhance mutual respect and bolster interpersonal bonds (Hofstede, 2001). In addition to the above, it is necessary to fulfill any promised incentives, and convey well wishes for their safe journey home (Krueger, 1991).

Following this, the facilitator extends appreciation to participants for their active engagement, formally bidding them farewell (Montañez-Serrano, 2010).

As discussions draw to a close, the moderator invites final remarks from participants, thereby signaling the conclusion of the session. Alternatively, a succinct recapitulation of key viewpoints may be offered, prompting participants to assess the accuracy of the synthesis. Further elucidation is provided in Table 4. *Functioning dynamics of a Group Discussions*, delineating the operational dynamics of *Group Discussions*.

Table 4. Functioning Dynamics of a Group Discussions

Dynamic	Description
Starting	● Upon entry, participants see an oval table, AV equipment, moderator, and assistants. ● Dress code and language standards must be adhered to. ● Moderator begins by welcoming, giving equipment overview, setting time frames, and introducing the topic.
Presentation of the topic	● Debate proposal offers a flexible discussion framework. ● Sometimes initiated by advertisement or miscellaneous content. ● Participants discuss interpretations, moderator analyzes scene elements for story comprehension.
Group Facilitation	● Facilitator guides group dynamics, intervening to address stagnation or aimless navigation. ● Utilizes strategic redirection and facilitation to maintain focus, promote collaboration, and achieve desired outcomes.
Group Closure	● Moderator invites final contributions after discussing all topics, signaling a meeting conclusion. ● Expresses gratitude to participants for their engagement and bids farewell.

As soon as the participants have left the meeting place, the moderator and assistant should retire to an isolated place. The purpose of all this is to arrive at crafting a brief summary on which both team members agree, describing the findings and interpretation of the key themes for the research (Ortega, 2005).

The analysis continues when all the preliminary summaries, recordings, interview scripts, participants' demographic data, and, if available, transcripts of the conversations are brought together.

Data Analysis

Data Selection and Preparation

Finally, in the fourth and last phase, interpretation and analysis of discourses take place. Alongside quantitative techniques, we have a detailed plan for processing and analyzing data before commencing the information-gathering process. However, it must be made very clear from the beginning that there is no predetermined plan for exploring the group discourse (Porto & Ruiz, 2014). Our objective here is not to dictate strict guidelines for interpreting *Group Discussions*, but rather to offer a set of ideas in the form of a framework that could be beneficial for the analysis of discussions.

An initial step that aids interpretation involves the precise transcription of every group meeting (Montañez-Serrano, 2010). The transcription should accurately capture the speech of each participant.

[...] The transcription was carried out following a systematic textual condensation, consisting of: 1) a generalized reading of all the material, in order to obtain a general impression, putting in parentheses any preconceived ideas regarding the study hypotheses [...] (Martín-Pérez, 2023, p.11).

Subsequently, employing both the transcription and the recording of the meeting, the discourses undergo interpretation. These interpretations, while inherently subjective, strive to be objective and aim to illustrate collective representations and images related to the research problem. (Krueger, 1991) The analysis begins by revisiting the study's objectives. Furthermore, it is crucial to emphasize that the interpretation that follows should be coherent and maintain logical consistency with the subject matter under analysis. It is also essential to consider opposing viewpoints, divergent perspectives, or relevant discourses whenever possible (Montañez-Serrano, 2010).

Group Discussions generate diverse discourses that hover over the collective discourse, reflecting the broader public opinion. This forms the essence of this qualitative research technique, which entails capturing the group discourse to interpret and analyze the trends emerging within this cohort, strategically representing our intended sample (Porto & Ruiz, 2014).

> *[...] Finally, a set of illustrative quotes was extracted to exemplify the general opinion of the participants [...]* (Martín-Pérez, 2023, p.12)

Every research involves a reduction of the entire dataset. The goal is to minimize this reduction as much as possible. Given that the data obtained from implementing this technique tends to be voluminous, it becomes necessary to segment the information, establish categories and ultimately encode the results (Porto & Ruiz, 2014).

Information Segmentation

A transcription offers significant advantages as it speeds up the process of organizing and classifying information. When multiple cultures are present in *Group Discussions*, it is crucial that they capture the literal meaning to avoid misunderstandings and distortions (Brislin, 1986). Often requiring a competent translator to overcome linguistic and cultural barriers, ensuring the reliability of the translator when interpreting testimonies is essential (Hofstede, 1980).

Segmentation marks the initial stage of classification where our goal is to identify meaningful units from the collected data. The complexity of analyzing *Group Discussions* occurs at several levels. The analyst must consider how to compare different responses. The separation can be carried out based on various criteria such as thematic nodes, participant characteristics, grammatical units (phrases or paragraphs), or by the temporal evolution of the narrative (Porto & Ruiz, 2014).

Categorization and Coding

During the phase of categories establishing, it is essential to define the concept of categories referring to situations, contexts, events, behaviors regarding a specific issue (Hammersley & Atkinson, 1994). Each category typically evolves throughout the research process, possessing significance and enabling the conceptual grouping and classification of units (text fragments or observations) related to the same theme or concept (Hammersley & Atkinson, 1994; Porto & Ruiz, 2014).

The process of organizing and reorganizing information into categories can vary significantly (Hammersley & Atkinson, 1994). We can establish categories in three main directions: 1) By defining them a priori, based on a existing conceptual framework; 2) Through open categorization, where categories are developed during analysis without restricting participants' responses to predefined concepts; 3) or by starting with broad a priori categories and refining them as the discourse progresses (Porto & Ruiz, 2014).

The categories must be comprehensive, ensuring that no important information is overlooked in the classification, and they must be mutually exclusive, meaning each piece of information belongs to only one category, even if it touches upon multiple thematic areas within the same fragment (Porto & Ruiz, 2014).

Local vocabularies unveil a culture's perception of the world and its construction of social reality (Hammersley & Atkinson, 1994). Ensuring a balance in the influence of researchers involves aligning concepts and categories with respect for the interpretations of subjects (Sanjuán-Núñez, 2019). Marvin Harris distinguishes between *emic* and *etic* approaches, preferring the latter, which relies on measurements and records to summarize cultural characteristics (Harris, 2014).

The most commonly advocated strategy relies on coding and text segments (Hammersley & Atkinson, 1994) Each category is allocated a distinct code (letters, numbers, colors, etc.) to differentiate each piece of information. Subsequently, a comprehensive examination of the text transcription is carried out, wherein the code of the pertinent category is allocated to each segment, along with providing identifications regarding the participant and the fragment's placement within the broader discourse. The most significant aspect when including a quotation in the report is for the researcher to grasp what the participant truly intended to convey (Krueger, 1991).

> *[...] Next, the 2) identification of meaningful units for the participants and transcription coding were carried out. This coding was performed by I.M. and S.M. and entered with their coding into an Excel spreadsheet. It should be noted that each quote could be coded with multiple codes simultaneously. Subsequently, researcher I.M. conducted 3) condensation and summarization of the contents of each code, and 4) generalization of descriptions and concepts related to knowledge about the disease, experiences, coping strategies, as well as expectations towards the healthcare system and personnel, following an analysis style where, instead of a strict framework, reliance was placed on theory. [...]* (Martín-Pérez, 2023, p.11-12)

Interpretation and Theme Extraction

After multiple readings of the transcripts derived from group recordings, we discern key themes within these narratives, in addition to the thematic blocks established during the initial segmentation. Consequently, it becomes apparent that the qualitative analysis process is non-linear, with results emerging from various phases. It is crucial to note that data obtained through qualitative measurement techniques do not assert validity in a manner allowing for extrapolation to the entire population; instead, they focus on diagnosis within a specific case. Given the interpretive nature of the information within a context, generalization is not feasible (Krueger, 1991).

> *[...] Firstly, our findings should not be extrapolated to the entire population of Fibromyalgia patients because the qualitative design has high internal validity but low external validity, thus they should be interpreted only within the cultural context in which our collaborators were situated. [...]"* (Martín-Pérez, 2023, p.20)

From a methodological viewpoint, all perspectives hold value as they do not aim for absolute truth or morality, but rather strive for a nuanced comprehension of others' viewpoints. Ultimately, they mirror the meanings participants assign to the situation, manifesting as a model that structures data, relationships, and interpretations of individuals (Porto & Ruiz, 2014).

Dimensions of Analysis

The analysis process at the onset grapples with the question of its depth. At one end of the spectrum lies the direct presentation of data, faithfully reproducing statements as they address each topic in conversation. At the opposite end, a descriptive approach offers the meaning of data rather than a mere summary (Ortega, 2005).

In the context of *Group Discussions* analysis, these dimensions offer valuable perspectives for unraveling the complexities of group interactions and participants' perceptions. Narrative analysis helps identify the stories shared by group members, revealing their individual and collective experiences. Discourse analysis aids in understanding how meanings are constructed and negotiated within the group, by examining the words and expressions used during the discussion. Conversation analysis highlights group dynamics, social influences, and emerging communication patterns during the exchange.

Researchers must consider the emphasis or intensity placed on each comment and evaluate the variability versus internal consistency of comments (Krueger, 1991). Interpretation extends beyond specific transcript words, including annotations from fieldwork, the atmosphere surrounding participants' comments, the degree of vagueness of examples used, and the consistency or variability of statements made.

Finally, content analysis provides a framework for identifying recurring themes and discussion categories, thus contributing to a more comprehensive understanding of topics addressed in the *Group Discussions*.

Integrating these dimensions into *Group Discussions* analysis enriches data interpretation and helps capture the richness and diversity of participants' perspectives.

Result Verifiability

The analysis process must be systematic, which means it should follow a prescribed and sequential process to ensure coherence and comprehensiveness in evaluating the data. This involves establishing clear and defined steps that guide from data collection to result interpretation (Ortega, 2005).

Moreover, the process must be verifiable, implying that other researchers should be able to reach similar conclusions when examining the same available data and documents. This verifiability is essential to validate the reliability and validity of the analysis results. If different researchers can arrive at the same conclusions using the same data, it increases confidence in the accuracy and objectivity of the analysis conducted (Krueger, 1991).

Tools and Analysis Software

The examination of Group Discussions relies on a range of tools and specialized software designed to extract, arrange, and understand collected data. There are specific programs tailored to significantly ease the analysis and management of this information, aiding in the extraction of results and the formulation of interpretations (Porto & Ruiz, 2014). Among these tools are qualitative analysis programs like

NVivo, ATLAS.ti, or MAXQDA, which streamline data categorization and coding, thereby enabling the recognition of emerging patterns and trends.

However, these platforms also have limitations, such as their learning curve and associated costs, as well as the need for proper training for optimal use. Despite these limitations, the advantages of using these tools are undeniable, as they allow for a deeper and more rigorous interpretation of data, significantly contributing to the validity and reliability of *Group Discussions* analysis results.

The Report

An effective report typically serves three main functions, with the primary objective being the clear communication of research results. Achieving this necessitates a careful consideration of the specific informational needs of the intended audience or stakeholders. Furthermore, the process of developing a report requires the researcher to construct a coherent and logical description of the entire investigation, ensuring that the document remains informative and useful for future reference (Ortega, 2005).

Reports serve as vital tools for communicating research findings, and their presentation can take numerous forms, including written narratives, oral presentations, or a combination of both. For written reports, Krueger (1991) suggests a recommended structure that includes various essential elements such as a cover page, abstract, table of contents, problem description, key points and methodology, results, limitations and alternative explanations, conclusions and suggestions, as well as an appendix.

The incorporation of various visual and multimedia tools can significantly enrich the dynamics of *Group Discussions* and amplify their impact. For instance, audiovisual technologies enable the presentation of multimedia content during discussions, thereby enhancing participants' comprehension and engagement. Images, graphics, and photographs can help illustrate abstract or complex concepts, facilitating communication and idea exchange. Furthermore, audio and video recording of discussion sessions provides the opportunity to review and analyze interactions and key points discussed in greater detail (Krueger, 1991; Ortega, 2005).

The use of tables and figures can also improve the organization and visualization of relevant data during discussions. Tables can be used to summarize and compare information, while figures can visually represent complex relationships or trends. These visual aids serve as reference points during discussions, enhancing participants' understanding and analysis of the information.

Moreover, the integration of specific technological platforms and tools for organizing and facilitating *Group Discussions* can enhance the efficiency and accessibility of sessions. For example, online video conferencing and collaboration platforms enable remote participation of individuals located in different geographical locations, thus expanding the diversity and representativeness of *Group Discussions*. Similarly, qualitative data analysis tools can facilitate the identification of patterns and emerging themes from discussion transcripts, streamlining the analysis and synthesis process. Finally, adhering to such a structure can help ensure clarity and coherence in the presentation of research findings.

CONCLUSION

This chapter delves into the significance of utilizing *Group Discussions* as a qualitative methodological tool, particularly within the sphere of social research addressing multicultural contexts.

Beginning with the designing phase, the chapter underscores the imperative of thoughtfully selecting participants who authentically represent the cultural diversity inherent in the context. It further emphasizes the criticality of meticulous preparation, not only in appointing a suitable moderator but also in addressing logistical considerations such as selecting an inclusive and accessible meeting location. It also dissects the essential phases necessary for the effective execution of *Group Discussions*.

The analysis phase serves not only to comprehend the diverse perspectives within the group but also to unravel the intricacies and subtleties of intercultural interactions. The chapter draws attention to the necessity of adopting a systematic and verifiable approach to ensure the reliability and validity of obtained results. This entails thorough data selection and preparation, segmentation of collected information and coding of relevant categories to discern emerging themes.

Finally, the chapter also underscores the importance of effectively communicating research findings through well-structured reports. By adhering to these comprehensive practices, researchers can enrich their understanding and foster meaningful insights in multicultural research settings.

REFERENCES

Bourdieu, P. (1993). *The field of cultural production: Essays on art and literature.* Columbia University Press.

Brislin, R. W. (1986). The Wording and Translation of Research Instruments. In Lonner, W. J., & Berry, J. W. (Eds.), *Field Methods in Cross-Cultural Research* (pp. 137–164). SAGE Publications Ltd.

Callejo, J. (2001). El grupo de discusión: Introducción a una práctica de investigación. *Ariel.*

Foucault, M. (1969). *The archaeology of knowledge.* Pantheon Books.

García-Canclini, N. (2005). *Culturas híbridas: Estrategias para entrar y salir de la modernidad.* Paidós.

Geertz, C. (2011). *La interpretación de las culturas.* Gedisa.

Goffman, E. (1967). *Interaction ritual: Essays on face-to-face behavior.* Anchor Books.

Gudykunst, W. B., & Ting-Toomey, S. (1988). *Culture and interpersonal communication.* SAGE Publications Ltd.

Hammersley, M., & Atkinson, P. (1994). *Etnografía: Métodos de investigación.* Academic Press.

Hofstede, G. (2001). *Culture's consequences: Comparing values, behaviors, institutions, and organizations across nations.* SAGE Publications Ltd.

Huer, M. B., & Saenz, T. I. (2003). Challenges and strategies for conducting survey and focus group research with culturally diverse groups. *American Journal of Speech-Language Pathology*, 12(2), 209–220. 10.1044/1058-0360(2003/067)12828534

Kimmel, M. S., & Aronson, A. (2018). *The Gendered Society Reader.* Oxford University Press.

Krueger, R. A. (1991). *El grupo de discusión: guía práctica para la investigación aplicada.* Pirámide.

Krueger, R. A., & Casey, M. A. (2015). *Focus Groups: A Practical Guide for Applied Research.* SAGE Publications Ltd.

LeBreton, D. (1999). *Antropología del Dolor.* Seix Barral.

Martín-Pérez, I. M., Martín-Pérez, S. E., Martínez Rampérez, R., Vaswani, S., & Dorta Borges, M. (2023). Conocimientos, actitudes y creencias hacia la enfermedad en mujeres con fibromialgia. Un estudio cualitativo basado en grupo focal. *Revista de la Sociedad Española del Dolor*, 79-94. 10.20986/resed.2023.4022/2022

Martín-Pérez, S. E., Martín-Pérez, I. M., Álvarez Sánchez, A., Acosta Pérez, P., & Rodríguez Alayón, E. (2023). Social support in low-income women with fibromialgia syndrome from sub-urban and peri-urban areas of Tenerife (Canary Islands, Spain): A mixed method study. *Journal of Patient-Reported Outcomes*, 7(1), 135. 10.1186/s41687-023-00661-038129366

Montañez-Serrano, M. (2010). *El grupo de discusión.* Cuadernos CIMAS-Observatorio Internacional de Ciudadanía y Medio Ambiente Sostenible.

Ortega, M. S. (2005). *El grupo de discusión: una herramienta para la investigación cualitativa.* Laertes.

Ortiz Fernández, F. (1999). *Contrapunteo cubano del tabaco y el azúcar.* EditoCubaEspaña.

Paidós Hofstede, G. (1980). *Culture's consequences: International differences in work-related values.* SAGE Publications Ltd.

Payne, G., & Payne, J. (2004). *Key Concepts in Social Research.* SAGE Publications Ltd. 10.4135/9781849209397

Porto Pedrosa, L., & Ruiz San Román, J. A. (2014). Los grupos de discusión. In Porto Pedrosa, L., & Ruiz San Román, J. A. (Eds.), *Métodos y técnicas cualitativas y cuantitativas aplicables a la investigación en ciencias sociales* (pp. 253–273). Tirant Humanidades México.

Rodriguez, K. L., Schwartz, J. L., Lahman, M. K. E., & Geist, M. R. (2011). Culturally Responsive Focus Groups: Reframing the Research Experience to Focus on Participants. *International Journal of Qualitative Methods*, 10(4), 400–417. 10.1177/160940691101000407

Sanjuán-Núñez, L. (2019). *El grupo de discusión, la investigación documental y otras técnicas cualitativas de investigación.* Operta UOC Publishing.

Schultz, P. (2002). Environmental Attitudes and Behaviors Across Cultures. *Online Readings in Psychology and Culture*, 8(1). Advance online publication. 10.9707/2307-0919.1070

Tümen-Akyıldız, S., & Ahmed, K. H. (2021). An overview of qualitative research and focus group discussion. *Journal of Academic Research in Education*, 7(1), 1–15. 10.17985/ijare.866762

ADDITIONAL READING

Barbour, R. (2018). *Doing Focus Groups.* SAGE Publications. 10.4135/9781526441836

Bloor, M., Frankland, J., Thomas, M., & Robson, K. (2001). *Focus Groups in Social Research.* SAGE Publications. 10.4135/9781849209175

Gutiérrez Brito, J. (2008). *Dinámica del grupo de discusión.* CIS.

Kitzinger, J. (1994). The Methodology of Focus Groups: The Importance of Interaction Between Research Participants. *Sociology of Health & Illness*, 16(1), 103–121. 10.1111/1467-9566.ep11347023

Litosseliti, L. (2003). Using Focus Groups in Research. *Continuum.*

Morgan, D. L. (1997). *Focus Groups as Qualitative Research.* SAGE Publications. 10.4135/9781412984287

Puchta, C., & Potter, J. (2004). *Focus Group Practice.* SAGE Publications. 10.4135/9781849209168

Stewart, D. W., & Shamdasani, P. N. (2014). *Focus Groups: Theory and Practice.* SAGE Publications.

Wilkinson, S. (1998). *Focus Groups in Health Research: Exploring the Meanings of Health and Illness.* Psychology Press. 10.1177/135910539800300304

KEY TERMS AND DEFINITIONS

Bias Mitigation: The steps taken to minimize bias in the research process to ensure that the findings are more trustworthy and unbiased.

Case Study: A research method that involves an up-close, in-depth, and detailed examination of a subject of study (the case), as well as its related contextual conditions.

Epistemology: The branch of philosophy concerned with the theory of knowledge, especially regarding its methods, validity, and scope.

Ethnography: A qualitative research method used to study cultures and groups from a holistic perspective.

Grounded Theory: A research methodology that involves constructing theories through methodical gathering and analysis of data.

Mixed Methods: Research methodology that combines both quantitative and qualitative research techniques in a single study to provide a better understanding of research problems.

Ontology: A branch of metaphysics dealing with the nature of being, including the relationships and categories of being.

Phenomenology: A qualitative research approach that focuses on the study of an individual's lived experiences within the world.

Reliability: The degree to which research methods and findings are consistent and replicable over time and across various conditions and analysts.

Theory Triangulation: Using multiple perspectives or theories to interpret a set of data, helping to ensure that the conclusions drawn are robust.

Chapter 6
The Role of Triangulation in Qualitative Research:
Converging Perspectives

Cem Harun Meydan
https://orcid.org/0000-0002-3604-1117
Ankara Science University, Turkey

Handan Akkaş
https://orcid.org/0000-0002-2082-0685
Ankara Science University, Turkey

ABSTRACT

Triangulation is a methodological approach that involves using multiple methods or data sources to enhance the credibility and validity of research findings. This approach is useful in qualitative studies that aim to gain a deeper understanding of complex social phenomena and to understand the intricacies of multicultural environments. By embracing diverse perspectives, methods, and data sources, researchers can verify and validate their findings, leading to more comprehensive and reliable conclusions and can navigate cultural dynamics more effectively, leading to more nuanced and culturally sensitive findings. Beyond methodological considerations, triangulation allows researchers to capture diverse perspectives and enrich their analysis, playing a crucial role in qualitative research by enhancing the credibility, validity, and depth of research findings. Additionally, it is beneficial for mixed methods designs to provide a holistic understanding of research problems. Triangulation serves as a cornerstone for advancing knowledge and understanding in multicultural research contexts.

DOI: 10.4018/979-8-3693-3306-8.ch006

INTRODUCTION

The concept of triangulation has been widely discussed in the literature, emphasizing its importance in ensuring the robustness of qualitative research. Triangulation can reveal shared perspectives and realities without claiming absolute 'truth' in findings (Lincoln & Guba, 1985). This approach is particularly valuable in qualitative studies that seek to gain a deeper understanding of complex social phenomena.

The significance of using triangulation to improve understanding and strengthen the validity of qualitative research findings has been highlighted in several studies (Clifford et al., 2010; Longhurst, 2016). Researchers can verify and validate their findings by combining different techniques and data sources, leading to more comprehensive and reliable conclusions. Triangulation is useful for mixed methods designs as it integrates quantitative and qualitative methods to provide a more comprehensive understanding of research problems (Fielding, 2012). Triangulating data from multiple sources, including stakeholder interviews, enhances scientific research (Sands & Roer-Strier, 2006).

This method enables researchers to capture diverse perspectives and enrich their analysis, playing a crucial role in qualitative research by enhancing the credibility, validity, and depth of research findings. By combining various methods, data sources, or perspectives, researchers can enhance their interpretations and achieve a more comprehensive understanding of the phenomena being studied.

TRIANGULATION

Triangulation is a crucial aspect of research as it enhances the credibility, validity, and depth of research findings by integrating multiple methods, data sources, or viewpoints (Hussein, 2009). This methodological approach, which is commonly used in qualitative research, involves the strategic use of different data sources, research methods, investigators, or theoretical frameworks to explore a research question or phenomenon (Denzin, 1978; Patton, 1999).

Definition of Triangulation in Qualitative Research

Triangulation is the use of multiple methods or perspectives, including both qualitative and quantitative methods, to collect and interpret data about a phenomenon. The purpose of triangulation is to increase the credibility of the study and obtain an accurate representation of reality (Cassidy et al., 2022; Polit & Hungler 1999).

The term 'triangulation' is metaphorically inspired by navigation, where multiple reference points are used for accurate location. The primary objective is to ensure comprehensive data collection by using both quantitative and qualitative approaches to identify similarities and differences. This is particularly valuable for gaining deeper insights into complex social phenomena (Hussein, 2009).

Triangulation, which originated with Denzin's work in the 1970s, emphasizes the need to use multiple data sources and methods to enrich the depth and breadth of qualitative research (Denzin, 1978). Patton (1999) proposed various forms of triangulation, including data triangulation, investigator triangulation, and methodological triangulation, each of which contributes to the overall rigor and credibility of the research. Data triangulation involves using multiple sources of data, such as interviews, observations, and documents, to validate or corroborate findings. Investigator triangulation involves the participation of multiple researchers to reduce individual bias and increase reliability (Patton, 1999). Methodological triangulation combines different research methods or theoretical frameworks to achieve a more nuanced understanding (Denzin, 1978; Patton, 1999). Triangulation aligns with the overarching principles of qualitative research, which emphasize depth, context, and multiple perspectives in exploring complex phenomena (Creswell, 2013). Incorporating triangulation strengthens the internal validity of a study, ensuring robust and trustworthy findings (Denzin, 1978; Patton, 1999).

The primary goal of triangulation is to ensure data completeness by using both quantitative and qualitative methods to identify similarities and differences. This approach allows researchers to produce holistic work or thick descriptions by combining qualitative methods for a comprehensive view of the topic. Triangulation is frequently employed in mixed methods designs to validate and confirm phenomena, contributing to the rigor and reliability of the research (Swavely et al., 2022). Researchers can examine meta-themes across different data components that are analyzed individually, increasing the depth of the study, by using a triangulation protocol (Cassidy et al., 2022). Triangulation is a valuable strategy in qualitative research as it allows for the testing of validity and reliability through the convergence of information from multiple sources (Zheng-ying, 2021).

The Purpose of Triangulation in Qualitative Research

Triangulation is a crucial methodological approach in qualitative research. Its purpose is to improve the validity, credibility, and reliability of research findings while aiming for a comprehensive understanding of the phenomenon under investigation. This is accomplished by collecting data using multiple methods and cross-checking the results (Denzin, 1978; Muthukrishna & Henrich, 2019). By integrating multiple data sources, methods, theories, or researchers' perspectives, triangulation aims to mitigate the limitations of individual approaches, ultimately contributing to the advancement of knowledge in various fields.

Enhancing Validity: Ensuring Credibility of Findings

Triangulation is a crucial method for enhancing the validity and credibility of research findings. It involves systematically corroborating evidence from diverse sources or methods (Creswell & Miller, 2000; Patton, 2015). The use of multiple data sources or methods bolsters the validity of the research by cross-validating findings. Validity refers to the extent to which research accurately measures or reflects the phenomenon under study (Maxwell, 2012). This process enhances the credibility of conclusions drawn, as demonstrated in studies such as those examining the effectiveness of teaching methods through classroom observations, interviews, and reflections (Patton, 2015).

Triangulation also helps to identify and mitigate potential biases that may arise from relying on a single method or data source (Denzin, 1978; Patton, 2015). For instance, researchers can mitigate social desirability bias and obtain a more precise representation of the phenomenon being studied by triangulating interview data with observations or document analysis. Triangulation also guarantees a comprehensive investigation of the research topic by integrating multiple perspectives, thereby reducing reliance on individual interpretations or biases (Creswell & Miller, 2000). To enhance the validity of research through triangulation, researchers integrate multiple data sources, methods, or perspectives to corroborate research findings, identify potential biases, and provide a more accurate and comprehensive understanding of the research phenomenon.

Achieving Comprehensive Understanding: The Holistic Perspective

Triangulation is an essential aspect of qualitative research as it allows for a comprehensive understanding of the research topic by adopting a holistic perspective (Creswell & Miller, 2000; Denzin, 1978). Researchers should approach the phenomenon under investigation from various angles, considering its diverse dimensions and complexities. This method allows for a thorough and detailed analysis of the research topic by combining various methods or data sources to investigate different aspects.

For example, when studying the effects of community health interventions, triangulation involves using surveys and focus groups together to assess the intervention's effectiveness and its impact on the community. Triangulation encourages researchers to consider multiple theoretical perspectives, promoting a more comprehensive analysis of the research phenomenon. By drawing on diverse theories, such as those from psychology, sociology, and organizational behavior, researchers can gain deeper insights into complex topics, such as employee motivation.

To achieve a comprehensive understanding through triangulation, researchers must adopt a holistic perspective that encompasses various methods, data sources, theoretical frameworks, or researchers' viewpoints. By triangulating data from diverse sources and perspectives, researchers can attain a nuanced and profound understanding of the phenomenon under investigation, thus advancing knowledge in their field.

Significance of Converging Perspectives

Converging perspectives through triangulation are essential in qualitative research, as they enhance the robustness and credibility of study findings. In-depth exploration of complex phenomena in qualitative research necessitates the integration of multiple perspectives, which is critical for ensuring a comprehensive understanding of the phenomenon under study (Flick, 2018; Golafshani, 2003).

Triangulation is a crucial method in research that enables crosschecking of information from various sources or perspectives. This helps to mitigate the limitations associated with relying on a single method or dataset (Creswell, 2013). By incorporating different perspectives, researchers can strengthen the internal validity of their findings, making them more defensible and trustworthy (Denzin, 1978).

Converging perspectives have a notable importance in addressing and minimizing bias, which is a common challenge in qualitative research. Triangulation, particularly researcher triangulation (Patton, 1999, 2015), can mitigate bias arising from the researcher's background, cultural influences, and personal beliefs. Including multiple researchers with different backgrounds and experiences reduces individual biases, thereby increasing the reliability of interpretations.

Furthermore, the convergence of perspectives can enhance the richness and depth of qualitative studies. By combining various data sources or methods, researchers can capture the complexity and nuances of the phenomenon being studied, in line with the holistic nature of qualitative research (Creswell, 2013; Guba, 1981).

Triangulation enhances the reliability of findings and helps to build a completer and more nuanced picture of the phenomenon under investigation. This is particularly important in multicultural settings where the interplay of different cultural factors can significantly affect research findings.

Converging perspectives also contribute to the overall rigor of qualitative research. Researchers can build a more convincing argument for the validity and trustworthiness of their interpretations by critically examining the phenomenon from multiple angles (Creswell, 2013; Denzin, 1978). This is especially crucial in qualitative research, where ensuring rigor is essential to maintaining the study's integrity.

The importance of converging perspectives through triangulation in qualitative research lies in its ability to enhance the internal validity of study findings, address bias, enrich the depth of exploration, and contribute to the overall robustness and credibility of the research.

Significance of Triangulation in Multicultural Settings

Triangulation is an essential aspect of qualitative research when studying multicultural settings. These environments present unique challenges due to their diverse cultural dynamics, making it necessary to employ multiple methods, data sources, and perspectives. By triangulating data from various sources such as interviews, observations, and document analysis, researchers can delve deeper into the cultural nuances and intricacies within these settings (Denzin, 1978; Patton, 1999). This method not only allows for the validation of findings but also helps to reduce potential biases, ultimately capturing the diversity of experiences and perspectives within the studied culture.

Additionally, triangulation significantly improves the validity and credibility of research conducted in multicultural contexts. By integrating various methodological approaches and cultural perspectives, researchers can gain deeper insights into the phenomenon under study, surpassing the limitations of any single method or viewpoint (Creswell & Miller, 2000). This approach promotes reflexivity among researchers, encouraging them to critically examine their own cultural assumptions, biases, and interpretations throughout the research process.

Triangulation is significant in multicultural settings, as demonstrated by empirical studies such as those conducted by Budge et al. (2012), Kuo et al. (2021), Erkanlı (2024), and Santoso et al. (2023). These studies show how triangulation helps to achieve a comprehensive understanding of complex cultural phenomena. For example, Budge et al. (2012) used triangulation to investigate the emotional and coping processes of transgender individuals, providing insight into the nuanced experiences within this community. Similarly, Erkanlı (2024) employed triangulation to examine primary school teachers' attitudes towards multicultural education, offering valuable insights into educational practices in culturally diverse classrooms. Santoso et al. (2023) explored the challenges of multicultural management in public administration by using data from various sources. They provided practical recommendations for managing cultural diversity in governmental settings.

FOUNDATIONS OF TRIANGULATION

Historical Context: Evolution of the Triangulation Concept

The evolution of the triangulation concept in qualitative research has been a journey that intertwines methodological innovation with practical applications from navigation, surveying, and military strategy. This historical exploration dates back to the foundational works of the 1970s. Triangulation has transformed from a metaphorical link to navigation into a versatile and indispensable strategy in contemporary research methodologies.

The metaphor of navigation, renowned for its precision and accuracy in determining locations, inspires triangulation in qualitative research. This approach involves using multiple reference points to pinpoint the exact position of an object. The use of diverse elements to enhance the credibility, validity, and depth of research findings is highlighted by this metaphor. Triangulation is positioned as a guiding beacon in the quest for a more robust understanding of complex phenomena.

Denzin's work in the 1970s laid the foundation for the concept of triangulation. Denzin, a sociologist and qualitative methodologist, recommended using multiple data sources and methods to enhance the depth and breadth of qualitative research. The initial conceptualization established the basis for the metaphorical use of triangulation in research methods. It highlights the importance of gathering evidence from multiple perspectives to gain a more precise understanding of the subject being investigated (Denzin, 1978).

Stake further developed this idea, emphasizing the role of triangulation in validating and supporting research findings. Stake's (1995) study of case study methodology highlights the significance of using multiple sources of evidence and perspectives to strengthen the reliability of qualitative research. Triangulation, as described by Stake (1995), is a crucial strategy to reinforce the internal validity of studies, ensuring that conclusions are not based on a single method or viewpoint.

Patton's contributions further enriched the concept of triangulation in the 1990s. In his book 'Qualitative Evaluation and Research Methods', Patton outlines various forms of triangulation, including data triangulation, investigator triangulation, and methodological triangulation (Patton, 1990). Data triangulation involves using multiple sources of data, such as interviews, observations, and documents, to validate or corroborate findings. Investigator triangulation involves multiple researchers to reduce individual biases and enhance reliability. Methodological triangulation combines various research methods or theoretical frameworks to provide a more comprehensive understanding of the phenomenon under investigation. Patton's framework elevated triangulation from a metaphorical notion to a systematically applied strategy in qualitative research.

Triangulation has historical roots in military strategy and surveying practices. Today, it is employed in academic research to ensure objectivity and accuracy. In military strategy, it was used to determine the position of objects. Surveying techniques dating back centuries involved using triangulation to plot the location of a third point based on two known or visible points. The concept of triangulation is borrowed from navigation and has enduring relevance across diverse disciplines. The text cites Löwe and Kerkhove (2019) to emphasize the adaptability and relevance of triangulation in different contexts.

This chapter discusses the use of triangulation in research, which involves the use of multiple methods to measure a single construct. The metaphorical underpinnings of triangulation were recognized by Scandura and Williams (2000). Shih (1998) defined triangulation as a navigational technique that involves using multiple reference points to locate an object's exact position. Archibald (2015) described triangulation as a surveying technique that uses known or visible points to plot the location of a third point.

Triangulation is a fundamental methodological principle in contemporary qualitative research. The historical evolution of the concept provides guidance for researchers as they explore new frontiers and grapple with complex phenomena. The metaphor's origins, deeply rooted in navigation and surveying practices, have been seamlessly integrated with a systematic and nuanced application in qualitative methodologies.

Triangulation has become synonymous with the overarching principles of qualitative research, emphasizing depth, context, and multiple perspectives. Researchers can gain a more accurate and comprehensive understanding by strategically incorporating diverse elements and triangulating evidence to navigate the complex terrain of their research questions. The metaphorical link to navigation, which was once a conceptual foundation, has evolved into a methodological compass that guides researchers through the complexities of contemporary qualitative inquiry.

Upon reflection of the historical journey of the triangulation concept, it is clear that its roots in navigation and surveying practices were foundational principles that continue to shape the landscape of qualitative research. From Denzin's early advocacy for a comprehensive approach to Patton's systematic framework, and from military strategy to contemporary applications, triangulation has traversed time and disciplines. The historical evolution of triangulation demonstrates its adaptability, resilience, and enduring relevance as a methodological cornerstone in qualitative research.

Triangulation is often compared to navigation, highlighting its methodological significance (Downward & Mearman, 2006). Triangulation in research involves the strategic incorporation of various methods, data sources, or viewpoints to converge on a more comprehensive understanding of a research question or phenomenon (Löwe & Kerkhove, 2019).

The metaphor of navigation is used to illustrate that relying on a single point of reference may introduce inaccuracies and uncertainties in determining location. Similarly, in research, triangulation emphasises the importance of using multiple perspectives or sources of information to improve accuracy and reliability. Triangulation aims to verify findings from different angles, ensuring a more comprehensive and nuanced understanding of the subject under investigation. This is achieved by combining diverse elements (Denzin, 1978; Eisenhardt, 1989; Patton, 1990).

Just like navigators use triangulation to determine their position by considering different landmarks, researchers use triangulation to incorporate various methods and sources in their data analysis. This metaphor vividly illustrates how triangulation aligns with the overarching principles of qualitative research, emphasizing depth, context, and multiple perspectives in exploring complex phenomena (Creswell, 2013). The navigation metaphor accurately reflects the methodology of triangulation. The aim of this approach is to improve the reliability, validity, and depth of research findings by strategically combining diverse elements. This provides researchers with a more accurate and comprehensive understanding of the complex terrain they are studying.

The concept of triangulation in qualitative research has historical roots in navigation and military strategy, where multiple reference points are used to pinpoint an object's exact position. The concept of triangulation has been borrowed from navigation to describe the use of multiple methods to measure a single construct in research (Scandura & Williams, 2000). Triangulation involves using multiple reference points to locate an object's exact position. This technique emphasizes the importance of combining various methods to enhance the credibility and validity of research findings (Shih, 1998). The concept of triangulation originated from surveying and navigation, where two known or visible points are used to plot the location of a third point (Archibald, 2015). Triangulation in research refers to the use of multiple methods, investigators, and theories to increase the reliability and validity of research results (Downward & Mearman, 2006). Triangulation is a navigational and surveying technique that assumes measurement is based on a common ontology and epistemology. It emphasizes the importance of using multiple approaches to strengthen research.

The concept of triangulation in qualitative research has evolved historically, encapsulating both metaphorical inspiration from navigation and practical applications in diverse fields. Triangulation is a methodological cornerstone that has proven to be adaptable, resilient, and enduring. Its foundational roots lie in Denzin's advocacy for comprehensive approaches and Patton's systematic framework. The metaphorical connection to navigation not only serves as a conceptual foundation but also acts as a methodological compass that guides researchers through the complexities of contemporary qualitative inquiry. The historical evolution of triangulation remains relevant and adaptable in the ever-evolving landscape of qualitative research. It continues to guide researchers as they explore new frontiers.

Theoretical Underpinnings: Methodological Pluralism

Methodological pluralism, based on the theoretical foundations of qualitative research, recognizes that no single methodological approach can fully capture the complexity inherent in human experience and social phenomena (Freshwater, 2022). Therefore, qualitative researchers adopt an inclusive stance, drawing on a variety of methods, perspectives, and theoretical frameworks to comprehensively explore and interpret multifaceted realities (Denzin & Lincoln, 2018). It is based on epistemological and ontological pluralism and is committed to understanding subjective experiences and constructed meanings within their social contexts. This approach moves away from positivist paradigms that seek universal laws and causal relationships (Creswell & Creswell, 2017).

Methodological pluralism is a philosophy that is closely linked to theoretical eclecticism. Researchers employ various qualitative methods, including interviews, observations, ethnography, and document analysis, to capture the complexity of the phenomenon under study (Maxwell, 2013). By using multiple methods, researchers can triangulate evidence, validate findings, and enhance the credibility and trustworthiness of their research (Patton, 2015). Methodological pluralism extends to theoretical pluralism, emphasizing the incorporation of diverse theoretical perspectives to inform research design, data collection, and analysis.

The theoretical underpinnings of triangulation demonstrate the value of using multiple perspectives and approaches to enhance the research process. Vivek (2023) highlights the importance of establishing a robust theoretical framework through a systematic literature review, which provides valuable insights into the theoretical foundations that inform the use of triangulation in research. Santos et al. (2019) demonstrate the use of abductive reasoning to integrate diverse data sources and methods, enhancing understanding in complex industrial networks. Farrukh et al. (2021) emphasize the significance of theoretical underpinnings in shaping identity narratives in the digital domain. They illustrate how triangulation can unravel complex social phenomena and construct nuanced narratives.

Additionally, the discourse of methodological pluralism extends beyond qualitative research to permeate different disciplines and domains. Freshwater (2022) discusses the ongoing debates and challenges related to integration versus triangulation approaches, offering current perspectives on the intricacies of mixed methods in evidence-based nursing research. Hoque et al. (2013) investigate the origins of debates in the accounting field, discussing the theoretical foundations and methodological considerations of organizational and accounting research. In addition, Ashour (2018) highlights the importance of methodological pluralism in the study of complex markets, emphasizing the need to reconcile different methodological techniques to enhance the credibility and robustness of research.

Furthermore, the concept of methodological pluralism, particularly in the context of triangulation, has been the subject of scholarly debate and exploration across various disciplines. Freshwater (2022) addresses the ongoing discussions of methodological pluralism, paradigmatic contests, and debates about the advantages and limitations of different research methods, including integration versus triangulation approaches. This commentary provides a contemporary perspective on the challenges and considerations of using mixed methods in evidence-based nursing research. Hoque et al. (2013) contribute to this discussion by exploring theoretical triangulation and methodological pluralism in organizational and accounting research. They trace the origins of these debates back to pioneering works, shedding light on the evolution of these concepts within the accounting field. Ashour (2018) examines the pluralist perspective of triangulation in technology-based services. The author emphasizes the significance of coordinating various methodological techniques to address the complexity inherent in studying complex markets.

Previous studies have contributed to the theoretical underpinnings of methodological pluralism, particularly within the framework of triangulation. They provide valuable insights into the historical development, debates, and practical applications of methodological pluralism in different research domains.

TYPES OF TRIANGULATION

Types of triangulation include methodological, data, investigator and theory triangulation. Methodological triangulation involves using multiple research methods to study the same phenomenon, which increases the credibility and validity of the findings (Saks, 2018). Data triangulation involves using multiple data sources or types to corroborate and validate research findings, ensuring a comprehensive understanding of the subject under study (Thurmond, 2001). Investigator triangulation involves multiple researchers or investigators examining the same data or research question to provide diverse perspectives and reduce bias in the research process (Archibald, 2015). Theory triangulation integrates multiple theoretical frameworks or perspectives to explore complex social phenomena (Denzin & Lincoln, 2018).

Methodological Triangulation: Combining Different Research Methods

Methodological triangulation is a strategic combination of various research methods used to study the same phenomenon, with the aim of increasing the credibility, validity, and comprehensiveness of research findings. This approach allows researchers to combine the strengths of various methodologies, including qualitative and quantitative methods, to gain a more comprehensive understanding of the research topic (Saks, 2018). Methodological triangulation involves integrating multiple research methods to overcome the limitations of individual methods and provide a more reliable basis for drawing conclusions and making inferences (Tuckett, 2005). Methodological triangulation is essential to ensure the rigour and reliability of research findings, particularly in complex and multifaceted investigations (Tuckett, 2005).

This is because no single research method can fully capture the complexities of human phenomena (Denzin & Lincoln, 2018). The text acknowledges the existence of multiple truths and realities within social contexts (Patton, 2015), embracing the notion of epistemological and ontological pluralism. This philosophical stance highlights the significance of integrating diverse research methods to obtain a holistic understanding of the research topic. Furthermore, methodological triangulation is in line with pragmatic perspectives, which recommend using multiple methods to approach research questions from different angles (Maxwell, 2013).

Methodological triangulation involves using two or more research methods to investigate a phenomenon (Denzin & Lincoln, 2018). Common research methods include interviews, observations, document analysis, surveys, and focus groups (Creswell & Creswell, 2017). Triangulating data collected from different sources and perspectives can validate findings, identify patterns, and provide a more nuanced understanding of the research topic (Patton, 2015). For instance, a qualitative study on organizational culture may involve combining interviews with observations and document analysis to investigate the cultural values, norms, and practices within an organization.

Methodological triangulation has several advantages for qualitative research. Firstly, it enhances the credibility and validity of research findings by reducing the risk of bias and increasing the reliability of data (Denzin and Lincoln, 2018). Researchers can enhance the trustworthiness of their research by corroborating findings across multiple methods (Creswell & Creswell, 2017). Methodological triangulation enables researchers to overcome the limitations of individual methods, allowing for a more comprehensive exploration of complex phenomena (Patton, 2015). For example, while interviews may provide rich qualitative data, they may be subject to interviewer bias. By complementing interviews with observations or document analysis, researchers can mitigate bias and obtain a more balanced perspective on the research topic. Methodological triangulation can help generate comprehensive and nuanced insights, enriching the depth of analysis and contributing to theory development (Maxwell, 2013). Researchers can gain a deeper understanding of the research phenomenon by triangulating data from different sources and methods. This can help uncover subtle nuances, contradictions, and patterns within the data (Patton, 2015).

Combining Phenomenology, Grounded Theory, Ethnography, and Case Study

Researchers can gain a comprehensive understanding of the research topic by effectively combining phenomenology, grounded theory, ethnography, and case study as methodological triangulation. This approach allows researchers to explore the lived experiences and perceptions of individuals, providing insights into the subjective dimensions of the phenomenon under study. Grounded theory and ethnography complement each other in research. Grounded theory facilitates the development of theoretical frameworks based on data analysis, while ethnography provides contextual insights into the cultural context and social interactions surrounding the research topic, enriching the understanding of its complexity. Grounded theory, ethnography, and case study methodologies each offer unique contributions to research. Grounded theory facilitates the development of theoretical frameworks based on data analysis. Ethnography provides contextual insights into the cultural context and social interactions surrounding the research topic, enriching the understanding of its complexity. Case study methodology provides detailed explorations of specific instances or contexts related to the phenomenon, offering concrete illustrations of real-world situations. By integrating these methodologies, researchers can triangulate data from multiple sources, perspectives, and methods, thereby enhancing the richness and validity of research findings. This approach enables a detailed analysis that captures the complexity of the research topic from various perspectives, resulting in a more comprehensive understanding.

Phenomenology is a philosophical and methodological approach that aims to uncover the lived experiences of individuals. Phenomenology involves studying how individuals experience phenomena in their conscious awareness (Tanwir et al., 2021). Positions on subjects should be made clear through hedging. The objective of phenomenology is to understand how people make meaning of their lived experiences by exploring the subjective and personal dimensions of human existence (Verdonck et al., 2010). This approach enables researchers to describe and interpret the detailed experiences, perceptions, feelings, and interpretations of individuals in specific situations, providing insights into the essence of being in the world (Guerrero-Castañeda et al., 2019). Phenomenology is a powerful tool for generating nuanced understanding of lived experiences, exploring the ways in which individuals perceive, describe, feel, and make sense of their encounters (Gao et al., 2020). Phenomenology aims to uncover the meanings and truths that are inherent in lived experiences. It sheds light on the geographies of experience and consciousness in the lived world (Popli, 2020). Phenomenological inquiry is used by researchers to uncover the essence of a subject by exploring primal, eidetic, or inceptual meanings that are often overlooked in everyday life (Pascal et al., 2010). This method enables a thorough analysis of how individuals perceive and interpret their surroundings, relationships, and personal encounters, providing valuable insights into the subjective dimensions of human existence (Ellestad, 2023). Phenomenology is useful in capturing the essence of lived experiences, offering a profound understanding of how individuals navigate and make sense of their realities (Firouzkouhi et al., 2022).

Grounded theory and phenomenology are two distinct qualitative research methodologies that can complement each other. Both methodologies have unique strengths and can provide a deeper understanding of a research topic. Grounded theory aims to develop a theory from data, while phenomenology aims to describe the essence of a phenomenon as experienced by individuals. Despite their differences, grounded theory and phenomenology can be used together to provide a more comprehensive understanding of a research topic. Grounded theory generates new insights and understandings from empirical observations, while phenomenology explores and describes the essence of lived experiences by uncovering the meanings and structures of subjective experiences (Oizumi et al., 2014; Pham et al., 2020). However, it is worth noting that phenomenology aims to explore and describe the essence of lived experiences, uncovering the meanings and structures of subjective experiences (Pham et al., 2020). Researchers can enhance the rigor and depth of their analysis by using grounded theory alongside phenomenology. This allows for the exploration of both the subjective experiences of individuals and the development of theoretical constructs grounded in data (Neergaard et al., 2009). The combination of grounded theory and phenomenology can provide a comprehensive approach to qualitative research. This approach enables researchers to capture the complexity of real-life experiences while also generating theoretical insights from empirical observations. Such integration can result in a more nuanced comprehension of intricate phenomena and contribute to the progress of knowledge across various fields of study (Austin-Keiller et al., 2023). Using both grounded theory and phenomenology in research can provide researchers with the benefits of each approach, ultimately leading to a more holistic and in-depth exploration of research topics and the lived experiences of individuals (Sale, 2008).

Ethnography involves immersing oneself in cultural contexts to study and understand the social practices, behaviors, and beliefs of a particular group or community. The focus is on observing and interacting with individuals in their natural settings to gain insights into their cultural norms, values, and everyday experiences (King et al., 2015). Ethnography enables researchers to investigate the shared meanings and practices of a particular cultural group, providing a detailed and contextual understanding of social phenomena (Maggs-Rapport, 2000). Ethnographers aim to uncover the complexities of human behavior and social interactions within a specific cultural context by engaging in participant observation and in-depth interviews (Neergaard et al., 2009). Ethnography complements phenomenology by providing researchers with a rich understanding of how individuals interpret their experiences within broader social and cultural contexts. The method of participant observation is used in ethnography to unveil the layers of meaning in everyday life, enriching phenomenological inquiry by contextualizing individual experiences within larger socio-cultural frameworks. The combination of ethnography and phenomenology enables researchers to investigate the relationship between individual experiences and cultural influences, providing a comprehensive and nuanced perspective on human behavior and social phenomena (McLellan-Lemal et al., 2017).

Case study research involves exploring contextual realities by conducting in-depth investigations of specific individuals, groups, events, or phenomena within their real-life settings. This approach enables researchers to investigate complex issues in their natural contexts, providing detailed and multifaceted explorations of the subject matter (Crowe et al., 2011). By immersing themselves in the study's context, researchers can gain a comprehensive understanding of the intricacies and dynamics of the situation being investigated. Case studies are a valuable tool for capturing the richness and complexity of real-world situations. They offer insights into the nuances and intricacies of the context under study, providing a detailed examination of specific cases. This allows researchers to explore the unique characteristics, challenges, and outcomes associated with each case (Fracheboud et al., 2022). It can reveal the contextual factors that influence individual experiences, behaviors, and decision-making processes (Mingo, 2023). Case study research is a valuable method for exploring complex and multifaceted issues, providing a rich and detailed understanding of the context in which the phenomenon occurs. Fracheboud et al. (2022) also note that this research method is particularly useful for this purpose. This method enables researchers to capture the complexities of real-life situations, providing a comprehensive perspective on the subject matter.

Case study research enhances qualitative methodologies such as ethnography by providing a thorough investigation of contextual realities within specific cases or situations (Crowe et al., 2011). This investigation offers valuable insights and information that may not be apparent through other research methods. It provides a holistic view of the context under study (Johnson et al., 1988; Mingo, 2023). Furthermore, case study research provides contextual richness that complements the broader perspectives offered by ethnography. Case studies thoroughly analyze interactions, behaviors, and outcomes within a specific context, enhancing the comprehension of social and cultural factors that influence individual experiences and behaviors. This is accomplished by concentrating on particular cases within their real-life settings. The use of case studies is a valuable tool for gaining insight into complex social phenomena (Mingo, 2023). In conclusion, the integration of case study methodology with ethnography provides a detailed and contextual exploration of specific cases, resulting in a profound understanding of the complexities and dynamics within real-life situations. This combination allows researchers to achieve a comprehensive understanding of the contextual realities that shape individual experiences and behaviors.

Triangulation is a research method that consolidates outcomes by merging multiple methods, data sources, and viewpoints to bolster credibility, validity, and depth (Carter et al., 2014). Researchers use method, investigator, theory, and data source triangulation to minimize bias, heighten result reliability, and furnish nuanced data interpretation (Dewasiri et al., 2018). Triangulation addresses individual method weaknesses and yields more robust research outcomes (Bekhet & Zauszniewski, 2012). Methodological triangulation can enhance analysis and interpretation, providing a comprehensive perspective (Heale & Forbes, 2013). It can augment the richness and clarity of the study, facilitating a deeper understanding of the phenomenon (Ajemba & Arene, 2022). Integrating various forms of evidence and perspectives can enhance the trustworthiness of research (Greyson, 2018). Using multiple methods can also increase the significance of findings (Briller et al., 2008), strengthen research trustworthiness (Hamilton & Bechtel, 1996), and promote a comprehensive understanding (Dewasiri et al., 2018). Triangulation can enhance the robustness of analysis and interpretation (Flick, 2016), facilitate thorough comprehension (Donkoh, 2023), and increase the credibility of scientific knowledge (Dewasiri & Abeysekera, 2020). It improves the reliability of quantitative methods (Hamilton & Bechtel, 1996), mitigates individual method weaknesses, and strengthens study outcomes (Bularafa & Haruna, 2022). Triangulation is a method that enhances research accuracy, credibility, and validity, particularly in qualitative social scientific research.

Practical Applications: When and How to Use Methodological Triangulation

Methodological triangulation is a strategy used to enhance the credibility, validity, and depth of research outcomes. It involves integrating diverse research methods, data sources, and perspectives to achieve a more comprehensive understanding of the research topic. Triangulation can minimize bias, increase the reliability of results, and offer a nuanced interpretation of data (Bekhet & Zauszniewski, 2012). By using method triangulation, investigator triangulation, theory triangulation, and data source triangulation, researchers can improve the analysis and interpretation of findings, providing a comprehensive view of the research topic (Murray, 1999). Triangulation also allows for the integration of multiple forms of evidence and various perspectives, resulting in more meaningful research findings (Donkoh, 2023). Furthermore, using diverse theoretical frameworks and data sources, as recommended by Bauwens (2010), can increase the reliability of research findings. Triangulation, as explained by Natow (2019), can aid in creating high-quality research models that are more applicable in real-world scenarios. It promotes a comprehensive understanding of the phenomenon under study and enhances research rigor, as noted by Shih (1998) and Bauwens (2010). Triangulation is a method that can enhance the reliability of quantitative research by reducing the weaknesses of individual methods and strengthening the overall outcome of the study. Methodological triangulation can enhance the accuracy, credibility, and validity of findings, particularly in qualitative social science research (Shih, 1998). Overall, methodological triangulation offers a flexible framework for researchers to navigate the complexities of research methodology and produce comprehensive, valid, and applicable findings across various domains of inquiry.

To use methodological triangulation effectively, researchers can follow these steps:

- Identifying the Research Question or Problem: The first step is to clearly define the research question or problem that needs to be addressed through triangulation (Bekhet & Zauszniewski, 2012; Kumar et al., 2022).
- Selecting Multiple Research Methods: The next step is to choose and combine appropriate research methods for addressing the research question, such as qualitative and quantitative methods (Kumar et al., 2022; Sahibzada et al., 2019).
- Data Collection: Collect data using selected research methods, ensuring diverse and complementary data sources (Kumar et al., 2022; Turner et al., 2016).
- Data Analysis: Analyze the data collected from various sources using the appropriate analytical techniques for each method (Kumar et al., 2022; Maggs-Rapport, 2000).
- Integration and Synthesis: Integrate and synthesize the findings from the different methods to provide a comprehensive understanding of the research question (Haq et al., 2022; Kumar et al., 2022).
- Compare and Contrast Findings: Compare and contrast the findings from different research methods to identify converging or diverging results (Kumar et al., 2022).
- Draw Conclusions: Draw conclusions based on the synthesized results and provide insights into the research problem (Jack & Raturi, 2006; Kumar et al., 2022).
- Validate Findings: Validate the findings through methodological triangulation to ensure the reliability and validity of the study (Kumar et al., 2022).
- Report Findings: Present the research findings in a clear and coherent manner, highlighting the benefits of using methodological triangulation in the study (Kumar et al., 2022).

Data Triangulation: Using Different Data Sources

Data triangulation is a research methodology that involves using multiple data sources or methods to corroborate and validate research findings, thereby strengthening the credibility and reliability of the study (Vigo et al., 2021). By combining data from different sources or approaches, such as qualitative and quantitative data, researchers can gain a more comprehensive understanding of the phenomenon under study and enhance the validity of their conclusions (Gamarel et al., 2022). Data triangulation is a method used by researchers to validate their findings and ensure that the results are reliable and robust (Prasitanarapun & Kitreerawutiwong, 2023). This approach involves comparing and contrasting data from various sources to identify patterns, trends, and discrepancies, ultimately leading to more informed and reliable research outcomes (Davies et al., 2015). Data triangulation is a valuable method for enhancing the accuracy and credibility of research findings by integrating diverse sources of data to provide a more complete and nuanced understanding of the research topic. Triangulating data from multiple sources mitigates bias, strengthens the validity of results, and offers a more comprehensive analysis of the research problem. Data triangulation is a systematic approach that involves cross-referencing information from different sources to ensure the reliability and validity of research findings (Kissling & Muthusamy, 2022). This method allows researchers to triangulate data from various sources to enhance the trustworthiness and robustness of their study (Allan et al., 2019). Data triangulation is an essential aspect of research methodology that involves using multiple data sources or methods to validate research findings and ensure the accuracy and credibility of the study (Chu & Hsu, 2021).

Integrating Observations, Interviews, and Focus Group Data

Integrating observations, interviews, and focus group data for data triangulation requires a systematic approach to combine and analyze information from diverse sources. Although there is no specific citation outlining a step-by-step process for integrating these data sources, guidance can be provided based on established research methodologies and principles of triangulation. The following is a general approach with references to relevant literature:

Establishing a Clear Research Framework: Before integrating data, it is important to clarify the research objectives, questions, and theoretical framework. This will provide a lens through which to interpret and integrate findings (Creswell & Creswell, 2017).

Ensuring systematic data collection: It is necessary to plan data collection methods for each source (observations, interviews, focus groups) based on their strengths and suitability for the research context (Patton, 2014). Consistency in data collection procedures should be maintained to enhance reliability and validity.

Thematic Analysis Across Data Sources: The task involves transcribing and organizing data from observations, interviews, and focus groups. The next step is to conduct a thematic analysis to identify common patterns, themes, and discrepancies across the different datasets, as suggested by Braun and Clarke (2006).

Comparison and Triangulation: To compare findings from each data source and identify points of convergence and divergence, it is important to triangulate data by examining how different sources corroborate or complement each other's insights, following Denzin's (1978) approach.

Data Validation and Trustworthiness: To enhance the credibility and trustworthiness of findings, data triangulation should be used. Additionally, interpretations should be validated with participants or colleagues through member checking or peer debriefing (Lincoln & Guba, 1985).

Interpretation and Synthesis: The integrated findings should be interpreted within the context of the research aims and theoretical framework. Key insights from observations, interviews, and focus groups should be synthesized to provide a comprehensive understanding of the phenomenon (Miles, et al., 2013).

Reporting findings: It is important to present findings clearly and transparently in research reports or publications. Additionally, it is necessary to discuss the strengths and limitations of data triangulation and its implications for theory, practice, and future research (Creswell, 2014).

By following these steps and drawing from established literature on qualitative research methods and triangulation, researchers can effectively integrate observations, interviews, and focus group data to gain a comprehensive understanding of the research topic.

It is important to note that data triangulation poses several challenges and considerations that are crucial for a comprehensive research methodology. To ensure consistency, it is necessary to interpret, validate, and analyze the data (Kim, 2009; Matre, 2022; Shepard et al., 2002; Youngs & Piggot-Irvine, 2011). Integrating data from diverse sources can be challenging due to differences in formats, structures, and quality. To ensure consistency and coherence across these sources, it is necessary to pay meticulous attention, particularly when dealing with heterogeneous datasets (Youngs & Piggot-Irvine, 2011). Thoughtful analysis is required for the interpretation and synthesis of findings to avoid the risk of misinterpretation or bias (Kim, 2009). Validating data across various methods and sources further complicates the process, requiring thoroughness and attention to detail (Shepard et al., 2002). Effectively addressing these challenges is essential for producing reliable data analysis and meaningful research outcomes.

Investigator Triangulation: Involving Multiple Researchers

Investigator triangulation is a qualitative research method that involves multiple investigators collaborating to analyze data, interpret findings, and ensure research credibility and reliability (Denzin & Lincoln, 2018). This approach recognizes the value of diverse perspectives and expertise in enhancing the rigor and validity of qualitative inquiry (Creswell & Creswell, 2017). Researcher triangulation involves the use of multiple investigators with different backgrounds, experiences, and areas of expertise. This approach serves to minimize bias, strengthen the trustworthiness of findings, and promote a more comprehensive understanding of the research topic (Campbell & Fiske, 1959). Furthermore, investigator triangulation enables the examination of data from various angles, facilitating richer insights, deeper analysis, and broader interpretations. Moreover, this collaborative approach promotes reflexivity and critical dialogue among researchers, leading to increased awareness of potential biases or preconceptions (Thurmond, 2001). When integrated into mixed methods research, investigator triangulation allows researchers to validate and cross-verify data through the perspectives of multiple investigators, enhancing the overall trustworthiness and comprehensiveness of the findings (Johnson & Onwuegbuzie, 2004). By using investigator triangulation, researchers can navigate the complexities of social phenomena, resulting in the production of robust, credible, and nuanced outcomes (Hamilton & Bechtel, 1996).

Collaborative research teams, comprising multiple investigators with diverse backgrounds, expertise, and experiences, are essential for achieving investigator triangulation. This approach enhances the rigor, credibility, and validity of qualitative inquiry (Denzin & Lincoln, 2018). Collaborative teams can enrich the research process by involving researchers with different viewpoints, skills, and methodological approaches. This can lead to comprehensive analyses and nuanced interpretations of data. Collaborative efforts among team members can facilitate a deeper understanding of the research topic and minimize potential biases or preconceptions (Creswell & Creswell, 2017). It is important to maintain reflexivity and engage in critical dialogue to navigate social phenomena more effectively, resulting in robust and credible findings.

In the context of investigator triangulation, managing biases is crucial, and reflexivity serves as a vital tool. Reflexivity involves reflecting on one's own assumptions, biases, and preconceptions, and plays a pivotal role in ensuring the integrity and credibility of qualitative research. By engaging in reflexive practices, researchers can critically examine their own positions, perspectives, and influences on the research process. This technique aims to minimise the impact of biases on data collection, analysis, and interpretation (Gupta & Sharma, 2006). Reflexivity encourages researchers to be self-aware, enabling them to openly and rigorously acknowledge and address their own biases throughout the research process (Alvesson & Sköldberg, 2009). In the context of investigator triangulation, reflexivity can promote open dialogue and critical self-reflection among team members. This enhances the rigor and trustworthiness of research outcomes (Denzin & Lincoln, 2018). By actively managing biases through reflexivity, researchers can maintain the integrity and validity of investigator triangulation. This ultimately contributes to the generation of robust and credible qualitative findings.

Theory Triangulation: Utilizing Multiple Theoretical Frameworks

Theory triangulation is a methodological approach widely used in qualitative research to enhance the depth and rigor of investigations by integrating multiple theoretical frameworks or perspectives to explore complex social phenomena (Denzin & Lincoln, 2018). This approach is based on the recognition that social phenomena are multifaceted and can be better understood when examined through diverse theoretical lenses (Maxwell, 2013). Researchers use theory triangulation to expand their analytical scope, deepen their understanding of the research phenomenon, and improve the quality of their research outcomes (Creswell & Creswell, 2017; Patton, 2015).

The purpose of theory triangulation is to integrate complementary theories to navigate the complexities of the research topic more effectively (Patton, 2015). This integration enables researchers to explore the research phenomenon from various angles, leading to a more nuanced interpretation of data and ultimately improving the validity of findings (Creswell & Creswell, 2017). For example, when studying the experiences of marginalized communities, researchers may use critical race theory to analyze systemic discrimination and oppression, and feminist theory to explore gender dynamics within these communities. By combining insights from different theoretical perspectives, researchers can gain a more comprehensive understanding of the research phenomenon, enriching the depth of analysis and interpretation.

Furthermore, theory triangulation is a valuable framework for designing and conducting mixed methods research. Mixed methods research combines qualitative and quantitative data collection and analysis techniques to provide a more holistic understanding of research questions. Theory triangulation enables researchers to approach research questions from multiple angles by drawing on diverse theoretical perspectives. This enhances the richness and complexity of the research design. For instance, in a study that analyzes the effect of educational interventions on student achievement, researchers may use socio-cultural theory to explore the impact of social factors on learning outcomes. They may also incorporate cognitive psychology to investigate individual differences in cognitive processes. Integrating theories from different disciplines can lead to a more comprehensive understanding of the research phenomenon, resulting in more robust and nuanced research outcomes.

However, the use of theory triangulation requires careful consideration and critical reflexivity throughout the research process to ensure the integrity and credibility of the findings. Reflexivity involves reflecting on one's own assumptions, biases, and theoretical orientations and critically examining their potential impact on the research process (Finlay, 2002; Gupta & Sharma, 2006). To enhance the trustworthiness of research findings, researchers must engage in reflexivity to minimize potential subjective evaluations and biased language (Gupta & Sharma, 2006). Technical terms and abbreviations should be explained when first used, and the language used in research should be formal, clear, and objective (Gupta & Sharma, 2006).

In practice, theory triangulation involves identifying, selecting, and integrating multiple theoretical frameworks or perspectives that offer complementary insights into the research topic. The selected theories must be compatible and coherent to enhance the depth and breadth of the analysis. For instance, in a study investigating the effect of environmental policies on community health, researchers may use ecological systems theory to analyze the interplay between individuals and their surroundings. Additionally, they may incorporate social determinants of health theory to explore the impact of social factors on health outcomes. By synthesizing insights from various disciplines and theoretical perspectives, researchers can develop a more comprehensive and nuanced understanding of the research phenomenon. This contributes to the advancement of scholarly understanding across disciplines (Choi & Pak, 2006; Klein, 2010).

Theory triangulation, when integrated into research practices, contributes to the richness and robustness of qualitative research by illuminating different viewpoints and increasing the depth of analysis (Kashaev et al., 2015; Zwaan et al., 2019). Researchers can broaden their analytical scope, deepen their understanding of the research phenomenon, and enhance the quality and credibility of their research outcomes by leveraging theory triangulation.

Researchers can gain a comprehensive understanding of a research phenomenon and improve the validity of findings by systematically combining multiple theoretical frameworks through theory integration in triangulation (Ambjørn et al., 2005; Hoque et al., 2013). This method enables a nuanced exploration of the research phenomenon and provides a valuable framework for designing mixed methods research (Cooperman et al., 2017). By synthesizing perspectives, researchers can use diverse theoretical viewpoints to enrich the depth and breadth of analysis, ultimately contributing to the richness and robustness of qualitative research (Denzin & Lincoln, 2018; Maxwell, 2013; Patton, 2015). In parallel, interdisciplinary research involves integrating insights from multiple disciplines to address complex problems. This approach offers valuable interdisciplinary insights that enrich the understanding of research phenomena (Choi & Pak, 2006; Klein, 2010). It enhances creativity and innovation, allowing researchers to develop novel interpretations and advance scientific understanding across disciplines (Nowotny et al., 2001).

Interdisciplinary research integrates insights from multiple disciplines to address complex problems and advance knowledge (Klein, 2010). In qualitative research, leveraging diverse theoretical frameworks from various disciplines offers valuable interdisciplinary insights that can enrich the understanding of research phenomena (Choi & Pak, 2006). Researchers can bring different perspectives to their research questions by drawing on theories from fields such as sociology, psychology, anthropology, and cultural studies (Patton, 2015). This interdisciplinary approach enables them to explore the multifaceted nature of phenomena and consider them from various angles, leading to a more comprehensive understanding (Maxwell, 2013). Integrating diverse theoretical frameworks can foster creativity and innovation in research design and analysis (Nowotny et al., 2001). By synthesizing insights from different disciplines, researchers can develop novel interpretations and generate new knowledge (Klein, 2010). Overall, the use of diverse theoretical frameworks in interdisciplinary research can enrich and deepen qualitative research, leading to a better understanding of scholarly concepts across different fields.

CHALLENGES AND CRITICISMS OF TRIANGULATION

Triangulation is a crucial method in research, but it faces several challenges and criticisms that require careful consideration to ensure the integrity of research outcomes. One of the primary hurdles is methodological complexity, which demands meticulous planning, coordination, and execution to effectively integrate multiple methods, data sources, or theoretical frameworks (Flick, 2018). The challenge posed by triangulation is its resource intensiveness, which demands significant investments in time, funding, and expertise to manage diverse data sources and conduct multiple analyses (Golafshani, 2003). Integration issues arise when reconciling conflicting evidence from different sources or methods, requiring careful navigation of discrepancies to present coherent and credible conclusions (Denzin, 1978).

Furthermore, triangulation is not impervious to bias, which may introduce new biases or reinforce existing ones throughout the process (Jick, 1979). Additionally, interpretation challenges further complicate triangulation, requiring researchers to navigate the unique context, assumptions, and limitations of each method or data source to avoid misinterpretation of complex data (Creswell & Plano Clark, 2018). Critics argue that triangulation, while aiming to enhance the validity of research findings, does not inherently guarantee validity. This is because the mere combination of methods or data sources does not ensure greater accuracy or truthfulness if the individual components are flawed or insufficiently rigorous (Denzin, 1978).

Ethical considerations are important in the triangulation process, with strict adherence to ethical guidelines and principles required for participant confidentiality, data security, and informed consent (Bryman, 2006). It is important to balance quantitative measures with qualitative insights to avoid overlooking the richness and depth of qualitative data. Achieving a balance between quantitative and qualitative approaches is essential for comprehensive triangulation (Teddlie & Tashakkori, 2009).

Qualitative research presents unique challenges, which are further complicated by the intricate nature of qualitative inquiry. Triangulation can introduce complexities in research design, data collection, and analysis, especially when integrating multiple theoretical frameworks or perspectives (Gergen et al., 2015). Paradigmatic assumptions or worldviews can influence the selection and interpretation of methods, adding layers of complexity to the process (Creswell & Miller, 2000). In qualitative data collection and analysis, ensuring consistency and reliability across diverse methods and sources is crucial due to its subjective nature (Creswell & Plano Clark, 2018). Ethical considerations, such as participant confidentiality and informed consent, require careful attention when triangulating qualitative data from different sources (Bryman, 2006).

To navigate the multifaceted challenges in triangulation, meticulous planning, methodological transparency, and continuous reflexivity throughout the research process are required. Triangulation remains a valuable methodology for enriching the credibility, validity, and depth of research findings across diverse disciplinary landscapes and research contexts, despite its inherent complexities. By addressing the challenges and criticisms of triangulation objectively, researchers can use its strengths to gain insights and generate robust qualitative research outcomes.

BEST PRACTICES FOR IMPLEMENTING TRIANGULATION

To optimize the effectiveness and rigor of triangulation in qualitative research, researchers should incorporate best practices and strategies. This will generate robust and reliable research outcomes.

Implementing triangulation requires careful planning, flexibility, and adherence to best practices to ensure the validity and reliability of research findings. To ensure a successful process, it is crucial to establish a clear plan that outlines the objectives, methods, and data sources involved (Patton, 2015). Researchers should articulate the research questions, hypotheses, or objectives that triangulation aims to address, ensuring alignment with the overarching research goals (Creswell & Creswell, 2017). Defining the methods and data sources to be triangulated, along with the criteria for selecting them, enhances clarity and coherence in the triangulation process (Denzin & Lincoln, 2018).

Furthermore, it is crucial to be flexible and adaptable when facing unforeseen challenges and opportunities in the field (Johnson & Onwuegbuzie, 2004). Researchers should be open to modifying the triangulation approach based on emerging insights, changing circumstances, or unexpected findings encountered during data collection or analysis (Creswell & Creswell, 2017). Researchers should be responsive to feedback from participants, collaborators, or stakeholders, incorporating their perspectives and adjusting triangulation strategies accordingly (Maxwell, 2013). Embracing iterative cycles of data collection, analysis, and reflection enables researchers to refine and enrich triangulation strategies over time, fostering continuous improvement and deeper insights into the research phenomenon (Creswell & Plano Clark, 2018).

In addition to these practices, there are several strategies that can enhance the effectiveness of triangulation in qualitative research. It is important to document the triangulation process at each step to ensure transparency and replicability (Renz et al., 2018). Integrating qualitative and quantitative data can provide a comprehensive understanding of the research phenomenon (Kessler et al., 2012). Using computerized text analysis software can aid in the analysis of qualitative data and management of large datasets (Wray et al., 2007). Employing a multi-theoretical approach enables a more nuanced examination of complex phenomena across different organizational levels (Jones, 2023). Additionally, researchers should prioritize the well-being of those involved in emotionally challenging research by providing adequate support and resources. Incorporating multiple research instruments, such as interviews and questionnaires, can enhance the credibility of research results (Creswell & Creswell, 2017).

ETHICAL CONSIDERATIONS

The use of triangulation in qualitative research raises ethical considerations that are crucial for maintaining the integrity, validity, and fairness of the research process (Farmer et al., 2006; Karnieli-Miller et al., 2022). Preserving participants' confidentiality and privacy is of utmost importance when integrating data from multiple sources. Therefore, researchers must handle the collected data with sensitivity and caution to maintain participants' trust (Sands & Roer-Strier, 2006). Additionally, researcher reflexivity is crucial, as it requires researchers to critically assess their biases, assumptions, and potential influence on the research process and results (Wray et al., 2007).

Transparency and accountability are crucial ethical aspects to consider in triangulation (Karnieli-Miller et al., 2022). Researchers should document their triangulation methods, data sources, and analytical procedures meticulously to ensure the reproducibility and credibility of the research findings (Karnieli-Miller et al., 2022). Maintaining transparency requires reporting any limitations and challenges encountered during the triangulation process to provide a comprehensive understanding of the research (Bryman, 2016; Karnieli-Miller et al., 2022).

Additionally, ethical considerations extend to the fair and respectful treatment of participants and stakeholders throughout the research process (Liamputtong, 2013; Mertens, 2015). Researchers should prioritize the well-being and autonomy of individuals involved in the study. They should provide opportunities for participants to withdraw from the study at any time without consequences (Mertens, 2015). Additionally, researchers should engage with participants and stakeholders in a culturally sensitive manner. They should recognize and respect diverse perspectives, values, and experiences (Liamputtong, 2013). Maintaining transparency and integrity in data collection, analysis, and reporting is essential to enhance the credibility and trustworthiness of research outcomes (Creswell & Creswell, 2017; Denzin & Lincoln, 2018). Adhering to ethical principles and standards in triangulation allows researchers to maintain the integrity of the research process, protect the rights of participants, and contribute to the advancement of knowledge in an ethical and responsible manner.

STUDIES ILLUSTRATING THE POWER OF TRIANGULATION

Triangulation is a methodological approach that integrates multiple perspectives, methods, and data sources to enhance the credibility, validity, and richness of research findings. Although there are a lot of studies used triangulation in their research, this section presents sample case studies that illustrate the diverse applications and importance of triangulation across various research domains. These studies, ranging from healthcare to education, social sciences to mathematics, demonstrate how triangulation enhances understanding of complex phenomena and supports evidence-based decision-making. Each case study illustrates how researchers have used triangulation to overcome methodological challenges, validate findings, and generate robust insights. This text explores the versatility and efficacy of triangulation as a cornerstone of rigorous and comprehensive research methodologies.

Munhall (1988) emphasizes the importance of ethical considerations in qualitative research, highlighting the role of triangulation in ensuring the validity and reliability of data. Triangulation is a methodological approach used to enhance trustworthiness by corroborating findings from multiple sources or methods. Researchers can mitigate bias, validate interpretations, and strengthen the credibility of their research outcomes by triangulating data from various perspectives.

Bekhet and Zauszniewski (2012) discuss methodological triangulation as an approach to understanding data in their article. The significance of triangulation in qualitative research is emphasised as a means to enhance the comprehensiveness and depth of understanding. By integrating multiple data sources or methods, researchers can gain insights from diverse perspectives, identify convergent or divergent patterns, and develop a more nuanced interpretation of the phenomenon under study.

Campbell et al. (2018) examine the challenges of assessing triangulation across methodologies, methods, and stakeholder groups in their study published in the American Journal of Evaluation. They discuss the complexities involved in interpreting convergent and divergent data obtained through triangulation. The importance of triangulation in reconciling discrepancies, validating findings, and capturing diverse perspectives is highlighted in the study, despite the inherent complexities and potential for interpretation bias.

Wardina and Sudihartinih (2019) used triangulation to assess students' mathematical connection ability in the linear function topic. The researchers aimed to obtain a comprehensive understanding of students' mathematical proficiency and conceptual grasp by triangulating data from multiple assessment methods, including tests, observations, and interviews. Triangulation enabled the researchers to corroborate findings across different data sources, validate interpretations, and enhance the reliability of their assessment outcomes.

Noble and Heale (2019) offer examples of triangulation in research, highlighting its importance in improving the credibility and validity of qualitative studies. Triangulation is presented as a methodological approach to support findings, validate interpretations, and ensure the reliability of research outcomes. The article demonstrates the application of triangulation in different research contexts to integrate diverse perspectives, reduce bias, and promote a more comprehensive understanding of complex phenomena.

Solano (2020) examines the use of triangulation to advance research on public service interpreting through qualitative case study methodologies. Triangulation enhances the trustworthiness of qualitative research by validating interpretations, corroborating findings, and ensuring the reliability of data. The study emphasises the significance of triangulation in capturing the intricacies and subtleties of public service interpreting practices, thereby contributing to the advancement of knowledge in the field.

Cassidy et al. (2022) employ a learning health system framework to investigate COVID-19 pandemic planning and response at a Canadian Health Centre. The study aims to validate findings, identify convergent or divergent patterns, and inform evidence-based decision-making through triangulation of data from various sources, including interviews, surveys, and document analysis. Triangulation enables the researchers to integrate insights from multiple stakeholders, capture diverse perspectives, and enhance the comprehensiveness of their analysis.

Curtin and Fossey (2007) offer guidelines for evaluating the trustworthiness of qualitative studies, highlighting the significance of triangulation in ensuring methodological rigor and credibility. Triangulation is a means of validating interpretations, corroborating findings, and enhancing the reliability of qualitative research outcomes. The guidelines provide practical strategies for implementing triangulation throughout the research process, from data collection to analysis and interpretation.

Sandelowski (1995) uses the metaphor of triangles and crystals to explain the concept of triangulation in qualitative research. Triangulation is a methodological approach to combining data from multiple sources or methods, which enhances the validity and reliability of research findings. The article demonstrates the versatility and flexibility of triangulation in qualitative research, highlighting its applicability across diverse research contexts and methodologies.

CONCLUSION

This chapter emphasizes the significance of triangulation in qualitative research to enhance the credibility, validity, and depth of research findings. It explores the multifaceted dimensions of triangulation, from its theoretical foundations to its practical applications across diverse research contexts. Triangulation is a methodological approach used by researchers to validate, corroborate, and enrich research outcomes by integrating multiple methods, data sources, and perspectives.

The primary role of triangulation is to provide a comprehensive understanding of complex research phenomena (Patton, 2015). Triangulating data from different sources and methodologies can provide a more nuanced and holistic perspective, capturing the intricacies inherent in the research topic (Creswell & Creswell, 2017). This approach not only enriches the depth of analysis but also enhances the validity and reliability of research findings by corroborating evidence across different sources (Denzin & Lincoln, 2018).

Triangulation is an essential tool for enhancing methodological rigor in qualitative inquiry by mitigating the limitations of individual methods (Creswell & Plano Clark, 2018). Researchers can triangulate data by integrating multiple methods, such as interviews, observations, and document analysis, to compensate for the weaknesses or biases inherent in each method (Johnson & Onwuegbuzie, 2004). The use of triangulation enhances the internal validity of the research and promotes a more comprehensive understanding of the research phenomenon (Maxwell, 2013).

Furthermore, it encourages researchers to be reflexive, critically reflecting on their biases, assumptions, and interpretations throughout the research process (Wray et al., 2007). Acknowledging and addressing potential sources of bias can enhance the transparency, credibility, and trustworthiness of research findings (Polit & Beck, 2017). Reflexivity also extends to the ethical dimensions of research, ensuring that researchers uphold principles of integrity, respect, and fairness in their interactions with participants and stakeholders (Bryman, 2016; Munhall, 1988).

The relevance of triangulation persists due to its adaptability and versatility across evolving research paradigms and methodologies. Future directions in triangulation research may involve exploring innovative approaches to data integration, harnessing the potential of big data analytics and machine learning, and addressing ethical considerations in increasingly complex research environments. Karnieli-Miller et al. (2022) suggest these possibilities. By embracing triangulation as a guiding principle, researchers can navigate the intricacies of qualitative inquiry with confidence. This generates robust and rich insights that contribute to the advancement of knowledge in their respective fields.

REFERENCES

Ajemba, N. & Arene, N. (2022). Possible advantages that may be enhanced with the adoption of research triangulation or mixed methodology. *Magna Scientia Advanced Research and Reviews*, 6(1), 58-61. 10.30574/msarr.2022.6.1.0066

Allan, S., McLeod, H. J., Bradstreet, S., Beedie, S. A., Moir, B., Gleeson, J., Farhall, J., Morton, E., & Gumley, A. (2019). Understanding implementation of a digital self-monitoring intervention for relapse prevention in psychosis: Protocol for a mixed method process evaluation. *JMIR Research Protocols*, 8(12), e15634. 10.2196/1563431821154

Alvesson, M., & Sköldberg, K. (2009). Reflexive methodology: New vistas for qualitative research. *Sage (Atlanta, Ga.)*.

Ambjørn, J., Görlich, A., Jurkiewicz, J., & Loll, R. (2012). Nonperturbative quantum gravity. *Physics Reports*, 519(4-5), 127–210. 10.1016/j.physrep.2012.03.007

Ambjørn, J., Jurkiewicz, J., & Loll, R. (2005). Semiclassical universe from first principles. *Physics Letters. [Part B]*, 607(3-4), 205–213. 10.1016/j.physletb.2004.12.067

Archibald, M. (2015). Investigator triangulation. *Journal of Mixed Methods Research*, 10(3), 228–250. 10.1177/1558689815570092

Ashour, S. (2018). Methodological pluralism in technology-based services: A pluralist perspective of triangulation. *Journal of Services Marketing*, 32(1), 86–96.

Austin-Keiller, A., Park, M., Yang, S., Mayo, N., Fellows, L., & Brouillette, M. (2023). "alone, there is nobody": A qualitative study of the lived experience of loneliness in older men living with HIV. *PLoS One*, 18(4), e0277399. 10.1371/journal.pone.027739937058482

Bauwens, A. (2010). The use of method triangulation in probation research. *European Journal of Probation*, 2(2), 39–52. 10.1177/206622031000200204

Bekhet, A., & Zauszniewski, J. (2012). Methodological triangulation: An approach to understanding data. *Nurse Researcher*, 20(2), 40–43. 10.7748/nr2012.11.20.2.40.c944223316537

Braun, V., & Clarke, V. (2006). Using thematic analysis in psychology. *Qualitative Research in Psychology*, 3(2), 77–101. 10.1191/1478088706qp063oa

Briller, S., Meert, K., Schim, S., Thurston, C., & Kabel, A. (2008). Implementing a triangulation protocol in bereavement research: A methodological discussion. *Omega*, 57(3), 245–260. 10.2190/OM.57.3.b18837173

Bryman, A. (2006). Integrating quantitative and qualitative research: How is it done? *Qualitative Research*, 6(1), 97–113. 10.1177/1468794106058877

Bryman, A. (2016). *Social research methods*. Oxford University Press.

Budge, S. L., Adelson, J. L., & Howard, K. A. S. (2012). Anxiety and depression in transgender individuals: The roles of transition status, loss, social support, and coping. *Journal of Consulting and Clinical Psychology*, 80(5), 860–873. 10.1037/a002802723398495

Bularafa, B., & Haruna, M. (2022). Multi-methods approach in entrepreneurship research: Triangulation in action. *Journal of Economics Finance and Management Studies*, 05(12), 3649–3655. 10.47191/jefms/v5-i12-23

Campbell, D., & Fiske, D. (1959). Convergent and discriminant validation by the multitrait-multimethod matrix. *Psychological Bulletin*, 56(2), 81–105. 10.1037/h004601613634291

Campbell, J. L., Quincy, C., Osserman, J., & Pedersen, O. K. (2013). Assessing Triangulation Across Methodologies, Methods, and Stakeholder Groups: The Joys, Woes, and Politics of Interpreting Convergent and Divergent Data. *The American Journal of Evaluation*, 34(1), 8–34.

Cassidy, C., & Durbin, C. (2022). Creating a Culture of Inquiry: A Case Study of Action Research in a Primary School. *Research in Education*, 94(1), 19–35. 10.1177/0034523715591017

Cassidy, C., Sim, M., Somerville, M., Crowther, D., Sinclair, D., Elliott Rose, A., Burgess, S., Best, S., & Curran, J. A. (2022). Using a learning health system framework to examine COVID-19 pandemic planning and response at a Canadian Health Centre. *PLoS One*, 17(9), e0273149. 10.1371/journal.pone.027314936103510

Charmaz, K. (2014). Constructing grounded theory. *Sage (Atlanta, Ga.)*.

Chu, A., & Hsu, C. (2021). Principal–agent relationship within a cruise supply chain model for china. *Journal of Hospitality & Tourism Research (Washington, D.C.)*, 45(6), 998–1021. 10.1177/1096348020985328

Clifford, N., Cope, M., Gillespie, T., French, S., & Valentine, G. (2010). Getting Started in Geographical Research: how this book can help. *Key methods in geography*, 1(1).

Cooperman, J., Lee, K., & Miller, J. (2017). A second look at transition amplitudes in (2 + 1)-dimensional causal dynamical triangulations. *Classical and Quantum Gravity*, 34(11), 115008. 10.1088/1361-6382/aa6d38

Creswell, J. W. (2013). *Qualitative Inquiry and Research Design: Choosing among Five Approaches.* Sage Publications.

Creswell, J. W. (2014). *Research design: Qualitative, quantitative, and mixed methods approaches.* Sage publications.

Creswell, J. W., & Creswell, J. D. (2017). *Research design: Qualitative, quantitative, and mixed methods approaches.* Sage publications.

Creswell, J. W., & Miller, D. L. (2000). Determining validity in qualitative inquiry. *Theory into Practice*, 39(3), 124–130. 10.1207/s15430421tip3903_2

Creswell, J. W., & Plano Clark, V. L. (2018). *Designing and conducting mixed methods research* (3rd ed.). SAGE Publications.

Crowe, S., Cresswell, K., Robertson, A., Huby, G., Avery, A., & Sheikh, A. (2011). The case study approach. *BMC Medical Research Methodology*, 11(1), 100. Advance online publication. 10.1186/1471-2288-11-10021707982

Curtin, M., & Fossey, E. (2007). Appraising the trustworthiness of qualitative studies: Guidelines for occupational therapists. *Australian Occupational Therapy Journal*, 54(2), 88–94. 10.1111/j.1440-1 630.2007.00661.x

Davies, L., Batalden, P., Davidoff, F., Stevens, D., & Ogrinc, G. (2015). The squire guidelines: an evaluation from the field, 5 years post release: table 1. *BMJ Quality & Safety*, 24(12), 769–775. 10.1136/bmjqs-2015-00411626089206

Denzin, N. K. (1978). *The Research Act: A Theoretical Introduction to Sociological Methods*. McGraw-Hill.

Denzin, N. K., & Lincoln, Y. S. (2018). *The Sage handbook of qualitative research*. Sage.

Dewasiri, N., & Abeysekera, N. (2020). Corporate social responsibility and dividend policy in Sri Lankan firms: A data triangulation approach. *Journal of Public Affairs*, 22(1), e2283. Advance online publication. 10.1002/pa.2283

Donkoh, S. (2023). Application of triangulation in qualitative research. *Journal of Applied Biotechnology & Bioengineering*, 10(1), 6–9. 10.15406/jabb.2023.10.00319

Downward, P., & Mearman, A. (2006). Retroduction as mixed-methods triangulation in economic research: Reorienting economics into social science. *Cambridge Journal of Economics*, 31(1), 77–99. 10.1093/cje/bel009

Dźwigoł, H. (2018). Quantitative methods in the triangulation process. *Proceedings of the IISES Annual Conference*, 53-68. 10.20472/IAC.2018.035.012

Edmondson, A. C., & McManus, S. E. (2007). Methodological fit in management field research. *Academy of Management Review*, 32(4), 1246–1264. 10.5465/amr.2007.26586086

Eisenhardt, K. M. (1989). Building theories from case study research. *Academy of Management Review*, 14(4), 532–550. 10.2307/258557

Ellestad, A., Beymer, L. L., & Villegas, S. (2023). The lived experiences of individuals with high-functioning autism during the job interview process: A phenomenological study. *Journal of Employment Counseling*, 60(4), 192–209. 10.1002/joec.12212

Erkanlı, İ. (2024). *Multicultural Education: An International Guide to Research, Policies, and Programs* (Vol. 2). Frontiers Media SA. https://doi.org/10.3389/978-2-88970-831-0

Fielding, N. (2012). Triangulation and mixed methods designs. *Journal of Mixed Methods Research*, 6(2), 124–136. 10.1177/1558689812437101

Finlay, L. (2002). Negotiating the swamp: The opportunity and challenge of reflexivity in research practice. *Qualitative Research*, 2(2), 209–230. 10.1177/146879410200200205

Firouzkouhi, M., Kako, M., Alimohammadi, N., Arbabi-Sarjou, A., Nouraei, T., & Abdollahimohammad, A. (2022). Lived experiences of covid-19 patients with pulmonary involvement: A hermeneutic phenomenology. *Clinical Nursing Research*, 31(4), 747–757. 10.1177/10547738221078898 35168379

Flick, U. (2018). *The SAGE handbook of qualitative data collection*. SAGE Publications. 10.4135/9781526416070

Fracheboud, T., Stiefel, F., & Bourquin, C. (2022). The fragility of trust between patients and oncologists: A multiple case study. *Palliative & Supportive Care*, 21(4), 585–593. 10.1017/S147895152200075X35770349

Freshwater, D. (2022). Methodological pluralism and triangulation in qualitative research: Paradigmatic contests and debates. *Qualitative Health Research*, 32(7), 1042–1056.

Gamarel, K., farrales, , Venegas, L., Dilworth, S. E., Coffin, L. S., Neilands, T. B., Johnson, M. O., & Koester, K. A. (2022). A mixed-methods study of relationship stigma and well-being among sexual and gender minority couples. *The Journal of Social Issues*, 79(1), 232–263. 10.1111/josi.1255237346391

Gao, W., Plummer, V., & McKenna, L. (2020). Using metaphor method to interpret and understand meanings of international operating room nurses' experiences in organ procurement surgery. *Journal of Clinical Nursing*, 29(23-24), 4604–4613. 10.1111/jocn.1549632956510

Gergen, K. J., Josselson, R., & Freeman, M. (2015). The promises of qualitative inquiry. *The American Psychologist*, 70(1), 1–9. 10.1037/a003859725581004

Golafshani, N. (2003). Understanding Reliability and Validity in Qualitative Research. *The Qualitative Report*, 8(4), 597–607.

Guba, E. G. (1981). *Effective Evaluation: Improving the Usefulness of Evaluation Results through Responsive and Naturalistic Approaches*. Jossey-Bass.

Guerrero-Castañeda, R., Menezes, T., & Prado, M. (2019). Phenomenology in nursing research: Reflection based on heidegger's hermeneutics. *Escola Anna Nery*, 23(4), e20190059. Advance online publication. 10.1590/2177-9465-ean-2019-0059

Gupta, A., & Sharma, M. (2006). Reflexivity: A concept and its meanings for practitioners involved in psychological research. *Indian Journal of Clinical Psychology*, 33(1), 20–26.

Hamilton, D., & Bechtel, G. (1996). Research implications for alternative health therapies. *Nursing Forum*, 31(1), 6–10. 10.1111/j.1744-6198.1996.tb00964.x8700752

Haq, M., Qazi, W., & Khan, S. (2022). Synthesizing qualitative and quantitative research evidence using triangulation: A systematic literature review. *Journal of Mixed Methods Research*, 16(1), 95–110.

Heale, R., & Forbes, D. (2013). Understanding triangulation in research. *Evidence-Based Nursing*, 16(4), 98–98. 10.1136/eb-2013-10149423943076

Hesse-Biber, S. N. (2010). *Mixed Methods Research: Merging Theory with Practice*. Guilford Press.

Hoque, Z., Covaleski, M., & Gooneratne, T. (2013). Theoretical triangulation and pluralism in research methods in organizational and accounting research. *Accounting, Auditing & Accountability Journal*, 26(7), 1170–1198. 10.1108/AAAJ-May-2012-01024

Hussein, A. (2009). The use of triangulation in social sciences research. *Journal of Comparative Social Work*, 4(1), 106–117. 10.31265/jcsw.v4i1.48

Jack, D. C., & Raturi, V. P. (2006). A methodological framework for combining qualitative and quantitative techniques. Journal of Organizational Culture. *Communications and Conflict*, 10(2), 77–90.

Jick, T. D. (1979). Mixing Qualitative and Quantitative Methods: Triangulation in Action. *Administrative Science Quarterly*, 24(4), 602–611. 10.2307/2392366

Johnson, M., Foley, M., Suengas, A., & Raye, C. (1988). Phenomenal characteristics of memories for perceived and imagined autobiographical events. *Journal of Experimental Psychology. General*, 117(4), 371–376. 10.1037/0096-3445.117.4.3712974863

Johnson, R., & Onwuegbuzie, A. (2004). Mixed methods research: A research paradigm whose time has come. *Educational Researcher*, 33(7), 14–26. 10.3102/0013189X033007014

Jones, A., Hartley, J., & Jones, N. (2023). Validity of the UCEEM in use: How does it triangulate with qualitative data in measuring the effect of an educational intervention? *Journal of Medical Education and Curricular Development*, 10. Advance online publication. 10.1177/23821205231202335377865574

Joseph, J., Sankar, D., & Nambiar, D. (2021). The burden of mental health illnesses in kerala: A secondary analysis of reported data from 2002 to 2018. *BMC Public Health*, 21(1), 2264. Advance online publication. 10.1186/s12889-021-12289-034895187

Karnieli-Miller, O., Strier, R., Pessach-Gelblum, L., Zimhony, A., Shalev, H., Weiser, M., & Bentwich, M. E. (2022). Digital ethnography in health care: Crossing the boundary between online and offline healthcare settings. *The Milbank Quarterly*, 100(1), 254–284.

Kashaev, R., Luo, F., & Vartanov, G. (2015). A TQFT of Turaev–Viro type on shaped triangulations. *Annales Henri Poincaré*, 17(5), 1109–1143. 10.1007/s00023-015-0427-8

Kessler, M. M., Reese, R. J., & Eggett, D. L. (2012). Triangulation: A methodological discussion. *Nurse Researcher*, 19(1), 30–37.

Kim, D. S. (2009). A Single Beta-Complex Solves All Geometry Problems in a Molecule. *Sixth International Symposium on Voronoi Diagrams*, 254-260. 10.1109/ISVD.2009.41

Kissling, E., & Muthusamy, T. (2022). Exploring boundedness for concept-based instruction of aspect: Evidence from learning the Spanish preterite and imperfect. *Modern Language Journal*, 106(2), 371–392. 10.1111/modl.12778

Kumar, A., Shrivastav, S. K., & Bhattacharyya, S. (2022). Measuring strategic fit using big data analytics in the automotive supply chain: A data source triangulation-based research. *International Journal of Productivity and Performance Management*, 72(10), 2977–2999. 10.1108/IJPPM-11-2021-0672

Kuo, C. C., Deng, L., Creighton, J., Lee, E., & Wehrly, S. E. (2021). Predicting doctorate completion for international students in counselor education programs. *Journal of Multicultural Counseling and Development*, 49(3), 211–225. 10.1002/jmcd.12181

Lincoln, Y. S., & Guba, E. G. (1985). *Naturalistic inquiry.* Sage Publications. 10.1016/0147-1767(85)90062-8

Longhurst, R. (2016). Semi-structured interviews and focus groups. In Clifford, N., Cope, M., Gillespie, T., & French, S. (Eds.), *Key Methods in Geography* (3rd ed., pp. 143–156). SAGE.

Löwe, B., & Kerkhove, B. (2019). Methodological Triangulation in Empirical Philosophy (of Mathematics). In Aberdein, A., & Inglis, M. (Eds.), *Advances in Experimental Philosophy of Logic and Mathematics* (pp. 15–38). Bloomsbury Methuen Drama., 10.5040/9781350039049.0005

Maggs-Rapport, F. (2000). The use of triangulation in a study of older people with depression. *International Journal of Geriatric Psychiatry*, 15(4), 354–360.

Matre, M. (2022). Speech-to-text technology as an inclusive approach: Lower secondary teachers' experiences. *Nordisk Tidsskrift for Pedagogikk Og Kritikk*, 8(0), 233. 10.23865/ntpk.v8.3436

Maxwell, J. A. (2013). *Qualitative Research Design: An Interactive Approach*. Sage Publications.

Miles, M. B., Huberman, A. M., & Saldana, J. (2013). *Qualitative data analysis: A methods sourcebook.* Sage publications.

Mingo, V., & Mistry, J. (2023). Home as the third place: Stories of movement among immigrant caregivers in an intercultural Chilean city. *Ethos (Berkeley, Calif.)*, 52(1), 68–88. 10.1111/etho.12415

Munhall, P. (1988). Ethical considerations in qualitative research. *Western Journal of Nursing Research*, 10(3), 275–284.3394317

Murray, J. S. (1999). Methodological triangulation in a study of social support for siblings of children with cancer. *Journal of Pediatric Oncology Nursing*, 16(4), 194–200. 10.1177/104345429901600440410565108

Natow, R. S. (2019). The use of triangulation in qualitative studies employing elite interviews. *Qualitative Research*, 20(2), 160–173. 10.1177/1468794119830077

Neergaard, M., Olesen, F., Andersen, R., & Søndergaard, J. (2009). Qualitative description – the poor cousin of health research? *BMC Medical Research Methodology*, 9(1), 52. Advance online publication. 10.1186/1471-2288-9-5219607668

Noble, H., & Heale, R. (2019). Triangulation in research, with examples. *Evidence-Based Nursing*, 22(2), 67–68. 10.1136/ebnurs-2019-10314531201209

Oizumi, M., Albantakis, L., & Tononi, G. (2014). From the phenomenology to the mechanisms of consciousness: Integrated information theory 3.0. *PLoS Computational Biology*, 10(5), e1003588. 10.1371/journal.pcbi.100358824811198

Östlund, U., Kidd, L., Wengström, Y., & Rowa-Dewar, N. (2011). Combining qualitative and quantitative research within mixed method research designs: A methodological review. *International Journal of Nursing Studies*, 48(3), 369–383. 10.1016/j.ijnurstu.2010.10.00521084086

Patton, M. Q. (1999). Enhancing the Quality and Credibility of Qualitative Analysis. *Health Services Research*, 34(5 Pt 2), 1189–1208. 10.1111/1475-6773.0013010591279

Patton, M. Q. (2015). *Qualitative Research & Evaluation Methods: Integrating Theory and Practice* (4th ed.). Sage Publications.

Pham, T., Kaiser, B., Koirala, R., Maharjan, S., Upadhaya, N., Franz, L., & Kohrt, B. (2020). Traditional healers and mental health in Nepal: A scoping review. *Culture, Medicine and Psychiatry*, 45(1), 97–140. 10.1007/s11013-020-09676-432444961

Polit, D. F., & Beck, C. T. (2017). *Nursing research: Generating and assessing evidence for nursing practice*. Lippincott Williams & Wilkins.

Polit, D. F., & Hungler, B. D. (1999). *Nursing Research* (6th ed.). Lippicott.

Popli, S. (2020). Phenomenology of vernacular environments: Wancho settlements in Arunachal Pradesh, in the north east of India. *Journal of Traditional Building Architecture and Urbanism*, (1), 539–550. 10.51303/jtbau.vi1.377

Prasitanarapun, R., & Kitreerawutiwong, N. (2023). The development of an instrument to measure interprofessional collaboration competency for primary care teams in the district health system of health region 2, Thailand. *BMC Primary Care*, 24(1), 55. Advance online publication. 10.1186/s12875-023-02013-936849902

Reimsbach, D., & Hauschild, B. (2015). Testing vs. building accounting theory with experimental research: Insights from management research. *International Journal of Behavioural Accounting and Finance*, 5(1), 82. 10.1504/IJBAF.2015.071050

Renz, S., Carrington, J. M., & Badger, T. A. (2018). Two strategies for qualitative content analysis: An intramethod approach to triangulation. *Qualitative Health Research*, 28(5), 824–831. 10.1177/104973231775358629424274

Sahibzada, S., Kaur, S., & Khan, S. (2019). Triangulation in social science research: Concepts and methods. *International Journal of Advanced Research*, 7(2), 1200–1213.

Saks, M. (2018). Methodological triangulation. *Nature Human Behaviour*, 2(11), 806–807. 10.1038/s41562-018-0458-531558816

Sale, J. (2008). How to assess rigour . . . or not in qualitative papers. *Journal of Evaluation in Clinical Practice*, 14(5), 912–913. 10.1111/j.1365-2753.2008.01093.x19018925

Sandelowski, M. (1995). Triangles and crystals: On the geometry of qualitative research. *Research in Nursing & Health*, 18(6), 569–574. 10.1002/nur.47701806127480857

Sands, R. G., & Roer-Strier, D. (2006). Using Data Triangulation of Mother and Daughter Interviews to Enhance Research about Families. *Qualitative Social Work: Research and Practice*, 5(2), 237–260. 10.1177/1473325006064260

Santos, C., Abubakar, S., Barros, A., Mendonça, J., Dalmarco, G., & Godsell, J. (2019). Lessons for industrial development policies: Joining global aerospace value networks. *Space Policy*, 48, 30–40. 10.1016/j.spacepol.2019.01.006

Santoso, S. W., Ma'ruf, A., & Zainuri, A. (2023). The Importance of Values and Culture in Public Administration: A Case Study of Indonesian Local Government. *Khazanah Sosial*, 2(2), 67–77.

Scandura, T., & Williams, E. (2000). Research methodology in management: Current practices, trends, and implications for future research. *Academy of Management Journal*, 43(6), 1248–1264. 10.2307/1556348

Shih, F. (1998). Triangulation in nursing research: Issues of conceptual clarity and purpose. *Journal of Advanced Nursing*, 28(3), 631–641. 10.1046/j.1365-2648.1998.00716.x9756233

Sobh, R., & Perry, C. (2006). Research design and data analysis in realism research. *European Journal of Marketing*, 40(11/12), 1194–1209. 10.1108/03090560610702777

Solano, A. M. M. (2020). Triangulation and trustworthiness—Advancing research on public service interpreting through qualitative case study methodologies. *Fitispos-International Journal*, 4(1), 12–29.

Swavely, D., Vandenberg, R. J., & Mostov, K. E. (2022). The Use of Triangulation in Research. *Research in Organizational Behavior*, 4, 287–306. 10.1016/S0191-3085(82)80012-6

Teddlie, C., & Tashakkori, A. (2009). *Foundations of mixed methods research: Integrating quantitative and qualitative approaches in the social and behavioral sciences*. SAGE Publications.

Thurmond, V. (2001). The point of triangulation. *Journal of Nursing Scholarship*, 33(3), 253–258. 10.1111/j.1547-5069.2001.00253.x11552552

Tuckett, A. (2005). Part ii. rigour in qualitative research: Complexities and solutions. *Nurse Researcher*, 13(1), 29–42. 10.7748/nr2005.07.13.1.29.c599816220839

Turner, D. W. (2016). Qualitative interview design: A practical guide for novice investigators. *The Qualitative Report*, 21(3), 572–586.

Valencia, M. (2022). Principles, scope, and limitations of the methodological triangulation. *Investigacion y Educacion en Enfermeria*, 40(2). Advance online publication. 10.17533/udea.iee.v40n2e03.36264691

Verdonck, M., Chard, G., & Nolan, M. (2010). Electronic aids to daily living: Be able to do what you want. *Disability and Rehabilitation. Assistive Technology*, 6(3), 268–281. 10.3109/17483107.2010. 52529120939677

Vigo, D., Jones, W., Dove, N., Maidana, D., Tallon, C., Small, W., & Samji, H. (2021). Estimating the prevalence of mental and substance use disorders: A systematic approach to triangulating available data to inform health systems planning. *Canadian Journal of Psychiatry*, 67(2), 107–116. 10.1177/070674 37211006872338272778

Vivek, R. (2023). Theoretical foundations of triangulation in qualitative and multi-method research. *Qualitative Research Journal*, 17(2), 89–104.

Wardina & Sudihartinih. (2019). Description of student's junior high school mathematical connection ability on the linear function topic. *Journal of Mathematics Science and Education, 4*(1), 53-60.

Wray, N., Marković, M., & Manderson, L. (2007). "Researcher saturation": The impact of data triangulation and intensive-research practices on the researcher and qualitative research process. *Qualitative Health Research*, 17(10), 1392–1402. 10.1177/1049732307308308188000078

Youngs, H. & Piggot-Irvine, E. (2011). The application of a multiphase triangulation approach to mixed methods. *Z, 6*(3), 184-198. 10.1177/1558689811420696

Zheng-ying, L. (2021). An Empirical Study of Software Project Management Based on the Triangulation Method. *Frontiers in Psychology*, 12, 670153. 10.3389/fpsyg.2021.670153

Zwaan, L., Viljoen, R., & Aiken, D. (2019). The role of neuroleadership in work engagement. *SA Journal of Human Resource Management*, 17. Advance online publication. 10.4102/sajhrm.v17i0.1172

ADDITIONAL READING

Braun, V., & Clarke, V. (2013). *Successful qualitative research: A practical guide for beginners.* Sage Publications.

Corbin, J., & Strauss, A. (2014). *Basics of qualitative research: Techniques and procedures for developing grounded theory* (4th ed.). Sage Publications.

Flick, U. (2017). *An introduction to qualitative research* (6th ed.). Sage Publications.

Guba, E. G., & Lincoln, Y. S. (1989). *Fourth generation evaluation.* Sage Publications.

Hennink, M., Hutter, I., & Bailey, A. (2020). *Qualitative Research Methods.* Sage Publications.

Morse, J. M. (2015). Critical analysis of strategies for determining rigor in qualitative inquiry. *Qualitative Health Research,* 25(9), 1212–1222. 10.1177/1049732315588501261 84336

Ritchie, J., Lewis, J., McNaughton Nicholls, C., & Ormston, R. (Eds.). (2014). *Qualitative research practice: A guide for social science students and researchers* (2nd ed.). Sage Publications.

Silverman, D. (Ed.). (2016). *Qualitative research* (4th ed.). Sage Publications.

Stake, R. E. (2013). *Multiple case study analysis.* Guilford Press.

Yin, R. K. (2018). *Case study research and applications: Design and methods* (6th ed.). Sage Publications.

KEY TERMS AND DEFINITIONS

Bias Mitigation: The steps taken to minimize bias in the research process to ensure that the findings are more trustworthy and unbiased.

Case Study: A research method that involves an up-close, in-depth, and detailed examination of a subject of study (the case), as well as its related contextual conditions.

Data Triangulation: Using different sources of information to increase the credibility of research outcomes.

Epistemology: The branch of philosophy concerned with the theory of knowledge, especially regarding its methods, validity, and scope.

Ethnography: A qualitative research method used to study cultures and groups from a holistic perspective.

Grounded Theory: A research methodology that involves constructing theories through methodical gathering and analysis of data.

Investigator Triangulation: The use of multiple observers or researchers to reduce the bias that can come from a single investigator's perspectives or predispositions.

Methodological Triangulation: Combining multiple methods to study a single problem to increase confidence in the findings.

Mixed Methods: Research methodology that combines both quantitative and qualitative research techniques in a single study to provide a better understanding of research problems.

Ontology: A branch of metaphysics dealing with the nature of being, including the relationships and categories of being.

Phenomenology: A qualitative research approach that focuses on the study of an individual's lived experiences within the world.

Reliability: The degree to which research methods and findings are consistent and replicable over time and across various conditions and analysts.

Theory Triangulation: Using multiple perspectives or theories to interpret a set of data, helping to ensure that the conclusions drawn are robust.

Triangulation: The use of multiple methods, data sources, or researchers to verify and enhance the validity and reliability of research findings.

Chapter 7
Ensuring Reliability and Validity in Qualitative Social Sciences Research

Aissa Mosbah
https://orcid.org/0000-0003-4092-8789
Dhofar University, Oman

ABSTRACT

Social sciences (SS) researchers have produced far less qualitative than quantitative research. This is due to many factors including particularly the lack of straightforward and easy-to-implement guidelines that would help researchers in the process of ensuring research rigor through reliability, validity, and/or other concepts. Nonetheless, the extant literature shows that most qualitative research measures on research rigor were developed in nursing, which is a natural science discipline, and that social science researchers often adopt these measures in their works. This chapter focuses on multiculturalism in business management discipline, as a rapidly growing field of the SS. While multiculturalism has become a key feature and a determinant of organizational success in today's rapidly globalized business environments, it may be a source of bias in qualitative research. Most importantly, the chapter develops a set of measures/techniques that will aid qualitative social science researchers, and business researchers specifically, on how to ensure research rigor.

INTRODUCTION

Unlike quantitative research that deals with numbers, qualitative research emphasizes the collection and analysis of data displayed in form of words to answer specific research questions. These differences have implications on the scientific accuracy, rigor, and robustness as well as generalizability of the research findings. Nonetheless, establishing research rigor is relatively easier for quantitative researchers than for their qualitative peers. This is attributed to the existence of clearly established, straightforward and agreed-upon quantitative measures as documented in a plethora of textbooks and research articles.

DOI: 10.4018/979-8-3693-3306-8.ch007

These measures are built upon statistical principles (Noble & Smith, 2015) to subsequently deliver most possibly accurate results.

However, this is not the case in qualitative research, which lacks similar measures (Riege, 2003), particularly in the social sciences including the business management field (Singh et al., 2021), where rigor is still a problem for both researchers and readers (Andersen & Anne, 2004). Indeed, qualitative research has, despite efforts, been repetitively critiqued for lacking consensus on how to assess quality and rigor (Marschan-Piekkari, 2017; Murphy & Yielder, 2010; Rolfe, 2006; Sinkovics et al., 2008; Welch & Rose & Johnson, 2020). For example, while Welch and Marschan-Piekkari (2017) describe it as complex and messy, Rolfe (2006, p. 304) contends that:

> "After a quarter of a century of debate in nursing about how best to judge the quality of qualitative research, we appear to be no closer to a consensus, or even to deciding whether it is appropriate to try to achieve a consensus".

Overall, the existing critics point to the lack of scientific rigor, poor justification of the methods, absence of transparent procedures of analysis, researchers' bias in form of personal opinions that shape the interpretation of findings, and insufficient examination of the practical application of rigor strategies such as reflexivity (Darawsheh, 2014; Noble & Smith, 2015).

To date, most of the existing works and discussions on reliability and validity in qualitative research comes from the field of nursing. Much less has been done in the Social Sciences (SS) disciplines particularly business management (Hlady-Rispal & Jouison-Laffitte, 2014; Rajasinghe et al., 2021); Beside being shaped by higher tendency for empirical testing, the business management field through lenses of the workplace remains a perfect place for multicultural dynamism and thriving. This is clearly seen in the disciplines of multinational firms (Marschan-Piekkari & Rebecca, 2004a), as well as international, ethnic, and migrant entrepreneurship. Specifically in entrepreneurship, it has been argued that researchers focus on rigor at the cost of practical relevance (Frank & Landström, 2016).

Scholars have not agreed upon a specific framework or model to guide researchers the question of maintaining reliability and validity (and research rigor in general) in qualitative SS research. However, despite the usefulness of the existing works in assisting researchers, four main limitations are apparent. First, some works simply draw on the quantitative research approach and how it deals with reliability and validity (Rolfe, 2006). As such, these works have not just ignored the specificities of qualitative research, but failed to draw a clear separation between reliability and validity and could not precisely specify the rigor measures that belong to each of them. For example, Rolfe (2006) recommends "the use of multiples sources of evidence" to increase construct validity but recommend this technique again to ensure credibility. Second, although the available models and frameworks have given detailed accounts of the research components and the steps that add to or distort research rigor, they do not provide detailed or simplified techniques to guide researchers. To us, providing simplified techniques are crucial to researchers.

Third, opposing approaches do exist for some research components related to rigor such as objectivity and reflexivity (Meyrick, 2006). Fourth, the overemphasizing triangulation of researchers, methods and/or data sources for scientific accuracy and rigor (Renz et al., 2018; Lemon & Hayes, 2020; Natow, 2020; Santos et al., 2020) not just require extensive resources and therefore limit qualitative research production which is already scant, but contradict the views that argue for limited interviews/cases as being sufficient to yield reliable results in business management (Boddy, 2016) and emphasis on larger samples (e.g. more than four cases) distort the strength in business research (Welch & Piekkari, 2017).

Indeed, the differences between social sciences and nursing sciences do not only revolve around the nature of the disciplines and their methods of inquiry but also on the context and the use of dissimilar approaches to check, verify, and validate research steps to ultimately ensure reliability and validity. For example, when a patient is interviewed, issues like quality, bias and accuracy of the information obtained from him/her can be contrasted with existing medical reports that encompass supporting information such as temperature records, blood tests, X-rays and so on. These elements are, unfortunately, not available in most social science settings. In business management for example, all that can be done on this matter may relate to firm-, customer-, or employee-related measures which are, unfortunately, often not easily disclosed. This being the case then, it could be extremely difficult for researchers, for example, to access alternative data to verify pricing strategies, specific government support, competitive strategies, financial indices, and strategic goals. This issue exacerbates in business contexts especially in workplaces that encompass multiculturalism. Furthermore, while patients may be more concerned with confidentiality of their personal data, businesses owners may prefer not to share accurate strategic, competitive and/or financial data. Employees may hide improper behaviors or culturally sensitive information when data privacy and safety are not ensured.

The existing differences along the sparse guidelines on how to ensure rigor in multicultural qualitative business research in general represent a solid basis for developing measures to ensure rigor in business research. We argue that the best measures to warrant the robustness of qualitative research must (i) go beyond the data to consider elements such as the culture, context, researcher, and process, and (ii) be addressed sequentially according to their occurrence in the research process.

Considering this gap, our chapter discusses the concepts of reliability and validity in qualitative Social Sciences (SS) research using insights from multicultural business settings. In doing so, the chapter proposes a set of measures/techniques to ensure quality and rigor. This way, the chapter also responds to the recommendation of Rose and Johnson (2020) by providing straightforward techniques to support SS researchers in directly addressing the problems of rigor measures instead of attempting to prescribe them. It must be noted that different terminologies have been used to reflect both reliability (credibility, consistency, dependability, and transferability) and validity (quality, trustworthiness and rigor) (Golafshani, 2003; Sinkovics et al., 2008). However, we adopt the approach of Davies and Dodd (2002) in which the term rigor encompasses both reliability and validity.

BUSINESS MANAGEMENT AS A SOCIAL SCIENCES' (SS) FIELD

The field of social Sciences (SS) involve studying human activities and their outcomes but with some differences. It emphasizes the study of human and institutional aspects in a social context and the interrelationship between them. Meyer (1999, P. 1) defines it as *"the rational and systematic study of human society in all its forms with the aim of arriving at an enduring understanding, acknowledged as such by a broad consensus of researchers of social phenomena"*. Therefore, the broader field of social sciences includes disciplines such as psychology, sociology and social work, economics human geography, political sciences, and anthropology (Encyclopedia Britannica, 2005;).

The SS research process is surrounded by the following key characteristics and challenges. First, it builds on both quantitative and qualitative approaches with more emphasis on the former type. Second, it relies heavily on theories, concepts, and methods. Second, it frequently involves human interaction and subjective interpretations of data and findings. Third, it requires close attention to be paid to the surrounding context. Fourth, it requires ethical considerations because humans are involved.

The business management as an SS field refers to managing all the internal and external aspects that relate to the establishment, functioning, performance, and growth of the business at both the organizational and enterprise levels. Management as a concept is defined based on four components or activities -often called functions- that give managers the right for decision-making. These are: planning, organizing, leading, and controlling. The business management encompasses a list of sub-fields, called disciplines in the context of this chapter, that can be grouped into three main categories namely: *(i) the business start-up* represented primarily by the entrepreneurship discipline, *(ii) business functioning* seen in a set of fields that cover different business functions such as purchase/procurement, finance and accounting, production, logistics and supply chain, human resources, research and development, marketing and sales, strategy, etc. and *(iii) business growth/expansion* captured through international business and firms' cross-border engagement.

MULTICULTURALISM AND BIAS IN QUALITATIVE BUSINESS RESEARCH

Cultural diversity and cross-border engagements are key features of multiculturalism in organizational settings (Marschan-Piekkari & Welch, 2004b). Qualitive research, by capturing individual experiences effectively, provides researchers and managers with insights on the mechanism of navigating the dynamics and complexities of starting a business overseas, managing multicultural teams, customer requirements, negotiations, partnerships, strategic alliances, and institutional requirements. Qualitative research targets unquantifiable phenomena and stresses the "why" questions. It uses techniques like interviews, focus groups (see, Elhami & Khoshnevisan, 2022), and ethnographies (see, for example, Roshan, 2023) to collect data and ultimately uncover the underpinning cultural values and beliefs, motivations, challenges, expectations, strategies, and reactions at the levels of individuals, firms, and institutions.

Yet, while business management, as a broad field, encompasses several disciplines that embed multiculturalism, the following disciplines necessitate qualitative researchers to deal with multiculturalism in a way or another, whether at the human resource (employees) level, markets (customers) level, and/ or institutional level. This mainly includes international business through the study of Multinational Companies (MNCs), international marketing, expatriates' management, immigrant entrepreneurship, transnational entrepreneurship, and international entrepreneurship. Nonetheless, although multiculturalism has become a key feature and a determinant of organizational success in today's rapidly globalized business environments, it may be a source of bias in qualitative research. Qualitative research bias in multicultural organizational setting can be largely determined by the researcher and the respondent/data, mostly through subjectivity of the researcher in the case of the former (Puwels & Matthyssens, 2004) and response bias in the case of the latter (Parkhe, 2004). Table 1 presents different reasons that may influence participant' responses and their sources (types of participants) in multicultural business disciplines.

Table 1. Possible response bias in qualitative business research

Business disciplines	Examples of reasons and scenarios of bias (source)
Expatriate management (HR)	- External status (expats). - Double taxation (expats) - Possible exploitation and/or discriminating HR policies (managers).
International Marketing	- Boycott (customers) - local cultural issues/scandals (managers) - Misleading information (competitors)
Ethnic entrepreneurship	- Biased laws (minority entrepreneurs)
Immigrant entrepreneurship	- Illegal migrant as employees (employees) - Illegal business practices (managers) - Tax avoidance (managers)
Transnational entrepreneurship	- Double taxation at the home country
Ethnic entrepreneurship	- Discriminating laws and policies (entrepreneurs)
International strategic alliances	- Confidentiality (managers)

DIFFERENCES BETWEEN QUALITATIVE RESEARCH AND QUANTITATIVE RESEARCH

Qualitative research often employs interviews and observations in data collection. It uses the exploratory approach to understand various phenomena and help develop theories as opposed to quantitative research which tends to test and refine theories. Table 2 highlights the key differences between qualitative research and quantitative research. While both quantitative and qualitative types of research have their strengths and weaknesses, choosing the right one depends primarily on factors like the nature and level of available knowledge of the investigated phenomenon, and the research questions and objectives of the study. Nonetheless, qualitative research is suitable for exploring and comprehending environments or phenomena that are poorly known. In the meanwhile, recent decades have witnessed an emerging trend among researchers who rely on a pragmatism paradigm and consequently apply a mixed-methods approach, integrating quantitative and qualitative elements of research, to yield a deep but complete understanding (Creswell & Clark, 2018).

Table 2. Fundamental differences between qualitative research and quantitative research

Criteria	Qualitative research	Quantitative research
Examples (research questions) in business research	How do family business managers neutralize the impact of family conflicts on business decisions? What makes an immigrant entrepreneur targets either the co-ethnic niche or the mainstream market?	What factors affect the entrepreneurs' intention to use franchising as a growth strategy? Does customer satisfaction mediate the relationship between service quality and loyalty in the F&B industry?
Research paradigm	Interpretivism, Phenomenology, ethnography, and critical theory.	Positivism, post-positivism, constructivism.
Role in the knowledge/theory development.	Building	Testing

continued on following page

Table 2. Continued

Criteria	Qualitative research	Quantitative research
Reasoning	Inductive (Bottom-up)	Deductive (Top-down)
Inquiry	Process-oriented	Results-oriented
Purpose	Exploratory (understand phenomena)	Explanatory or casual (test relationships between phenomena)
Type of questions	Unstructured (Open-ended).	Structured/ Close-ended (such as multiple choices)
Data collection method	- Interviews (primary data) - Available reports/content (secondary data)	- Surveys or recorded observations (primary data) -Available reports statistics (secondary data)
Types of data	Qualitative (words)	Quantitative (numbers)
Sample size	Small	Large
Reliability and Validity	Apply to the whole research process	Apply to the measurement model
	Context-dependent	Established measures (statistical and non-statistical)
Data analysis	Based on codes and themes.	Based on statistics.
Interpretation	Subjective	Objective
Position towards hypotheses	Can aid in developing hypotheses for further research	Use hypothesis (from existing theories/models)
Time frame	Longer	Shorter
Overall difficulty	Relatively more difficult	Relatively less difficult

QUALITATIVE RESEARCH IN BUSINESS MANAGEMENT VERSUS NURSING

A highlighted early, qualitative research rigor differs between the social sciences including business management and nursing as a natural science field. In Table 3 we explain these differences based on five different elements that are pivotal to qualitative research namely, research aims and focus, context and setting, characteristics of participants, data analysis and interpretation, and ethical applications.

Table 3. Qualitative research in business management as opposed to nursing.

Research aspects	Differences
Research aims and focus	*Business*: seeks to provide systematic insights into business-related phenomena, including customer behavior, market trends, and organizational performance. These insights are then applied to decision-making, strategy formulation, and problem-solving in the business context. *Nursing*: Patient experiences, medical procedures, adherence to treatment, and attitudes toward illness are frequently the topics of interviews in these fields. Understanding treatment effectiveness, patient satisfaction, or healthcare provider-patient communication may be the goal.
Context and setting	*Business*: Interviews for entrepreneurship research can be conducted online or in a variety of locations, including offices and event locations. Discussions regarding funding and financial indicators, HR issues and trends, market conditions and competition, customer behaviors may be part of the context. *Nursing:* Hospitals, clinics, and community health centers are common locations for interviews conducted for nursing research projects. Discussions regarding a patient's medical history, symptoms, treatment options, and interactions with healthcare professionals may be included in the context.
Characteristics of participants	*Business*: participants are primarily managers at hierarchical levels and from different departments, employees, customers, and policy makers. *Nursing Sciences*: participants are usually patients, caregivers, family members of patients, and medical professionals (such as doctors, nurses, and therapists).
Data analysis and interpretation	*Business*: in the data analysis researchers attempt to identify patterns and themes, and unveil factors impacting performance, decision-making, resource acquisition, innovation and asset management, and intention. *Nursing Sciences*: the analysis of interview data may entail the identification of patient narratives, the viewpoints of healthcare providers, and themes pertaining to the management of illness, the results of treatment, healthcare disparities, or the relationships between patients and providers.
Ethics and data regulations	*Business*: is not subject to stringent regulatory frameworks related to interview data privacy. However, informed consent, confidentiality, and the possible effects of study results on participants' reputations or business interests are a few examples of ethical issues in entrepreneurship research. *Nursing*: Strict regulations are in place to protect patient confidentiality and privacy. Ethical concerns include informed consent, confidentiality, and patient privacy as well the possible emotional or psychological effects of discussing delicate health-related topics.

RELIABILITY AND VALIDITY IN QUALITATIVE RESEARCH

Reliability and validity are good indicators of quality and rigor of qualitative research (Murphy & Yielder, 2010). While Davies and Dodd (2002) believe that reliability and validity reflect research rigor in qualitative research, Golafshani (2003) noted that reliability is sometimes reflected in terms such as credibility, consistency, dependability, and transferability whereas validity is explained through the terms of quality, trustworthiness, and rigor. More specifically, reliability lies with consistency and indicates the exact replicability of the processes and the results (Leung, 2015).

Validity, on the other side, reflects the extent to which the research tools and processes are appropriate, and findings and interpretations are accurate and truthful. According to Leung (2015), to ensure validity, researchers must look at the questions, methodology with design and sampling, data analysis and conclusions. Validity can be distorted in the case of bias in both the instrument (Murphy & Yielder, 2009) and the researcher whose personal perspectives influence the interpretations (Johnson 1997; Roberts & Priest, 2006). Therefore, the lack of validity can be seen, for example, in a case where a question that claims to address the role of culture in opportunity identification and exploitation ends up asking about the role of family instead (father, brothers, family support, ...etc).

While we find this explanation of reliability and validity useful, we design our work in a way to respond to the recommendation made by Rose and Johnson (2020) in which they argued that the Issues of research rigor -in form of trustworthiness- are often either nonexistent, unsubstantial, or unexplained, and urged searchers to address challenges related to reliability and validity within their ontological, epistemological, and paradigmatic perspectives. The next section develops a model encompassing measures/techniques to aid researchers to directly address aspects that maintain research rigor.

RELIABILITY AND VALIDITY IN QUALITATIVE BUSINESS RESEARCH: PROPOSED RIGOR MEASURES.

The nature of the qualitative data (words), the researcher distance from the investigated phenomenon, and the extent of his influence on the findings require a different conception of reliability and validity, and the overall research rigor, than in the quantitative approaches. Therefore, unlike in quantitative research where reliability and validity are concerned the data and its process of collection (measurement model), reliability and validity in quantitative research go beyond the data itself and its process of collection to include additional elements. The extant literature shows five principal determinants that may compromise or improve rigor in qualitative research (see. Figure 1) namely: the research context (Bryman et al., 1996; Phillippi & Lauderdale, 2018), researcher (Morse et al., 2002), process (Leung, 2015), triangulation (Cater et al., 2015) and data. With respect to the researcher for instance, Golafshani (2003) contends that validity and reliability as means of credibility in qualitative research are influenced by the researcher's ability and effort.

Figure 1. Factors influencing quality and rigor in qualitative research

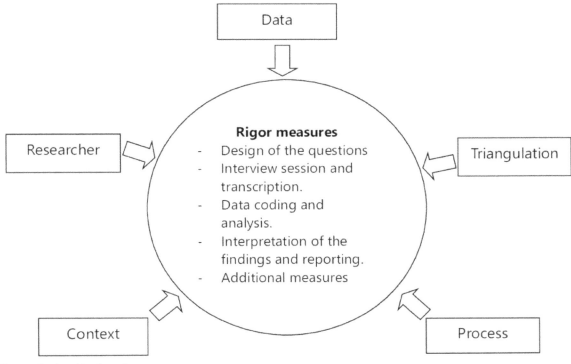

Source: developed by the author

We argue in this chapter that while it is possible to make a definitional distinction between reliability and validity in qualitative research, the practical distinction between both terms may not be possible. That is because of the overlap in the rigor measures or techniques that are supposed to belong to each. One reason for this could perhaps be attributed to the fact that qualitative research does not always follow distinct phases; for instance, data collection and analysis frequently take place at the same time (Meyrick, 2006). Furthermore, in the model depicted in figure 1 we have outlined four steps in the research process where careful operationalization is needed to ensure quality and rigor and proposed a set of measures/techniques of rigor in each step. This is consistent with calls made by other scholars to emphasize research rigor during the analysis process (Sinkovics et al., 2008). As detailed in table 4, the four steps are: (1) design of the questions, (2) interview session and transcribing, (3), data coding and analysis, and (4) interpretation of the findings and reporting. We have supported this with additional measures/techniques that apply to the overall research process but not specifically related to each of these steps. Thus, these measures are grouped sequentially, that is; according to their occurrence in the research process.

Table 4. Proposed measures of rigor in qualitative research

Aspects	Techniques to ensure rigor
Design of the questions	- Research questions must reflect the research objectives. - Questions must be driven from a strong conceptual framework (Johnson et al., 2020) - More than one person to be involved in their development - Questions to be arranged logically to enable smooth flow of conversation flow. - Questions to be reviewed by independent researchers. - Questions to be first distributed to a few participants to assess their clarity. - Conduct mock interviews with a minimum of two participants to fine-tune the questions and guarantee clarity. - Translation to be verified by a third party or expert translators in case of multi-ethnic participation or when adopting a previous questions written in a different language.
Interview sessions and Transcription	- A quiet and private location and casual conversation at the beginning are needed to build rapport and trust with the participant. - Digest the questions well before each interview session begins. - Take notes to document contextual information and non-verbal cues of participants during sessions (Phillippi and Lauderdale, 2018) - Ensure accuracy in transcribing.
Data coding and Analysis	- Intensive engagement with the data before the analysis - Multiple researchers to participate in the coding process. Preferably, use Kappa coefficient to assess inter-rater reliability (consistency/agreement among coders regarding the codes). - Begin with a wide approach to identify initial themes and categories. - Use specialized software like Nvivo and Atlas. – Move back and forth between the data and interpretation to make strong links between them (Roberst and Priest, 2006) - Reflect clearly on your biases, interpretations, and assumptions throughout the analysis.
Interpretation of Findings and reporting	- Recognize your bias and subjectivity and how they may affect the way you interpret observations. - Seek feedback from participants regarding the findings and the interpretations - Avoid 'cherry picking' when reporting (Roberts and Priest, 2006)
Additional measures	- Collaborate with research members from the culture(s) under investigation. - Keeping detailed notes on decisions made throughout the process (Roberts and Priest, 2006). - Prolonged engagement of the researcher to gain exposure to the study setting. - Acknowledge your role in the research by reflecting upon the personal experiences, beliefs, assumptions, and biases throughout the research process (reflexivity). - Maintain consistency in the writing and support the writing with a strong chain of evidence along the manuscript.

We acknowledge that our model focuses on all the research aspects or steps where research quality and rigor can directly or indirectly be distorted; from designing the questions to interpretation and reporting of the findings. Therefore, the theoretical justification (if needed) and sampling procedures, although important, are beyond the scope of this chapter because they appear to align with the overall search methodology and structure and are well explained in research methodology books.

CONCLUSION

This chapter discussed the concepts of reliability and validity as indicators of qualitative research rigor in qualitative Social Sciences (SS) research using insights from the business management field. The conception of reliability and validity in their relation to rigor was adopted from the approach of Davies and Dodd (2002) in which the term rigor encompasses both reliability and validity. More specifically, the chapter outlined four steps in the research process where careful operationalization is needed to ensure quality and rigor and proposed a set of measures/techniques of rigor in each step. The steps/areas are: (1) design of the questions, (2) interview sessions and transcription, (3) data coding and analysis, and

(4) interpretation of findings and reporting. Additional supportive measures that are also needed in the research process have been added to the model. While presented in a more natural and intuitive manner -based on their occurrence in the research process, these measures are likely to add to the body of knowledge particularly in the SS field where researchers tend to use guidelines developed in the nursing field. Their strength lays in being simple, clear, and straightforward.

REFERENCES

Andersen, P. H., & Anne, M. (2004). *23.* Ensuring Validity in Qualitative International Business Research. In Marschan-Piekkari, R., & Welch, C. (Eds.), *Handbook of Qualitative Research Methods for International Business* (pp. 464–485). Edward Elgar Publishing. 10.4337/9781781954331.00045

Bardwell, W. A., & Dimsdale, J. E. (2001). The impact of ethnicity and response bias on the self-report of negative affect. *Journal of Applied Biobehavioral Research*, 6(1), 27–38. 10.1111/j.1751-9861.2001.tb00105.x

Boddy, C. R. (2016). Sample size for qualitative research. *Qualitative Market Research*, 19(4), 426–432. 10.1108/QMR-06-2016-0053

Bryman, A., Stephens, M., & Campo, C. (1996). The importance of context: Qualitative research and the study of leadership. *The Leadership Quarterly*, 7(3), 353–370. 10.1016/S1048-9843(96)90025-9

Cater, N., Bryant-Lukosius, D., DiCenso, A., Blythe, J., & Neville, A. (2015). The use of triangulation in qualitative research. *Oncology Nursing Forum*, 41(5), 545–547. 10.1188/14.ONF.545-54725158659

Creswell, J. W., & Clark, V. L. P. (2018). *Designing and conducting mixed methods research.* Sage publications.

Darawsheh, W. (2014). Reflexivity in research: Promoting rigour, reliability and validity in qualitative research. *International Journal of Therapy and Rehabilitation*, 21(12), 560–568. 10.12968/ijtr.2014.21.12.560

Davies, D., & Dodd, J. (2002). Qualitative research and the question of rigor. *Qualitative Health Research*, 12(2), 279–289. 10.1177/104973230201200211111837376

Elhami, A., & Khoshnevisan, B. (2022). Conducting an interview in qualitative research: The Modus Operandi. *Mextesol Journal*, 46(1), 1–7.

Encyclopedia Britannica. (2005). *The Social Sciences* (15th ed., Vol. 27). Author.

Frank, H., & Landström, H. (2016). What makes entrepreneurship research interesting? Reflections on strategies to overcome the rigour–relevance gap. *Entrepreneurship and Regional Development*, 28(2), 51–75. 10.1080/08985626.2015.1100687

Golafshani, N. (2003). Understanding reliability and validity in qualitative research. *The Qualitative Report*, 8(4), 597–607. 10.46743/2160-3715/2003.1870

Hlady-Rispal, M., & Jouison-Laffitte, E. (2014). Qualitative research methods and epistemological frameworks: A review of publication trends in entrepreneurship. *Journal of Small Business Management*, 52(4), 594–614. 10.1111/jsbm.12123

Johnson, J. L., Adkins, D., & Chauvin, S. (2020). A review of the quality indicators of rigor in qualitative research. *American Journal of Pharmaceutical Education*, 84(1), 138–146. 10.5688/ajpe712032292186

Johnson, R. B. (1997). Examining the validity structure of qualitative research. *Education*, 118(2), 282–292.

Lemon, L. L., & Hayes, J. (2020). Enhancing trustworthiness of qualitative findings: Using Leximancer for qualitative data analysis triangulation. *The Qualitative Report*, 25(3), 604–614. 10.46743/2160-3715/2020.4222

Leung, L. (2015). Validity, reliability, and generalizability in qualitative research. *Journal of Family Medicine and Primary Care*, 4(3), 324. 10.4103/2249-4863.16130626288766

Marschan-Piekkari, R., & Welch, C. (2004a). Qualitative research methods in international business: The state of the art. In *Handbook of Qualitative Research Methods for International Business* (pp. 464-485). Edward Elgar Publishing.

Marschan-Piekkari, R., & Welch, C. (2004b). *Handbook of Qualitative Research Methods for International Business*. Edward Elgar Publishing. 10.4337/9781781954331

Meyer, P. J. (1999). *An Essay in the Philosophy of Social Sciences*. https://www.academia.edu/27210801/An_Essay_in_the_Philosophy_of_Social_Science

Meyrick, J. (2006). What is good qualitative research? A first step towards a comprehensive approach to judging rigour/quality. *Journal of Health Psychology*, 11(5), 799–808. 10.1177/135910530606664316908474

Morse, J. M., Barrett, M., Mayan, M., Olson, K., & Spiers, J. (2002). Verification strategies for establishing reliability and validity in qualitative research. *International Journal of Qualitative Methods*, 1(2), 13–22. 10.1177/160940690200100202

Murphy, F. J., & Yielder, J. (2010). Establishing rigour in qualitative radiography research. *Radiography*, 16(1), 62–67. 10.1016/j.radi.2009.07.003

Natow, R. S. (2020). The use of triangulation in qualitative studies employing elite interviews. *Qualitative Research*, 20(2), 160–173. 10.1177/1468794119830077

Noble, H., & Smith, J. (2015). Issues of validity and reliability in qualitative research. *Evidence-Based Nursing*, 18(2), 34–35. 10.1136/eb-2015-10205425653237

Omusulu, R. (2013). The main features and constraints of social science's research methods. *International Journal of Development and Sustainability*, 2(3), 1907–1918.

Parkhe, A. (2004). Interviews: a key data source in international business research. In *Handbook of Qualitative Research Methods for International Business* (pp. 464-485). Edward Elgar Publishing. 10.4337/9781781954331.00010

Pauwels, P., & Matthyssens, P. (2004). The architecture of multiple case study research in international business. In *Handbook of Qualitative Research Methods for International Business* (pp. 464-485). Edward Elgar Publishing. 10.4337/9781781954331.00020

Phillippi, J., & Lauderdale, J. (2018). A guide to field notes for qualitative research: Context and conversation. *Qualitative Health Research*, 28(3), 381–388. 10.1177/1049732317697102229298584

Rajasinghe, D., Aluthgama-Baduge, C., & Mulholland, G. (2021). Researching entrepreneurship: An approach to develop subjective understanding. *International Journal of Entrepreneurial Behaviour & Research*, 27(4), 866–883. 10.1108/IJEBR-10-2019-0601

Riege, A. M. (2003). Validity and reliability tests in case study research: A literature review with "hands-on" applications for each research phase. *Qualitative Market Research*, 6(2), 75–86. 10.1108/13522750310470055

Roberts, P., Priest, H., & Traynor, M. (2006). Reliability and validity in research. *Nursing Standard*, 20(44), 41–46. 10.7748/ns.20.44.41.s5616872117

Roberts, P., & Woods, L. (2000). Alternative methods of gathering and handling data: Maximising the use of modern technology. *Nurse Researcher*, 8(2), 84–95. 10.7748/nr2001.01.8.2.84.c6152

Rolfe, G. (2006). Validity, trustworthiness and rigour: Quality and the idea of qualitative research. *Journal of Advanced Nursing*, 53(3), 304–310. 10.1111/j.1365-2648.2006.03727.x16441535

Rose, J., & Johnson, C. W. (2020). Contextualizing reliability and validity in qualitative research: Toward more rigorous and trustworthy qualitative social science in leisure research. *Journal of Leisure Research*, 51(4), 432–451. 10.1080/00222216.2020.1722042

Roshan, A. (2023). *Trajectories of Iranian migrants in Madrid* [Unpublished Doctoral Dissertation]. Universidad Autónoma de Madrid.

Santos, K. D. S., Ribeiro, M. C., Queiroga, D. E. U. D., Silva, I. A. P. D., & Ferreira, S. M. S. (2020). The use of multiple triangulations as a validation strategy in a qualitative study. *Ciencia & Saude Coletiva*, 25, 655–664. 10.1590/1413-81232020252.1230201832022205

Singh, N., Benmamoun, M., Meyr, E., & Arikan, R. H. (2021). Verifying rigor: Analyzing qualitative research in international marketing. *International Marketing Review*, 38(6), 1289–1307. 10.1108/IMR-03-2020-0040

Sinkovics, R. R., Penz, E., & Ghauri, P. N. (2008). Enhancing the trustworthiness of qualitative research in international business. *MIR. Management International Review*, 48(6), 689–714. 10.1007/s11575-008-0103-z

Welch, C., & Marschan-Piekkari, R. (2017). How should we (not) judge the 'quality' of qualitative research? A reassessment of current evaluative criteria in International Business. *Journal of World Business*, 52(5), 714–725. 10.1016/j.jwb.2017.05.007

ADDITIONAL READING

Beck, C. T., Keddy, B. A., & Cohen, M. Z. (1994). Reliability and validity issues in phenomenological research. *Western Journal of Nursing Research*, 16(3), 254–267. 10.1177/019394599401600303038036802

Cope, D. G. (2014). Methods and meanings: Credibility and trustworthiness of qualitative research. *Oncology Nursing Forum*, 41(1), 77–88. 10.1188/14.ONF.89-9124368242

Cutcliffe, J. R., & McKenna, H. P. (1999). Establishing the credibility of qualitative research findings: The plot thickens. *Journal of Advanced Nursing*, 30(2), 374–380. 10.1046/j.1365-2648.1999.01090.x10457239

Cypress, B. S. (2017). Rigor or reliability and validity in qualitative research: Perspectives, strategies, reconceptualization, and recommendations. *Dimensions of Critical Care Nursing*, 36(4), 253–263. 10.1097/DCC.0000000000000025328570380

Giddings, L. S., & Grant, B. M. (2009). From rigour to trustworthiness: Validating mixed methods. *Mixed Methods Research for Nursing and the Health Sciences, 13*(1), 119-134. https://doi.org/10.1097/DCC.0000000000000253

Graneheim, U. H., & Lundman, B. (2004). Qualitative content analysis in nursing research: Concepts, procedures and measures to achieve trustworthiness. *Nurse Education Today*, 24(2), 105–112. 10.1016/j.nedt.2003.10.00114769454

Gunawan, J. (2015). Ensuring trustworthiness in qualitative research. *Belitung Nursing Journal*, 1(1), 10–11. 10.33546/bnj.4

Høye, S., & Severinsson, E. (2007). Methodological aspects of rigor in qualitative nursing research on families involved in intensive care units: A literature review. *Nursing & Health Sciences*, 9(1), 61–68. 10.1111/j.1442-2018.2007.00300.x17300547

Long, T., & Johnson, M. (2000). Rigour, reliability and validity in qualitative research. *Clinical Effectiveness in Nursing*, 4(1), 30–37. 10.1054/cein.2000.0106

McBrien, B. (2008). Evidence-based care: Enhancing the rigour of a qualitative study. *British Journal of Nursing (Mark Allen Publishing)*, 17(20), 1286–1289. 10.12968/bjon.2008.17.20.3164519043334

Porter, S. (2007). Validity, trustworthiness and rigour: Reasserting realism in qualitative research. *Journal of Advanced Nursing*, 60(1), 79–86. 10.1111/j.1365-2648.2007.04360.x17824942

Schou, L., Høstrup, H., Lyngsø, E. E., Larsen, S., & Poulsen, I. (2012). Validation of a new assessment tool for qualitative research articles. *Journal of Advanced Nursing*, 68(9), 2086–2094. 10.1111/j.1365-2648.2011.05898.x22168459

Squires, A., & Dorsen, C. (2018). Qualitative research in nursing and health professions regulation. *Journal of Nursing Regulation*, 9(3), 15–26. 10.1016/S2155-8256(18)30150-9

KEY TERMS AND DEFINITIONS

Business Management: Is the process of managing business entities by applying the principles of planning, organizing, leading, and controlling of their resources to ultimately achieve specific goals competitively and sustainably.

Multiculturalism in a Business Setting: Refers to the active inclusion of individuals from diverse cultural backgrounds and nationalities within a business entity. It is based on accepting and valuing different cultural backgrounds and practices among employees, customers, and business partners. Corporate multiculturalism is associated with various challenges but boosts creativity and innovation and the international presence of the firm.

Qualitative Research: Is a method of inquiry that is concerned with exploring the meanings behind concepts with a primary aim of gaining an in-depth understanding of human behavior and experiences, as well as social phenomena.

Reliability: In qualitative research refers, in theoretical terms, to exact replicability of the processes and the results (Leung, 2015).

Research Rigor: Is about employing strategies to ensure transparent and sound research processes and deliver the most accurate and reality-reflecting research findings.

Social Sciences: Refer to the rational and systematic study of human society in all its forms with the aim of arriving at an enduring understanding, acknowledged as such by a broad consensus of researchers of social phenomena" (Meyer (1999, P. 1). It includes disciplines such as business management, psychology, sociology and social work, economics human geography, political sciences, and anthropology (The Encyclopedia Britannica, 2005; Omosulu, 2013).

Validity: In qualitative research means, in theoretical terms, the "appropriateness" of the tools, processes, and data (Leung, 2015).

Chapter 8
An Overview of Using IRAMUTEQ Software in Qualitaitve Analysis Designs

Maha Mennani
https://orcid.org/0009-0001-6289-4949
Cadi Ayyad University, Morocco

Elhoussain Attak
Cadi Ayyad University, Morocco

ABSTRACT

Qualitative research methodology provides an effective way to explore participants' perceptions and unlock their experiences. In multicultural research settings, particularly in social sciences (e.g., sociology, psychology, theology, etc.), there is a strong tendency among qualitative researchers to collect the required data through interviews. This study employs qualitative research methodology, particularly lexicometric analysis via the IRaMuTeQ software, to analyze text data from semi-structured interviews. This software allows for detailed statistical analysis of the text corpus, including classic text analysis, specificity analysis, similarity analysis, and word cloud. In addition, this research aims to explore participants' perceptions and experiences through around twenty interviews, juxtaposing process and content in order to identify different themes. The IRaMuTeQ software helps to visualize lexicographic elements and ensure homogeneity between initial and resulting themes through correspondence factorial analysis.

INTRODUCTION

In academic research, qualitative analysis offers a valuable method for comprehensively understanding the details of topics under study. It achieves this by relying upon narrative perspectives and interpretations of participants (interviewees), thereby enriching the grasping of the subject matter (Muzari et al., 2022). Unlike quantitative research, which focuses on analyzing numerical data, statistics, and quantitative measurements, qualitative research focuses on understanding the social phenomena and the meanings attributed by individuals to their reality depending on their response to the complexity and the diversity of human experiences. However, qualitative research consists of exploring the subjective

DOI: 10.4018/979-8-3693-3306-8.ch008

dimensions of reality and the recognition of the diversity of points of view (Bhangu et al., 2023). This approach often favors semi-structured interviews, focus group discussions, and participant observation for collecting qualitative data.

In this sense, the qualitative approach is an excellent method for addressing multicultural issues where the emphasis is not placed on deepening the theoretical or conceptual understanding of the research subject, but on examining the contribution to change and quality improvement within the framework studied (Morgan, 2022). Indeed, qualitative research produces detailed data on the "who, what, and where of events or experiences" from a subjective point of view. From a philosophical perspective, this research approach suggests that reality is multiple and subjective, given that it is perceived differently by each individual. This type of research encourages deploying flexible, inductive, and dynamic processes while preserving the integrity of the data so that they remain devoted to the phenomenon studied (Tomaszewski et al., 2020).

Moreover, qualitative data analysis represents a powerful method used across various research fields to deeply explore participants' perceptions and experiences. Consequently, integrating computer-assisted qualitative data analysis software (CAQDAS) seems indispensable in qualitative research (Monteiro et al., 2021). However, software like IRAMUTEQ serves as a promising methodological approach for qualitative analysis research. Its advantages extend beyond the limitations of its algorithms, but further research is needed to enhance its effectiveness in other contexts (Niedbalski & Ślęzak, 2022).

Within this analytical framework, zakat, an Islamic principle, constitutes a fundamental aspect of Muslims' spiritual and social life. It symbolizes an act of financial purification and community support, aiming to redistribute wealth within society. Qualitative analysis of zakat provides insights relying on the perceptions and interpretations surrounding this practice within the context of Islamic countries (Nurul Izza, 2021). In this study, the IRAMUTEQ software is employed as a qualitative text analysis tool to explore discourses and representations related to zakat in a multicultural context (Faiz & Abdullah, 2023). IRAMUTEQ enables rigorous analysis of texts by identifying recurring themes, keyword associations, and linguistic nuances within the studied documents.

This program offers various forms of data analysis, such as classic text analysis, specificity analysis, similarity analysis, and word cloud creation (Chaves et al., 2017). To realize this approach, a series of interviews with different participants is conducted to explore the qualitative research process. Furthermore, comparing both the process and the content proves useful in studying the various themes covered during the interviews. This research encourages coherence between the initially proposed themes and those revealed by the correspondence factorial analysis. This chapter aims to provide a general overview of the qualitative approach designs (Sarrica et al., 2016).

The primary objective of this book, as a whole, consists of examining various qualitative research approaches and principles suitable for multicultural contexts (Allsop et al., 2022). Consequently, this research aims to enhance understanding of contemporary perspectives related to zakat's practice through available texts, illuminating diverse conceptions and applications of zakat across different cultural and social settings (Abu-Ghazaleh Mahajneh et al., 2021). As part of this research, the use of IRaMuTeQ software facilitates analyzing the transcriptions of the semi-structured interviews carried out during the exploratory survey.

The book chapter structure is divided into five main sections. After introducing the research topic, section 2 reviews the literature regarding the qualitative research approach by shedding light on the IRaMuTeQ software analysis process. Section 3 describes the research methodology, including the research conception and design as well as the sampling technique followed to analyze the qualitative data. The results of the semi-structured interviews, with the muzzakis, are presented in section 4. Finally, section 5 concludes the book chapter by addressing the theoretical and practical implications of the research, highlighting its limitations, and proposing directions for future research.

LITERATURE REVIEW

Examining the relevance of existing research related to qualitative studies seems important to contextualize a research topic. This literature review aims to prove useful for understanding the current landscape of knowledge for this study.

Qualitative Analysis Background

Qualitative research refers to a moving process of collecting, organizing, and interpreting textual materials from conversations or interviews conducted. It is used to explore the meanings of social phenomena as they are experienced by individuals in their natural context (Lewis, 2015). This approach can be considered one of the most accessible input methods for humanities researchers, in the sense that it draws on concise conversations and aims to collect the stories of the interviewees. These stories can be expressed in various forms, such as conversations (individual or group interviews) and/or written texts.

Indeed, qualitative approaches aim to understand a specific phenomenon, based on an exploratory rather than a confirmatory approach (Crowther & Lauesen, 2017). They seek to examine the reality studied. Qualitative methodology involves an in-depth analysis of reasons and processes, allowing the researcher to analyze, in detail, the perceptions, beliefs, and representations of individuals, whether conscious or unconscious. Human and social phenomena can be approached in different ways, either by analyzing them using the same methods for studying natural phenomena or by recognizing their specificity and adopting a distinct scientific approach (Dodgson, 2017).

This second conception highlights the distinction between the explanation phase, which seeks to discover universal laws and explain the meaning that actors attribute to their actions in a given context. The central argument is that the social sciences differ from the natural sciences because of the intentional nature of human actions. Despite this particularity, it is possible to develop an objective scientific approach based on intentional dimension. Qualitative research follows this tradition by adopting a comprehensive perspective (Pomerantsev & Rodionova, 2021). It therefore seeks to understand how individuals think, speak, and act, by framing them in their context or their specific situation.

Similarly, qualitative research methods provide an overview of specific phenomena that can be employed in different ways, either as an independent research methodology or as a prelude to more in-depth qualitative studies (Dodgson, 2017). Despite their widespread use in academic studies, research articles provide little specific methodological guidance for this methodological approach. This lack of representation pushes researchers to opt for more complex qualitative designs, such as grounded theory or phenomenology, without meeting the criteria required by these approaches, and without resorting to an appropriate justification of their choice. Hence, it is crucial to encourage deeper discussions about how and why qualitative research approaches are adopted (Murgado-Armenteros et al., 2015). This would not only guide researchers but also guarantee some acceptable standards for applying this approach in different research areas.

Moreover, the qualitative research approach aims to probe complex phenomena. Adopting a qualitative strategy facilitates access to stakeholders' perceptions to better understand the study context as a whole, which guarantees coherence between the central concept of the research and the measurement elements. Additionally, the qualitative approach reaches a detailed presentation of data collected from a single individual, a case study, or a group of people. Entire works are devoted to qualitative research methodology, as well as the different methods that make it up (Roller, 2019).

Furthermore, choosing an appropriate approach to address research questions characterizes a crucial step in the research process likely to allow researchers to justify their methodological choices. Engaging in qualitative studies does not require deep theoretical foundations but aims to remain faithful to participants' experiences, particularly in areas of analysis where the knowledge is limited. Therefore, using qualitative research methodology seems to be the most suitable technique as it ensures a direct presentation of results closely linked to the terminology used in the predefined research question. The use of the qualitative approach is often recommended in different studies covering economic, social, and human as well as multicultural perspectives.

Qualitative Approach: A Contextual Application

Qualitative analysis of textual data is a crucial component in numerous research studies across social sciences, humanities, and other fields of study. Utilizing Computer-Assisted Qualitative Data Analysis Software (CAQDAS) enhances researchers' understanding of textual data and facilitates the extraction of significant insights (Woods et al., 2016). These software tools allow researchers to organize, compile, encode, and manage various data types, including audio, images, videos, and text, to increase flexibility and efficiency in data analysis. They offer advantages over analog research methods, enabling easier term searches, faster data segmentation and coding, and uniformity in text data processing.

It proves useful to note that the present research adopts a qualitative approach, aiming to develop a research model based on an in-depth analysis of the subject studies. As several researchers have pointed out, using a qualitative approach makes it possible to reach complex problems while formulating a coherent set of specific propositions aimed at exploring a particular topic (Grodal et al., 2021). This approach involves collecting data in the form of speeches or sentences by using a semi-structured interview guide. Thus, this method relies on selecting and categorizing the collected information, relating it, and then organizing it to provide a contextual appropriate explanation of the research topic.

To do this, harmonizing the content analysis and the discursive analysis aims to identify the key dimensions that contribute to enriching the results of the research process as a whole. The content analysis facilitates examining the data from the semi-structured interviews conducted (Sarrica et al., 2016). This method is widely used to thoroughly carry out the complex and detailed information collected in this study. It is particularly suited to the social research field, where the complexity of the research field requires an in-depth approach.

Several researchers (Graneheim et al., 2017) have defined content analysis as a set of techniques aimed at obtaining indicators and quantitative data for a systematic description of the content of texts and speeches. From this perspective, adopting the content analysis to the theoretical and methodological specificities of a research subject is recommended to understand the qualitative approach. This methodological tactic is particularly suitable for processing structured and unstructured data such as interviews and collected documents. However, the main contribution of discursive textual analysis lies in creating new interpretations of the corpus analyzed (Devi Prasad, 2019).

An Overview of IRaMuTeQ Software

Through IRaMuTeQ or similar software, textual data analysis becomes more coherent, concise, and accessible to the target research audience (M. Paulus & N. Lester, 2020). IRaMuTeQ is selected for its excellence among available CAQDAS options and its Hierarchical Descending Classification (DHC) features (Mazieri et al., 2022). IRaMuTeQ is specialized software for textual data analysis, providing advanced capabilities to explore and interpret meanings within qualitative data. This subsection of the chapter aims to provide detailed instructions for downloading and installing this software, enabling researchers to conduct a qualitative analysis of textual data required for this study type (Pomerantsev & Rodionova, 2021).

IRaMuTeQ is an open-source software based on R, offering a user-friendly interface for text and interview analysis. Its features include lexical analysis, statistical processing of occurrences, automatic and manual text categorization, and the generation of visual representations such as word clouds and factorial analyses (Souza et al., 2018). Several steps are involved in successfully navigating the process from downloading to data analysis using the IRaMuTeQ software within this analytical framework.

Step 1: Installing IRaMuTeQ

To initiate this process, it is useful to begin by downloading and installing IRaMuTeQ from the official website. Researchers are instructed to follow the installation guidelines provided on the website. The installation process may depend on the operating system (Windows, MacOS, Linux) being used.

Step 2: Data Preparation

Once the software is installed, the researcher needs to prepare textual data in a compatible format such as text files (.txt) or Word documents (.docx), ensuring that the data is cleaned of any punctuation or stop words. At this stage, researchers should consider the time required between coding and data analysis using IRaMuTeQ, as this temporal variable may depend on the data complexity and the coding method employed. Researcher experience and team size also influence the duration of this process. After coding is completed, data analysis may require additional efforts to explore results and interpret conclusions.

Step 3: Creating a Project in IRaMuTeQ

The third step involves launching IRaMuTeQ and creating a new project. Subsequently, the researcher imports the prepared data files into the newly created project.

Step 4: Data Analysis

At this stage, IRaMuTeQ automatically segments texts into textual units (words, phrases) and contexts (documents, document groups), facilitating further data processing and analysis. Moreover, the software applies textual analysis methods such as lexical analysis and statistical processing of occurrences.

Step 5: Exploration and Visualization

Upon completion of this step, researchers utilize visualization features to explore textual data. IRaMuTeQ enables the generating of word clouds, factorial representations, and hierarchical classifications to enhance understanding of the analyzed data.

Step 6: Interpretation of Results

The final step involves qualitative interpretation of results to help researchers identify trends, patterns, or significant relationships within the data, enabling the formulation of relevant conclusions and insights from advanced analysis.

MATERIALS AND METHODS

After defining the theoretical framework, it is essential to outline the research methodology that will guide the study. This chapter's section will provide a clear methodological approach by describing the perspectives employed to address the qualitative research objectives.

Research Methodology

To meet the objectives of the qualitative research methodology, the IRaMuTeQ software is used to visualize the lexicographic elements of the corpus studied (Souza et al., 2018). Using this approach allows the researcher to capture participants' perspectives from their own experiences. In the 1980s, the emergence of computer programs offered valuable assistance in analyzing qualitative data for specific research. Among this software IRaMuTeQ, with a comprehensive dictionary in several languages, is developed using the Python programming language, allowing it to benefit from the functionalities of the R statistical software, thus facilitating the processing of this type of data.

Furthermore, by using the IRaMuTeQ software, the relevance of this study is based on three major aspects (Monteiro et al., 2021): An innovative exploitation of sub-corpus analyses in research, a better understanding of the formation of intermediate categories, an aspect often neglected in the use of qualitative software, and an exhaustive presentation of the analytical process of discursive textual analysis reflecting, thus, an area of study little explored in the literature. These elements reveal the originality of the analytical perspectives offered by the IRaMuTeQ software as a fundamental tool for discursive textual analysis. Several types of analyses are provided by the IRaMuTeQ software, in this case:

Textual Analysis

The text analysis uses the IRaMuTeQ software version 07 alpha 2 (R Interface for Multidimensional Analysis of Texts and Questionnaires), an open-source lexicometric software developed by Ratinaud (2009). This program allows multidimensional analysis of texts and has recently found applications in various research fields such as health, social sciences, education, ecology, and business, etc. (Ratinaud, P.,2009). By facilitating and accelerating the interpretation of texts thanks to lexicometric analysis, this software saves considerable time (Souza et al., 2020). This analysis is structured in three parts: A lexicographic analysis, a descending hierarchical classification according to the Reinert method, and a similarity analysis. The detailed results of these analyses are presented below.

Cluster Analysis

The cluster analysis is carried out using the method of descending hierarchical classification of active forms (words), known as the Reinert method (Figura et al., 2023). This method allowed us to group the data into five large lexical clusters, as illustrated in Figure 4. Additionally, the figure provides additional information for interpreting the composition of these clusters, presenting the most significant forms included in each group. Given display limitations, only the 17 most relevant forms from each group were included in the figure, excluding verbs and base forms.

Similarly, the correspondence factor analysis (CFA) (Mazieri et al., 2022) is carried out and the results are presented in Figure 5. This graphical representation highlights the groups formed by the most frequently used words in each cluster, after applying the descending hierarchical classification. Each cluster is represented by a different color: Cluster 1 in red, cluster 2 in green, cluster 3 in light blue, cluster 4 in dark blue, and Cluster 5 in purple. This two-axis representation makes it possible to identify relationships between clusters.

Research Design

In the context of analyzing multicultural practices, zakat seems to be a fundamental aspect of cultures, particularly Muslim ones (Muda & Riau, 2024). This conception has a differentiated meaning on the religious and socio-economic level because it is influenced by the diversity of the cultural, historical, and geographical contexts in which it operates. Indeed, the concept of zakat covers the principle of equitable redistribution of wealth for the benefit of the most deprived (Sarif et al., 2024). This notion of sharing and supporting vulnerable members of society resonates with universal values of compassion, social justice, and social inclusion, transcending cultural differences. Thus, this concept has emerged even in societies where Islam is not the majority religion, to become a universal humanitarian practice, helping to alleviate inequalities and promote social well-being (Mohd et al.,2023).

Therefore, this qualitative analysis aims to fill this gap by examining the different dimensions of zakat and its adaptation in diverse cultural contexts. By understanding zakat as a multicultural practice, we can better appreciate its impact on promoting social and economic well-being (Meerangani, 2019). To follow this conception, the design of this study involves holding 20 semi-structured interviews with the selected people, in this case, the muzzakis. This research framework aims to analyze the impact of zakat on mitigating economic and social inequalities noted within the Moroccan context. Thanks to its qualitative scope, this study ensures the definition of the main contributions of zakat in reducing the economic and social gaps observed (Belabes, 2022).

Sampling Technique

To meet the objectives of this qualitative study, the purposive sampling technique is implemented, reflecting a widely preferred method among qualitative researchers (Guest et al., 2020). This approach is based on specifying the characteristics of participants, to the extent that qualitative researchers do not seek to generalize their results at the statistical level. It focuses on administrating semi-structured interviews with the targeted population. Through purposive sampling, the researcher can select participants based on his judgment, which allows him to obtain targeted and relevant information about the pre-established objectives of the study.

Data Analysis

Data analysis is conducted inductively by reviewing written transcripts and listening to audio recordings from semi-structured interviews conducted with interviewees. To ensure reliable results, information is triangulated using various data sources. By using the IRaMuTeQ software, a lexicometric or textual-statistical analysis is carried out, to allow the researcher to obtain certain regularity and correlation within the corpus studied (Canuto et al., 2020).

RESULTS AND DISCUSSIONS

After completing the various phases of adjusting the functioning of the program, an analysis of textual data is implemented in three distinct stages. The first step consists of preparing and coding the textual corpus, and the second relates to the processing of textual data in the software. While the third stage is assimilated to interpreting the research results, by mobilizing different sets of analyses.

Statistical Analysis

This analysis reveals information such as the frequency and number of occurrences of lexical units, as well as the distribution of words in the corpus. By using the Zipf diagram, it becomes possible to visualize the behavior of words according to their frequency of occurrence in the text, providing insight into the structure of the corpus and the most recurring words. In addition, the curve makes it possible to illustrate a distinct distribution of words according to their frequency of occurrence in the text corpus. On the left side of the curve, we observe that a few words are repeated several times, while on the right side, a large number of words are repeated several times.

Figure 1. Statistical Analysis Generated by IRaMuTeQ Software

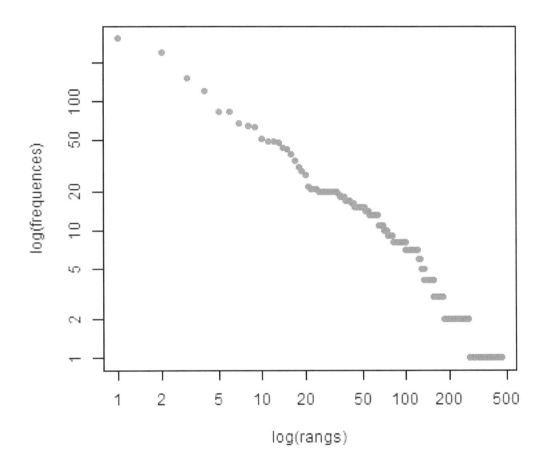

Source: Authors
Note. This statistical analysis provides quantitative insights into the analyzed textual data.

This distribution highlights the importance of words with frequency 1 (hapax), represented by the final part of the X axis (horizontal line), where f =190, or 40.95% of the forms, indicating their recurrence in the text. On the other hand, only three active forms, through the application of lemmatization, appeared more than fifty times in the dynamic transcription, thus forming the group of the most recurring terms, positioned at the top of the Y axis (vertical line). These active forms, listed in order of frequency, are: "institution" (f = 83), "zakat" (f = 57), and "social" (f = 50). Based on these results, the frequent use of these terms is justified by the framing of the Zakat institution, where participants detail their opinion towards Zakat as a multicultural approach to development in the Moroccan context.

Word Cloud

This analysis sheds light on the words arranged visually in the form of a cloud, with variable sizes. The most important words refer to those which are frequently repeated in the textual corpus, which gives them a certain preponderance. Based on the frequency indicator, we were able to identify the most salient words, distinguished by their larger size and central position relative to other words (see Figure 2).

It is notable that terms such as "institution", "zakat" and "social" stand out, particularly among all the words, which confirm the conclusions of the previous statistical analysis.

Figure 2. Word Cloud Generated by IRaMuTeQ Software

Source: Authors
Note. This figure facilitates exploring and interpreting textual data by highlighting the most significant key terms, thereby enabling researchers to discern patterns or trends present in the analyzed dataset.

Similarity Analysis

Similarity analysis, based on graph theory, reflects a dynamic concept of lexicometric data processing. It allows us to examine relationships between word occurrences, making it easier to identify connections between them and infer the structure of lexical content (see Figure 3). For this analysis, we included words that appeared at least 10 times in the corpus. We found that three words, namely "institution", "zakat" and "social", particularly stood out, as mentioned previously. They occupy central positions in three distinct sets of terms, generating different ramifications. It seems important to note that the term "institution", stands out by being the most central and having the greatest number of connections.

Figure 3. Similarity Dendrogram Generated by IRaMuTeQ Software

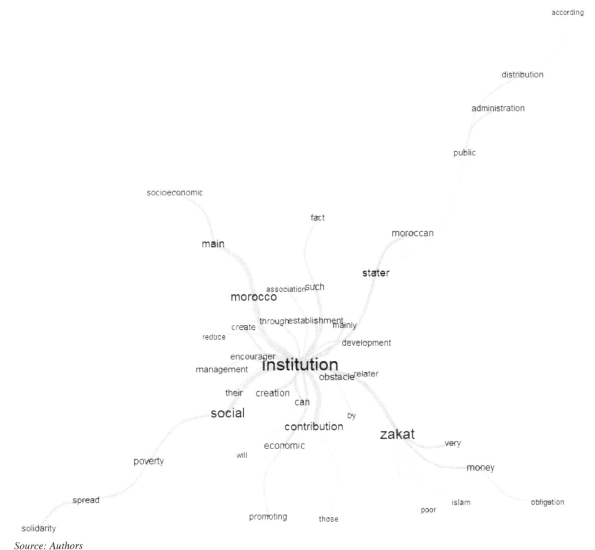

Source: Authors
Note. This figure provides a similarity analysis by identifying patterns and relationships among textual data, thereby allowing researchers to explore similarities and differences among various elements within the dataset.

Through similarity analysis, significant advances are being made to understand the relationships between central words and those connected to them, which has greatly expanded our interpretation of lexicometric data. In addition, the paths by which words are expressed to their connections, highlighting the strongest and most frequent, are identified.

DESCENDING HIERARCHICAL CLASSIFICATION

Another lexicometric analysis method deployed is descending hierarchical classification (CHD), which groups text segments based on their respective vocabularies and divides them on the presence or absence of stem forms to create different lexical worlds, called classes or clusters. This method establishes a stable and definitive classification based on the similarity of vocabulary between text segments, taking into consideration lexical differences between classes, and measurement by using chi-square ($\chi2$) tests.

The software organizes this analysis by generating different dendrograms in the CHD, by illustrating relationships between classes (clusters). Of the 96 text segments identified, 68 are successfully classified using the lemmatization approach, representing the use of 70.83%. CHD analysis produces five distinct classes of text segments (see Figure 4), highlighting the semantic content of each class.

Figure 4. A Dendrogram of Descending Hierarchical Classification Generated by IRaMuTeQ Software

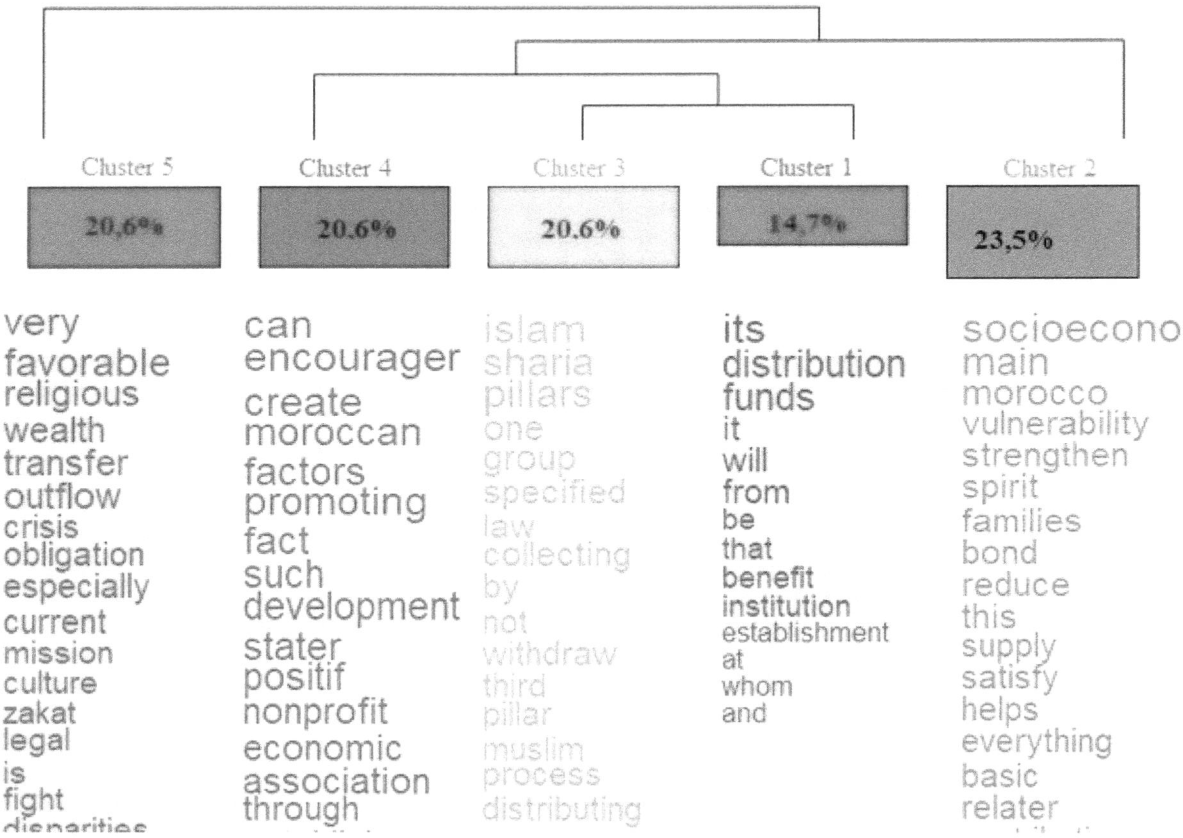

Cluster 5	Cluster 4	Cluster 3	Cluster 1	Cluster 2
20.6%	20.6%	20.6%	14.7%	23.5%

very	can	islam	its	socioecono
favorable	encourager	sharia	distribution	main
religious	create	pillars	funds	morocco
wealth	moroccan	one	it	vulnerability
transfer	factors	group	will	strengthen
outflow	promoting	specified	from	spirit
crisis	fact	law	be	families
obligation	such	collecting	that	bond
especially	development	by	benefit	reduce
current	stater	not	institution	this
mission	positif	withdraw	establishment	supply
culture	nonprofit	third	at	satisfy
zakat	economic	pillar	whom	helps
legal	association	muslim	and	everything
is	through	process		basic
fight		distributing		relater
disparities				

Source: Authors
Note. This figure categorizes terms into distinct groups, delineating their similarities and differences.

This analysis demonstrates remarkable stability, with the five identified clusters. This means that these classes are composed of text segments containing similar words. In the dendrogram above, the textual corpus is subdivided into two independent blocks (sub-corpus). The first block includes class

2 (23.53%), a second subdivision including class 4 (20.59%), and another subdivision with classes 1 (14.71%) and 3 (20.59), which present a closer and differentiated semantic content. The second block is mainly made up of class 5 (20.59%). The latter is the most isolated from the others, which demonstrates proximity and homogeneity between the two.

At the end of interpreting the data from the CHD analysis, the active forms of each class of the text segments are examined, including nouns, adjectives, adverbs, verbs, and unrecognized forms, with particular emphasis on those obtained in the chi-square ($\chi 2$) test with a $p < 0.05$, indicating the strength of the word association in a respective class. Terms with lower χ^2 values are less related to the class, while lower p-values indicate a greater relationship, thus contributing to the validation and reliability of the results for the class in question. Words with p-values less than 0.0001 are extremely significant in each class, indicating their certainty at 99.99%.

Furthermore, after processing data by the IRaMuTeQ software, the significant words of the classes and their incorporation into the text segments are examined in detail. Based on the semantic content, the different identified classes will be named as follows:

Cluster 1: Distribution of zakat.

Cluster 2: Socio-economic contributions of the institution of zakat.

Cluster 3: Islamic foundations on zakat.

Cluster 4: Zakat and the promotion of development.

Cluster 5: Cultural aspects of zakat.

It should be noted that this nomination is made by the authors, taking into account the semantic universe of each cluster. The main associated words, their exhaustive analysis, and the semantic context reflect elements to be taken into consideration to extract the meaning of the classes and name them accordingly. This division allows us to understand how the participants, in particular the muzzakis, envisage supervising the zakat institution within the Moroccan context.

CORRESPONDENCE FACTORIAL ANALYSIS

This lexicometric software offers another way of presenting the results, through Correspondence Factor Analysis (CFA), represented on a Cartesian plane, bringing together the different words and their positioning in the classes according to frequencies and correlation values ($\chi 2$) of each word in the corpus (see Figure 5). This visualization facilitates the understanding of the characteristic vocabulary of each class in different semantic analysis contexts.

Figure 5. Correspondence Factorial Analysis Generated by IRaMuTeQ Software

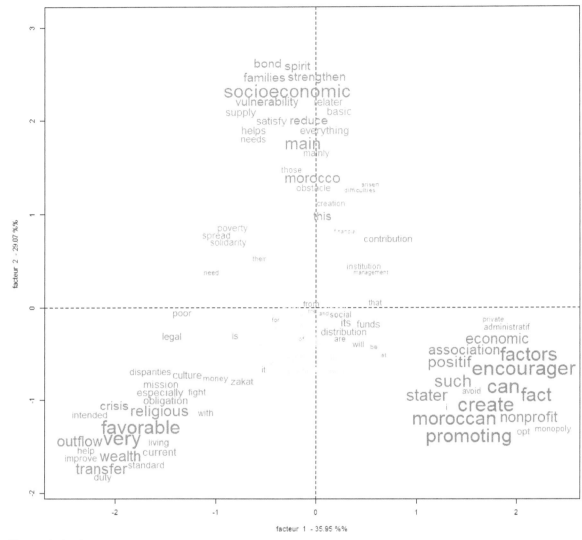

(*Source: Authors*)
Note. Correspondence factorial analysis represents connections between categorical variables present in textual data, by revealing dependencies among various categories or terms.

In the Correspondence Factorial Analysis (CFA) framework, we identified the most significant words having a higher $\chi 2$, which translates into their larger size in the image. Each class is represented in a centralized segment, while others extend toward the periphery. In addition, a few words from each class are scattered in the other quadrants. Notably, cluster 5 (lower left quadrant), in purple, stands out as the most isolated on the Cartesian level, not expanding towards any other quadrant, which indicates less association with other classes and specificity in its lexical content analysis.

In this sense, clusters 2 and 4 represented in gray and blue (upper left quadrant), appear to be interconnected. This interconnection is observed between the two classes making it possible to highlight the place of zakat, as a multicultural practice, in terms of promoting socioeconomic development. Words from these two classes are mixed in this quadrant. Thus, clusters 1 and 3 represented respectively in red and green are correlated on the factorial level, because they share closer vocabularies linked to the zakat institution within the Moroccan context. Furthermore, the last remaining class, namely class 5, represented in purple appears distant from the others since it deals with different aspects in close relation to the cultural axis of zakat.

CONCLUSION

To conclude, the use of IRaMuTeQ software in this qualitative research proves particularly valuable for the researchers involved, because it allows them to improve their mastery of analytical software in terms of lexicometric studies (Montalescot et al., 2024). In addition, it facilitates operationalizing the data, concerning the organization and segmentation of a large volume of text, by providing that the corpus is previously well prepared for qualitative analysis. This approach interprets the results more objectively because the text segments are easily retrieved. Another advantage reflects the accessibility of this software to all researchers, being free and available with different dictionaries, which promotes major discussions during the textual processing data.

At the end of this study, a lexicometric study (Sousa et al., 2021) is generated by using the IRaMuTeQ software (R Interface for Multidimensional Text Analysis and Questionnaires) in addition to graphic representations of the texts studied, and the statistical analyses of the textual corpus coming from semi-structured interviews conducted. This software offers the possibility of leading a statistical analysis of the textual corpus, including both speeches and texts, based on a prior segmentation of the texts. Although this software does not provide an exhaustive analysis of the interviews or questionnaires, it helps to visualize the lexical aspects of the corpus examined (Souza et al., 2018).

Besides, zakat refers to a compulsory religious act to redistribute wealth and support disadvantaged communities (Muda & Riau, 2024). Its potential as a tool for socio-economic development has garnered increasing interest, especially in multicultural contexts like Morocco. The study uses a thorough qualitative analysis to examine how Zakat can promote sustainable development within Islamic countries, particularly Morocco. Moreover, using qualitative research methodology seems essential for the underlying dynamics between Zakat and development within the Moroccan context, likely to gather rich and contextual information on Zakat practices and their perceived impact.

Furthermore, the initiation of different lexical analysis techniques discerns the semantic contents linked to contextualizing zakat as a multicultural development practice in the Moroccan context. The use of this software ensures the statistical rigor necessary to process extensive textual responses, facilitating the integration of quantitative and qualitative approaches into the analytical process and reinforcing the objectivity of data interpretation (Fona, 2023). The diagram resulting from the statistical analysis reveals words that are not very recurring and others that are very repeated, among which the three most mentioned were identified as being relevant throughout the lexicometric analysis process. In addition, similarity analysis helped to identify co-occurrences between words, providing a better understanding of the associations between different terms used to describe zakat's practice within the Moroccan context.

Descending hierarchical classification (CHD) is widely used in our study for generating a five-class dendrogram, allowing the most significant words to be grouped in each class by promoting a more precise interpretation of the lexicometric data. In addition, correspondence factorial analysis (CFA) completed this study approach by visualizing the existing links between the different classes and by highlighting the convergences and divergences between the different lexical domains (Iqbal et al., 2024). Overall, using the IRaMuTeQ software holds significant value for this qualitative research. It provides a robust platform for analyzing and interpreting textual data while facilitating collaboration between researchers and ensuring the accuracy and validity of the results obtained. This highlights the importance for researchers to master the different word-processing features offered by the software to use it effectively. It also highlights the need for the researcher to be involved at all stages of the research, benefiting from the theoretical support necessary to prepare the textual corpus. The use of IRaMuTeQ software for data analysis must be guided by the research problem to pattern the research process as a whole, going from the data collection and inference phase to the interpretation of data.

Based on this review, this study presumes experience using IRaMuTeQ software to facilitate analyzing textual data from a qualitative research perspective. The use of this software has proven to be beneficial, appropriate, and reliable, for promoting both the analysis process and the results of the research, in terms of interpreting responses with scientific rigor (Fakis et al., 2014). As a result, the use of this tool has significantly improved in terms of processing data from the dynamics of creativity and sensitivity. It should be noted that little research in Morocco describes the use of this software by detailing the different analysis methods, which represents a major challenge for the Author. This finding highlights the importance of our study, providing a comprehensive description of the analytical process taking into consideration all available features of the software. To this end, it is necessary to conduct more studies using the IRaMuTeQ software to broaden the understanding of this tool for qualitative analyses from different research areas (Elo et al., 2014).

IMPLICATIONS AND LIMITATIONS

In the context of analyzing multicultural aspects, this study aims to delve deeper into the literature examining the influence of Zakat, a multicultural practice, on promoting development through qualitative analysis (Izza & Rusydiana, 2023). It seeks to explore the causal relationship between these two elements in the Moroccan context. Our research provides a detailed understanding of qualitative research methodology. While this study has uncovered noteworthy findings, it is important to acknowledge its limitations. The absence of zakat institutions within the Moroccan context in Morocco poses challenges in assessing its impact on fostering integrated socio-economic development principles. Additionally, the scarcity of data on Moroccan muzzakis has restricted both the methodological and empirical breadth of our qualitative investigation.

REFERENCES

Abu-Ghazaleh Mahajneh, M., Greenspan, I., & Haj-Yahia, M. M. (2021). Zakat giving to non-muslims: Muftis' attitudes in Arab and non-Arab countries 0F. *Journal of Muslim Philanthropy and Civil Society*, 5(2), 66–86. 10.2979/muslphilcivisoc.5.2.04

Allsop, D. B., Chelladurai, J. M., Kimball, E. R., Marks, L. D., & Hendricks, J. J. (2022). Qualitative methods with Nvivo software: A practical guide for analyzing qualitative data. *Psych*, 4(2), 142–159. 10.3390/psych4020013

Belabes, A. (2022). Limitations Of The SDGs in the light of a Zakat approach in terms of resilience. *AZKA International Journal of Zakat & Social Finance*, 3(1), 53–84. 10.51377/azjaf.vol3no1.94

Bhangu, S., Provost, F., & Caduff, C. (2023). Introduction to qualitative research methods - Part i. *Perspectives in Clinical Research*, 14(1), 39–42. 10.4103/picr.picr_253_2236909216

Canuto, A., Braga, B., Monteiro, L., Digitais, F., & IRaMuTeQ, A. E. (2020). *Aspects of CAQDAS usage in qualitative research : An empiric comparison of ALCEST And IRAMUTEQ as digital ToolsEasyChair preprint critic A.*

Chaves, M. M. N., dos Santos, A. P. R., dos Santosa, N. P., & Larocca, L. M. (2017). Use of the software IRAMUTEQ in qualitative research: An experience report. *Studies in Systems, Decision, and Control*, 71, 39–48. 10.1007/978-3-319-43271-7_4

Crowther, D., & Lauesen, L. M. (2017). Qualitative methods. *Handbook of Research Methods in Corporate Social Responsibility*, 225–229. 10.1177/0010414006296344

de Souza, M. A. R., Wall, M. L., & Thuler, A. C. (2018). O uso do software IRAMUTEQ na análise de dados em pesquisas qualitativas. *Revista Da Escola de Enfermagem Da USP, 52*(0), 1–17. https://doi .org/10.1590/s1980-220x2017015003353

De Souza, M. A. R., Wall, M. L., Thuler, A. C. D. M. C., Lowen, I. M. V., & Peres, A. M. (2018). The use of IRAMUTEQ software for data analysis in qualitative research*. *Revista Da Escola de Enfermagem, 52*, 1–7. https://doi.org/10.1590/S1980-220X2017015003353

Devi Prasad, B. (2019). Qualitative content analysis: Why is it still a path less taken? *Forum Qualitative Social Research*, 20(3). Advance online publication. 10.17169/fqs-20.3.3392

Dodgson, J. E. (2017). About Research: Qualitative Methodologies. *Journal of Human Lactation*, 33(2), 355–358. 10.1177/0890334417769869328418801

Elo, S., Kääriäinen, M., Kanste, O., Pölkki, T., Utriainen, K., & Kyngäs, H. (2014). Qualitative Content Analysis. *SAGE Open*, 4(1), 215824401452263. 10.1177/2158244014522633

Faiz, M. F., & Abdullah, I. (2023). Establishing a Zakat Culture based on Good Zakat Governance and Good Zakat Empowerment in Indonesia. *Journal of Islamic Economics Perspectives, 5*(2), 1–11.

Fakis, A., Hilliam, R., Stoneley, H., & Townend, M. (2014). Quantitative Analysis of Qualitative Information From Interviews: A Systematic Literature Review. *Journal of Mixed Methods Research*, 8(2), 139–161. 10.1177/1558689813495111

Figura, M., Fraire, M., Durante, A., Cuoco, A., Arcadi, P., Alvaro, R., Vellone, E., & Piervisani, L. (2023). New frontiers for qualitative textual data analysis: A multimethod statistical approach. *European Journal of Cardiovascular Nursing*, 22(5), 547–551. 10.1093/eurjcn/zvad02136748993

Fona, C. (2023). Qualitative data analysis: Using thematic analysis. *Researching and Analysing Business: Research Methods in Practice*, 130–145. 10.4324/9781003107774-11

Graneheim, U. H., Lindgren, B. M., & Lundman, B. (2017). Methodological challenges in qualitative content analysis: A discussion paper. *Nurse Education Today*, 56(May), 29–34. 10.1016/j.nedt.2017.06.00228651100

Grodal, S., Anteby, M., & Holm, A. L. (2021). Achieving rigor in qualitative analysis: The role of active categorization in theory building. *Academy of Management Review*, 46(3), 591–612. 10.5465/amr.2018.0482

Guest, G., Namey, E., & Chen, M. (2020). A simple method to assess and report thematic saturation in qualitative research. *PLoS One*, 15(5), 1–17. 10.1371/journal.pone.023207632369511

Iqbal, M., Chaghtai, K., Jabbar, A. A., Achour, M., & Geraldine, E. (2024)... *Concept, Implementation, and Development of Productive Zakat Management for Social, Educational, and Humanitarian.*, 2(1), 67–78.

Izza, N. N., & Rusydiana, A. S. (2023). A Qualitative Review on Halal Food: NVivo Approach. *Management, and Business, 1*, 90–106. https://ejournal.unida.gontor.ac.id/index.php/JTS/index

Lewis, S. (2015). Qualitative Inquiry and Research Design: Choosing Among Five Approaches. *Health Promotion Practice*, 16(4), 473–475. 10.1177/1524839915580941

Mazieri, M. R., Quoniam, L. M., Reymond, D., & Cunha, K. C. T. (2022). Use of IRAMUTEQ for content analysis based on descending hierarchical classification and correspondence factor analysis. *Brazilian Journal of Marketing*, 21(5), 1978–2011.

Meerangani, K. A. (2019). The Role of Zakat in Human Development. *SALAM: Jurnal Sosial Dan Budaya Syar-I*, 6(2), 141–154. 10.15408/sjsbs.v6i2.11037

Mohd, P., Fikri, F., Omar, A., Nur, M., & Hasbollah, H. (n.d.). *The Roles of Zakat Towards Maqasid Al-Shariah and Sustainable Development Goals (SDGs): A Case Study of Zakat Institutions in East Malaysia.* Academic Press.

Montalescot, L., Lamore, K., Flahault, C., & Untas, A. (2024). What is the place of interpretation in text analysis? An example using ALCESTE® software. *Qualitative Research in Psychology*, 21(2), 200–226. 10.1080/14780887.2024.2316624

Monteiro, L., de Melo, R., Braga, B., de Sá, J., Monteiro, L., Cunha, M., Gêda, T., & Canuto, A. (2021). ALCESTE X IRAMUTEQ: Comparative Analysis of the Use of CAQDAS in Qualitative Research. *Advances in Intelligent Systems and Computing, 1345 AISC*, 67–79. 10.1007/978-3-030-70187-1_6

Morgan, H. (2022). Conducting a Qualitative Document Analysis. *The Qualitative Report*, 27(1), 64–77. 10.46743/2160-3715/2022.5044

Muda, E., & Thalib, A. (2024). Innovative Approaches to Managing Zakat within the Context of Sustainable Development and Societal Well-Being in Indonesia. *European Journal of Studies in Management & Business*, 29, 74–89. Advance online publication. 10.32038/mbrq.2024.29.05

Murgado-Armenteros, E. M., Gutiérrez-Salcedo, M., Torres-Ruiz, F. J., & Cobo, M. J. (2015). Analysing the conceptual evolution of qualitative marketing research through science mapping analysis. *Scientometrics*, 102(1), 519–557. 10.1007/s11192-014-1443-z

Muzari, T., Shava, G. N., & Shonhiwa, S. (2022). Qualitative Research Paradigm, a Key Research Design for Educational Researchers, Processes and Procedures : A Theoretical Overview. *Indiana Journal of Humanities and Social Sciences*, 3(1), 14–20.

Niedbalski, J., & Ślęzak, I. (2022). Encounters with CAQDAS: Advice for Beginner Users of Computer Software for Qualitative Research. *The Qualitative Report*, 27(4), 1114–1132. 10.46743/2160-3715/2022.4770

Nurul Izza, N. (2021). Review on Zakat Performance Studies using NVivo-12. *Islamic Social Finance*, 1(1). Advance online publication. 10.58968/isf.v1i1.109

Paulus, M. T., & Lester, J. (2020). Using software to support qualitative data analysis. *Handbook of Qualitative Research in Education, 2*, 420–429. 10.4337/9781788977159.00048

Pomerantsev, A. L., & Rodionova, O. Y. (2021). New trends in qualitative analysis: Performance, optimization, and validation of multi-class and soft models. *Trends in Analytical Chemistry*, 143, 116372. 10.1016/j.trac.2021.116372

Roller, M. R. (2019). A quality approach to qualitative content analysis: Similarities and differences compared to other qualitative methods. *Forum Qualitative Social Research*, 20(3). Advance online publication. 10.17169/fqs-20.3.3385

Sarif, S., Ali, N. A., & Kamri, N. (2024). Zakat for generating sustainable income: An emerging mechanism of productive distribution. *Cogent Business and Management*, 11(1), 2312598. Advance online publication. 10.1080/23311975.2024.2312598

Sarrica, M., Mingo, I., Mazzara, B. M., & Leone, G. (2016). *The effects of lemmatization on textual analysis conducted with IRaMuTeQ : results in comparison.* Academic Press.

Souza, L. G. S. (2020). Places from which We Speak: The Concepts of Consensual and Reified Universes and the Interpretation of the Outcomes Obtained with ALCESTE and IRAMUTEQ. *Papers on Social Representations*, 29(2), 11–25.

Tomaszewski, L. E., Zarestky, J., & Gonzalez, E. (2020). Planning Qualitative Research: Design and Decision Making for New Researchers. *International Journal of Qualitative Methods*, 19, 1–7. 10.1177/1609406920967174

Woods, M., Macklin, R., & Lewis, G. K. (2016). Researcher reflexivity: Exploring the impacts of CAQDAS use. *International Journal of Social Research Methodology*, 19(4), 385–403. 10.1080/13645579.2015.1023964

ADDITIONAL READING

Afiyah, I., & Mahmudulhassan, M. (2024). Professional Zakat as a Catalyst for Welfare: Strategic Mapping for Sustainable Economic Growth in Semarang. *Demak Universal Journal of Islam and Sharia*, 2(03), 199–210.

Anisa, Y., & Mukhsin, M. (2023). The Role Of Zakat In Realizing Sustainable Development Goals (SDGs) To Increase Community Economic Income. Al-Infaq. *Jurnal Ekonomi Islam*, 13(2), 286–296.

Dos Santos Martins, I. C., do Rosário Lima, V. M., Amaral-Rosa, M. P., Moreira, L., & Ramos, M. G. (2019, September). Handcrafted and software-assisted procedures for discursive textual analysis: analytical convergences or divergences? In *World Conference on Qualitative Research* (pp. 189-205). Cham: Springer International Publishing.

Erni, E., Artis, A., & Rahman, R. (2024). Zakat Management Practices and Sustainable Development in Indonesia. *Sinergi International Journal of Islamic Studies*, 2(1), 24–37. 10.61194/ijis.v2i1.129

Kanygin, G., & Koretckaia, V. (2021). Analytical coding: Performing qualitative data analysis based on programming principles. *The Qualitative Report*, 26(2), 316–333. 10.46743/2160-3715/2021.4342

Mokodenseho, S., Paputungan, P., Paputungan, A., Modeong, N., Manggo, T., Kobandaha, S., Dilapanga, S., & Imban, Y. (2024). The Strategic Role of Zakat Management in Socio-Economic Empowerment of the Ummah. *West Science Islamic Studies*, 2(02), 114–1. 10.58812/wsiss.v2i02.821

Muttaqin, Z., & Nasir, M. D. A. (2024). Can Zakat Contribute to Achieving Sustainable Development Goals? A Case Study on Java Island, Indonesia. *Jurnal Ekonomi Syariah Teori dan Terapan*, 11(1).

Neta, A. A. C., & Cardoso, B. L. C. (2021). The use of the IRAMUTEQ software in data analysis in qualitative or quali-quanti research. *Cenas Educacionais*, 4, e11759–e11759.

Nizar, N. M. S., & Mohamad, S. N. A. (2024). Potential use of zakat wakalah for sustainable development of Islamic social finance. *Journal of Islamic*, 9(61), 761–775.

KEY TERMS AND DEFINITIONS

IRaMuTeQ Software: IRaMuTeQ is a software designed for text and data table analysis, built on the R statistical software and Python language. It offers a range of processing and tools to assist in the description and qualitative analysis of text corpora and matrices of individual/character types.

Lexicometric Analysis: This is a quantitative approach based on the alliance of language sciences, statistics, and computer science. It makes it possible to process a global corpus of text by establishing their vocabulary and classifying words according to their frequency, their distribution, and their grammatical categories.

Multicultural Settings: Refer to contexts where individuals from different cultures, ethnicities, races, and religions, in particular, coexist and interact. These environments are often characterized by diverse beliefs, traditions, values, and customs, forming a rich and varied cultural mosaic.

Qualitative Methodology: The qualitative research methodology represents an approach aimed at deepening the understanding of social and human phenomena by exploring the perspectives, experiences, and interpretations of individuals involved in the research. It employs methods such as interviews, observations, and document analysis to collect qualitative data.

Research Design: Refers to the overall structure of a scientific study. It englobes theoretical, methodological, and analytical choices that guide the collection and interpretation of data, as well as the formulation of research questions and specific objectives. Research design is crucial as it ensures the rigor, consistency, and relevance of the study while enabling appropriate responses to research questions.

Chapter 9
A Conceptual Framework of Racial Ideologies and Frames:
Implications for Qualitative Research on Racial Discourse

Kelly Burmeister Long
http://orcid.org/0000-0002-2332-9955
University of North Georgia, USA

Katherine Rose Adams
University of North Georgia, USA

ABSTRACT

This chapter explores prominent scholars' articulations of racial ideologies and frames used in discourse on race and racism. Focusing on qualitative research designs, the chapter aims to consolidate the insights from leading scholars into a consolidated conceptual framework for racial discourse. The conceptual framework draws on influential works, such as Helms' White identity statuses, to categorize racial ideologies, fostering a nuanced understanding of the complexities surrounding racial discourse and contributing to the ongoing efforts to understand societal views of race and racism. Then, this chapter discusses pertinent research designs that could be used in racial discourse analysis in deploying the conceptual framework of racial ideologies and frames.

INTRODUCTION

Ideology, as articulated by scholars, embodies "a set of ideas employed in the justification and perpetuation of vested interests" (Spears, 1999, p. 6) and is also characterized by Giroux (2001) as the creation, use, and portrayal of ideas that can either mislead or clarify behavior (as cited in Earick, 2012, p. 143). Originating in the field of political science, ideology serves to document the ways individuals

DOI: 10.4018/979-8-3693-3306-8.ch009

and societies rationalize their existence (Knight, 2006). Ideologies can be either shared or highly individualized, often veering towards impractical and delusional notions (Knight, 2006).

The term *race ideology* refers to societal influences gradually molding both acknowledged and unacknowledged facets of race, influencing how individuals identify themselves or are identified within specific racial categories (Hernandez, 2001). Race ideology encompasses constraints on what qualifies as racism and extends to language and discourse that attribute significance to distinct forms of racial categorization (Hernandez, 2001). This conceptualization aligns with a key theme in critical race theory, asserting that "race and races are the product of social thought and relations" (Delgado & Stefancic, 2023, p. 8). Racial ideology is dynamic and fluid, shaped by both political and social conditions, with applications ranging from positive to negative contexts (Doane, 2017; Earick, 2012). Described by Bonilla-Silva (2006) as powerful expressions, racial ideologies function to both generate and sustain the prevailing status quo.

Past research has illuminated the diverse ways in which White individuals engage in discussions about race, ranging from overtly racist perspectives to more progressive antiracist ideologies (Hughey, 2022). The transmission of these ideologies occurs through various channels, encompassing language, images, and behaviors (Spears, 1999). For example, amid the COVID-19 crisis, researchers observed a notable increase in incidents of racism against Asian Americans (Tessler et al., 2020). Similarly, in the context of police brutality, instances of law enforcement officers killing Black Americans garnered attention and momentarily led to a surge in positive sentiment about Black Americans on social media, returning to a baseline of 49.33% negativity within a few weeks (Nguyen et al., 2021). During the Trump presidency, an examination of news media discourse, particularly surrounding the border wall issue, revealed a direct link between racial ideologies and the prevalence of racism, with potential implications for antiracism efforts (Kang & Yang, 2022). As these national examples show, racial ideologies are influential forces shaping societal attitudes and behaviors, emphasizing the need for continued examination and intervention to foster a more inclusive and equitable society.

Qualitative methods are considered the gold standard for understanding nuanced racial experiences and racial perceptions of individuals (Gillborn et al., 2018). Critical race theory (CRT) scholars have explained how most racial experience narratives have been from White Americans. However, CRT scholars argue that people of color are best suited to document racism (Parker & Lynn, 2002). This tenet is critical because the culture of Whiteness is so powerful that White people often have the final say about when racism has occurred and when it should be ignored (Helms, 2017). As Helms (2017) defined it, "*Whiteness* is the overt and subliminal socialization processes and practices, power structures, laws, privileges, and life experiences that favor the White racial group over all others" (p.718). Pertaining to racial perceptions, many researchers have sought to document the racial beliefs of White people, to reveal both problematic and helpful belief systems tied to Whiteness (Feagin, 2020; Helms, 2017). When participants talk about race and racism, saturation is often reached, such that perceptions can be coded to various frames that reflect broader ideologies (Bonilla-Silva, 2021).

A chief feature of ideologies are *frames*, or "set paths for interpreting information" (Bonilla-Silva, 2006, p. 26) which result in common patterns of speech (Vliegenthart & Van Zoonen, 2011). Formed through personal experiences, popular wisdom, and media discourse (Vliegenthart & Van Zoonen, 2011), these speech patterns play out in predictable patterns of discourse (Bonilla-Silva, 2006). Racial framing, put broadly "refers to the racial perceptions, stereotypes, images, ideologies, narratives, and emotive reactions used to make sense of a given situation, experience, or issue involving racial matters, especially in the United States and other Western countries" (Feagin 2006, 2010 as cited by Wingfield

& Feagin, 2012, p. 144). In the context of our research, comprehending the intricate nature of racial framing lays the groundwork for our proposed conceptual framework, which aims to guide qualitative researchers in deciphering racial ideologies and their manifestations in discourse.

As we delve into the intricacies of racial framing and its interconnectedness with ideologies, our journey now transitions toward the development of a comprehensive conceptual framework. This conceptual framework of racial discourse frames, based in ideologies, is designed to support researchers in organizing racial ideologies within qualitative studies, facilitating the mapping participant responses to known racial frames and, by extension, broader ideological constructs. In the following sections, we navigate this conceptual landscape, aiming to shed light on the interplay between racial ideologies and discourse, offering valuable insights for researchers seeking a deeper understanding of the multifaceted nature of race and racism in contemporary society.

CONCEPTUAL FRAMEWORK

This proposed conceptual framework guides researchers in analyzing racial discourses. The framework centers on the ways that White people discourse about race and racism, as this dominant groups' discourse has negative impacts on people of color. In the framework, Helm's (2017) White identity status are tied to ideologies, as Helm's theory offers a different set of identity statuses for people of color.

The conceptual framework was comprised using two main approaches. First, we compiled a systematic set of literature that documented prevailing racial ideologies and frames. Second, we organized the ideologies and frames in a way that clustered similar ideologies and frames. Third, we organized these ideologies and frames into a continuum ranging from overtly racist to those oriented toward intentional social justice action. Fourth, we mapped Feagin's (2013) frames to relevant ideologies, as well as Helm's (2017) White identity status to each set of ideologies to aid in understanding of the mindset of individuals in these frames. Figure 1 first shows a continuum of these ideologies, with arrows representing a direction in which the ideologies are split, between the most polarizing of ideologies, including racist ideologies on one side (broken into White supremacist ideologies and color-blind ideologies) and antiracist ideologies on the other side (including diversity ideologies and social justice ideologies). Below, Table 1 shows the alignment of ideologies and frames.

Figure 1. Conceptual Framework

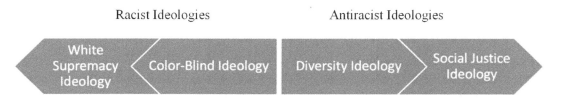

Table 1. Racial Ideologies and Frames

Ideologies	Frames	Sources
White Supremacy Ideologies	**Hard Racial Frame:** "Explicit racist imagery and language that openly positions people of color as racially inferior to whites, involving emotional, "gut-level" responses of racial disgust, distaste, or discomfort"	**Wingfield & Feagin, 2012, p. 145**
	Symbolic Racism: Decline in overt racism used to justify the belief that claims of racism from people of color are illegitimate	Tarman & Sears, 2005, as described by Feagin, 2014
	Laissez-Faire Racism: "Whites continuing negative stereotyping of blacks and blaming blacks for their socioeconomic problems"	Bobo et al., 1996, as described by Feagin, 2014, p. 129
	Great Chain-of-Being: Asserts the superiority of a societal structure built by White people, wherein individuals of color are expected to conform	Feagin, 2013
	Emotionally Normative Frame: Subtly defines human beauty by White form and features, reinforcing normative standards of beauty	Feagin, 2013
	White Moral Teflon: White people use discourse to frame themselves as virtuous, deflecting criticism and maintaining an impervious shield around Whiteness	Feagin, 2013
Color-Blind Ideologies	**Soft Racial Frame:** Downplays the reality of structural racism and glorifies individuals of color who ignore institutionalized racism	Wingfield & Feagin, 2012
	Disconnected Power Analysis Frame: acknowledging structural racism while alleviating oneself from "guilt and responsibility"	Jayakumar & Adamian, 2017, p. 929
	Denial of Magnitude and Impact: Assumption that White experience is universal, that racism is limited to individual incidents	Feagin 2013
	Disintegration: Conscious acknowledgement of Whiteness and associated privileges, which is in conflict with one's moral socialization	Helms 2017
	Structural Responsibility: People of color are dependent on social supports	Haltinner 2016
	Abstract Liberalism: Individuals choose to succeed	Bonilla-Silva 2018
	Cultural Racism: Culture affects your attitude toward success	Bonilla-Silva 2018
	Denial of Systemic Racism: The past does not impact the present	Bonilla-Silva 2018
	Deficit: People of color are to blame for their plight	Ladson-Billing 2006
	Naturalization: Students of color have less ability to succeed	Bonilla-Silva 2018
	Deflection: When asked specifically to talk about race and racism, evades with "neutral" discourse	Long 2020
Diversity Ideologies	**Diversity:** Race shapes individuals' world views and cultural practices, and that interaction across racial lines is positive and important	Warikoo and de Novais 2015, p. 861
	Racial Evasion: Race is salient, diversity is valued, but self-preservation is evident through lack of action	Jayakumar & Adamian 2017; Oware 2016;
Social Justice Ideologies	**Oppression:** Race group members are affected by oppression	Bonilla-Silva 2018; Helms 2017; Hughey 2012
	Privilege: Race group members are affected by privilege/power	Hastie & Rimmington 2014
	Radical Contextualization: Historical and social features produce inequity	Lopez, et al. 2018
	QuantCrit: Interpretations of racial data are impacted by dominant thinking	Covarrubias et al., 2018

Racist Ideologies

Racist Ideologies encapsulate a global system that categorizes individuals based on perceived superiority or inferiority, evolving over centuries through intricate political, cultural, and economic influences (Grosfoguel, 2016). As emphasized by Bourke (2016) and Doane (2017), the roots of racist ideologies trace back to the 17th century when François Bernier (1684) conceptualized race in their essay, *New Division of Earth by the Different Species or Races of Men*. Addressing the nature of racist ideologies, Doane (2017) argued, that "ideologies are only racist inasmuch as they maintain racialized social systems" (p. 979). Consequently, any ideologies failing to advance social justice are arguably racist, irrespective of intent or conscious awareness. White supremacy ideology and color-blind ideology stand out as prominent examples of racist ideologies, each characterized by distinctive frames that define and perpetuate them.

White Supremacy Ideology

At times referred to as social dominance orientation (Duckitt, 2001), this chapter deliberately employs the term *White supremacy ideology* to encapsulate the "social and systemic manifestation of the belief that white people hold a level of superiority over other races, thus granting them the right to exert dominion over people of other racial groups, by use of both social and systemic structures" (Love, 2022, p. 4). While this analysis draws on Helm's (2017) White racial identity statuses to define ideologies and consequently identify associated frames, one notable absence in Helm's statuses excludes White supremacist ideologies. In exploring the intricate manifestations of White supremacy ideology, these expressions can be categorized into two distinctive groupings: those that exhibit explicit and overt characteristics and those that operate through subtler, though still explicit means.

At the forefront of explicit manifestations lies the *hard racial frame*, where "explicit racist imagery and language, openly conceptualizes people of color as racially inferior to whites, and involves emotional, 'gut-level' response of racial disgust, distaste, or discomfort directed toward people of color" (Wingfield & Feagin, 2012, p. 145). For example, the hard racial frame may involve using "openly racist terminology (for example, the N-word)" (Wingfield & Feagin, 2012, p. 145). This visceral reaction is not merely a cognitive bias but signifies a deeply ingrained emotional aversion. The *symbolic racism* frame constitutes a bridge between explicit and implicit forms, employing the decline in overt racism to invalidate claims of racism from people of color (Tarman & Sears, 2005, as described by Feagin, 2014). Examples of symbolic racism included disagreeing with statements like "Generations of slavery and discrimination have created conditions that make it difficult for blacks to work their way out of the lower class" or agree with statements like, "It's really a matter of some people not trying hard enough; if blacks would only try harder, they could be as well off as whites" (Tarman & Sears, 2005, p. 738). *Laissez-faire racism*, another explicit frame, involves "whites' continuing negative stereotyping of blacks and blaming blacks for their socioeconomic problems" (Bobo et al., 1996, as cited by Feagin, 2014, p. 129). An example of Laissez-faire racism would be beliefs that "blacks as more likely to prefer living off of welfare than whites" (Bobo et al., 1996, p. 14). Overlapping with symbolic and laissez-faire racism is the *great chain-of-being* frame, a concept asserting the superiority of a societal structure built by White people, where individuals of color are expected to conform (Feagin, 2013). For example, the great chain-of-being is reflected in views of African Americans as "dependent on welfare, as not as work oriented as whites, as less intelligent than whites, and as an intermarriage threat to white families" (Feagin, 2013, p. 30).

The *emotionally normative* frame defines human beauty by White form and features, reinforcing the normative standards of beauty (Feagin, 2013). Further delving into subtlety, the concept of *White moral teflon* unfolds, wherein White people frame themselves as virtuous, deflecting criticism and maintaining an impervious shield around Whiteness (Feagin, 2013).

Overall, in White supremacy ideology, explicit manifestations were characterized by an overt acknowledgment of racial hierarchies and biases (Feagin, 2013). On the other hand, color-blind ideology operates through implicit means and is characterized by a deliberate refusal to acknowledge the significance of race and White dominance in society (Bonilla-Silva, 2006; Doane, 2017). The next section addressed the turn from racist ideologies to color-blind ideology.

Color-Blind Ideology

Color-blind ideology, often considered one of the most widely discussed ideologies alongside White supremacy, is characterized by a deliberate refusal to acknowledge the role of race and White domination in society. Instead, proponents of color-blindness often claim that society has achieved a post-racial state (Bonilla-Silva, 2006; Doane, 2017; Feagin, 2013). Within the framework of Helms' (2017) White identity statuses, the contact status best encapsulates color-blind ideologies, reflecting an obliviousness or denial of the significance and differential meaning of race, particularly Whiteness.

Scholarly examinations of color-blind ideology reveal various frames that align with this perspective. The *soft racial frame*, for instance, downplays the reality of *structural racism*—or the "continued existence of a race structure in society" (Bonilla-Silva, 1997, p. 476 as cited by Braveman et al., 2022)—and glorifies individuals of color who ignore *institutionalized racism* (Wingfield & Feagin, 2012), which includes involvement of organizations and structures in oppression (Braveman et al., 2022). The institutional racism frame strategically employs colorblind language while avoiding overtly racist terminology, distinguishing it from the hard racial frame (Wingfield & Feagin, 2012). Similarly ignoring structural racism, in the *deficit* frame, people of color are blamed for their challenges, ignoring systemic racism which captures all possible factors contributing to disparities in outcomes (Ladson-Billings, 2006), such as "political, legal, economic, health care, school, and criminal justice systems" (Braveman et al., 2022, p. 172). A frame close to the deficit frame is the *abstract liberalism* frame which proposes that individuals choose to succeed, obscuring both structural barriers and systemic inequalities (Bonilla-Silva, 2018). Similarly, the *denial of magnitude and impact* frame is rooted in the assumption that the White experience is universal and limiting racism to individual incidents, thus neglecting its systemic nature (Feagin, 2013). And perhaps most aptly named, the *denial of systemic racism* frame is rooted in the belief that the past does not impact the present, minimizing the enduring effects of historical racism (Bonilla-Silva, 2018). While there is similarity in these frames, researchers need to consider the extent useful to keep each frame as separate.

In contrast to frames that ignore structural, institutional, or systemic racism, the *disconnected power analysis* frame captures perspective wherein White awareness of structural racism while alleviating oneself from "guilt and responsibility" (Jayakumar & Adamian, 2017, p. 929). Jayakumar and Adamian (2017) highlighted a participant comment that exemplified this frame:

I think that people have this sort of veil over their eyes. I think that I have this magnifying glass on…I recognize that ignorance now in my friends and family—the things that they say I just, like, can't believe, just sort of this, it's just like over the head, you know, so, one of that. (p. 928)

In other words, recognition without action, wherein the self-image as racially conscious is emphasized.

The *structural responsibility* frame suggests that people of color are dependent on social supports, implying a lack of self-reliance. As Haltinner (2016) explained, "Rather than blaming people of color for the plight of the urban poor, these struggles are framed as the result of an abusive state that uses welfare-like programs to hurt poor people by intentionally continuing a cycle of poverty (Katz 1989)" (p. 407). Importantly, activists who espouse this frame believe that "Democrats…deceive and enslave poor people of color with social services" (Haltinner, 2016, p. 408). Additionally, this frame includes ideations that the past racist practices do influence the present, as one participant in Haltinner (2016) explained, "The Supreme Court has screwed up a number of times... Look back into 1855. We have the Dred Scott decision and that was where the Supreme Court declared that black people aren't people"

(p. 407). Interestingly, this frame includes some recognition of structure, but does so in a way that is distinctly racist.

The *cultural racism* frame highlights the influence of culture on attitudes toward success, perpetuating stereotypes and sidestepping systemic issues (Bonilla-Silva, 2018). The *naturalization* frame suggests that students of color inherently possess less ability to succeed, perpetuating harmful stereotypes (Bonilla-Silva, 2018). Lastly, the *deflection* frame characterizes responses that evade discussions on race and racism with seemingly neutral discourse, avoiding direct engagement with the issues (Long, 2020).

These frames, as reflective of color-blind racist ideologies, often discussed alongside White supremacy, often involve a deliberate denial of the role of race and White domination, frequently asserting a post-racial narrative. Helms' (2017) contact status represents an obliviousness or denial of the significance and differential meaning of race, especially Whiteness. Examining color-blind ideology reveals various frames aligning with this perspective, each contributing to the construction of the ideology while perpetuating racial disparities and typically maintaining a blind spot to systemic inequalities (though there is some variation of this among the different frames).

Antiracist Ideologies

Based on our conceptualization of the antiracist conceptual framework, there are two ideologies: diversity ideologies and social justice ideologies. If racist ideologies are ones that maintain a racialized social system, then anti-racist ideologies are those that challenge this system. Antiracism appeared as a concept in the mid-twentieth century (Bonnett & Carrington, 2000). Antiracism has been formally defined as "those forms of thought and/or practice that seek to confront, eradicate and/or ameliorate racism" (Bonnett & Carrington, 2000, p. 3). The main ideologies captured in the literature were described as social justice and diversity ideologies.

Diversity Ideology

As Bonnet and Carrington (2000) contended, "although many contemporary forms of anti-racism have a theoretical interest in affirming 'diversity,' it is a concern rarely translated into an appreciation of the multitude of ways people in different parts of the world resist racism" (p. 2). Similarly, *diversity ideology* is conceptualized in this study as those beliefs that express support of diversity, equity, and inclusion efforts, and actions focus on symbolic efforts, often only in times of ease, as people with this ideology do not want a target on their back. One of the least commonly discussed ideologies are those that do not quite meet the definition of color-blind nor do they meet the definition of social justice. Helms' (2017) White identity statuses that best describes diversity ideology include a) disintegration, reflected by a conscious acknowledgment of Whiteness and associated privileges, which conflicts with one's moral socialization, b) reintegration, reflected by an assuaging internal emotional turmoil, victim blaming, and avoiding noticing racism, and c) pseudo independence, reflect by well-intentioned White people who perceive racial tensions as existing externally between People of Color 'bad White people..

Diversity frames include the belief that "race shapes individuals' worldviews and cultural practices, emphasizing the positivity and importance of interaction across racial lines" (Warikoo & de Novais, 2015, p. 861). Additionally, *racial evasion* is aligned with this ideology, wherein race is acknowledged as salient, and diversity is valued, but actions often fall short, revealing a self-preserving tendency (Jayakumar & Adamian, 2017; Oware, 2016; Smith & Mayorga-Gallo, 2017).

In terms of the relationship of the diversity frames to Helms' (2017) White identity statuses, disintegration reflected a conscious acknowledgment of Whiteness and associated privileges, leading to internal conflict conflicting with one's moral socialization. In the diversity frame, individuals may align with the disintegration status as they consciously acknowledge racial differences. Moreover, reintegration reflected an assuaging internal emotional turmoil, victim blaming, and avoiding noticing racism. Individuals in this status seek to reconcile internal conflicts by blaming victims and avoiding a critical examination of systemic racism (Helms, 2017). Individuals adopting the diversity frame may also share similarities with the reintegrative status, particularly in terms of assuaging internal emotional turmoil. The diversity frame, by recognizing the positive and important aspects of interaction across racial lines, attempts to create a harmonious view of diversity. This harmonious perspective aligned with the reintegrative status's desire to soothe internal conflicts.

For the racial evasion frame, Helms' (2017) status of pseudo independence, where well-intentioned White allies localize race and racial tensions in People of Color or "bad" White people rather than themselves, demonstrates a form of self-preservation. The racial evasion frame, characterized by the salience of race and the valuing of diversity, yet exhibiting self-preservation through a lack of action, aligns with the pseudo independence status. Both concepts involve a reluctance to directly confront systemic issues, deflecting responsibility and preserving personal comfort.

Social Justice Ideologies

The second justice is the second ideology that falls under the antiracist conceptual framework. Social justice ideology takes a stance against opposition and involves specific actions to address power and oppression (Freire, 1970). Helms White identity status that best describes social justice ideologies is a) Immersion-Emersion which reflects an acknowledgment of Whiteness as a source of racism and examination of one's own and other Whites' roles in perpetrating and maintaining it (Helms, 2017), and b) autonomy status which is characterized by learned discovery and the intention to view oneself in a flattering manner (Helms, 2017).

Frames encapsulating social justice ideology include *overt counterframing* which challenges prevailing racial hierarchies and White racial frames (Feagin 2010 as cited by Wingfield & Feagin, 2012). Wingfield and Feagin (2012, p. 146) cite an example of this frame offered by Frederick Douglas in 1852 when he explained, "What, to the American slave, is your Fourth of July? I answer: A day that reveals to him, more than all other days of the year, the gross injustices and cruelty to which he is the constant victim. To him your celebration is a sham." Similarly, the *social justice* frame (though perhaps between phrased in this context as the *oppression frame*) recognizes the impact of oppression on marginalized racial groups (Bonilla-Silva, 2018; Hughey, 2012) and then on the other side of the same coin, the *privilege* frame acknowledges that race group members benefit from privilege and power (Hastie & Rimmington, 2014). Extending to a more nuanced recognition of privilege and oppression, the *radical contextualization* frame emphasizes historical and social factors producing racial inequity (Lopez et al., 2018). Lastly, the *QuantCrit* frame explores how dominant thinking influences interpretations of racialized data (Covarrubias et al., 2018).

Together, these frames and statuses form a robust social justice ideology committed to dismantling oppressive structures and fostering equity. Helms (2017) White identity statuses serve as a valuable framework for understanding the nuanced manifestations of social justice ideology. The Immersion-Emersion status aligns closely with frames such as overt counterframing, as individuals in this status actively challenge prevailing racial hierarchies and white racial frames. Immersion-Emersion involves an acknowledgment of Whiteness as a source of racism, reflecting a critical examination of one's role in perpetuating racial inequalities, which resonates with the commitment of overt counterframing to challenge existing racial narratives. On the other hand, the autonomy status, characterized by a lifelong commitment to defining oneself positively as a White person, finds resonance in frames like the privilege frame. The White identity frame acknowledges that race group members, particularly White individuals, benefit from privilege and power, highlighting the intersection of autonomy and the acknowledgment of systemic advantages.

APPLYING FRAMES IN QUALITATIVE RESEARCH

Next, this conceptual chapter turns to the task of applying the frames to conducting qualitative research. While scholars have captured a variety of theoretical and ideological frames, critical researchers analyzing qualitative discourse on race and racism can employ different qualitative approaches and analysis techniques to compliment racial frames guiding critical research. This work was inspired by prior research that compiled frames to use in qualitative coding of participant discourse on racial data (Long, 2020), and this chapter is intended to provide alternative types of qualitative approaches and analysis techniques that would complement the use with existing frames and ideologies.

Qualitative Approaches of Racial Frames

Originally categorized as 'traditions' by Jacob (1987), advanced qualitative research design can be designated into categories that help further situated and align the research inquiry process. Approaches, or genres, create the structure for which theoretical frameworks, or for the purpose of this study, racial frames, can be unique perspectives for which research designs flourish (Mohajan, 2018). Common qualitative approaches are phenomenology, ethnography, case study, grounded theory, and narrative inquiry (Creswell & Poth, 2018). However, critical antiracist ideologies call for research approaches that acknowledge the existence of and purposefully dismantle racism by examining power structures, challenging dominant narratives, and centering marginalized voices (Dei, 2005). Several emergent approaches have sought to further recognize that experiences of racism are shaped by gender, class, sexuality, and other intersecting identities, through taking on a 'critical' lens of the original approach.

Critical ethnography and critical discourse analysis are two approaches that are sought out by critical scholars conducting of qualitative research. Accordioning to Esposito and Evans-Winters (2022), critical theorists actively engage in a collective understanding that, "1) society privileges members of the dominant group, 2) social identities such as race and gender are social constructions, and 3) social structures impede on people's daily lives, thus influencing individuals' and groups' behaviors and opportunities" (p. 63). While critical ethnography attempts to account for structural inequalities and systematic resistance within society through immersing within the environments of lived participants, critical discourse interrogates how language is used to reinforces racist ideologies and maintain power systems (Esposito & Evans-Winters, 2022). Critical ethnography involves an in-depth investigation of social and cultural community or phenomena (Madison, 2011) and implores the critical researcher to question their involvement, assumptions, and biases within the 'reconstructive analysis' process towards focusing on amplifying the voices of marginalized insiders (Carspecken, 2013). Critical discourse focuses on analyzing language to investigate how racialized discourses are constructed, reproduced, and challenged within texts, media, and narrative interactions to uncover power dynamics, ideologies, and social inequalities (Liu & Guo, 2016).

While narrative inquiry already is an approach that lends itself to research that seeks to "collect stories from individuals about individuals' lived and told experiences" (Creswell & Poth, 2018, p. 68), critical narrative inquiry advances the methodological approach by combining critical reflection throughout the design, data collection and analysis, and discussion of findings (Hickson, 2016). The approach of critical narrative inquiry recognizes the power of storytelling individuals' lived experiences as a means of understanding larger systematic structural and social phenomena. Pino Gavidia and Adu (2022) found that the role of reflexivity in narrative inquiry is the supposition of a critical lens that stories are not composed in silos but exist amongst the backdrop of socially constructed temporality, stating that "researchers are reflexively aware of their roles and influences in the research process to deconstruct stories into question for knowledge co-creation, and pluralistic and multiple ways of understanding reality" (p. 4). Critical researchers purposefully engage dominant narratives perpetuate racism and seek out counter-stories that challenge prevailing narratives.

Community-based participatory research is an approach that collaborates with those outside of the academy as the investigation is involved with seeking to address or solve a community-based problem or issue (Leavy, 2023). Through active participation with community members throughout all stages of the research process, community-based participatory research utilizes a recursive, iterative process of continuous communication checks that review data, insights, and findings as a means of addressing internal power dynamics (Banks et al., 2016). In the context of critical antiracist research, community-based participatory research empowers marginalized communities to define their own experiences of racism, identify priorities for action, and work collaboratively with researchers to address systemic inequalities and promote social justice (Fleming et al., 2023). Critical researchers must employ pre-research strategies of gaining cultural competence of communities of study as well as identifying key stakeholders and gatekeepers that can be co-collaborators and co-conspirators of community-based social justice research (Leavy, 2023).

Through the purposeful use of appropriate qualitative approaches, critical researchers can create quality research designs to address various forms of racism and advocate for systematic transformative change. While approaches assist with the design and structure, qualitative analysis requires designated and validated means of coding.

Qualitative Methods of Racial Frames

Qualitative methods, within the context of critical research, can effectively navigate the complexities of racial dynamics producing insightful comprehensions into how race shapes participant identities, social structures, and practices of power dynamics. Methods, or forms of data, are typically categorized into four key types of information: interviews (including focus groups), observations, audiovisuals, and documents (Creswell & Poth, 2018). The use of qualitative methods should be developed in alignment of the research's purpose, theoretical framework, and approach, and there is no one method that is best aligned with critical research however, researchers have employed forms of data collection that focus on techniques that lift and empower minoritized voices (Esposito & Evans-Winters, 2022).

For example, when engaging in community-based participatory research, the methods utilized to complement the approach can empowering to then qualitative inquiry process by engaging marginalized communities as active participants and co-researchers within the research process (Wallerstein et al., 2020). Community-based participatory research employs a responsive design that centers the data collection choices within the recursive practices of collaborating with research participants and stakeholders, to address their defined problems, and meet their goals needs (Leavy, 2023). While any data collection form can be utilized, the focus becomes the methods' ability to be transformational and emancipatory through employing cultural sensitivity and power sharing (Leavy, 2023), such as through the use of photovoice (Evans-Agnew & Rosemberg, 2016; Wang & Burris, 1997) or observational service (Emerson et al., 2011). By centering the voices and experiences of those most impacted by racial injustice, community-based participatory research facilitates collaborative knowledge production.

With her social justice grounded theory framework, Charmaz (2005) stated that the ability to compare multiple methods of data allows the researcher to "gain some sense of structural and organizational sources of suffering and their differential effects on individuals. The comparisons suggest how research participants' relative resources and capabilities became apparent through studying inductive data" (p. 17). When data collection methods can encompass personal stories, testimonials, and more accessible means of narrative representations, researchers can deconstruct prevailing racial frames and interrogate the ways in which participants experience race and racial injustice are constructed, negotiated, and challenged in various social systems (Kovach, 2017; Miller et al., 2020). Qualitative discourse on race and racism can employ a multiple array of methods that work synergistically to enhance our understanding of racial dynamics and inform anti-racist praxis.

Qualitative Analysis of Racial Frames

Qualitative coding methods can be invaluable tools for analyzing data through critical antiracist lenses. Through critical forms of analysis, researchers can identify and understand patterns, themes, and power dynamics that may emerge within their data (Saldaña, 2021). However, when critical researchers utilize various forms of value coding, like cross-cultural content analysis informed coding (Bernard, 2017), operational racism at both individual and systemic levels can be uncovered. Coding techniques are seldom directly connected to theories or ideologies, however there are strategies that critical researchers can engage to focus antiracist ideologies. Hunt et al. (2024) suggest that "justice-focused researchers and advocates call for the disaggregation of data, or breaking data down into sub-populations" (para 12) to better understand the disparity of issues and barriers faced among community subgroups.

Intersectionality can be both a theoretical framework as well as an intentional form of qualitative analysis (Esposito & Evans-Winters, 2022). Intersectionality, a concept popularized by Kimberlé Crenshaw (1991), highlights how different social identities (such as race, gender, class, sexuality, etc.) intersect and interact to shape individuals' experiences of privilege and oppression. Crenshaw defined intersectionality as "the location of women of color both within overlapping systems of subordination and at the margins of feminism and antiracism" (p. 1265). Within the analysis of data, intersectional coding involves the consideration of multiple intersecting axes of identity (Abrams et al., 2020). In an antiracist context, intersectionality helps critical researchers reflect on how racism intersects with other forms of oppression and privilege during the coding phases of analysis.

Decolonial analysis techniques strive to challenge colonial legacies and Eurocentric epistemologies by centering Indigenous, enslaved, and colonized voices from the data (Esposito & Evans-Winters, 2022). Decolonial coding involves critically examining data through lenses that prioritize decolonization, Indigenous knowledge systems, and resistance to colonial oppression (Boveda & Bhattacharya, 2019). Tuck and Yang (2014) explain that the very terminology of the research code is set in settler colonialism, and "to refuse the colonizing code requires deconstructing power, not objective cataloging of observations. Indeed, 'objectivity' is code for power" (p. 812). The authors continue that within research's legacy within colonialism, that even "academic codes decide what stories are civilized (intellectual property) and what stories are natural, wild, and thus claimable under the doctrine of discovery" (Tuck & Yang, 2014, p. 812). In an antiracist context, decolonial coding aims to decenter Whiteness and colonial ideologies, fostering solidarity with Indigenous and other marginalized voices.

Antiracist analysis and coding techniques are not mutually exclusive and should be implemented based on the designated needs of the research's racial frames and ideologies. Linström and Marais (2017) found that when applying guiding frames to qualitative research that there still remains "areas of concern regarding this methodology remain the subjectivity of the process, coupled with the fact that consensus on a standard frame typology does not exist yet" (p. 34). Qualitative approaches and analysis techniques that employ critical antiracist frameworks can contribute to the understanding of racism's complexities, advocate for social justice, and support efforts to dismantle oppressive systems and promote equity and inclusion.

CONCLUSION

This chapter delved into the intricate landscape of racial ideologies in the U.S. context, employing the conceptual framework of Helms' (2017) White identity statuses to elucidate the diverse ways individuals engaged with and perpetuated these ideologies. The exploration began with the explicit and overt manifestations of White supremacy ideology, characterized by frames like the hard racial frame, symbolic racism, and laissez-faire racism. These frames exemplified the perpetuation of racial hierarchies, overtly positioning people of color as inferior to Whites. Transitioning to subtler expressions, the chapter uncovered frames like the great chain-of-being, emotionally normative frame, white moral teflon, and disconnected power analysis frame, shedding light on the implicit facets of White supremacy ideology. The subsequent section dissected color-blind ideology, emphasizing a deliberate refusal to acknowledge the role of race and White domination in society, and unveiling frames such as the soft racial frame and denial of magnitude and impact frame. Finally, the antiracist conceptual framework introduced diversity ideology and social justice ideology, with frames like diversity and racial evasion under diversity ideology, and overt counterframing, oppression frame, privilege frame, radical contextualization frame, and QuantCrit frame under social justice ideology. Helms White identity statuses provided a comprehensive lens to understand how individuals navigated these ideologies, offering insights into their consciousness, acknowledgment, and commitment to addressing racial inequities. In traversing these ideologies, this chapter aimed to contribute to a nuanced understanding of the complexities surrounding race and to foster critical reflections on dismantling systemic racism.

Then, this conceptual chapter turned to the task of suggesting qualitative approaches, methods, and analysis techniques to complement racial frames. While several suggestions are listed, there are still a bevy of emerging analysis techniques, such as positionality coding and counter-storytelling analysis, that support the work to amplify marginalized voices and disrupt hegemonic narratives of racism.

Conducting multicultural research within racial frameworks requires a purposeful attention to the ethical considerations needed to protect individuals while being mindful of the larger societal context. Aluwihare-Samaranayake (2012) stated that "the possibility exists that ethics in research must not only consider the protection of human subjects but also consider what constitutes socially responsible and acceptable research" (p. 76). Researchers must employ a critical consciousness that challenges their own bias and positionality with their research (Esposito & Evans-Winters, 2022). Strategies that seek to combat researcher assumptions and preconceptions like member checking, when participants review and validate data and researcher interpretation, (Birt et al., 2016) or using validating literature from within-group and/or marginalized authors (Sakr et al., 2023). More pragmatic strategies include ensuring research is Institutional Review Board (IRB) approved, the researcher trained in the ethics of conducting human-subject research, such as CITI training, and participants have had all aspects of the research purpose, design, potential benefits and harms, and participant rights through the collection of informed consent (Creswell & Poth, 2018). Full transparency of the power dynamics, protection of participants, and ownership of data are invaluable for conducting qualitative research that seeks to address racial and social inequities (Esposito & Evans-Winters, 2022).

Future research should continue to expand and refine this catalog of ideologies and frames, to provide additional guidance to researchers as ideologies that reflect the nebulous ways individuals and societies rationalize their existence. As well, this chapter focused on the U.S. context for racial frames. Future research should be mindful of the racial dynamics of the populations in which investigations are conducted to further cultural sensitivity and global perspectives.

REFERENCES

Abrams, J. A., Tabaac, A., Jung, S., & Else-Quest, N. M. (2020). Considerations for employing intersectionality in qualitative health research. *Social Science & Medicine*, 258, 1–25. 10.1016/j.socscimed.2020.11313832574889

Aluwihare-Samaranayake, D. (2012). Ethics in qualitative research: A view of the participants' and researchers' world from a critical standpoint. *International Journal of Qualitative Methods*, 11(2), 64–81. 10.1177/160940691201100208

Banks, S., Armstrong, A., Carter, K., Graham, H., Hayward, P., Henry, A., & Strachan, A. (2016). Everyday ethics in community-based participatory research. In *Knowledge Mobilisation and Social Sciences* (pp. 97–111). Routledge.

Bernard, H. R. (2017). *Research methods in anthropology: Qualitative and quantitative approaches.* Rowman & Littlefield.

Bernier, F. (1684). New division of earth by the different species or races of men. *Journal des Savants*, 24, 1863–1864.

Birt, L., Scott, S., Cavers, D., Campbell, C., & Walter, F. (2016). Member checking: A tool to enhance trustworthiness or merely a nod to validation? *Qualitative Health Research*, 26(13), 1802–1811. 10.1177/1049732316665487027340178

Bobo, L., Kluegel, J. R., & Smith, R. A. (1996). *Laissez-faire racism: The crystallization of a kinder, gentler, antiblack ideology.* Russel Sage Foundation.

Bonilla-Silva, E. (2021). *Racism without racists: Color-blind racism and the persistence of racial inequality in the United States.* Rowman & Littlefield.

Bonnett, A., & Carrington, B. (2000). Fitting into categories or falling between them? Rethinking ethnic classification. *British Journal of Sociology of Education*, 21(4), 487–500. 10.1080/713655371

Bourke, B. (2016). Meaning and implications of being labelled a predominantly White institution. *College and University*, 91(3), 12–21.

Boveda, M., & Bhattacharya, K. (2019). Love as de/colonial onto-epistemology: A post-oppositional approach to contextualized research ethics. *The Urban Review*, 51(1), 5–25. 10.1007/s11256-018-00493-z

Braveman, P. A., Arkin, E., Proctor, D., Kauh, T., & Holm, N. (2022). systemic and structural racism: definitions, examples, health damages, and approaches to dismantling: Study examines definitions, examples, health damages, and dismantling systemic and structural racism. *Health Affairs*, 41(2), 171–178. 10.1377/hlthaff.2021.0139435130057

Carspecken, F. P. (2013). *Critical ethnography in educational research: A theoretical and practical guide.* Routledge. 10.4324/9781315021263

Charmaz, K. (2005). Grounded theory in the 21st century: A qualitative method for advancing social justice research. In N. Denzin & Y. Lincoln (Eds.), *Handbook of qualitative research* (3rd ed., pp. 507–535). Sage.

Covarrubias, A., Nava, P. E., Lara, A., Burciaga, R., Vélez, V. N., & Solorzano, D. G. (2018). Critical race quantitative intersections: A testimonio analysis. *Race, Ethnicity and Education*, 21(2), 253–273. 10.1080/13613324.2017.1377412

Crenshaw, K. (1991). Mapping the margins: Intersectionality, identity politics, and violence against women of color. *Stanford Law Review*, 43(6), 1241–1299. 10.2307/1229039

Creswell, J. W., & Poth, C. N. (2018). *Qualitative inquiry and research design: Choosing among five approaches* (4th ed.). Sage.

Delgado, R., & Stefancic, J. (2023). *Critical race theory: An introduction*. NYU Press.

Doane, A. (2017). Beyond color-blindness:(Re) theorizing racial ideology. *Sociological Perspectives*, 60(5), 975–991. 10.1177/0731121417719697

Duckitt, J. (2001). A dual-process cognitive-motivational theory of ideology and prejudice. In Advances in Experimental Social Psychology. Academic Press. 10.1016/S0065-2601(01)80004-6

Earick, M. E. (2012). Ideology, race, and education. *International Critical Childhood Policy Studies Journal*, 3(1), 74–105.

Emerson, R. M., Fretz, R. I., & Shaw, L. L. (2011). *Writing ethnographic fieldnotes*. University of Chicago press. 10.7208/chicago/9780226206868.001.0001

Esposito, J., & Evans-Winters, V. (2022). Introduction to intersectional qualitative research. *Sage (Atlanta, Ga.)*.

Evans-Agnew, R. A., & Rosemberg, M. A. S. (2016). Questioning photovoice research: Whose voice? *Qualitative Health Research*, 26(8), 1019–1030. 10.1177/1049732315624223 26786953

Feagin, J. R. (2014). *Racist America: Roots, current realities, and future reparations*. Routledge. 10.4324/9780203762370

Feagin, J. R. (2020). *The white racial frame: Centuries of racial framing and counter-framing*. Routledge.

Fleming, P. J., Stone, L. C., Creary, M. S., Greene-Moton, E., Israel, B. A., Key, K. D., Reyes, A. G., Wallerstein, N., & Schulz, A. J. (2023). Antiracism and community-based participatory research: Synergies, challenges, and opportunities. *American Journal of Public Health*, 113(1), 70–78. 10.2105/AJPH.2022.30711436516389

Freire, P. (1970). *Pedagogy of the oppressed*. Bloomsbury.

Gillborn, D., Warmington, P., & Demack, S. (2018). QuantCrit: Education, policy,'Big Data'and principles for a critical race theory of statistics. *Race, Ethnicity and Education*, 21(2), 158–179. 10.1080/13613324.2017.1377417

Giroux, H. A. (2001). *Theory and resistance in education: Towards a pedagogy for the opposition*. Greenwood Publishing Group.

Grosfoguel, R. (2016). What is racism? *Journal of World-systems Research*, 22(1), 9–15. 10.5195/jwsr.2016.609

Haltinner, K. (2016). Individual responsibility, culture, or state organized enslavement? How Tea Party activists frame racial inequality. *Sociological Perspectives*, 59(2), 395–418. 10.1177/0731121415593275

Hastie, B., & Rimmington, D. (2014). '200 years of white affirmative action': White privilege discourse in discussions of racial inequality. *Discourse & Society*, 25(2), 186–204. 10.1177/0957926513516050

Helms, J. E. (2017). The challenge of making Whiteness visible: Reactions to four Whiteness articles. *The Counseling Psychologist*, 45(5), 717–726. 10.1177/0011000017718943

Hernandez, T. K. (2001). Multiracial matrix: The role of race ideology in the enforcement of antidiscrimination laws, a United States-Latin America comparison. *Cornell Law Review*, 87, 1093.

Hickson, H. (2016). Becoming a critical narrativist: Using critical reflection and narrative inquiry as research methodology. *Qualitative Social Work: Research and Practice*, 15(3), 380–391. 10.1177/1473325015617344

Hughey, M. (2012). *White bound: Nationalists, antiracists, and the shared meanings of race.* Stanford University Press. 10.1515/9780804783316

Hughey, M. W. (2022). Superposition strategies: How and why White people say contradictory things about race. *Proceedings of the National Academy of Sciences, 119*(9), 1-8. 10.1073/pnas.2116306119

Hunt, S., Riegelman, A., & Myers-Kelley, S. (2024, February 28). Conducting research through an anti-racism lens. *University of Minnesota.* https://libguides.umn.edu/antiracismlens

Jacob, E. (1987). Qualitative Research Traditions: A Review. *Review of Educational Research*, 6(2), 245–259. 10.3102/00346543057001001

Jayakumar, U. M., & Adamian, A. S. (2017). The fifth frame of colorblind ideology: Maintaining the comforts of colorblindness in the context of white fragility. *Sociological Perspectives*, 60(5), 912–936. 10.1177/0731121417721910

Kang, Y., & Yang, K. C. (2022). Communicating racism and xenophobia in the era of Donald Trump: A computational framing analysis of the US-Mexico cross-border wall discourses. *The Howard Journal of Communications*, 33(2), 140–159. 10.1080/10646175.2021.1996491

Knight, K. (2006). Transformations of the concept of ideology in the Twentieth century. *The American Political Science Review*, 100(4), 619–626. 10.1017/S0003055406062502

Kovach, M. (2017). Doing indigenous methodologies. *The SAGE Handbook of Qualitative Research*, 214-234.

Ladson-Billings, G. (2006). From the achievement gap to the education debt: Understanding achievement in US schools. *Educational Researcher*, 35(7), 3–12. 10.3102/0013189X035007003

Leavy, P. (2023). *Research design: Quantitative, qualitative, mixed methods, arts-based, and community-based participatory research approaches.* Guilford.

Linström, M., & Marais, W. (2012). Qualitative news frame analysis: A methodology. *Communitas*, 17, 21–38.

Liu, K., & Guo, F. (2016). A review on critical discourse analysis. *Theory and Practice in Language Studies*, 6(5), 1076–1084. 10.17507/tpls.0605.23

Long, K. B. (2020). *How Senior Institutional Research Leaders Interpret Graduation Outcomes Split by Race Category* (Doctoral dissertation, Oakland University).

López, N., Erwin, C., Binder, M., & Chavez, M. J. (2018). Making the invisible visible: Advancing quantitative methods in higher education using critical race theory and intersectionality. *Race, Ethnicity and Education*, 21(2), 180–207. 10.1080/13613324.2017.1375185

Love, A. (2022). Recognizing, understanding, and defining systemic and individual White supremacy. *Women of Color Advancing Peace and Security* (Working Paper). https://www.zbw.eu/econis-archiv/bitstream/11159/509639/1/EBP080507786_0.pdf

Madison, D. S. (2011). Critical ethnography: Method, ethics, and performance. *Sage (Atlanta, Ga.)*.

Miller, R., Liu, K., & Ball, A. F. (2020). Critical counter-narrative as transformative methodology for educational equity. *Review of Research in Education*, 44(1), 269–300. 10.3102/0091732X20908501

Mohajan, H. K. (2018). Qualitative research methodology in social sciences and related subjects. *Journal of Economic Development. Environment and People*, 7(1), 23–48. 10.26458/jedep.v7i1.571

Nguyen, T. T., Criss, S., Michaels, E. K., Cross, R. I., Michaels, J. S., Dwivedi, P., Huang, D., Hsu, E., Mukhija, K., Nguyen, L. H., Yardi, I., Allen, A. M., Nguyen, Q. C., & Gee, G. C. (2021). Progress and push-back: How the killings of Ahmaud Arbery, Breonna Taylor, and George Floyd impacted public discourse on race and racism on Twitter. *SSM - Population Health*, 15, 1–9. 10.1016/j.ssmph.2021.10092234584933

Oware, M. (2016). "We Stick Out Like a Sore Thumb..." Underground White Rappers' Hegemonic Masculinity and Racial Evasion. *Sociology of Race and Ethnicity (Thousand Oaks, Calif.)*, 2(3), 372–386. 10.1177/2332649215617781

Parker, L., & Lynn, M. (2002). What's race got to do with it? Critical race theory's conflicts with and connections to qualitative research methodology and epistemology. *Qualitative Inquiry*, 8(1), 7–22. 10.1177/107780040200800102

Pino Gavidia, L. A., & Adu, J. (2022). Critical narrative inquiry: An examination of a methodological approach. *International Journal of Qualitative Methods*, 21, 1–5. 10.1177/16094069221081594

Sakr, N., Son Hing, L. S., & González-Morales, M. G. (2023). Development and validation of the *marginalized*-group-focused diversity climate scale: Group differences and outcomes. *Journal of Business and Psychology*, 38(3), 689–722. 10.1007/s10869-022-09859-3

Saldaña, J. (2021). *The Coding Manual for Qualitative Researchers* (4th ed.). Sage Publications.

Smith, C. W., & Mayorga-Gallo, S. (2017). The new principle-policy gap: How diversity ideology subverts diversity initiatives. *Sociological Perspectives*, 60(5), 889–911. 10.1177/0731121417719693

Spears, A. K. (1999). Race and ideology: An introduction. In *Race and ideology: Language, symbolism, and popular culture* (pp. 11–58). Wayne State University Press.

Tarman, C., & Sears, D. O. (2005). The conceptualization and measurement of symbolic racism. *The Journal of Politics*, 67(3), 731–761. 10.1111/j.1468-2508.2005.00337.x

Tessler, H., Choi, M., & Kao, G. (2020). The anxiety of being Asian American: Hate crimes and negative biases during the COVID-19 pandemic. *American Journal of Criminal Justice*, 45(4), 636–646. 10.1007/s12103-020-09541-532837158

Tuck, E., & Yang, K. W. (2014). Unbecoming claims: Pedagogies of refusal in qualitative research. *Qualitative Inquiry*, 20(6), 811–818. 10.1177/1077800414530265

Vliegenthart, R., & Van Zoonen, L. (2011). Power to the frame: Bringing sociology back to frame analysis. *European Journal of Communication*, 26(2), 101–115. 10.1177/0267323111404838

Wallerstein, N., Oetzel, J. G., Sanchez-Youngman, S., Boursaw, B., Dickson, E., Kastelic, S., Koegel, P., Lucero, J. E., Magarati, M., Ortiz, K., Parker, M., Peña, J., Richmond, A., & Duran, B. (2020). Engage for equity: A long-term study of community-based participatory research and community-engaged research practices and outcomes. *Health Education & Behavior*, 47(3), 380–390. 10.1177/109019811 989707532437293

Wang, C., & Burris, M. A. (1997). Photovoice: Concept, methodology, and use for participatory needs assessment. *Health Education & Behavior*, 24(3), 369–387. 10.1177/109019819702400309158980

Warikoo, N. K., & De Novais, J. (2015). Colour-blindness and diversity: Race frames and their consequences for white undergraduates at elite US universities. *Ethnic and Racial Studies*, 38(6), 860–876. 10.1080/01419870.2014.964281

Wingfield, A. H., & Feagin, J. (2012). The racial dialectic: President Barack Obama and the white racial frame. *Qualitative Sociology*, 35(2), 143–162. 10.1007/s11133-012-9223-7

ADDITIONAL READING

Cho, S., Crenshaw, K. W., & McCall, L. (2013). Toward a field of intersectionality studies: Theory, applications, and praxis. *Signs (Chicago, Ill.)*, 38(4), 785–810. 10.1086/669608

Corces-Zimmerman, C., & Guida, T. F. (2019). Toward a critical whiteness methodology: Challenging whiteness through qualitative research. In *Theory and method in higher education research* (Vol. 5, pp. 91–109). Emerald Publishing Limited. 10.1108/S2056-375220190000005007

DiAngelo, R. (2018). *White fragility: Why it's so hard for white people to talk about racism*. Beacon Press.

Matias, C. E., & Boucher, C. (2023). From critical whiteness studies to a critical study of whiteness: Restoring criticality in critical whiteness studies. *Whiteness and Education*, 8(1), 64–81. 10.1080/23793406.2021.1993751

Modood, T., & Sealy, T. (2022). Beyond Euro-Americancentric forms of racism and anti-racism. *The Political Quarterly*, 93(3), 433–441. 10.1111/1467-923X.13138

Morning, A. (2018). Kaleidoscope: Contested identities and new forms of race membership. *Ethnic and Racial Studies*, 41(6), 1055–1073. 10.1080/01419870.2018.1415456

Roth, W. D., van Stee, E. G., & Regla-Vargas, A. (2023). Conceptualizations of race: Essentialism and constructivism. *Annual Review of Sociology*, 49(1), 39–58. 10.1146/annurev-soc-031021-034017

Walker, S., Sriprakash, A., & Tikly, L. (2021). Theorizing race and racism in comparative and international education. *The Bloomsbury handbook of theory in comparative and international education, 383.*

Wimmer, A. (2019). Racism in nationalised states: A framework for comparative research. In *Comparative perspectives on racism* (pp. 47–72). Routledge. 10.4324/9781315196374-3

Zuberi, T., & Bonilla-Silva, E. (Eds.). (2008). *White logic, white methods: Racism and methodology.* Rowman & Littlefield Publishers.

KEY TERMS AND DEFINITIONS

Color-Blind Ideology: Deliberate refusal to acknowledge the role of race and White domination in society. Instead, proponents of color-blindness often claim that society has achieved a post-racial state (Bonilla-Silva, 2006; Doane, 2017; Feagin, 2013).

Diversity Ideology: Those beliefs that express support of diversity, equity, and inclusion efforts, and actions focus on symbolic efforts, often only in times of ease, as people with this ideology do not want a target on their back.

Frames: "Set paths for interpreting information" (Bonilla-Silva, 2006, p. 26) which result in common patterns of speech (Vliegenthart & Van Zoonen, 2011).

Ideology: "A set of ideas employed in the justification and perpetuation of vested interests" (Spears, 1999, p. 6).

Race Ideology: Societal influences gradually molding both acknowledged and unacknowledged facets of race, influencing how individuals identify themselves or are identified within specific racial categories (Hernandez, 2001).

Racial Framing: "The racial perceptions, stereotypes, images, ideologies, narratives, and emotive reactions used to make sense of a given situation, experience, or issue involving racial matters, especially in the United States and other Western countries" (Feagin 2006, 2010 as cited by Wingfield & Feagin, 2012, p. 144).

Social Justice Ideology: Positions that take a stance against opposition and involves specific actions to address power and oppression (Freire, 1970).

White Supremacy Ideology: The "social and systemic manifestation of the belief that white people hold a level of superiority over other races, thus granting them the right to exert dominion over people of other racial groups, by use of both social and systemic structures" (Love, 2022, p. 4).

Whiteness: "The overt and subliminal socialization processes and practices, power structures, laws, privileges, and life experiences that favor the White racial group over all others" (Helms, 2017, p.718).

Chapter 10
Qualitative Techniques in Action:
Practical Example

Mariam Sahraoui
Université Hassan 2, Morocco

ABSTRACT

The chapter delves into a qualitative analysis of research data focusing on the discourse exchanged during a sales transaction between a Moroccan intern and a native French client. The aim is to explore the linguistic and cultural dynamics inherent in intercultural business interactions, particularly in the context of sales operations. The analysis homes in on how the Moroccan intern navigates linguistic subtleties and cultural disparities while engaging with a French client. It scrutinizes verbal exchanges, language preferences, communication strategies, and cultural nuances to uncover pivotal factors that influence the success of such interactions. The research seeks to pinpoint the strengths and challenges encountered by the Moroccan intern when selling to a French-speaking clientele. The objective is to extract practical insights to augment the linguistic and intercultural competencies of interns enrolled in commerce and management programs, underscoring the significance of these skills in an increasingly globalized business landscape.

INTRODUCTION

This chapter of the book is dedicated to the analysis of qualitative research data, shedding light on the discourse exchanged during a sales operation between a Moroccan intern enrolled in the Commerce and Management program at OFPPT and a native French client. This study is situated within the complex context of intercultural commercial transactions, where linguistic and cultural dynamics play a central role.

The primary objective of this research is to deepen our understanding of the specific linguistic and cultural interactions in this context, closely examining how the Moroccan intern navigates through linguistic nuances and cultural differences during interactions with a French client. To achieve this, we will delve into verbal interactions, language choices, communication strategies, as well as cultural variations that emerge during these exchanges.

DOI: 10.4018/979-8-3693-3306-8.ch010

Furthermore, this study aims to identify the strengths and challenges the Moroccan intern may face when selling to a native French-speaking audience. By highlighting these aspects, we seek to draw practical insights to enhance the linguistic and intercultural skills of commerce and management interns at OFPPT. It also aims to underscore the importance of such skills in an increasingly globalized business world, where the ability to successfully navigate intercultural environments is essential for professional success.

THEORETICAL FRAMEWORK

Intercultural Communication Theories

Intercultural communication is a multidisciplinary field that focuses on human interactions in contexts characterized by cultural diversity. This subchapter examines the key theories underlying intercultural communication and their relevance in the context of commercial transactions between a Moroccan intern and a native French client.

- Intercultural Adjustment Theory: This theory emphasizes individuals' ability to effectively adapt to cultural differences during intercultural interactions. We will analyze how the Moroccan intern can implement adjustment strategies to navigate the commercial context with a French client. In her work, Kim (2005) develops a theory of adaptation to a new culture, also known as the integrative intercultural adaptation theory. This theory proposes that when individuals find themselves in a new cultural environment, they may adopt different adaptation strategies, including assimilation, maintaining their own culture, or adopting certain aspects of the new culture while retaining elements of their original culture. Kim argues that optimal intercultural adaptation occurs when individuals adopt an integrative approach, integrating aspects of their original culture with those of the new culture, thereby creating a hybrid cultural identity. This theory highlights the importance of flexibility and open-mindedness in the process of intercultural adaptation.
- Cultural Identity Management Theory: This theory explores how individuals manage their cultural identity during intercultural interactions by adjusting their behavior according to the context. Ting-Toomey and Chung (2012) offer valuable insights into the intercultural dynamics underlying cultural identity management. By examining the patterns and skills necessary to navigate intercultural interactions effectively, this work sheds light on the strategies individuals use to adjust their behavior according to the cultural context. This approach resonates with the theory of cultural identity management, emphasizing the importance for the Moroccan intern to negotiate his cultural identity while interacting with a French client. By exploring these concepts in the specific context of intercultural commercial transactions, we can better understand how these processes influence communication and sales outcomes.
- Social Exchange Theory: This theory examines the processes of social exchange and cooperation among individuals from different cultures. Molm, Takahashi, and Peterson's (2000) research focuses on the dynamics of risk and trust in social exchanges, proposing experimental tests to verify certain classical propositions of social exchange theory. Their work explores how individuals evaluate risks and trust in social interactions, and how these perceptions influence their participation in social exchanges. They have conducted empirical studies to test hypotheses of social exchange theory, particularly focusing on the relationship between perceived risk and trust in interpersonal exchanges.

We will analyze how the Moroccan intern and the French client negotiate social norms and implicit expectations during the sales operation, and how this affects the quality of communication and the business relationship.

By exploring these theories of intercultural communication, we aim to shed light on the specific dynamics underlying interactions between the Moroccan intern and the French client, and to better understand the strategies and challenges inherent in intercultural communication within the context of commercial transactions.

Importance of Linguistic and Intercultural Skills in International Commerce

Success in international commerce largely depends on the ability of actors to effectively navigate culturally diverse and linguistically complex environments. This subchapter examines the crucial importance of linguistic and intercultural skills in the context of international commerce, highlighting their impact on communication, business relationships, and transaction success (Bartel-Radic, 2009).

- Effective Communication: Linguistic skills are essential for establishing clear and precise communication with business partners from different linguistic backgrounds. Effective communication helps overcome language barriers and facilitates mutual understanding, which is crucial for concluding business agreements and managing relationships with clients and partners.
- Cultural Adaptation: Intercultural skills are indispensable for adapting to the norms, values, and business practices specific to each culture. Professionals in international commerce must be able to understand and respect cultural differences, recognize social codes and implicit expectations, and adjust their behavior accordingly to establish trust and foster cooperation.
- Conflict Management: Linguistic and intercultural skills also play a crucial role in managing conflicts and misunderstandings that may arise in the context of international business transactions. The ability to resolve disputes effectively and prevent misunderstandings contributes to maintaining sustainable business relationships and preserving the reputation and image of the company.
- Competitive Advantages: Companies and professionals who possess linguistic and intercultural skills are better equipped to seize opportunities in international markets and adapt to rapid changes in global commerce. They can establish trusted relationships with international partners, identify specific customer needs, and anticipate market trends, giving them a significant competitive advantage.

Furman and Anderson (2020) explore companies' expectations of graduates in international business, highlighting several key ideas. First, the authors compare employers' expectations regarding linguistic and intercultural skills in different countries, emphasizing differences and similarities in the sought-after skills. They also underscore the growing importance of intercultural skills in a context of business globalization, where companies increasingly value candidates capable of working in multicultural and multilingual environments. Furthermore, companies seek versatile graduates capable of combining technical, linguistic, and intercultural skills such as communication, collaboration, and problem-solving. The study also highlights the need for international business education programs to integrate elements that develop students' linguistic and intercultural skills, including language courses, cultural exchange experiences, and international internships. Finally, the authors discuss the challenges faced by educational institutions in meeting these companies' expectations, as well as opportunities for collaboration between businesses and educational institutions to bridge the gap between supply and demand for skills in the global job market.

Linguistic Dynamics in Intercultural Business Transactions

During the early 20th century, knowledge began to specialize and become autonomous, with increasingly distinct research and theories. Linguistics, too, turned to other disciplines to better understand linguistic phenomena in their entirety. Since verbal messages are considered essential for interaction and communication in society, linguists and sociolinguists became interested in understanding the role of language in the construction of social reality. This reflection led to the emergence of sociolinguistics, which criticizes linguistics for its inability to comprehensively address the various linguistic phenomena present in society (Saussure (1916) and Labov (1976)). In the context of this study, it is necessary to highlight a set of concepts to better understand the social mechanisms underlying the use of the target language in specific contexts. For example, the use of French in professional business courses differs in linguistic practice from everyday French. Individuals not initiated in French for specific purposes often encounter difficulties in real communications. Thus, the study of specialized languages has seen significant development in the second half of the 20th century, with many linguists focusing on defining the characteristics of such languages.

Technolect, specialized language, or language for specific purposes: What are the differences?

Specialized French differs from common French and refers to the language used in communication situations involving verbal exchanges within a particular field of experience, which may be scientific, technical, etc. Specialized languages, as defined by PHAL, "Correspond to a static role of language, its function of designation, and concern a difference in content and specialization of lexicon (definition, terminology, nomenclature, specialized vocabulary of science and technology considered). These characteristics define what is called languages for specific purposes" (Phal, 1968, p.8).

As such, specialized language does not constitute a separate language: it utilizes morphological, syntactical resources, and specialized vocabulary encompassing terminology from a domain of human activity. It does not oppose common language; rather, it uses it to orally or in writing formulate specialized knowledge in a professional situation or context (Coste & Galisson, 1976).

According to DUBOIS, specialized language is "a linguistic subsystem that gathers the linguistic specificities of a particular field" (Dubois et al., 2001, p.40), it is used to express a distribution of sciences and a compartmentalization and allows no flexibility or suppleness, representing a means of expressing specialized knowledge. It opposes common language, which is the unmarked and non-specialized language while forming together the general language that designates the entirety of language (common language + specialized language = General language). However, the term specialized language implies a broader adaptability to the complexities of different sciences, techniques, and technologies.

The term "technolect" refers, like the other definitions mentioned above, to linguistic uses to describe a particular domain of human activity. Unlike the term specialized language, this designation also incorporates non-standard and non-identifiable language usages solely to standardized language but also to dialectal or slang levels. Messaoudi (2002) emphasizes that written and oral productions, including scholarly language, highly scientific texts, as well as common vocabulary and popular terminology, will be considered as part of technolect. It serves to qualify purely technical domains but is also usable in other areas of human activity with much less technical tendency.

From now on, the term "technolect" will be used to qualify linguistic uses specific to the field of commerce. This is justified by the fact that the study takes a sociodidactic perspective, and technolect encompasses both written and oral language aspects of speakers in and out of the classroom.

Specialized Communication Situation

Before addressing the question of "specialized" communication situations, it seems pertinent to specify the term "communication." A multitude of definitions has been given, but we will retain the more general one from Joly, "Communication is the action of communicating, transmitting, informing" (Joly, 2009). This sharing of information requires the use of discourse, which is the physical realization of language and speech. The latter forms a system and a tool for communication. Moreover, to teach oral activities to learners, they must be placed in communication situations during which they must perform tasks. According to Narcy-Combes (2005), the tasks proposed to learners are supposed to be realistic, authentically discursive, and consistent with what they do in everyday life. The teaching process of activities requires the inclusion of content corresponding to knowledge that must be presented in a culturally authentic manner.

The Importance of Qualitative Research

Qualitative research is a methodological approach that focuses on the in-depth understanding and meaning of complex social phenomena. Unlike quantitative research, which emphasizes the measurement and quantification of variables, qualitative research seeks to explore the experiences, perceptions, and motivations of individuals in depth. To achieve this, it employs a variety of methods such as semi-structured interviews, focus groups, and participant observation.

A key characteristic of qualitative research is its inductive approach, where researchers remain open to emerging discoveries and new perspectives throughout the research process. This allows for flexible and adaptive exploration of data, enabling researchers to capture the complexity and richness of human experiences.

Qualitative research is particularly useful for studying complex and often misunderstood social phenomena, such as family dynamics, organizational decision-making processes, and intercultural interactions. It provides depth of analysis that allows for the understanding of the diversity of perspectives and individual experiences, which can inform policies, practices, and social interventions significantly.

Furthermore, qualitative research is often used in an exploratory context, where it can provide valuable insights to guide future research and develop hypotheses to be tested using quantitative methods. This combination of qualitative and quantitative methods can strengthen the validity and reliability of research results, offering a more comprehensive and nuanced understanding of the phenomena under study.

In summary, qualitative research offers a flexible, holistic, and rich approach to exploring the complex dimensions of social life. It enables researchers to give voice to the people involved and generate profound insights that can inform theory, policy, and practice in a variety of fields.

METHODOLOGY

Chosen Method

Qualitative research, often used in social and human sciences, provides a comprehensive approach to understanding complex social phenomena. Unlike quantitative research, which focuses on measurement and quantification of variables, qualitative research concentrates on exploring individuals' experiences, perceptions, and motivations (Denzin & Lincoln, 2018). This method enables researchers to delve deeply into the social, cultural, and historical contexts in which the phenomena under study occur, thereby offering a rich and detailed understanding of research subjects.

One of the strengths of qualitative research lies in its inductive approach, where researchers remain open to emerging discoveries throughout the research process (Charmaz, 2014). This methodological flexibility allows researchers to capture the complexity and richness of the collected data, focusing on the meaning and context of participants' experiences rather than statistical generalization (Creswell & Poth, 2018).

Qualitative research is characterized by its ability to generate rich and contextual data through a variety of methods, such as semi-structured interviews, participant observations, and content analyses (Merriam, 2009). These methods enable researchers to collect data in natural settings, thereby promoting a thorough understanding of the phenomena under study.

Moreover, qualitative research is often used in an exploratory context, where it can provide valuable insights to guide future research and develop hypotheses to be tested using quantitative methods (Maxwell, 2013). This combination of qualitative and quantitative methods can enhance the validity and reliability of research findings, offering a more comprehensive and nuanced understanding of the phenomena under study (Creswell & Creswell, 2018).

In summary, qualitative research offers a flexible and holistic approach to exploring the complex dimensions of social life. It allows researchers to give voice to the individuals involved and generate profound insights that can inform theory, policy, and practice in a variety of fields (Patton, 2015).

In our research, the use of qualitative methodology is particularly important for several reasons. Firstly, our aim is to deeply understand the experiences, perceptions, and motivations of individuals involved in our field of study. By adopting a qualitative approach, we can explore the nuances and subtleties of the phenomena we seek to understand, focusing on the specific contexts in which they occur. Additionally, the methodological flexibility of qualitative research allows us to adapt our data collection and analysis methods to suit the needs of our research. For example, we may choose to use semi-structured interviews to gather detailed narratives of participants' experiences, or to observe interactions directly in natural settings to better understand social dynamics at play. Moreover, qualitative research enables us to explore the underlying mechanisms and complex processes that influence the phenomena under study. By identifying and analyzing these mechanisms, we can develop a thorough understanding of the factors that shape social realities in our field of interest. Finally, by combining qualitative and quantitative approaches, our research can benefit from the complementarity of these two methodologies. Qualitative data can provide valuable insights to inform the design of our quantitative measurement instruments, while also shedding light on the interpretations of the quantitative results obtained.

Description of the Sample and Study Context

The sample for this study consists of a trainee enrolled in the Commerce and Management program at the Office of Vocational Training and Employment Promotion (OFPPT) and a native French speaker. The trainee, representing the sample, is a young Moroccan student aged 20, enrolled in a vocational training program in commerce. He has a secondary education level, with a basic mastery of the French language acquired in a formal educational setting. The trainee is selected because of his learner status in the field of commerce and his regular interaction with French-speaking clients in a simulated professional context. It is noteworthy that he had undergone training in French for Specific Purposes (FSP), demonstrating particularly remarkable linguistic and intercultural mastery throughout the analyzed commercial interactions.

The native speaker participating in this study is a 28-year-old French individual residing in France. He has a higher education level with a background in business management. A native French speaker, he has an advanced mastery of the language and professional experience in the field of commerce. The native speaker is chosen to represent a typical interlocutor in the context of commercial transactions with French-speaking clients.

This study takes place within the framework of a simulated environment of commercial transactions, where the OFPPT trainee interacts with a native French speaker in sales situations. Interactions primarily occur in an educational context, involving sales simulations and commercial negotiation scenarios.

The choice of OFPPT as the study site is motivated by its role in the vocational training of young Moroccans in various fields, including commerce and management. The institution provides a conducive learning environment for observing and analyzing the linguistic and intercultural skills of trainees in commercial situations.

The study focuses on verbal interactions between the Moroccan trainee and the native French speaker at different stages of the sales process, such as customer reception, product presentation, price negotiation, and sales closure. The objective is to understand how linguistic and cultural dynamics influence communication and the outcomes of intercultural commercial transactions.

The study context offers a unique opportunity to observe the communication strategies used by the Moroccan trainee to adapt to the linguistic and cultural expectations and norms of the French client. Additionally, it allows for exploring the challenges and opportunities encountered by the trainee in selling to a native French-speaking audience, as well as the implications for improving linguistic and intercultural skills in the field of commerce.

Data Collection Methods

The data collection methods adopted in this study were designed to offer a comprehensive and rigorous approach to capturing the nuances of intercultural commercial interactions between the OFPPT trainee and the native French speaker. The use of audiovisual recordings allowed for detailed capture of verbal and non-verbal exchanges, providing a complete view of interactions. Cameras were positioned to cover the entire space where interactions took place, ensuring comprehensive event coverage. This method was complemented by direct observations, enabling researchers to grasp nuances of behaviors and facial expressions not always captured by recordings.

Furthermore, to ensure the reliability and validity of collected data, we meticulously followed the standardized protocol for recording interactions and conducting interviews, developed to ensure systematic and rigorous data collection. The various steps of this protocol were rigorously adhered to. Firstly, particular attention was given to equipment preparation before each interaction or interview session. We ensured that audiovisual equipment was operational and correctly configured, positioning cameras to capture the entirety of the space where interactions took place and placing microphones to distinctly record participants' voices. Next, informed consent was obtained from both participants before the start of interaction recordings. We took time to explain the study's objectives, the nature of recordings made, and emphasized participants' right to withdraw consent at any time. During interactions, we adopted a discreet posture to preserve the authenticity of exchanges. We avoided intervening in dialogues and recorded the entirety of interactions, taking care to note key moments and relevant elements for subsequent analysis. Finally, we guaranteed the confidentiality and anonymity of collected data. Audiovisual recordings were securely stored, and only the researcher had access to the data. Participants' personal information was strictly protected, and all data were handled with utmost care and full respect for confidentiality.

Analysis of Intercultural Interactions in a Commercial Context

To analyze the audiovisual recordings according to the given criteria, we will examine each criterion in detail through the interactions between the trainee and the client. These criteria are essential for evaluating the quality of intercultural communication and interaction management in a commercial context. Here's how we could proceed:

- Intercultural Adjustment: We will identify the adaptive behaviors of the trainee and the client to accommodate cultural differences. This may include gestures of mutual respect, language adaptations, or discussions about cultural differences between the two parties.
- Management of Cultural Identities: We will look for verbal and non-verbal signals indicating adaptation to the cultural norms and expectations of the other party. This could manifest in the use of appropriate greetings, adherence to politeness norms, or references to specific cultural aspects.
- Social Exchange: We will assess the quality and fluidity of social interaction between the trainee and the client. This could include moments of conviviality, exchange of jokes, or signs of emotional connection between the participants.
- Linguistic and Intercultural Skills: We will evaluate the trainee's linguistic skills in terms of pronunciation, vocabulary usage, and grammar. Additionally, we will examine the communication techniques used to establish and maintain a positive relationship throughout the exchange, demonstrating the trainee's intercultural skills in overcoming linguistic or cultural barriers.

For a comprehensive analysis, please refer to the complete analysis grid in the appendix. By analyzing these aspects of interactions, we can better understand how the trainee and the client adapt and interact in an intercultural commercial context, highlighting their linguistic and intercultural skills as well as their ability to navigate successfully in complex situations.

RESULTS: PRESENTATION, ANALYSIS, AND INTERPRETATION

Presentation and Analysis of Results

The analysis of intercultural interactions is of crucial importance in the commercial field, where exchanges between individuals from different cultures can significantly influence the success of transactions. This section focuses on the results of the analysis of interactions between the trainee and the client in a commercial context, highlighting the nuances of intercultural adjustments, management of cultural identities, the quality of social exchange, and the linguistic and intercultural skills involved.

Through this in-depth analysis, we aim to identify key elements that foster successful intercultural communication in the specific context of commercial exchanges. By understanding these dynamics, we can propose relevant recommendations to improve the quality of interactions and promote the success of international transactions in an increasingly interconnected world.

Intercultural Adjustment

- The adaptive behaviors of the trainee and the client were observed on multiple occasions. For example, the trainee used appropriate greetings based on the client's culture, which helped establish a trust relationship from the beginning of the interaction.
- Discussions about cultural differences also took place, especially during price negotiations, where the trainee explained differences in perception of value between cultures, thereby facilitating mutual understanding.

The recordings show that the trainee and the client demonstrate a certain ability to adapt to cultural differences. For example, the trainee uses formal and respectful language towards the French client, demonstrating an awareness of politeness norms. Additionally, gestures of mutual respect, such as appropriate greetings and expressions of gratitude, are observed throughout the interactions.

Management of Cultural Identities

- Verbal and non-verbal signals indicating adaptation to the cultural norms of the other party were observed throughout the interactions. For example, the client showed patience and respect towards local customs during product discussions and used relevant cultural references to establish a connection with the French client, such as compliments on French culture or discussions about cultural events. Similarly, the client shows an interest in Moroccan culture, which enhances the sense of mutual understanding.
- The trainee also demonstrated cultural sensitivity by adapting their body language and speech to match the expectations of the French client, which strengthened the business relationship.

Social Exchange

- The quality of social interaction between the trainee and the client was high, with moments of conviviality and exchange of jokes contributing to creating a positive and relaxed atmosphere.
- Signs of emotional connection were observed, especially when the client expressed satisfaction with the company's social responsibility values, which strengthened trust and rapport between the two parties.

Linguistic and Intercultural Skills

- The trainee's linguistic skills were assessed as high, with clear pronunciation, appropriate vocabulary usage, and correct grammar throughout the interactions.
- The trainee's intercultural skills were demonstrated by their ability to overcome linguistic and cultural barriers, including adapting their speech and clarifying misunderstandings effectively.

In conclusion, the analysis of intercultural interactions highlights the ability of the trainee and the client to navigate successfully in a diverse commercial context. Their intercultural adjustment, management of cultural identities, quality of social exchange, and linguistic and intercultural skills play a crucial role in the success of international business transactions. These results underscore the importance of intercultural communication in the business field and highlight effective strategies to promote harmonious and productive interaction between individuals from different cultures.

Interpretation of Results

The analysis of intercultural interactions in a business context reveals several key aspects that significantly influence the dynamics of commercial relationships. First and foremost, the intercultural adjustment of participants is essential. This goes beyond mere recognition of cultural differences; it involves actively adapting to these differences. Individuals who demonstrate this ability are better equipped to navigate diverse business environments, fostering smooth communication and effective collaboration. Their ability to understand and respect the cultural codes of business partners also facilitates the establishment of trust, a crucial aspect in any successful business partnership.

Furthermore, the management of cultural identities is another key element. This entails mutual recognition of the cultural identities of the parties involved in a business transaction. When each party feels recognized in their culture and when their cultural norms and expectations are respected, it enhances mutual trust and engagement in the business relationship. Such recognition also fosters an atmosphere of respect and openness that is conducive to transparent communication and constructive collaboration.

Positive social exchange moments are also crucial. These informal moments, whether they occur during official meetings or outside the professional setting, contribute to strengthening personal bonds among individuals involved in the business transaction. These personal connections often form the basis of solid and enduring professional relationships. Indeed, an environment where positive social interactions prevail creates an atmosphere conducive to collaborative decision-making and effective resolution of potential conflicts.

Lastly, the linguistic and intercultural skills of the intern are of paramount importance. In a globalized business context, the clarity and mutual understanding of exchanges largely depend on individuals' ability to communicate effectively in foreign languages and successfully navigate cultural nuances. Interns with strong linguistic and intercultural skills are better prepared to establish meaningful connections with international business partners and contribute to the success of business transactions.

These various elements underscore the crucial importance of intercultural communication and the development of linguistic and intercultural skills in the context of international business interactions. Awareness and mastery of these aspects are essential to ensuring the success of business relationships in an increasingly globalized and diversified world.

The Impact of Previous Work on Intercultural Interactions in Business Settings: A Validation of Our Findings

The results of our analysis of intercultural interactions in the commercial context find significant validation in prior research conducted by several distinguished scholars. Indeed, our conclusions closely align with those of other similar studies, thereby bolstering the robustness and relevance of our findings.

Firstly, our findings regarding the importance of intercultural adjustment for fostering effective communication resonate with the works of researchers such as Hofstede and Hofstede (2005), who have been among the most influential in understanding cultural dimensions and their impact on intercultural interactions. Their research has led to the formulation of several key cultural dimensions, such as power distance, individualism versus collectivism, masculinity versus femininity, and uncertainty avoidance. These dimensions have been widely utilized to comprehend how cultural differences can influence individual behaviors and interpersonal interactions. By emphasizing cultural sensitivity and adaptability, Hofstede and Hofstede underscored the importance for individuals to understand and respect the cultural norms of others in intercultural interactions, which is consistent with our findings regarding the importance of intercultural adjustment for effective communication in the business context.

The works of Gudykunst and Kim (2003) also focus on intercultural interactions, particularly emphasizing the management of cultural identities. They developed the theory of affirmative ethnocentrism, which describes various strategies individuals can adopt to manage their cultural identity in intercultural contexts. This theory highlights the importance of recognizing and valuing the cultural identities of others to establish positive and productive relationships. Our observations on the management of cultural identities and its impact on trust and engagement in business relationships align with this perspective, emphasizing the significance of mutual recognition of cultural identities in fostering successful intercultural interactions in the business domain.

By integrating the insights of these researchers with our own findings, we enhance our understanding of the underlying mechanisms of intercultural interactions in the commercial context, thereby reinforcing the relevance and validity of our conclusions.

Furthermore, the works of Hall (1976) have significantly contributed to understanding intercultural interactions by highlighting the importance of informal interactions and social exchanges in building successful interpersonal relationships. Hall emphasized that moments of conviviality and unstructured social interactions can play a crucial role in establishing trust and mutual understanding between individuals from different cultures. Our results on the quality of social exchanges and its influence on creating an environment conducive to decision-making align with these findings, highlighting the importance of informal interactions in the intercultural business context.

The works of Chen and Starosta (2000) also focus on the linguistic and intercultural skills necessary for successful intercultural interactions. Their research emphasized the importance of linguistic proficiency and intercultural sensitivity in reducing misunderstandings and communication barriers between individuals from different cultures. By emphasizing the central role of these skills in facilitating clarity and mutual understanding in exchanges, our findings are consistent with those of Chen and Starosta. By integrating these perspectives into our results, we enhance our understanding of the factors underlying intercultural interactions in the business context and underscore the importance of developing linguistic and intercultural skills to succeed in a globalized and diversified business environment.

In conclusion, our results are consistent with the conclusions of previous studies on intercultural interactions in the business domain, thereby strengthening the robustness of our findings and highlighting the crucial importance of intercultural communication for the success of international business transactions. By integrating the insights of these researchers into our own findings, we contribute to enriching the academic understanding of this vital domain in an increasingly globalized world.

DISCUSSIONS

Strengths in Intercultural Communication

In the realm of intercultural communication, the Moroccan trainee demonstrated a series of remarkable skills that greatly contributed to their effectiveness in interactions with the French client. Firstly, their linguistic competence was outstanding, as evidenced by clear and precise pronunciation as well as appropriate vocabulary usage in various business contexts. This linguistic proficiency was likely reinforced by their training in French for Specific Purposes (FSP), enabling them to communicate fluently and accurately while fully understanding the needs and expectations of the French client.

Furthermore, the trainee showed a high sensitivity to cultural differences by adjusting their language, tone, and behavior to align with the social norms and expectations of the client. This ability to recognize and respect the verbal and non-verbal cues of the French client facilitated the establishment of a trust relationship and fostered open and effective communication.

Moreover, the trainee demonstrated remarkable flexibility and adaptability in managing negotiations and potential conflicts. They were able to respond appropriately to the demands and concerns of the client, adopting a collaborative approach and proposing alternative solutions when necessary. This ability to navigate agilely in complex business situations was a major asset for the trainee, allowing them to maintain dialogue and achieve mutually beneficial compromises. In summary, these skills were key elements of the trainee's success in their intercultural interactions, enabling them to effectively manage challenges and capitalize on opportunities throughout the sales process.

To shed further light on the intercultural skills demonstrated by the Moroccan intern, it is pertinent to compare his results with those of previous research in the field of intercultural communication. The work of several researchers has highlighted similar strengths, thus offering a broader perspective on the effectiveness of the observed skills.

Firstly, the impact of linguistic training on communication skills has been extensively documented. Previous studies, such as those by Byram (1997), have shown that training in French for Specific Purposes (FSP) significantly improves the linguistic skills of non-native speakers. This specialized training allows learners to interact more effectively in multicultural environments by reducing misunderstandings and facilitating clear and precise communication. The Moroccan intern, benefiting from this training, demonstrated clear pronunciation and appropriate use of vocabulary, thus confirming the importance of FSP in preparing professionals for intercultural interactions.

Secondly, cultural sensitivity and adaptation are crucial skills for establishing trust in intercultural interactions. Bennett's (1993) work on intercultural sensitivity reveals that taking cultural differences into account, including social norms and expectations, is essential. Bennett's Developmental Model of Intercultural Sensitivity illustrates how individuals can evolve from ethnocentrism to ethnorelativism, thereby enhancing their ability to communicate and interact effectively with people from different cultures. The Moroccan intern demonstrated this sensitivity by adjusting his language, tone, and behavior to align with the social norms and expectations of the French client.

Furthermore, flexibility and adaptability in negotiations are essential skills for navigating complex situations. Ting-Toomey's (1999) research on intercultural conflict management shows that flexibility and adaptability enable individuals to respond appropriately to demands and concerns, thereby increasing the chances of reaching mutually beneficial agreements. The Moroccan intern adopted a collaborative approach, proposing alternative solutions when necessary, which was a major asset in maintaining dialogue and achieving compromises.

Finally, verbal and non-verbal communication plays a crucial role in intercultural interactions. Edward T. Hall (1976) emphasized the importance of verbal and non-verbal cues in intercultural communication. The ability to interpret and respond appropriately to these cues is essential for successful communication. The Moroccan intern's skills in this regard confirm Hall's observations on the importance of contextual communication. His ability to recognize and respect the verbal and non-verbal signals of the French client facilitated the establishment of trust and promoted open and effective communication.

These previous studies corroborate the skills observed in the Moroccan intern, highlighting the importance of linguistic skills, cultural sensitivity, flexibility, and adaptability in successful intercultural interactions. Based on these results, it can be concluded that the intern's skills are in line with best practices recognized in the field of intercultural communication.

Challenges and Obstacles to Overcome

Despite their strengths, the Moroccan trainee also faced several challenges and obstacles in their intercultural interactions with the French client. Firstly, one of the main difficulties they encountered was related to cultural and linguistic differences between the two parties. Despite their training in FSP and their sensitivity to French cultural norms, the trainee sometimes struggled to fully understand the nuances of communication and the implicit expectations of the French client. These gaps could lead to misunderstandings and frustrations, sometimes affecting the fluency and effectiveness of exchanges.

Additionally, the trainee also faced challenges related to managing conflicts and potential disagreements during business negotiations. Due to their lack of experience or limited confidence level in certain situations, they might hesitate to defend their positions or express their views clearly, fearing to compromise the relationship with the client. This tendency to avoid direct confrontations could sometimes lead to excessive concessions or difficulty in effectively advocating for the interests of their company

Furthermore, the trainee might encounter difficulties related to time management and deadline pressure during business interactions. In a dynamic and demanding business environment, they were sometimes faced with urgent demands or high expectations from the client, which could lead to stress and anxiety. This additional pressure could affect their ability to stay focused and make informed decisions, thereby compromising the quality of their interactions with the client.

To shed further light on the challenges and obstacles faced by the Moroccan intern during his intercultural interactions with the French client, it is pertinent to compare his experiences with those documented in previous research. Several researchers have studied similar situations, and their findings offer precise perspectives on these issues.

Studies, such as those by Gudykunst and Kim (2003), have shown that despite good linguistic training, individuals may encounter difficulties in grasping the nuances and implicit expectations in intercultural communication. Gudykunst and Kim highlight that communication between different cultures involves subtleties and unspoken elements that can be misinterpreted, leading to misunderstandings and frustrations. This phenomenon was observed in the Moroccan intern, who, despite his training in French for Specific Purposes (FSP) and cultural sensitivity, sometimes struggled to fully understand the subtleties of communication with the French client.

Ting-Toomey's (1988) research on intercultural conflict management reveals that individuals from different cultures may adopt varied conflict management styles, which can lead to misunderstandings and difficulties in negotiations. Ting-Toomey emphasizes that a lack of experience or reluctance to confront directly can result in excessive concessions and insufficient defense of personal or organizational interests. The Moroccan intern experienced similar situations, where his lack of confidence or hesitation to clearly express his viewpoints sometimes led to overly significant compromises.

Hall's (1959) work on cultural differences in time perception shows that expectations regarding time management can vary significantly between cultures. Hall describes how monochronic cultures (which view time linearly and segmented) and polychronic cultures (which view time more flexibly and fluidly) can have different approaches to managing deadlines and priorities. The Moroccan intern, in a demanding commercial environment, faced high expectations and tight deadlines, which could lead to stress and affect his ability to remain focused, thereby impacting the quality of his interactions with the client.

These previous studies confirm the challenges observed in the Moroccan intern and offer explanations for difficulties related to understanding the subtleties of communication, managing conflicts and disagreements, as well as handling time management and deadline pressures. By recognizing these obstacles, it becomes possible to better prepare and support individuals in their intercultural interactions, minimizing misunderstandings and maximizing the effectiveness of exchanges.

Implications for Intercultural Skills Development

The challenges and obstacles faced by the Moroccan trainee in their intercultural interactions with the French client underscore the crucial importance of developing intercultural skills in the professional domain. Firstly, these experiences highlight the need for individuals to develop a thorough understanding of cultural and linguistic differences to navigate effectively in international business contexts. It is essential for professionals to acquire increased cultural sensitivity, as well as practical knowledge of social norms and cultural expectations of stakeholders with whom they interact.

Furthermore, the challenges encountered by the trainee also emphasize the importance of developing intercultural communication skills, including the ability to recognize and interpret verbal and non-verbal cues, adapt language and behavior based on the cultural context, and effectively manage conflicts and potential disagreements. Professionals must be able to communicate clearly, precisely, and respectfully while maintaining positive and constructive professional relationships with international colleagues and clients.

Additionally, these experiences highlight the importance of developing stress and time management skills, as well as the ability to work effectively under pressure in a dynamic and demanding business environment. Professionals must be able to effectively manage their time, resources, and priorities while remaining focused and productive, even in stressful or tight deadline situations.

The challenges and obstacles faced by the Moroccan intern during his intercultural interactions with the French client highlight the critical importance of developing intercultural competencies in the professional realm. These experiences underscore the necessity for individuals to cultivate a deep understanding of cultural and linguistic differences to navigate effectively in international business contexts. It is essential for professionals to enhance their cultural sensitivity and acquire practical knowledge of the social norms and cultural expectations of the stakeholders they interact with.

Firstly, the need for a profound understanding of cultural and linguistic differences is evident. Research by Hofstede (1980) on cultural dimensions theory demonstrates how cultural differences in power distance, individualism versus collectivism, uncertainty avoidance, and other dimensions can impact business interactions. Hofstede's findings reveal that awareness and comprehension of these differences can lead to more effective communication and collaboration in multicultural settings. This aligns with the intern's need to understand the French client's implicit expectations and communication nuances, despite his FSP training.

Secondly, the importance of developing intercultural communication skills is highlighted. Ting-Toomey and Kurogi's (1998) work on face-negotiation theory illustrates the necessity of recognizing and interpreting verbal and non-verbal cues in intercultural communication. Their research indicates that professionals must adapt their language and behavior according to cultural contexts and manage potential conflicts and disagreements effectively. The intern's experience of struggling to express his viewpoints and hesitating to confront issues directly reflects these challenges, underscoring the need for clear, precise, and respectful communication.

Additionally, the significance of stress and time management skills in a dynamic commercial environment is evident. Adler (2008) discusses the importance of cross-cultural management and the ability to perform effectively under pressure. Adler's research emphasizes that professionals need to manage their time, resources, and priorities efficiently while maintaining productivity and focus, even in high-stress situations or tight deadlines. The intern's experience of stress and difficulty in managing urgent demands highlights the necessity of developing these competencies.

These prior studies corroborate the challenges observed in the Moroccan intern and provide precise insights into the importance of intercultural understanding, communication skills, and stress and time management in professional success. By addressing these obstacles, it is possible to better prepare and support individuals in their intercultural interactions, minimizing misunderstandings and maximizing the effectiveness of exchanges.

The Role of Technology in Facilitating Intercultural Communication in International Commerce

His role in trade is pivotal, as supported by the findings. Firstly, modern communication tools such as video conferencing platforms and instant messaging software provide effective means to interact in real-time with individuals located in geographically distant regions. These technologies enable direct interaction, reducing delays and facilitating swift problem resolution, thereby enhancing the smoothness of international business transactions.

Moreover, these tools transcend linguistic barriers through their automatic translation features. By allowing users to communicate in their native language while receiving instant translations in their interlocutor's language, these technologies promote more efficient mutual understanding and mitigate potentially costly misunderstandings.

Furthermore, social networks and online collaboration platforms offer virtual spaces where individuals can interact informally, fostering the development of professional relationships based on trust and mutual understanding of cultures. These platforms enable individuals to share information, experiences, and perspectives, thereby fostering a sense of community and strengthening ties among international business stakeholders.

Lastly, customer relationship management (CRM) tools and e-commerce platforms play a crucial role in enabling companies to personalize their interactions with clients from different cultures. By analyzing customer data and utilizing machine learning algorithms, these tools can provide personalized recommendations and offers that take into account the specific cultural and linguistic preferences of each client.

In conclusion, technology offers innovative means to overcome barriers to intercultural communication, thereby contributing to the strengthening of international business relations in an increasingly connected world. By effectively utilizing these tools, companies can establish solid and enduring partnerships with business stakeholders from diverse cultural backgrounds, fostering growth and success in global markets.

PRACTICES AND RECOMMENDATIONS

Strategies to Improve Linguistic and Intercultural Skills

To improve linguistic and intercultural skills, it is essential to implement a series of effective strategies and practices. Firstly, trainees and professionals can benefit from ongoing language training, specifically tailored to the needs and requirements of their professional field. This training may include general language courses as well as French for Specific Purposes (FSP) courses to enhance the linguistic skills necessary in a business context.

Studies by Byram (1997) and Kramsch (1993) have highlighted the importance of continuous and specialized language training for professionals. Byram demonstrated that French for Specific Purposes (FSP) courses are particularly effective in enhancing the linguistic skills necessary in a business context. Kramsch emphasized that learning languages in relation to specific professional contexts enables learners to better understand and use the relevant vocabulary and linguistic structures.

It is also essential to promote regular immersion in the target language and culture through various activities such as reading newspapers, watching films and TV series, listening to podcasts, or participating in cultural events. This helps individuals deepen their understanding of the target language and culture while familiarizing them with different accents, idiomatic expressions, and communication styles. Duff's (2008) research highlights the importance of this regular immersion. Duff found that learners who engage in reading newspapers, watching films and TV series, listening to podcasts, and participating in cultural events gain a better grasp of idiomatic expressions, various accents, and communication styles specific to the target language.

Additionally, trainees and professionals can benefit from cultural awareness sessions and training on cultural differences, social norms, and specific business practices in their target market. These sessions may include case studies, simulations of intercultural interactions, and practical advice on managing cultural differences in a professional context. Research by Hofstede (2001) and Bennett (1993) highlights the importance of cultural awareness sessions and training on cultural differences. Hofstede identified several cultural dimensions (such as power distance and individualism vs. collectivism) that influence professional interactions. Bennett developed a model of intercultural sensitivity development, emphasizing that awareness and training enable individuals to shift from ethnocentrism to ethnorelativism, thereby improving their ability to manage cultural differences effectively.

It is also recommended to foster an open and curious attitude towards foreign cultures and languages, as well as a willingness to learn and adapt continuously. Individuals can benefit from interactions with people from different cultures, whether at work, in social contexts, or through professional networks and online platforms. Research by Deardorff (2006) and Fantini (2000) shows that adopting an open and curious attitude towards foreign cultures and languages is crucial for developing intercultural competencies. Deardorff highlighted the concept of "intercultural competence" as a continuous process of learning and adaptation. Fantini emphasized that interactions with people from different cultures, whether in professional or social contexts, enhance individuals' ability to adapt and navigate effectively in intercultural environments.

Integration of Intercultural Teaching Into the Curriculum

The integration of intercultural teaching into the curriculum in Morocco is crucial to prepare students to thrive in an increasingly globalized and interconnected world (Bourray, 2018). To achieve this, several measures can be considered.

Firstly, it is essential to include dedicated modules on intercultural awareness in educational programs, focusing on understanding different cultures, social norms, and business practices. These modules could address topics such as intercultural communication, managing cultural differences, stereotypes and prejudices, as well as the skills needed to work effectively in multicultural environments.

Furthermore, it would be beneficial to incorporate practical activities into the training program, such as intercultural exchanges, internships abroad, or collaborative projects with international partners. These experiences provide students with the opportunity to put their intercultural knowledge into practice in real contexts, while developing valuable skills such as intercultural communication, problem-solving, and teamwork.

Additionally, it is important to train teachers and trainers to effectively integrate intercultural teaching into their courses, providing pedagogical resources, tools, and teaching techniques. This will enable them to create an inclusive and diverse learning environment, where students are encouraged to explore and appreciate the cultural diversity around them.

Finally, it is necessary to promote a holistic approach to intercultural teaching by connecting it to other disciplines such as foreign languages, literature, history, and social sciences. This will allow students to understand cultural dimensions in a broader context and gain a global perspective on intercultural issues.

By effectively integrating intercultural teaching into the curriculum in Morocco, educational institutions can help prepare students to succeed in a diverse and interconnected world by strengthening their intercultural understanding, linguistic skills, and adaptability to cultural differences.

Importance of Intercultural Awareness for Better Success in International Trade

Intercultural awareness is of crucial importance for better success in international trade. In an increasingly globalized world, businesses operate in diverse and interconnected environments where understanding cultural differences becomes a major strategic asset. Here are some reasons that highlight the importance of intercultural awareness in the context of international trade:

Understanding foreign markets: Intercultural awareness enables companies to better understand the foreign markets in which they operate. By understanding the social norms, cultural values, beliefs, and behaviors of consumers in different countries, businesses can adapt their products, services, and marketing strategies to meet the specific needs of each market.

Effective communication: Good intercultural awareness fosters effective communication with business partners, clients, and international collaborators. By understanding differences in communication styles, body language, and etiquette, international business professionals can avoid misunderstandings and conflicts, and establish lasting trust-based relationships.

Successful negotiation: Intercultural awareness is essential for conducting successful negotiations in an international context. By understanding the values, attitudes, and business practices of foreign partners, negotiators can adapt their negotiation strategies and find mutually beneficial solutions that meet the interests of both parties.

Effective management of multicultural teams: In an international business environment, it is common to work with teams composed of members from different cultures. Intercultural awareness allows managers to better understand the needs, motivations, and expectations of their international colleagues, thereby facilitating effective team management and promoting an inclusive work environment.

Adaptability to changes: Companies that are sensitive to cultural differences are better equipped to cope with changes and challenges in an ever-evolving business environment. They are more adept at quickly adapting to new markets, regulations, and emerging trends, giving them a competitive edge in the international market.

CONCLUSION

The in-depth analysis of intercultural business interactions between the Moroccan trainee and the French client has highlighted several essential aspects of intercultural communication in a business context. We observed that the trainee demonstrated remarkable linguistic and intercultural skills, particularly in adapting language, behavior, and communication strategies to meet the client's needs and expectations. The results also underscored the challenges faced by the trainee, such as managing cultural differences and negotiating cultural identities, which require increased sensitivity and flexibility in an intercultural business environment.

+ Contributions to Research and Practical Implications:

This study makes a significant contribution to research on intercultural communication in the context of international trade. By highlighting the skills, challenges, and communication strategies of the Moroccan trainee, it offers valuable insights for practitioners and researchers interested in developing intercultural skills in the business domain. On a practical level, this study underscores the importance of integrating intercultural teaching into business training programs and provides recommendations for improving the linguistic and intercultural skills of international business professionals.

To further enrich our understanding of intercultural communication in international trade, future research could explore different business contexts involving a diversity of participants and cultures. It would also be interesting to examine the effectiveness of different training and intervention strategies for enhancing the intercultural skills of business professionals. Finally, particular attention could be paid to the ethical and sustainable aspects of intercultural communication in international trade, to promote responsible business practices that respect cultural diversities.

REFERENCES

Bartel-Radic, A. (2009). La compétence interculturelle: état de l'art et perspectives. *Management International*, *13*(4), 11–26. 10.7202/038582ar

Bennett, M. J. (1993). Towards Ethnorelativism: A Developmental Model of Intercultural Sensitivity. In Paige, R. M. (Ed.), *Education for the Intercultural Experience* (pp. 21–71). Intercultural Press.

Bourray, M. (2018). L'interculturel dans l'enseignement/apprentissage du FLE au Maroc. *FRANCISOLA*, 3(2), 122–140. 10.17509/francisola.v3i2.15746

Byram, M. (1997). *Teaching and Assessing Intercultural Communicative Competence*. Multilingual Matters.

Charmaz, K. (2014). Grounded Theory in Global Perspective: Reviews by International Researchers. *Qualitative Inquiry*, 20(9), 1074–1084. 10.1177/1077800414545235

Chen, G., & Starosta, W. (2000). The Development and Validation of the Intercultural Sensitivity Scale. *Human Communication*, 3, 1–15. 10.1037/t61546-000

Coste, D., & Galisson, R. (1976). *Dictionary of Language Teaching*. Hachette.

Creswell, J. W., & Creswell, J. D. (2018). *Research Design: Qualitative, Quantitative, and Mixed Methods Approaches*. Sage.

Creswell, J. W., & Poth, C. N. (2018). *Qualitative Inquiry and Research Design Choosing among Five Approaches* (4th ed.). SAGE Publications, Inc.

Deardorff, D. K. (2006). Identification and Assessment of Intercultural Competence as a Student Outcome of Internationalization. *Journal of Studies in International Education*, 10(3), 241–266. 10.1177/1028315306287002

Denzin, N. K., & Lincoln, Y. S. (Eds.). (2018). *The SAGE Handbook of Qualitative Research* (5th ed.). Sage.

Dubois, J., Lecercle, J.-J., & Marcellesi, J.-B. (2001). *General Linguistics Course*. Payot.

Fantini, A. E. (2000). *A Central Concern: Developing Intercultural Competence*. School for International Training Occasional Papers Series.

Furman, F. K., & Anderson, A. R. (2020). What do firms want from business graduates? A comparative analysis of the views of employers" in different countries. *Journal of International Business Education*, 15, 39–70.

Gudykunst, W. B., & Kim, Y. Y. (2003). *Communicating with Strangers: An Approach to Intercultural Communication*. McGraw-Hill.

Gudykunst, W. B., & Kim, Y. Y. (2003). *Communicating With Strangers: An Approach to Intercultural Communication* (4th ed.). McGraw-Hill.

Hall, E. T. (1959). *The Silent Language*. Doubleday.

Hall, E. T. (1976). *Beyond Culture*. Anchor Books.

Hofstede, G. (2001). *Culture's Consequences: Comparing Values, Behaviors, Institutions, and Organizations Across Nations*. Sage Publications.

Hofstede, G., & Hofstede, G. J. (2005). *Culture and Organizations—Software of the Mind: Intercultural Cooperation and its Importance for Survival* (2nd ed.). McGraw Hill.

Joly, B. (2009). *Communication*. De Boeck Supérieur.

Kim, Y. Y. (2005). Adapting to a new culture: An integrative communication theory. *Theorizing about intercultural communication*, 375-400.

Kramsch, C. (1993). *Context and Culture in Language Teaching*. Oxford University Press.

Labov, W. (1976). *Sociolinguistics*. Minuit.

Maxwell, J. (2012). *Qualitative Research Design: An Interactive Approach*. Sage, Inc.

Merriam, S. B. (2009). *Qualitative research: A guide to design and implementation*. Jossey-Bass.

Messaoudi, L. (2002). Technolect and linguistic resources. The example of the highway code in Morocco. *Language in Society*, 2002(1), 53–75. 10.3917/ls.099.0053

Molm, L. D., Takahashi, N., & Peterson, G. (2000). Risk and trust in social exchange: An experimental test of a classical proposition. *American Journal of Sociology*, 105(5), 1396–1427. 10.1086/210434

Narcy-Combes, J.-P. (2005). *Language Teaching and ICT: towards responsible action research*. OPHRYS.

Phal, A. (1968). *Scientific Language and Linguistic Analysis*. CREDIF.

Saussure, F. (1916). *Course in General Linguistics*. Payot.

Ting-Toomey, S. (1988). Intercultural Conflict Styles: A Face-Negotiation Theory. In Kim, Y. Y., & Gudykunst, W. B. (Eds.), *Theories in Intercultural Communication* (pp. 213–235). Sage.

Ting-Toomey, S. (1999). *Communicating Across Cultures*. Guilford Press.

Ting-Toomey, S., & Chung, L. C. (2012). *Understanding Intercultural Communication*. Oxford University Press.

ADDITIONAL READING

Barrett, D., & Twycross, A. (2018). Data collection in qualitative research. *Evidence-Based Nursing*, 21(3), 63–64. 10.1136/eb-2018-10293929858278

Bryman, A. (2016). *Social Research Methods*. Oxford University Press.

Creswell, J. W. (2013). *Qualitative Inquiry & Research Design: Choosing Among Five Approaches* (3rd ed.). Sage Publications.

Denzin, N. K., & Lincoln, Y. S. (2005). Introduction: The Discipline and Practice of Qualitative Research. In Denzin, N. K., & Lincoln, Y. S. (Eds.), *Handbook of Qualitative Research* (3rd ed., pp. 1–32). Sage.

Elhami, A. (2020a). Communication accommodation theory: A brief review of the literature. *Journal of Advances in Education and Philosophy*, 4(5), 192–200. 10.36348/jaep.2020.v04i05.002

Elhami, A. (2020b). A Socio-pragmatic perspective of Spanish and Persian greeting. *Theory and Practice in Language Studies*, 10(9), 1009. 10.17507/tpls.1009.01

Elhami, A., & Roshan, A. (2024). Religion and higher education migrants' acculturation orientation. *Intercultural Education*, 35(3), 283–301. 10.1080/14675986.2024.2348428

Elhami, A., & Roshan, A. (2024). The History of Acculturation: A review article. *Social SciencesHumanities and Education Journal*, 5(1), 180–196.

Elhami, A., Roshan, A., Ghahraman, V., & Afrashi, A. (2024). Sociocultural adjustment by two international students: A critical look at multilingualism in Spain. *International Journal of Language Studies*, 18(3), 1–38.

Flick, U. (2014). *An Introduction to Qualitative Research* (5th ed.). Sage Publications.

Glaser, B. G., & Strauss, A. L. (1967). *The Discovery of Grounded Theory: Strategies for Qualitative Research*. Aldine Publishing Company.

Guba, E. G., & Lincoln, Y. S. (1994). Competing Paradigms in Qualitative Research. In Denzin, N. K., & Lincoln, Y. S. (Eds.), *Handbook of Qualitative Research* (pp. 105–117). Sage Publications.

Holliday, A. (2010). *Intercultural Communication and Ideology*. Sage Publications.

Mak, B. C. N. (2014). Instant messaging in office hours: Use of ellipsis dots at work and Hong Kong culture. *International Journal of Language Studies*, 8(2), 25–50.

Mapuya, M. (2024). Exploring the contribution of decolonisation epistemologies: Promoting social justice in accounting education. *International Journal of Language Studies*, 18(1), 131–155. 10.5281/zenodo.10468331

Patton, M. Q. (2015). *Qualitative Research & Evaluation Methods: Integrating Theory and Practice* (4th ed.). Sage Publications.

Silverman, D. (2020). *Qualitative Research* (5th ed.). Sage Publications.

KEY TERMS AND DEFINITIONS

Communication Barriers: They refer to obstacles or difficulties that hinder the effective transmission of information and mutual understanding during a verbal or non-verbal interaction or exchange. This may include linguistic differences, cultural differences, biases, stereotypes, misunderstandings, or other factors that disrupt communication and impede the quality of interactions.

Competitive Advantages: Are distinctive assets or capabilities that enable a company or individual to outperform competitors in a given market. This may include specific skills, unique resources, innovative technologies, or effective business strategies.

Conflict Management: Involves effectively resolving disputes and disagreements that may arise in interpersonal or professional interactions. This includes identifying sources of conflict, open and respectful communication, seeking mutually acceptable solutions, and preserving relationships.

Content Analysis: A research method used to systematically and objectively interpret the content of textual data. It aims to identify themes, patterns, or meanings in the data. Used in social sciences, psychology, communication, and media studies to analyze documents, speeches, interviews, and media messages. It may include qualitative (thematic) or quantitative (word counting/frequencies) approaches.

Cultural Adaptation: Refers to an individual's ability to adjust to the specific cultural norms, values, and practices of a given environment. This involves understanding and respecting cultural differences, as well as adjusting behavior to promote mutual understanding and cooperation.

Cultural Dynamics: The study of changes and evolutionary processes within and between cultures, including cultural interactions, adaptations, and transformations. Used in anthropology, sociology, and cultural studies to analyze reciprocal influences between different cultures. Influencing factors include globalization, migration, intercultural exchanges, technology, and media.

Cultural Identity Management Theory: Examines how individuals manage their cultural identity during intercultural interactions, adjusting their behavior based on the cultural context. This theory explores processes of negotiation and adaptation of identity in multicultural environments.

Cultural Interaction: The study of exchanges and relationships between individuals or groups from different cultures, focusing on communication and adaptation processes. Used in intercultural studies, intercultural psychology, and human resource management, this discipline aims to enhance understanding and cooperation between cultures. Key components of cultural interaction include acculturation (the process by which individuals adopt the cultural traits of another group), culture shock (psychological and emotional reactions to cultural differences), identity negotiation (adjustments and revisions of one's identity in interaction with other cultures), and cultural mediation (practices and strategies to facilitate communication and understanding between different cultures).

Cultural Sensitivity: It refers to an individual's ability to recognize, understand, and respect cultural differences during interactions with people from other cultures. This involves being aware of the norms, values, and cultural behaviors specific to each culture, and adapting one's behavior accordingly to facilitate effective communication and harmonious relationships.

Effective Communication: Involves clear and precise transmission of information between parties involved. This includes the ability to understand, express, and interpret messages appropriately in a given context, taking into account linguistic, cultural, and contextual differences.

Engagement: It refers to the active and voluntary involvement of a person or company in a relationship or interaction. This involves being emotionally and mentally invested in the relationship, proactively contributing to its development and maintenance, and assuming responsibilities and obligations towards the other party.

Informal Interactions: They refer to spontaneous and unstructured exchanges and encounters between individuals or groups, outside of formal or professional contexts. This may include casual conversations, joking exchanges, social gatherings, or other forms of interaction that contribute to building social bonds and strengthening interpersonal relationships.

Intercultural Adjustment: Refers to an individual's or group's ability to adapt to cultural differences when interacting with people from other cultures. This involves understanding, respecting, and integrating the norms, values, and behaviors specific to each culture to facilitate effective communication and harmonious relationships.

Intercultural Adjustment Theory: Focuses on individuals' ability to effectively adapt to cultural differences during intercultural interactions. This theory explores adaptation strategies used to navigate diverse cultural environments, emphasizing the integration of aspects of both the home and host cultures.

Intercultural Business Transactions: Refers to commercial exchanges that occur between individuals or commercial entities belonging to different cultures. These transactions often involve challenges related to linguistic, cultural, social, and economic differences, and require proper understanding and adaptation to succeed in a globalized and diverse business environment.

Intercultural Communication Theories: Conceptual frameworks used to understand and explain interactions between people from different cultures. These theories examine communication processes, potential obstacles to intercultural understanding, and strategies for overcoming these obstacles. They offer valuable insights into intercultural dynamics in various contexts.

Intercultural Competence: Refers to an individual's ability to interact effectively with people from cultures different from their own. This involves understanding cultural differences, tolerance, adaptability, intercultural communication, and conflict resolution. Intercultural competencies are crucial in an increasingly globalized and diverse world.

Language Skills: Refers to an individual's ability to understand, produce, and manipulate language effectively. This includes mastery of grammar, vocabulary, pronunciation, and oral and written comprehension. Language skills are essential for effective communication in multicultural and multilingual contexts.

Linguistic Dynamics: The study of change and evolution processes within languages and between languages in a social context. It is used in historical linguistics, sociolinguistics, and linguistic variation studies to understand how and why languages change over time. Influencing factors include linguistic contact, migration, technology, media, and language policies.

Linguistic Interaction: The study of verbal and non-verbal exchanges between individuals or groups, analyzing language use in communications. This discipline examines how people use languages in various communication situations, considering social and cultural contexts. Used in sociolinguistics, pragmatics, and communication studies to understand conversation dynamics and communication strategies. Key elements of linguistic interaction include turn-taking, style adjustment, politeness, and managing misunderstandings. In essence, linguistic interaction encompasses a wide range of practices and phenomena showing how individuals use language to interact and communicate effectively. It provides tools to analyze and understand the subtleties of human communication in various contexts.

Management of Cultural Identities: Involves recognizing, valuing, and respecting the different cultural identities present during intercultural interactions. This involves understanding and accepting cultural differences while preserving.

Mutual Recognition: It refers to the acceptance and mutual respect of the identities, values, and perspectives of other parties involved in an interaction. This involves acknowledging the legitimacy and validity of cultural differences and different viewpoints, and promoting open and constructive dialogue to achieve mutual understanding.

Qualitative Method: Offers an in-depth approach to understanding complex social phenomena. Unlike quantitative research focused on measurement and quantification, qualitative research explores individuals' experiences, perceptions, and motivations. It allows for exploring social, cultural, and historical contexts in which studied phenomena occur, providing a rich and detailed understanding of subjects. This inductive approach is flexible and allows researchers to capture the complexity of collected data, focusing on the meaning and context of participants' experiences rather than statistical generalization. Qualitative research uses a variety of methods, such as semi-structured interviews and participant observations, to collect data in natural settings, thus promoting a thorough understanding of studied phenomena.

Qualitative Research Data Analysis: The process by which data collected in qualitative research are examined, interpreted, and organized to identify themes, patterns, or meanings. This analysis often involves deep immersion in the data, using techniques such as coding, categorization, and interpretation to uncover research insights and implications.

Social Exchange Theory: Examines exchange and cooperation processes between individuals from different cultures. This theory explores dynamics of trust, perceived risk, and cooperation in intercultural interactions, highlighting factors influencing these processes.

Specialized Communication Situations: Involve verbal or non-verbal exchanges in specific contexts, such as professional or educational settings. These interactions require adapted language and appropriate linguistic skills to meet the requirements of the situation. Indeed, the tasks proposed to learners in such situations must be realistic and consistent with what they encounter in everyday life, necessitating authentic cultural understanding. Thus, specialized communication relies on real content and culturally relevant knowledge to foster effective interaction in a given context.

Technolect, Specialized Language, or Language of Specialization: In the context of our study, it is crucial to clarify the nuances between technolect, specialized language, and language of specialization. Specialized French, for example, differs from common French in that it is used in specific communication contexts related to a particular domain, such as scientific or technical. Specialized languages are characterized by specialized lexicons and terminology specific to a field of activity. They use ordinary linguistic resources to formulate specialized knowledge in a given professional context. The language of specialization is a linguistic subsystem that brings together the specificities of a particular domain, without necessarily opposing common language. Finally, the term technolect encompasses linguistic usages specific to a field of activity, but it also includes non-standard, dialectal, or slang expressions. This distinction allows for qualifying technical languages used in commerce while considering their diversity and adaptability.

Transaction Success: It refers to the achievement of commercial or economic objectives set during a transaction. This may include reaching a mutually beneficial agreement, satisfying the involved parties, generating profits or added value, and maintaining long-term business relationships.

Trust: It refers to the feeling of security, reliability, and credibility that one person or company inspires in another within the context of a relationship or interaction. This involves believing in the integrity, competence, and honesty of the other party, and engaging in interactions or transactions with confidence.

Compilation of References

Aboderin, I. (2007). Contexts, motives and experiences of Nigerian overseas nurses: Understanding links to globalization. *Journal of Clinical Nursing*, 16(12), 2237–2245. 10.1111/j.1365-2702.2007.01999.x18036114

Abrams, J. A., Tabaac, A., Jung, S., & Else-Quest, N. M. (2020). Considerations for employing intersectionality in qualitative health research. *Social Science & Medicine*, 258, 1–25. 10.1016/j.socscimed.2020.11313832574889

Abu-Ghazaleh Mahajneh, M., Greenspan, I., & Haj-Yahia, M. M. (2021). Zakat giving to non-muslims: Muftis' attitudes in Arab and non-Arab countries 0F. *Journal of Muslim Philanthropy and Civil Society*, 5(2), 66–86. 10.2979/muslphilcivisoc.5.2.04

Acharya, A. S., Prakash, A., Saxena, P., & Nigam, A. (2013). Sampling: Why and how of it. *Indian Journal of Medical Specialties*, 4(2), 330–333. 10.7713/ijms.2013.0032

Adamson, J., & Donovan, J. L. (2002). Research in black and white. *Qualitative Health Research*, 12(6), 816–825. 10.1177/104323020120060081212109726

Adams, T. E., Jones, S. H., & Ellis, C. (2015). *Autoethnography: Understanding qualitative research*. Oxford University Press.

Adhikari, R., & Melia, K. M. (2015). The (mis)management of migrant nurses in the UK: A sociological study. *Journal of Nursing Management*, 23(3), 359–367. 10.1111/jonm.1214124033826

Ahmed, A. O. A. (2024). A classroom ethnographic study on silence among EFL graduate students: A Case Study. *British Journal of Translation. Linguistics and Literature*, 4(1), 2–17. 10.54848/bjtll.v4i1.75

Ajemba, N. & Arene, N. (2022). Possible advantages that may be enhanced with the adoption of research triangulation or mixed methodology. *Magna Scientia Advanced Research and Reviews*, 6(1), 58-61. 10.30574/msarr.2022.6.1.0066

Allan, S., McLeod, H. J., Bradstreet, S., Beedie, S. A., Moir, B., Gleeson, J., Farhall, J., Morton, E., & Gumley, A. (2019). Understanding implementation of a digital self-monitoring intervention for relapse prevention in psychosis: Protocol for a mixed method process evaluation. *JMIR Research Protocols*, 8(12), e15634. 10.2196/1563431821154

Allsop, D. B., Chelladurai, J. M., Kimball, E. R., Marks, L. D., & Hendricks, J. J. (2022). Qualitative methods with Nvivo software: A practical guide for analyzing qualitative data. *Psych*, 4(2), 142–159. 10.3390/psych4020013

Aluwihare-Samaranayake, D. (2012). Ethics in qualitative research: A view of the participants' and researchers' world from a critical standpoint. *International Journal of Qualitative Methods*, 11(2), 64–81. 10.1177/160940691201100208

Alvesson, M., & Sköldberg, K. (2009). Reflexive methodology: New vistas for qualitative research. *Sage (Atlanta, Ga.)*.

Ambjørn, J., Görlich, A., Jurkiewicz, J., & Loll, R. (2012). Nonperturbative quantum gravity. *Physics Reports*, 519(4-5), 127–210. 10.1016/j.physrep.2012.03.007

Ambjørn, J., Jurkiewicz, J., & Loll, R. (2005). Semiclassical universe from first principles. *Physics Letters. [Part B]*, 607(3-4), 205–213. 10.1016/j.physletb.2004.12.067

Andersen, P. H., & Anne, M. (2004). *23.* Ensuring Validity in Qualitative International Business Research. In Marschan-Piekkari, R., & Welch, C. (Eds.), *Handbook of Qualitative Research Methods for International Business* (pp. 464–485). Edward Elgar Publishing. 10.4337/9781781954331.00045

Angrosino, M. (2007). *Doing ethnographic and observational Research*. SAGE Publications Ltd. 10.4135/9781849208932

Archibald, M. (2015). Investigator triangulation. *Journal of Mixed Methods Research*, 10(3), 228–250. 10.1177/1558689815570092

Ashour, S. (2018). Methodological pluralism in technology-based services: A pluralist perspective of triangulation. *Journal of Services Marketing*, 32(1), 86–96.

Atkinson, P. A., Coffey, A., & Delamont, S. (2003). *Key themes in qualitative research: Continuities and change*. AltaMira Press.

Augustyniak, A. (2016). *'Basque for all?' Ideology and Identity in Migrants' Perceptions of Basque*. [Doctoral Dissertation]. University of Southampton, Southampton.

Austin-Keiller, A., Park, M., Yang, S., Mayo, N., Fellows, L., & Brouillette, M. (2023). "alone, there is nobody": A qualitative study of the lived experience of loneliness in older men living with HIV. *PLoS One*, 18(4), e0277399. 10.1371/journal.pone.027739937058482

Babbie, E. R. (2020). *The Practice of Social Research*. Cengage AU.

Bandura, A. (1986). *Social foundations of thought and action: A social cognitive theory*. Prentice-Hall, Inc.

Banks, S., Armstrong, A., Carter, K., Graham, H., Hayward, P., Henry, A., & Strachan, A. (2016). Everyday ethics in community-based participatory research. In *Knowledge Mobilisation and Social Sciences* (pp. 97–111). Routledge.

Bardwell, W. A., & Dimsdale, J. E. (2001). The impact of ethnicity and response bias on the self-report of negative affect. *Journal of Applied Biobehavioral Research*, 6(1), 27–38. 10.1111/j.1751-9861.2001.tb00105.x

Barrett, D., & Twycross, A. (2018). Data collection in qualitative research. *Evidence-Based Nursing*, 21(3), 63–64. 10.1136/eb-2018-10293929858278

Bartel-Radic, A. (2009). La compétence interculturelle: état de l'art et perspectives. *Management International*, *13*(4), 11–26. 10.7202/038582ar

Battista, A. (2022). Donna Williams' Nobody nowhere and Somebody somewhere: A corpus-based discourse analysis of the author's language as a tool to negotiate one's relationship with the world and the self. *International Journal of Language Studies*, 16(4), 95–116.

Bauwens, A. (2010). The use of method triangulation in probation research. *European Journal of Probation*, 2(2), 39–52. 10.1177/206622031000200204

Beiser, M., & Hou, F. (2001). Language acquisition, unemployment and depressive disorder among Southeast Asian refugees: A 10-year study. *Social Science & Medicine*, 53(10), 1321–1334. 10.1016/S0277-9536(00)00412-311676403

Bekhet, A., & Zauszniewski, J. (2012). Methodological triangulation: An approach to understanding data. *Nurse Researcher*, 20(2), 40–43. 10.7748/nr2012.11.20.2.40.c944223316537

Belabes, A. (2022). Limitations Of The SDGs in the light of a Zakat approach in terms of resilience. *AZKA International Journal of Zakat & Social Finance*, 3(1), 53–84. 10.51377/azjaf.vol3no1.94

Bennett, M. J. (1993). Towards Ethnorelativism: A Developmental Model of Intercultural Sensitivity. In Paige, R. M. (Ed.), *Education for the Intercultural Experience* (pp. 21–71). Intercultural Press.

Benoot, C., Hannes, K., & Bilsen, J. (2016). The use of purposeful sampling in a qualitative evidence synthesis: A worked example on sexual adjustment to a cancer trajectory. *BMC Medical Research Methodology*, 16(1), 1–12. 10.1186/s12874-016-0114-626891718

Berdes, C., & Eckert, J. M. (2001). Race relations and caregiving relationships: A Qualitative Examination of Perspectives from Residents and Nurse's Aides in Three Nursing Homes. *Research on Aging*, 23(1), 109–126. 10.1177/0164027501231006

Berger, J., & Heath, C. (2008). Who drives divergence? Identity signalling, out-group similarity, and the abandonment of cultural tastes. *Journal of Personality and Social Psychology*, 95(3), 593–607. 10.1037/0022-3514.95.3.59318729697

Berger, R. (2015). Now I see it, now I don't: Researcher's position and reflexivity in qualitative research. *Qualitative Research*, 15(2), 219–234. 10.1177/1468794112468475

Bergkamp, J. A. (2010). The paradox of emotionality & competence in multicultural competency training: A grounded theory. Academic Press.

Bernard, H. R. (2000). *Research Methods in Anthropology: Qualitative and Quantitative Approaches*. AltaMira.

Bernard, H. R. (2002). *Research Methods in Anthropology: Qualitative and Quantitative Methods* (3rd ed.). AltaMira Press.

Bernard, H. R. (2017). *Research methods in anthropology: Qualitative and quantitative approaches*. Rowman & Littlefield.

Bernhold, Q., & Giles, H. (2019). Communication Accommodation Theory as a lens to examine painful self-disclosures in grandparent-grandchild relationships. In Avtgis, T., Rancer, A., MacGeorge, E., & Liberman, C. (Eds.), *Casing communication theory* (pp. 31–48). Kendall Hunt.

Bernier, F. (1684). New division of earth by the different species or races of men. *Journal des Savants*, 24, 1863–1864.

Berry, J. W., Breugelmans, S. M., & Poortinga, Y. H. (2011). *Cross-Cultural Psychology*. Cambridge University Press. 10.1017/CBO9780511974274

Bhangu, S., Provost, F., & Caduff, C. (2023). Introduction to qualitative research methods - Part i. *Perspectives in Clinical Research*, 14(1), 39–42. 10.4103/picr.picr_253_2236909216

Bicay, E. G., Cambalon, A. J., Gulada, Q. M., & Monteza, A. (2024). Tagakaulo in trade: A phenomenological exploration on the journey of language preservation. *International Journal of Innovative Research in Multidisciplinary Education.*, 3(4), 607–620. 10.58806/ijirme.2024.v3i4n16

Bilous, F. R., & Krauss, R. M. (1988). Dominance and accommodation in the conversational behaviours of same- and mixed-gender dyads. *Language & Communication*, 8(3), 183–194. 10.1016/0271-5309(88)90016-X

Birt, L., Scott, S., Cavers, D., Campbell, C., & Walter, F. (2016). Member checking: A tool to enhance trustworthiness or merely a nod to validation? *Qualitative Health Research*, 26(13), 1802–1811. 10.1177/104973231665487027340178

Blackwell, J., Allen-Collinson, J., Evans, A., & Henderson, H. (2024). How Person-Centred Is Cardiac Rehabilitation in England? Using Bourdieu to Explore Socio-Cultural Influences and Personalisation. *Qualitative Health Research*, 34(3), 239–251. 10.1177/104973232312102603793668

Blommaert, J., & Dong, J. (2010). Language and movement in space. In Coupland, N. (Ed.), *The handbook of language and globalization* (pp. 366–385). Wiley-Black. 10.1002/9781444324068.ch16

Blommaert, J., & Jie, D. (2020). *Ethnographic fieldwork*. Multilingual Matters. 10.21832/BLOMMA7130h

Boas, F. (1962). *Anthropology and Modern Life*. The Norton Library.

Bobo, L., Kluegel, J. R., & Smith, R. A. (1996). *Laissez-faire racism: The crystallization of a kinder, gentler, antiblack ideology*. Russel Sage Foundation.

Boddy, C. R. (2016). Sample size for qualitative research. *Qualitative Market Research*, 19(4), 426–432. 10.1108/QMR-06-2016-0053

Bonilla-Silva, E. (2021). *Racism without racists: Color-blind racism and the persistence of racial inequality in the United States*. Rowman & Littlefield.

Bonnett, A., & Carrington, B. (2000). Fitting into categories or falling between them? Rethinking ethnic classification. *British Journal of Sociology of Education*, 21(4), 487–500. 10.1080/713655371

Bourdieu, P. (1993). *The field of cultural production: Essays on art and literature*. Columbia University Press.

Bourhis, R. Y. (1979). Language in ethnic interaction: A social psychological approach. In Giles, H., & St. Jacques, B. (Eds.), *Language and ethnic relations* (pp. 117–141). Pergamon.

Bourhis, R. Y., Sachdev, I., Ehala, M., & Giles, H. (2019). Forty years of group vitality research. *Journal of Language and Social Psychology*, 38, 408–421. 10.1177/0261927X19868974

Bourke, B. (2016). Meaning and implications of being labelled a predominantly White institution. *College and University*, 91(3), 12–21.

Bourray, M. (2018). L'interculturel dans l'enseignement/apprentissage du FLE au Maroc. *FRANCISOLA*, 3(2), 122–140. 10.17509/francisola.v3i2.15746

Boveda, M., & Bhattacharya, K. (2019). Love as de/colonial onto-epistemology: A post-oppositional approach to contextualized research ethics. *The Urban Review*, 51(1), 5–25. 10.1007/s11256-018-00493-z

Bowen, G. A. (2008). Naturalistic inquiry and the saturation concept: A research note. *Qualitative Research*, 8(1), 137–152. 10.1177/1468794107085301

Braun, V., & Clarke, V. (2006). Using thematic analysis in psychology. *Qualitative Research in Psychology*, 3(2), 77–101. 10.1191/1478088706qp063oa

Braveman, P. A., Arkin, E., Proctor, D., Kauh, T., & Holm, N. (2022). systemic and structural racism: definitions, examples, health damages, and approaches to dismantling: Study examines definitions, examples, health damages, and dismantling systemic and structural racism. *Health Affairs*, 41(2), 171–178. 10.1377/hlthaff.2021.0139435130057

Briller, S., Meert, K., Schim, S., Thurston, C., & Kabel, A. (2008). Implementing a triangulation protocol in bereavement research: A methodological discussion. *Omega*, 57(3), 245–260. 10.2190/OM.57.3.b18837173

Brinkmann, S., & Kvale, S. (2005). Interviews: Learning the craft of qualitative research interviewing. *Sage (Atlanta, Ga.)*.

Brislin, R. W. (1986). The Wording and Translation of Research Instruments. In Lonner, W. J., & Berry, J. W. (Eds.), *Field Methods in Cross-Cultural Research* (pp. 137–164). SAGE Publications Ltd.

Bryman, A. (2006). Integrating quantitative and qualitative research: How is it done? *Qualitative Research*, 6(1), 97–113. 10.1177/1468794106058877

Bryman, A. (2016). *Social research methods*. Oxford University Press.

Bryman, A., Stephens, M., & Campo, C. (1996). The importance of context: Qualitative research and the study of leadership. *The Leadership Quarterly*, 7(3), 353–370. 10.1016/S1048-9843(96)90025-9

Budge, S. L., Adelson, J. L., & Howard, K. A. S. (2012). Anxiety and depression in transgender individuals: The roles of transition status, loss, social support, and coping. *Journal of Consulting and Clinical Psychology*, 80(5), 860–873. 10.1037/a002802723398495

Bularafa, B., & Haruna, M. (2022). Multi-methods approach in entrepreneurship research: Triangulation in action. *Journal of Economics Finance and Management Studies*, 05(12), 3649–3655. 10.47191/jefms/v5-i12-23

Bulatov, D. (2009). The effect of fundamental frequency on phonetic convergence. *UC Berkeley Phonology Lab Annual Report*, 404-434. 10.5070/P72W68F1C6

Burns, N., & Grove, S. K. (2001). Introduction to qualitative research. *The Practice of Nursing Research. Conduct, Critique and Utilization*, 67-68.

Byram, M. (1997). *Teaching and Assessing Intercultural Communicative Competence*. Multilingual Matters.

Caglitutuncigil, T. (2015). Intersectionality in language trajectories: African women in Spain. *Applied Linguistics Review*, 6(2), 217–239. 10.1515/applirev-2015-0011

Callejo, J. (2001). El grupo de discusión: Introducción a una práctica de investigación. *Ariel*.

Campbell, D., & Fiske, D. (1959). Convergent and discriminant validation by the multitrait-multimethod matrix. *Psychological Bulletin*, 56(2), 81–105. 10.1037/h004601613634291

Campbell, J. L., Quincy, C., Osserman, J., & Pedersen, O. K. (2013). Assessing Triangulation Across Methodologies, Methods, and Stakeholder Groups: The Joys, Woes, and Politics of Interpreting Convergent and Divergent Data. *The American Journal of Evaluation*, 34(1), 8–34.

Candel, O. S. (2021). Acculturation stress among international students: A literature review. In *Teachers and students in multicultural environment. Romania*. Editura Universiă ii Alexandru Ioan Cuza din Ia i.

Canuto, A., Braga, B., Monteiro, L., Digitais, F., & IRaMuTeQ, A. E. (2020). *Aspects of CAQDAS usage in qualitative research : An empiric comparison of ALCEST And IRAMUTEQ as digital ToolsEasyChair preprint critic A.*

Carlsen, B., & Glenton, C. (2011). What about N? A methodological study of sample-size reporting in focus group studies. *BMC Medical Research Methodology*, 11(1), 1–10. 10.1186/1471-2288-11-2621396104

Carspecken, F. P. (2013). *Critical ethnography in educational research: A theoretical and practical guide*. Routledge. 10.4324/9781315021263

Cashman, H. R. (2005). Identities at play: Language preference and group membership in bilingual talk in interaction. *Journal of Pragmatics*, 37(3), 301–315. 10.1016/j.pragma.2004.10.004

Cassidy, C., & Durbin, C. (2022). Creating a Culture of Inquiry: A Case Study of Action Research in a Primary School. *Research in Education*, 94(1), 19–35. 10.1177/0034523715591017

Cassidy, C., Sim, M., Somerville, M., Crowther, D., Sinclair, D., Elliott Rose, A., Burgess, S., Best, S., & Curran, J. A. (2022). Using a learning health system framework to examine COVID-19 pandemic planning and response at a Canadian Health Centre. *PLoS One*, 17(9), e0273149. 10.1371/journal.pone.027314936103510

Cater, N., Bryant-Lukosius, D., DiCenso, A., Blythe, J., & Neville, A. (2015). The use of triangulation in qualitative research. *Oncology Nursing Forum*, 41(5), 545–547. 10.1188/14.ONF.545-54725158659

Chang, H. (2008). *Autoethnography as method*. Left Coast Press.

Charmaz, K. (2005). Grounded theory in the 21st century: A qualitative method for advancing social justice research. In N. Denzin & Y. Lincoln (Eds.), *Handbook of qualitative research* (3rd ed., pp. 507–535). Sage.

Charmaz, K. (2006). *Constructing Grounded Theory*. Sage.

Charmaz, K. (2014). Constructing grounded theory. *Sage (Atlanta, Ga.)*.

Charmaz, K. (2014). Grounded Theory in Global Perspective: Reviews by International Researchers. *Qualitative Inquiry*, 20(9), 1074–1084. 10.1177/1077800414545235

Charmaz, K., & Thornberg, R. (2020). The pursuit of quality in grounded theory. *Qualitative Research in Psychology*, 18(3), 305–327. 10.1080/14780887.2020.1780357

Chaves, M. M. N., dos Santos, A. P. R., dos Santosa, N. P., & Larocca, L. M. (2017). Use of the software IRAMUTEQ in qualitative research: An experience report. *Studies in Systems, Decision, and Control*, 71, 39–48. 10.1007/978-3-319-43271-7_4

Chen, G., & Starosta, W. (2000). The Development and Validation of the Intercultural Sensitivity Scale. *Human Communication*, 3, 1–15. 10.1037/t61546-000

Chiseri-Strater, E. (1996). Turning In upon Ourselves: Positionality, Subjectivity, and Reflexivity in Case Study and Ethnographic Research. In P. Mortensen & G. Kirsch (Eds.), *Ethics and Representation in Qualitative Studies of Literacy* (pp. 115-133). New York: Stony Brook.

Christensen, K. (2017). Life trajectories of migrant care workers in the long—Term care sectors in Norway and the UK. *Social Policy and Society*, 16(4), 635–644. 10.1017/S1474746417000252

Chu, A., & Hsu, C. (2021). Principal–agent relationship within a cruise supply chain model for china. *Journal of Hospitality & Tourism Research (Washington, D.C.)*, 45(6), 998–1021. 10.1177/1096348020985328

Clarke, A. E. (2005). *Situational analysis: grounded theory after the postmodern turn*. Sage Publications. 10.4135/9781412985833

Clarke, A. E., & Charmaz, K. (2019). *Grounded theory and situational analysis*. Sage Publications.

Clifford, N., Cope, M., Gillespie, T., French, S., & Valentine, G. (2010). Getting Started in Geographical Research: how this book can help. *Key methods in geography*, 1(1).

Codó, E. (2018). Lifestyle residents in Barcelona: A biographical perspective on linguistic repertoires, identity narrative and transnational mobility. *International Journal of the Sociology of Language*, 250(250), 11–34. 10.1515/ijsl-2017-0053

Cohen, L., Manion, L., & Morrison, K. (2002). *Research Methods in Education*. Routledge. 10.4324/9780203224342

Collins, A. (1999). The changing infrastructure of education research. In Lagemann, E., & Shulman, L. (Eds.), *Issues in Education Research* (pp. 289–298). Jossey-Bass.

Cooperman, J., Lee, K., & Miller, J. (2017). A second look at transition amplitudes in (2 + 1)-dimensional causal dynamical triangulations. *Classical and Quantum Gravity*, 34(11), 115008. 10.1088/1361-6382/aa6d38

Corbin, J., & Strauss, A. (2014). *Basics of qualitative research: Techniques and procedures for developing grounded theory*. Sage publications.

Corona, V. (2017). An ethnographic approach to the study of linguistic varieties used by young Latin Americans in Barcelona. In E. Moore & M. Dooly (Eds.), *Qualitative approaches to research on plurilingual education* (pp. 170-188). Research-publishing.net. 10.14705/rpnet.2017.emmd2016.627

Coste, D., & Galisson, R. (1976). *Dictionary of Language Teaching*. Hachette.

Coupland, N., & Giles, H. (1988). Communication accommodation: Recent advances. *Language & Communication*, 8, 3–4. https://digilib.ars.ac.id/index.php?p=fstream-pdf&fid=13684&bid=6370

Covarrubias, A., Nava, P. E., Lara, A., Burciaga, R., Vélez, V. N., & Solorzano, D. G. (2018). Critical race quantitative intersections: A testimonio analysis. *Race, Ethnicity and Education*, 21(2), 253–273. 10.1080/13613324.2017.1377412

Coyne, E., Rands, H., Gurung, S., & Kellett, U. (2016). I-Kiribati nursing graduates experience of transition from university to residential aged care facilities in Australia. *Nurse Education Today*, 36, 463–467. 10.1016/j.nedt.2015.10.02026549264

Coyne, I. T. (1997). Sampling in qualitative research. Purposeful and theoretical sampling; merging or clear boundaries? *Journal of Advanced Nursing*, 26(3), 623–630. 10.1046/j.1365-2648.1997.t01-25-00999.x9378886

Crenshaw, K. (1991). Mapping the margins: Intersectionality, identity politics, and violence against women of color. *Stanford Law Review*, 43(6), 1241–1299. 10.2307/1229039

Creswell, J. W., & Poth, C. N. (2018). *Qualitative inquiry and research design: Choosing among five approaches* (4ᵗʰ ed.). Sage.

Creswell, J. W. (2002). *Educational Research: Planning, Conducting, and Evaluating Quantitative and Qualitative Research*. Pearson Education.

Creswell, J. W. (2007). *Qualitative Inquiry and Research Design: Choosing Among Five Approaches* (2nd ed.). Sage.

Creswell, J. W. (2013). *Qualitative Inquiry and Research Design: Choosing among Five Approaches*. Sage Publications.

Creswell, J. W. (2014). *Research design: Qualitative, quantitative, and mixed methods approaches*. Sage publications.

Creswell, J. W., & Clark, V. L. P. (2017). *Designing and Conducting Mixed Methods Research*. Sage publications.

Creswell, J. W., & Creswell, J. D. (2018). *Research Design: Qualitative, Quantitative, and Mixed Methods Approaches*. Sage.

Creswell, J. W., Hanson, W. E., Clark Plano, V. L., & Morales, A. (2007). Qualitative research designs: Selection and implementation. *The Counseling Psychologist*, 35(2), 236–264. 10.1177/0011000006287390

Creswell, J. W., & Miller, D. L. (2000). Determining validity in qualitative inquiry. *Theory into Practice*, 39(3), 124–130. 10.1207/s15430421tip3903_2

Creswell, J. W., & Plano Clark, V. L. (2018). *Designing and conducting mixed methods research* (3rd ed.). SAGE Publications.

Creswell, J. W., & Poth, C. N. (2018). *Qualitative Inquiry and Research Design Choosing among Five Approaches* (4th ed.). SAGE Publications, Inc.

Crotty, M. J. (1998). *The foundations of social research: Meaning and perspective in the research process*. Sage Publications.

Crowe, S., Cresswell, K., Robertson, A., Huby, G., Avery, A., & Sheikh, A. (2011). The case study approach. *BMC Medical Research Methodology*, 11(1), 100. Advance online publication. 10.1186/1471-2288-11-10021707982

Crowther, D., & Lauesen, L. M. (2017). Qualitative methods. *Handbook of Research Methods in Corporate Social Responsibility*, 225–229. 10.1177/0010414006296344

Cuesta, M., Rämgård, M., & Ramgard, M. (2016). Intersectional perspective in elderly care. *International Journal of Qualitative Studies on Health and Well-being*, 11(1), 30544. 10.3402/qhw.v11.3054427167554

Curtin, M., & Fossey, E. (2007). Appraising the trustworthiness of qualitative studies: Guidelines for occupational therapists. *Australian Occupational Therapy Journal*, 54(2), 88–94. 10.1111/j.1440-1630.2007.00661.x

Daly, P. (2005). Mothers living with suicidal adolescents: Aphenomenological study of their experiences. *Journal of Psychosocial Nursing and Mental Health Services*, 43(3), 22–28.15794529

Darawsheh, W. (2014). Reflexivity in research: Promoting rigour, reliability and validity in qualitative research. *International Journal of Therapy and Rehabilitation*, 21(12), 560–568. 10.12968/ijtr.2014.21.12.560

Davies, Ch. A. (1999). *Reflexive Ethnography: a guide to researching selves and others*. Routledge.

Davies, D., & Dodd, J. (2002). Qualitative research and the question of rigor. *Qualitative Health Research*, 12(2), 279–289. 10.1177/104973230201200021111837376

Davies, L., Batalden, P., Davidoff, F., Stevens, D., & Ogrinc, G. (2015). The squire guidelines: an evaluation from the field, 5 years post release: table 1. *BMJ Quality & Safety*, 24(12), 769–775. 10.1136/bmjqs-2015-00411626089206

De Fina, A. (2009). Narratives in interviews: The case of accounts. *Narrative Inquiry*, 19(2), 233–258. 10.1075/ni.19.2.03def

De Fina, A. (2019). The interview as an interactional event. In Patrick, P. L., Schmid, M. S., & Zwaan, K. (Eds.), *Language analysis for the determination of origin: Current perspectives and new directions* (pp. 21–40). Springer. 10.1007/978-3-319-79003-9_2

De Fina, A., & Perrino, S. (2011). Introduction: Interviews vs. 'natural' contexts: A false dilemma. *Language in Society*, 40(1), 1–11. 10.1017/S0047404510000849

de Souza, M. A. R., Wall, M. L., & Thuler, A. C. (2018). O uso do software IRAMUTEQ na análise de dados em pesquisas qualitativas. *Revista Da Escola de Enfermagem Da USP, 52*(0), 1–17. https://doi.org/10.1590/s1980-220x2017015003353

De Souza, M. A. R., Wall, M. L., Thuler, A. C. D. M. C., Lowen, I. M. V., & Peres, A. M. (2018). The use of IRAMUTEQ software for data analysis in qualitative research*. *Revista Da Escola de Enfermagem, 52*, 1–7. https://doi.org/10.1590/S1980-220X2017015003353

De Vos, A. S. (2001). *Research at Grass Roots: A Primer for The Caring Professions*. Van Schaik.

Deardorff, D. K. (2006). Identification and Assessment of Intercultural Competence as a Student Outcome of Internationalization. *Journal of Studies in International Education*, 10(3), 241–266. 10.1177/1028315306287002

Delgado, R., & Stefancic, J. (2023). *Critical race theory: An introduction*. NYU Press.

Demuth, C. (2013). Ensuring Rigor in Qualitative Research Within the Field of Cross-. *Culture and Psychology*.

Denzin, N. K. (1978). *The Research Act: A Theoretical Introduction to Sociological Methods*. McGraw-Hill.

Denzin, N. K., & Lincoln, Y. S. (2005). Introduction: The Discipline and Practice of Qualitative Research. In Denzin, N. K., & Lincoln, Y. S. (Eds.), *Handbook of Qualitative Research* (3rd ed., pp. 1–32). Sage.

Denzin, N. K., & Lincoln, Y. S. (2005a). *The Sage handbook of qualitative research* (3rd ed.). Sage.

Denzin, N. K., & Lincoln, Y. S. (Eds.). (2018). *The SAGE Handbook of Qualitative Research* (5th ed.). Sage.

Devi Prasad, B. (2019). Qualitative content analysis: Why is it still a path less taken? *Forum Qualitative Social Research*, 20(3). Advance online publication. 10.17169/fqs-20.3.3392

Dewasiri, N., & Abeysekera, N. (2020). Corporate social responsibility and dividend policy in Sri Lankan firms: A data triangulation approach. *Journal of Public Affairs*, 22(1), e2283. Advance online publication. 10.1002/pa.2283

Doane, A. (2017). Beyond color-blindness:(Re) theorizing racial ideology. *Sociological Perspectives*, 60(5), 975–991. 10.1177/0731121417719697

Dodgson, J. E. (2017). About Research: Qualitative Methodologies. *Journal of Human Lactation*, 33(2), 355–358. 10.1177/0890334417769869328418801

Donalek, J. G. (2004). Demystifying nursing research: Phenomenology as a qualitative research method. *Urologic Nursing*, 24, 516–517.15658739

Donkoh, S. (2023). Application of triangulation in qualitative research. *Journal of Applied Biotechnology & Bioengineering*, 10(1), 6–9. 10.15406/jabb.2023.10.00319

Downward, P., & Mearman, A. (2006). Retroduction as mixed-methods triangulation in economic research: Reorienting economics into social science. *Cambridge Journal of Economics*, 31(1), 77–99. 10.1093/cje/bel009

Dragojevic, M., Gasiorek, J., & Giles, H. (2016a). Communication accommodation theory. In Berger, C. R., & Roloff, M. (Eds.), *The international encyclopedia of interpersonal communication* (pp. 176–196). Wiley Blackwell.

Dragojevic, M., Gasiorek, J., & Giles, H. (2016b). Accommodative strategies as core of the theory. In Giles, H. (Ed.), *Communication accommodation theory: Negotiating personal and social identities across contexts* (pp. 36–59). Cambridge University Press. 10.1017/CBO9781316226537.003

Draucker, C. B., Martsolf, D. S., Ross, R., & Rusk, T. B. (2007). Theoretical sampling and category development in grounded theory. *Qualitative Health Research*, 17(8), 1137–1148. 10.1177/104973230730845017928484

Dubois, J., Lecercle, J.-J., & Marcellesi, J.-B. (2001). *General Linguistics Course*. Payot.

Duckitt, J. (2001). A dual-process cognitive-motivational theory of ideology and prejudice. In Advances in Experimental Social Psychology. Academic Press. 10.1016/S0065-2601(01)80004-6

Duranti, A. (1997). *Linguistic anthropology*. Cambridge University Press. 10.1017/CBO9780511810190

Duranti, A. (2011). Linguistic anthropology: The study of language as a non-neutral medium. In Mesthrie, R. (Ed.), *The Cambridge handbook of sociolinguistics* (pp. 28–46). Cambridge University Press. 10.1017/CBO9780511997068.006

Dźwigoł, H. (2018). Quantitative methods in the triangulation process. *Proceedings of the IISES Annual Conference*, 53-68. 10.20472/IAC.2018.035.012

Earick, M. E. (2012). Ideology, race, and education. *International Critical Childhood Policy Studies Journal*, 3(1), 74–105.

Edmondson, A. C., & McManus, S. E. (2007). Methodological fit in management field research. *Academy of Management Review*, 32(4), 1246–1264. 10.5465/amr.2007.26586086

Eide, P., & Allen, C. B. (2005). Recruiting transcultural qualitative research participants: A conceptual model. *International Journal of Qualitative Methods*, 4(2), 44–56. 10.1177/160940690500400204

Eisenhardt, K. M. (1989). Building theories from case study research. *Academy of Management Review*, 14(4), 532–550. 10.2307/258557

Elhami, A. (2023). *A Study of Communicative Practices of Iranian Migrants in Madrid* [Unpublished Doctoral Dissertation]. Universidad Autónoma de Madrid.

Elhami, A. (2020a). A Socio-pragmatic perspective of Spanish and Persian greeting. *Theory and Practice in Language Studies*, 10(9), 1009–1014. 10.17507/tpls.1009.01

Elhami, A. (2020b). Communication Accommodation Theory: A brief review of the literature. *Journal of Advances in Education and Philosophy.*, 4(5), 192–200. 10.36348/jaep.2020.v04i05.002

Elhami, A. (2020c). Acculturation Strategies: The Study of Bi-Dimensional and Uni-Dimensional of Filipino Immigrants in Madrid. *International Journal of Social Science Research*, 8(2), 1–15. 10.5296/ijssr.v8i2.16428

Elhami, A., & Khoshnevisan, B. (2022). Conducting an interview in qualitative research: The Modus Operandi. *Mextesol Journal*, 46(1), 1–7.

Elhami, A., & Khoshnevisan, B. (2022). Conducting an Interview in qualitative research: The Modus Operandi. *Mextesol Journal*, 46(1), 1–7.

Elhami, A., & Roshan, A. (2021). Communication Accommodation Theory in Covid-19 Pandemic. *Academia Letters. Article*, 1641. Advance online publication. 10.20935/AL1641

Elhami, A., & Roshan, A. (2023). A narrative study of Iranian females' acculturation orientation and Spanish learning experiences in Spain. In Chandan, H. (Ed.), *Strategies for cultural assimilation of immigrants and their children: Social, economic, and political considerations* (pp. 45–68). IGI Global. 10.4018/978-1-6684-4839-7.ch003

Elhami, A., & Roshan, A. (2024a). Religion and higher education migrants' acculturation orientation. *Intercultural Education*, 35(3), 283–301. 10.1080/14675986.2024.2348428

Elhami, A., & Roshan, A. (2024b). The history of acculturation: A review article. Social Sciences. *Humanities and Education Journal*, 5(1), 180–196.

Elhami, A., Roshan, A., Ghahraman, V., & Afrashi, A. (2024). Sociocultural adjustment by two international students: A critical look at multilingualism in Spain. *International Journal of Language Studies*, 18(3), 1–38.

Ellestad, A., Beymer, L. L., & Villegas, S. (2023). The lived experiences of individuals with high-functioning autism during the job interview process: A phenomenological study. *Journal of Employment Counseling*, 60(4), 192–209. 10.1002/joec.12212

Ellis, C., Adams, T. E., & Bochner, A. P. (2011). Autoethnography: an overview. *Historical Social Research. Social Science Open Access Repository, 36*(4), 273-290. 10.12759/hsr.36.2011.4.273-290

Elo, S., Kääriäinen, M., Kanste, O., Pölkki, T., Utriainen, K., & Kyngäs, H. (2014). Qualitative Content Analysis. *SAGE Open*, 4(1), 215824401452263. 10.1177/2158244014522633

Emerson, R. M., Fretz, R. I., & Shaw, L. L. (2011). *Writing ethnographic fieldnotes*. University of Chicago press. 10.7208/chicago/9780226206868.001.0001

Emmel, N. (2013). *Sampling and Choosing Cases in Qualitative Research: A Realist Approach*. Sage. 10.4135/9781473913882

Encyclopedia Britannica. (2005). *The Social Sciences* (15th ed., Vol. 27). Author.

Engler, S., & Stausberg, M. (2021). *The Routledge Handbook of Research Methods in the Study of Religion*. Routledge. 10.4324/9781003222491

Erkanlı, İ. (2024). *Multicultural Education: An International Guide to Research, Policies, and Programs* (Vol. 2). Frontiers Media SA. https://doi.org/10.3389/978-2-88970-831-0

Esposito, J., & Evans-Winters, V. (2022). Introduction to intersectional qualitative research. *Sage (Atlanta, Ga.)*.

Et-Bozkurt, T., & Yağmur, K. (2022). Family language policy among second- and third-generation Turkish parents in Melbourne, Australia. *Journal of Multilingual and Multicultural Development*, 43(9), 821–832. 10.1080/01434632.2022.2044832

Evans-Agnew, R. A., & Rosemberg, M. A. S. (2016). Questioning photovoice research: Whose voice? *Qualitative Health Research*, 26(8), 1019–1030. 10.1177/104973231562422326786953

Faiz, M. F., & Abdullah, I. (2023). Establishing a Zakat Culture based on Good Zakat Governance and Good Zakat Empowerment in Indonesia. *Journal of Islamic Economics Perspectives, 5*(2), 1–11.

Fakis, A., Hilliam, R., Stoneley, H., & Townend, M. (2014). Quantitative Analysis of Qualitative Information From Interviews: A Systematic Literature Review. *Journal of Mixed Methods Research*, 8(2), 139–161. 10.1177/1558689813495111

Falk, I., & Kilpatrick, S. (2000). What is Social Capital? A Study of Interaction in a Rural Community (Version 1). *University of Tasmania*. https://hdl.handle.net/102.100.100/596469

Fantini, A. E. (2000). *A Central Concern: Developing Intercultural Competence*. School for International Training Occasional Papers Series.

Feagin, J. R. (2020). *The white racial frame: Centuries of racial framing and counter-framing*. Routledge.

Feagin, J. R. (2014). *Racist America: Roots, current realities, and future reparations*. Routledge. 10.4324/9780203762370

Fielding, N. (2012). Triangulation and mixed methods designs. *Journal of Mixed Methods Research*, 6(2), 124–136. 10.1177/1558689812437101

Fife, S. T., Gossner, J. D., Theobald, A., Allen, E., Rivero, A., & Koehl, H. (2023). Couple healing from infidelity: A grounded theory study. *Journal of Social and Personal Relationships*, 40(12), 3882–3905. 10.1177/02654075231177874

Figura, M., Fraire, M., Durante, A., Cuoco, A., Arcadi, P., Alvaro, R., Vellone, E., & Piervisani, L. (2023). New frontiers for qualitative textual data analysis: A multimethod statistical approach. *European Journal of Cardiovascular Nursing*, 22(5), 547–551. 10.1093/eurjcn/zvad02136748993

Finlay, L. (2002). Negotiating the swamp: The opportunity and challenge of reflexivity in research practice. *Qualitative Research*, 2(2), 209–230. 10.1177/146879410200200205

Firouzkouhi, M., Kako, M., Alimohammadi, N., Arbabi-Sarjou, A., Nouraei, T., & Abdollahimohammad, A. (2022). Lived experiences of covid-19 patients with pulmonary involvement: A hermeneutic phenomenology. *Clinical Nursing Research*, 31(4), 747–757. 10.1177/10547738221107889835168379

Fleming, P. J., Stone, L. C., Creary, M. S., Greene-Moton, E., Israel, B. A., Key, K. D., Reyes, A. G., Wallerstein, N., & Schulz, A. J. (2023). Antiracism and community-based participatory research: Synergies, challenges, and opportunities. *American Journal of Public Health*, 113(1), 70–78. 10.2105/AJPH.2022.30711436516389

Flick, U. (2018). *The SAGE handbook of qualitative data collection*. SAGE Publications. 10.4135/9781526416070

Fona, C. (2023). Qualitative data analysis: Using thematic analysis. *Researching and Analysing Business: Research Methods in Practice*, 130–145. 10.4324/9781003107774-11

Forouzanfar, A., Fatehizade, M., & Farahbakhsh, K. (2024). A Grounded Theory Study of Couple Caregiving: A Qualitative Study. *Journal of Counseling Research*, 22(88). Advance online publication. 10.18502/qjcr.v22i88.15452

Foucault, M. (1969). *The archaeology of knowledge*. Pantheon Books.

Fracheboud, T., Stiefel, F., & Bourquin, C. (2022). The fragility of trust between patients and oncologists: A multiple case study. *Palliative & Supportive Care*, 21(4), 585–593. 10.1017/S147895152200075X35770349

Frank, H., & Landström, H. (2016). What makes entrepreneurship research interesting? Reflections on strategies to overcome the rigour–relevance gap. *Entrepreneurship and Regional Development*, 28(2), 51–75. 10.1080/08985626.2015.1100687

Freire, P. (1970). *Pedagogy of the oppressed*. Bloomsbury.

Freshwater, D. (2022). Methodological pluralism and triangulation in qualitative research: Paradigmatic contests and debates. *Qualitative Health Research*, 32(7), 1042–1056.

Fuller, J. M. (2000). Changing perspectives on data: Interviews as situated speech. *American Speech*, 75(4), 388–390. 10.1215/00031283-75-4-388

Furman, F. K., & Anderson, A. R. (2020). What do firms want from business graduates? A comparative analysis of the views of employers" in different countries. *Journal of International Business Education*, 15, 39–70.

Gallois, C., Ogay, T., & Giles, H. (2005). Communication accommodation theory: A look back and a look ahead. In Gudykunst, W. B. (Ed.), *Theorizing about intercultural communication* (pp. 121–148). Sage.

Gallois, C., Weatherall, A., & Giles, H. (2016). CAT and talk in action. In Giles, H. (Ed.), *Communication accommodation theory: Negotiating personal relationships and social identities across contexts* (pp. 105–122). Cambridge University Press. 10.1017/CBO9781316226537.006

Galvin, R. (2015). How many interviews are enough? Do qualitative interviews in building energy consumption research produce reliable knowledge? *Journal of Building Engineering*, 1, 2–12. 10.1016/j.jobe.2014.12.001

Gamarel, K., farrales, , Venegas, L., Dilworth, S. E., Coffin, L. S., Neilands, T. B., Johnson, M. O., & Koester, K. A. (2022). A mixed-methods study of relationship stigma and well-being among sexual and gender minority couples. *The Journal of Social Issues*, 79(1), 232–263. 10.1111/josi.1255237346391

Gance-Cleveland, B. (2004). Qualitative evaluation of a school-based support group for adolescents with an addicted parent. *Nursing Research*, 53(6), 379–386. 10.1097/00006199-200411000-0000615586134

Gao, W., Plummer, V., & McKenna, L. (2020). Using metaphor method to interpret and understand meanings of international operating room nurses' experiences in organ procurement surgery. *Journal of Clinical Nursing*, 29(23-24), 4604–4613. 10.1111/jocn.1549632956510

García-Canclini, N. (2005). *Culturas híbridas: Estrategias para entrar y salir de la modernidad*. Paidós.

Gasiorek, J., & Giles, H. (2012). Effects of inferred motive on evaluations of nonaccommodative communication. *Human Communication Research*, 38(3), 309–331. 10.1111/j.1468-2958.2012.01426.x

Geertz, C. (1973). *The interpretation of cultures*. Basic Books.

Geertz, C. (2011). *La interpretación de las culturas*. Gedisa.

Gergen, K. J., Josselson, R., & Freeman, M. (2015). The promises of qualitative inquiry. *The American Psychologist*, 70(1), 1–9. 10.1037/a003859725581004

Ghahraman, V., Karlsson, M., Kazemi, A., Saeedi, S., & Elhami, A. (2023). On the functions of hedging in research articles (RAs): A study on RA discussions. *International Journal of Language Studies*, 17(1), 165–187. 10.5281/zenodo.7513381

Giles, H. (1973). Accent mobility: A model and some data. *Anthropological Linguistics*, 15(2), 87–109.

Giles, H. (1980). Accommodation theory: Some new directions. In de Silva, S. (Ed.), *Aspects of linguistic behavior* (pp. 105–136). York University Press.

Giles, H. (Ed.). (2012). *The handbook of intergroup communication*. Routledge. 10.4324/9780203148624

Giles, H., Clementson, D., & Markowitz, D. (in press). CAT-aloguing the past, present and future. In Giles, H., Markowitz, D., & Clementson, D. (Eds.), *New directions for, and panaceas arising from, Communication Accommodation Theory*. Peter Lang.

Giles, H., Coupland, J., & Coupland, N. (1991). Accommodation theory: Communication, context, and consequence. In Giles, H., Coupland, J., & Coupland, N. (Eds.), *Contexts of accommodation: Developments in applied sociolinguistics* (pp. 1–68)., 10.1017/CBO9780511663673.001

Giles, H., Edwards, A. L., & Walther, J. B. (2023). Communication Accommodation Theory: Past accomplishments, current trends, and future prospects. *Language Sciences*, 99, 101571. 10.1016/j.langsci.2023.101571

Giles, H., & Gasiorek, J. (2013). Parameters of non-accommodation: Refining and elaborating communication accommodation theory. In Forgas, J., Vincze, O., & László, J. (Eds.), *Social cognition and communication* (pp. 155–172). Psychology Press.

Giles, H., & Harwood, J. (Eds.). (2018). *The Oxford encyclopedia of intergroup communication* (Vol. 1–2). Oxford University Press.

Giles, H., Scherer, K. R., & Taylor, D. M. (1979). Speech markers in social interaction. In Scherer, K. R., & Giles, H. (Eds.), *Social markers in speech*. Cambridge University Press.

Giles, H., & Smith, P. M. (1979). Accommodation theory: Optimum levels of convergence. In Giles, H., & St. Clair, R. N. (Eds.), *Language and social psychology* (pp. 45–65). Blackwell.

Giles, H., Willemyns, M., Gallois, C., & Anderson, M. C. (2007). Accommodating a new frontier: The context of law enforcement. In Fiedler, K. (Ed.), *Social communication* (pp. 129–162). Psychology Press.

Gillborn, D., Warmington, P., & Demack, S. (2018). QuantCrit: Education, policy, 'Big Data' and principles for a critical race theory of statistics. *Race, Ethnicity and Education*, 21(2), 158–179. 10.1080/13613324.2017.1377417

Gillham, B. (2005). *Research Interviewing: The range of techniques: A practical guide*. McGraw-Hill Education.

Gillham, D., De Bellis, A., Xiao, L., Willis, E., Harrington, A., Morey, W., & Jeffers, L. (2018). Using research evidence to inform staff learning needs in cross-cultural communication in aged care homes. *Nurse Education Today*, 63, 18–23. 10.1016/j.nedt.2018.01.00729407255

Giroux, H. A. (2001). *Theory and resistance in education: Towards a pedagogy for the opposition*. Greenwood Publishing Group.

Glaser, B. G., & Strauss, A. L. (2017). The discovery of grounded theory. In *Routledge eBooks*. 10.4324/9780203793206

Glaser, B. G., & Strauss, A. C. (1967). *The discovery of grounded theory: Strategies for qualitative research*. Aldine.

Glaser, B. G., & Strauss, A. L. (1967). *The Discovery of Grounded Theory: Strategies for Qualitative Research*. Aldine de Gruyter.

Glesne, C. (1999). *Becoming qualitative researchers: An introduction* (2nd ed.). Longman.

Goel, K., & Penman, J. (2015). Employment experiences of immigrant workers in aged care in regional *South Australia*. *Rural and Remote Health*, 15(1), 1–14. 10.22605/RRH269325798891

Goffman, E. (1967). *Interaction ritual: Essays on face-to-face behavior*. Anchor Books.

Gokhale, S. J., & Srivastava, N. (2017). *UNIT 2 Research Design and Sampling*. https://egyankosh.ac.in/bitstream/123456789/4114/1/MWG-005B3E-U2.pdf

Golafshani, N. (2003). Understanding Reliability and Validity in Qualitative Research. *The Qualitative Report*, 8(4), 597–607.

Golafshani, N. (2003). Understanding reliability and validity in qualitative research. *The Qualitative Report*, 8(4), 597–607. 10.46743/2160-3715/2003.1870

Gómez, M. V., & Kuronen, M. (2011). Comparing local strategies and practices: Recollections from two qualitative cross-national research projects. *Qualitative Research*, 11(6), 683–697. 10.1177/1468794111413366

Graneheim, U. H., Lindgren, B. M., & Lundman, B. (2017). Methodological challenges in qualitative content analysis: A discussion paper. *Nurse Education Today*, 56(May), 29–34. 10.1016/j.nedt.2017.06.00228651100

Green, J., & Thorogood, N. (2009). *Qualitative Methods for Health Research* (2nd ed.). Sage Publications.

Grodal, S., Anteby, M., & Holm, A. L. (2021). Achieving rigor in qualitative analysis: The role of active categorization in theory building. *Academy of Management Review*, 46(3), 591–612. 10.5465/amr.2018.0482

Grosfoguel, R. (2016). What is racism? *Journal of World-systems Research*, 22(1), 9–15. 10.5195/jwsr.2016.609

Guba, E. G. (1981). *Effective Evaluation: Improving the Usefulness of Evaluation Results through Responsive and Naturalistic Approaches*. Jossey-Bass.

Guba, E. G., & Lincoln, Y. S. (2005). Paradigmatic Controversies, Contradictions, and Emerging Confluences. In Denzin, N. K., & Lincoln, Y. S. (Eds.), *The Sage Handbook of Qualitative Research* (pp. 191–215). Sage.

Gudykunst, W. B., & Kim, Y. Y. (2003). *Communicating With Strangers: An Approach to Intercultural Communication* (4th ed.). McGraw-Hill.

Gudykunst, W. B., & Kim, Y. Y. (2003). *Communicating with Strangers: An Approach to Intercultural Communication*. McGraw-Hill.

Gudykunst, W. B., & Ting-Toomey, S. (1988). *Culture and interpersonal communication*. SAGE Publications Ltd.

Guerrero-Castañeda, R., Menezes, T., & Prado, M. (2019). Phenomenology in nursing research: Reflection based on heidegger's hermeneutics. *Escola Anna Nery*, 23(4), e20190059. Advance online publication. 10.1590/2177-9465-ean-2019-0059

Guest, G., Bunce, A., & Johnson, L. (2006). How many interviews are enough? An experiment with data saturation and variability. *Field Methods*, 18(1), 59–82. 10.1177/1525822X05279903

Guest, G., Namey, E., & Chen, M. (2020). A simple method to assess and report thematic saturation in qualitative research. *PLoS One*, 15(5), 1–17. 10.1371/journal.pone.023207632369511

Gupta, A., & Sharma, M. (2006). Reflexivity: A concept and its meanings for practitioners involved in psychological research. *Indian Journal of Clinical Psychology*, 33(1), 20–26.

Gürbüz, B. (2018). *Statistics (Population and Sample)* [İstatistik (Evren ve Örneklem)]. Ankara University Open Class Sources.

Guydish, A. J., & Fox Tree, J. E. (2021). Good conversations: Grounding, convergence, and richness. *New Ideas in Psychology*, 63, 100877. 10.1016/j.newideapsych.2021.100877

Hagaman, A. K., & Wutich, A. (2017). How many interviews are enough to identify metathemes in multisited and cross-cultural research? Another perspective on Guest, Bunce, and Johnson's (2006) landmark study. *Field Methods*, 29(1), 23–41. 10.1177/1525822X16640447

Halkoaho, A., Pietilä, A. M., Ebbesen, M., Karki, S., & Kangasniemi, M. (2016). Cultural aspects related to informed consent in health research: A systematic review. *Nursing Ethics*, 23(6), 698–712. 10.1177/0969733015557931225904548

Hall, E. T. (1959). *The Silent Language*. Doubleday.

Hall, E. T. (1976). *Beyond Culture*. Anchor Books.

Haltinner, K. (2016). Individual responsibility, culture, or state organized enslavement? How Tea Party activists frame racial inequality. *Sociological Perspectives*, 59(2), 395–418. 10.1177/0731121415593275

Ham, A. (2019). Social processes affecting the workforce integration of first-generation immigrant health care professionals in aging citizens in The Netherlands. *Journal of Transcultural Nursing*, 31(5), 460–467. 10.1177/1043659619 87519631530232

Hamilton, D., & Bechtel, G. (1996). Research implications for alternative health therapies. *Nursing Forum*, 31(1), 6–10. 10.1111/j.1744-6198.1996.tb00964.x8700752

Hammersley, M., & Atkinson, P. (1994). *Etnografía: Métodos de investigación*. Academic Press.

Hammersley, M., & Atkinson, P. (1995). *Ethnography: principles in practice*. Routledge.

Hancock, B., Windridge, K., & Ockleford, E. (2007). An introduction to qualitative research. *Sage (Atlanta, Ga.)*.

Haq, M., Qazi, W., & Khan, S. (2022). Synthesizing qualitative and quantitative research evidence using triangulation: A systematic literature review. *Journal of Mixed Methods Research*, 16(1), 95–110.

Hastie, B., & Rimmington, D. (2014). '200 years of white affirmative action': White privilege discourse in discussions of racial inequality. *Discourse & Society*, 25(2), 186–204. 10.1177/0957926513516050

Heale, R., & Forbes, D. (2013). Understanding triangulation in research. *Evidence-Based Nursing*, 16(4), 98–98. 10.1136/eb-2013-10149423943076

Heller, M. (2002). *Éléments d'une sociolinguiste critique*. Didier.

Heller, M. (2008). Language and the nation-state: Challenges to sociolinguistic theory and practice1. *Journal of Sociolinguistics*, 12(4), 504–524. 10.1111/j.1467-9841.2008.00373.x

Heller, M. (2018). Continuity and renewal. *Journal of Sociolinguistics*, 22(1), 3–4. 10.1111/josl.12267

Helms, J. E. (2017). The challenge of making Whiteness visible: Reactions to four Whiteness articles. *The Counseling Psychologist*, 45(5), 717–726. 10.1177/0011000017718943

Hennink, M., & Kaiser, B. N. (2022). Sample sizes for saturation in qualitative research: A systematic review of empirical tests. *Social Science & Medicine,* 292-302.

Hernandez, H. P. (2023). Nouns as nominal premodifiers in disciplinary research articles written by Filipino research writers: A cross-investigation. *International Journal of Language Studies*, 17(1), 31–52. 10.5281/zenodo.7513342

Hernandez, T. K. (2001). Multiracial matrix: The role of race ideology in the enforcement of antidiscrimination laws, a United States-Latin America comparison. *Cornell Law Review*, 87, 1093.

Hesse-Biber, S. N. (2010). *Mixed Methods Research: Merging Theory with Practice*. Guilford Press.

Hewett, D. G., Watson, B. M., & Gallois, C. (2015). Communication between hospital doctors: Underaccommodation and interpretability. *Language & Communication*, 41, 71–83. 10.1016/j.langcom.2014.10.007

Hickson, H. (2016). Becoming a critical narrativist: Using critical reflection and narrative inquiry as research methodology. *Qualitative Social Work: Research and Practice*, 15(3), 380–391. 10.1177/1473325015617344

Hlady-Rispal, M., & Jouison-Laffitte, E. (2014). Qualitative research methods and epistemological frameworks: A review of publication trends in entrepreneurship. *Journal of Small Business Management*, 52(4), 594–614. 10.1111/jsbm.12123

Hofstede, G. (2001). *Culture's consequences: Comparing values, behaviors, institutions, and organizations across nations.* SAGE Publications Ltd.

Hofstede, G. (2001). *Culture's Consequences: Comparing Values, Behaviors, Institutions, and Organizations Across Nations.* Sage Publications.

Hofstede, G., & Hofstede, G. J. (2005). *Culture and Organizations—Software of the Mind: Intercultural Cooperation and its Importance for Survival* (2nd ed.). McGraw Hill.

Hoque, Z., Covaleski, M., & Gooneratne, T. (2013). Theoretical triangulation and pluralism in research methods in organizational and accounting research. *Accounting, Auditing & Accountability Journal*, 26(7), 1170–1198. 10.1108/AAAJ-May-2012-01024

Huer, M. B., & Saenz, T. I. (2003). Challenges and strategies for conducting survey and focus group research with culturally diverse groups. *American Journal of Speech-Language Pathology*, 12(2), 209–220. 10.1044/1058-0360(2003/067)12828534

Hughey, M. (2012). *White bound: Nationalists, antiracists, and the shared meanings of race.* Stanford University Press. 10.1515/9780804783316

Hughey, M. W. (2022). Superposition strategies: How and why White people say contradictory things about race. *Proceedings of the National Academy of Sciences, 119*(9), 1-8. 10.1073/pnas.2116306119

Hunt, S., Riegelman, A., & Myers-Kelley, S. (2024, February 28). Conducting research through an anti-racism lens. *University of Minnesota.* https://libguides.umn.edu/antiracismlens

Hussein, A. (2009). The use of triangulation in social sciences research. *Journal of Comparative Social Work*, 4(1), 106–117. 10.31265/jcsw.v4i1.48

Hymes, D. (1980). *language in education.* Centre for Applied Linguistics Haynes, K. (2012). Reflexivity in qualitative research. In G. Symon & C. Cassell (Eds.), *Qualitative Organizational Research: Core Methods and Current Challenges* (pp. 72-89). Sage.

Iacono, J., Brown, A., & Holtham, C. (2009). Research methods – a case example of participant observation. *Electronic Journal of Business Research Methods*, 7(1), 39–46.

Iqbal, M., Chaghtai, K., Jabbar, A. A., Achour, M., & Geraldine, E. (2024)... *Concept, Implementation, and Development of Productive Zakat Management for Social, Educational, and Humanitarian.*, 2(1), 67–78.

Izza, N. N., & Rusydiana, A. S. (2023). A Qualitative Review on Halal Food: NVivo Approach. *Management, and Business, 1*, 90–106. https://ejournal.unida.gontor.ac.id/index.php/JTS/index

Jack, D. C., & Raturi, V. P. (2006). A methodological framework for combining qualitative and quantitative techniques. Journal of Organizational Culture. *Communications and Conflict*, 10(2), 77–90.

Jacob, E. (1987). Qualitative Research Traditions: A Review. *Review of Educational Research*, 6(2), 245–259. 10.3102/00346543057001001

Jayakumar, U. M., & Adamian, A. S. (2017). The fifth frame of colorblind ideology: Maintaining the comforts of colorblindness in the context of white fragility. *Sociological Perspectives*, 60(5), 912–936. 10.1177/0731121417721910

Jick, T. D. (1979). Mixing Qualitative and Quantitative Methods: Triangulation in Action. *Administrative Science Quarterly*, 24(4), 602–611. 10.2307/2392366

Johnson, J. L., Adkins, D., & Chauvin, S. (2020). A review of the quality indicators of rigor in qualitative research. *American Journal of Pharmaceutical Education*, 84(1), 138–146. 10.5688/ajpe712032292186

Johnson, M., Foley, M., Suengas, A., & Raye, C. (1988). Phenomenal characteristics of memories for perceived and imagined autobiographical events. *Journal of Experimental Psychology. General*, 117(4), 371–376. 10.1037/0096-344 5.117.4.3712974863

Johnson, R. B. (1997). Examining the validity structure of qualitative research. *Education*, 118(2), 282–292.

Johnson, R. B., & Christensen, L. B. (2004). *Educational Research: Quantitative, Qualitative, and Mixed Approaches*. Allyn and Bacon. 10.3102/0013189X033007014

Joly, B. (2009). *Communication*. De Boeck Supérieur.

Jones, A., Hartley, J., & Jones, N. (2023). Validity of the UCEEM in use: How does it triangulate with qualitative data in measuring the effect of an educational intervention? *Journal of Medical Education and Curricular Development*, 10. Advance online publication. 10.1177/23821205231202335377786574

Joseph, J., Sankar, D., & Nambiar, D. (2021). The burden of mental health illnesses in kerala: A secondary analysis of reported data from 2002 to 2018. *BMC Public Health*, 21(1), 2264. Advance online publication. 10.1186/s12889-021-12289-034895187

Jovchelovich, S., & Bauer, M. W. (2002). Entrevista Narrativa [Narrative Interview]. In Bauer, M. W., & Gaskell, G. (Eds.), *Pesquisa qualitativa com texto, imagem e som: Um manual prático* (pp. 90–113). Vozes. https://www.redalyc.org/pdf/3610/361035360027_2.pdf

Kang, Y., & Yang, K. C. (2022). Communicating racism and xenophobia in the era of Donald Trump: A computational framing analysis of the US-Mexico cross-border wall discourses. *The Howard Journal of Communications*, 33(2), 140–159. 10.1080/10646175.2021.1996491

Karnieli-Miller, O., Strier, R., Pessach-Gelblum, L., Zimhony, A., Shalev, H., Weiser, M., & Bentwich, M. E. (2022). Digital ethnography in health care: Crossing the boundary between online and offline healthcare settings. *The Milbank Quarterly*, 100(1), 254–284.

Kartini, K., Anwar, M., & Muliastuti, L. (2024). A Map of students' language impoliteness: A phenomenological study. *Journal of Languages and Language Teaching*, 12(2), 996–1006. 10.33394/jollt.v12i2.8864

Kashaev, R., Luo, F., & Vartanov, G. (2015). A TQFT of Turaev–Viro type on shaped triangulations. *Annales Henri Poincaré*, 17(5), 1109–1143. 10.1007/s00023-015-0427-8

Kawulich, B. (2005). Participant observation as a data collection method. *FORUM: Qualitative Social Research*, 6, Article 43. Retrieved from: http://nbn-resolving.de/urn:nbn:de:0114-fqs0502430

Kazemi, A., & Salmani Nodoushan, M. A. (2018). A conversation analytic perspective on Quranic verses and chapters. *Studies in English Language and Education*, 5(1), 1–11. 10.24815/siele.v5i1.8620

Keblusek, L., Giles, H., & Maass, A. (2017). Communication and group life: How language and symbols shape intergroup relations. *Group Processes & Intergroup Relations*, 20(5), 632–643. 10.1177/1368430217708864

Kelly, M. (2010). The role of theory in qualitative health research. *Family Practice*, 27(3), 285–290. 10.1093/fampra/cmp07719875746

Kessler, M. M., Reese, R. J., & Eggett, D. L. (2012). Triangulation: A methodological discussion. *Nurse Researcher*, 19(1), 30–37.

Kim, Y. Y. (2005). Adapting to a new culture: An integrative communication theory. *Theorizing about intercultural communication*, 375-400.

Kim, D. S. (2009). A Single Beta-Complex Solves All Geometry Problems in a Molecule. *Sixth International Symposium on Voronoi Diagrams*, 254-260. 10.1109/ISVD.2009.41

Kimmel, M. S., & Aronson, A. (2018). *The Gendered Society Reader*. Oxford University Press.

Kissling, E., & Muthusamy, T. (2022). Exploring boundedness for concept-based instruction of aspect: Evidence from learning the Spanish preterite and imperfect. *Modern Language Journal*, 106(2), 371–392. 10.1111/modl.12778

Knight, K. (2006). Transformations of the concept of ideology in the Twentieth century. *The American Political Science Review*, 100(4), 619–626. 10.1017/S0003055406062502

Kotera, Y., Ozaki, A., Miyatake, H., Tsunetoshi, C., Nishikawa, Y., Kosaka, M., & Tanimoto, T. (2022). Qualitative Investigation into the mental health of healthcare workers in Japan during the COVID-19 pandemic. *International Journal of Environmental Research and Public Health*, 19(1), 1–14. 10.3390/ijerph1901056835010828

Kothari, C. R. (2004). *Research Methodology: Methods and Techniques*. New Age International.

Kovach, M. (2017). Doing indigenous methodologies. *The SAGE Handbook of Qualitative Research*, 214-234.

Kramsch, C. (1993). *Context and Culture in Language Teaching*. Oxford University Press.

Krueger, R. A. (1988). Focus Groups. A Practical Guide for Applied Research. *Sage (Atlanta, Ga.)*.

Krueger, R. A. (1991). *El grupo de discusión: guía práctica para la investigación aplicada*. Pirámide.

Krueger, R. A., & Casey, M. A. (2015). *Focus Groups: A Practical Guide for Applied Research*. SAGE Publications Ltd.

Kumar, B. N., James, R., Hargreaves, S., Bozorgmehr, K., Mosca, D., Hosseinalipour, S.-M., . . . Severoni, S. (2022). Meeting the health needs of displaced people fleeing Ukraine: Drawing on existing technical guidance and evidence. *The Lancet Regional Health-Europe, 17*, 1-6. https://doi.org/. lanepe.2022.10040310.1016/j

Kumar, A., Shrivastav, S. K., & Bhattacharyya, S. (2022). Measuring strategic fit using big data analytics in the automotive supply chain: A data source triangulation-based research. *International Journal of Productivity and Performance Management*, 72(10), 2977–2999. 10.1108/IJPPM-11-2021-0672

Kuo, C. C., Deng, L., Creighton, J., Lee, E., & Wehrly, S. E. (2021). Predicting doctorate completion for international students in counselor education programs. *Journal of Multicultural Counseling and Development*, 49(3), 211–225. 10.1002/jmcd.12181

Labov, W. (1976). *Sociolinguistics*. Minuit.

Ladson-Billings, G. (2006). From the achievement gap to the education debt: Understanding achievement in US schools. *Educational Researcher*, 35(7), 3–12. 10.3102/0013189X035007003

Leavy, P. (2023). *Research design: Quantitative, qualitative, mixed methods, arts-based, and community-based participatory research approaches*. Guilford.

LeBreton, D. (1999). *Antropología del Dolor*. Seix Barral.

Leedy, P. D., & Ormrod, J. E. (2023). *Practical Research: Planning and Design*. Pearson.

Lemon, L. L., & Hayes, J. (2020). Enhancing trustworthiness of qualitative findings: Using Leximancer for qualitative data analysis triangulation. *The Qualitative Report*, 25(3), 604–614. 10.46743/2160-3715/2020.4222

Leung, L. (2015). Validity, reliability, and generalizability in qualitative research. *Journal of Family Medicine and Primary Care*, 4(3), 324. 10.4103/2249-4863.16130626288766

Lewin, K. (1946). Action research and minority problems. *The Journal of Social Issues*, 2(4), 34–46. 10.1111/j.1540-4560.1946.tb02295.x

Lewis, S. (2015). Qualitative Inquiry and Research Design: Choosing Among Five Approaches. *Health Promotion Practice*, 16(4), 473–475. 10.1177/1524839915580941

Liamputtong, P. (2008). Doing research in a cross-cultural context: Methodological and ethical challenges. *Doing Cross-Cultural Research: Ethical and Methodological Perspectives*, 3-20.

Liamputtong, P. (2007). *Researching The Vulnerable: A Guide to Sensitive Research Methods*. Sage Publications. 10.4135/9781849209861

Lie-A-Ling, H. J. M., Zuurbier, P. H., Roopnarine, J. L., & Lindauer, L. R. (2023). Cultural Sensitivity: Guidelines for Qualitative Research. *Pedagogische Studiën*, 100(2), 248–260. 10.59302/ps.v100i2.14225

Lightman, N. (2022). Caring during the COVID-19 crisis: Intersectional exclusion of immigrant women health care aides in Canadian long-term care. *Health & Social Care in the Community*, 30(4), 1343–1351. 10.1111/hsc.1354134396607

Li, J. (2022). Grounded theory-based model of the influence of digital communication on handicraft intangible cultural heritage. *Heritage Science*, 10(1), 126. Advance online publication. 10.1186/s40494-022-00760-z35968496

Lincoln, Y. S., & Guba, E. G. (1985). *Naturalistic inquiry*. Sage Publications. 10.1016/0147-1767(85)90062-8

Linström, M., & Marais, W. (2012). Qualitative news frame analysis: A methodology. *Communitas*, 17, 21–38.

Liu, K., & Guo, F. (2016). A review on critical discourse analysis. *Theory and Practice in Language Studies*, 6(5), 1076–1084. 10.17507/tpls.0605.23

Llompart, J. (2016). *Pràctiques plurilingües d'escolars d'un institut superdivers: de la recerca a l'acció educativa* [Doctoral tesis. Universidad Autónoma de Barcelona]. Retreived from https://www.tdx.cat/handle/10803/399835#page=1

Long, K. B. (2020). *How Senior Institutional Research Leaders Interpret Graduation Outcomes Split by Race Category* (Doctoral dissertation, Oakland University).

Longhurst, R. (2016). Semi-structured interviews and focus groups. In Clifford, N., Cope, M., Gillespie, T., & French, S. (Eds.), *Key Methods in Geography* (3rd ed., pp. 143–156). SAGE.

López, N., Erwin, C., Binder, M., & Chavez, M. J. (2018). Making the invisible visible: Advancing quantitative methods in higher education using critical race theory and intersectionality. *Race, Ethnicity and Education*, 21(2), 180–207. 10.1080/13613324.2017.1375185

Love, A. (2022). Recognizing, understanding, and defining systemic and individual White supremacy. *Women of Color Advancing Peace and Security* (Working Paper). https://www.zbw.eu/econis-archiv/bitstream/11159/509639/1/EBP080507786_0.pdf

Löwe, B., & Kerkhove, B. (2019). Methodological Triangulation in Empirical Philosophy (of Mathematics). In Aberdein, A., & Inglis, M. (Eds.), *Advances in Experimental Philosophy of Logic and Mathematics* (pp. 15–38). Bloomsbury Methuen Drama., 10.5040/9781350039049.0005

Madison, D. S. (2011). Critical ethnography: Method, ethics, and performance. *Sage (Atlanta, Ga.)*.

Maggs-Rapport, F. (2000). The use of triangulation in a study of older people with depression. *International Journal of Geriatric Psychiatry*, 15(4), 354–360.

Malinowski, B. (1922). Argonauts of the Western Pacific. George Routledge & Sons Ltd.

Manera, A. B., & Vecaldo, R. T. (2020). Cultural structuring of Urok practice: An intercultural communication of the Bago tribe in Kalinga province, Philippines. *International Journal of Psychosocial Rehabilitation*, 24(6), 13193–13217.

Mani, P. S. (2006). Methodological dilemmas experienced in researching Indo-Canadian Young Adults' decision-making process to study the sciences. *International Journal of Qualitative Methods*, 5(2), 55–72. 10.1177/160940690600500209

Mapuya, M. (2024). Exploring the contribution of decolonisation epistemologies: Promoting social justice in accounting education. *International Journal of Language Studies*, 18(1), 131–155. 10.5281/zenodo.10468331

Marschan-Piekkari, R., & Welch, C. (2004a). Qualitative research methods in international business: The state of the art. In *Handbook of Qualitative Research Methods for International Business* (pp. 464-485). Edward Elgar Publishing.

Marshall, A., & Batten, S. (2004). Researching across cultures: Issues of ethics and power. In *Forum Qualitative Sozialforschung. Forum Qualitative Social Research*, 5(3). Advance online publication. 10.17169/fqs-5.3.572

Marshall, B., Cardon, P., Poddar, A., & Fontenot, R. (2013). Does sample size matter in qualitative research? *A Review of Qualitative Interviews in IS Research. Journal of Computer Information Systems*, 54(1), 11–22. 10.1080/08874417.2013.11645667

Marsh, D., & Furlong, E. (2002). Ontology and Epistemology in Political Science. In David, M., & Gerry, S. (Eds.), *Theory and Methods in Political Science* (pp. 17–41). Palgrave. 10.1007/978-0-230-62889-2_2

Martín-Pérez, I. M., Martín-Pérez, S. E., Martínez Rampérez, R., Vaswani, S., & Dorta Borges, M. (2023). Conocimientos, actitudes y creencias hacia la enfermedad en mujeres con fibromialgia. Un estudio cualitativo basado en grupo focal. *Revista de la Sociedad Española del Dolor*, 79-94. .10.20986/resed.2023.4022/2022

Martín-Pérez, S. E., Martín-Pérez, I. M., Álvarez Sánchez, A., Acosta Pérez, P., & Rodríguez Alayón, E. (2023). Social support in low-income women with fibromyalgia syndrome from sub-urban and peri-urban areas of Tenerife (Canary Islands, Spain): A mixed method study. *Journal of Patient-Reported Outcomes*, 7(1), 135. 10.1186/s41687-023-00661-038129366

Masiloane, E. T. (2008). *A comparison of qualitative and quantitative research: similarities and differences* (Doctoral dissertation, University of the Free State, Bloemfontein).

Mason, J. (2002). *Qualitative researching* (2nd ed.). Sage. Retrieved from http://www.sxf.uevora.pt/wp-content/uploads/2013/03/Mason_2002.pdf

Mason, J. (2002). *Qualitative Researching. Sage Publications*.

Matre, M. (2022). Speech-to-text technology as an inclusive approach: Lower secondary teachers' experiences. *Nordisk Tidsskrift for Pedagogikk Og Kritikk*, 8(0), 233. 10.23865/ntpk.v8.3436

Maxwell, J. A. (2013). *Qualitative Research Design: An Interactive Approach*. Sage Publications.

Mazieri, M. R., Quoniam, L. M., Reymond, D., & Cunha, K. C. T. (2022). Use of IRAMUTEQ for content analysis based on descending hierarchical classification and correspondence factor analysis. *Brazilian Journal of Marketing*, 21(5), 1978–2011.

McArt, E. W., & Brown, J. K. (1990). The challenge of research on international populations: Theoretical and methodological issues. *Oncology Nursing Forum*, 17(2), 283–286.2315194

McGlone, M. S., & Giles, H. (2011). Language and interpersonal communication. In Knapp, M. L., & Daly, J. A. (Eds.), *The SAGE handbook of interpersonal communication* (4th ed., pp. 201–237). Sage. https://ci.uky.edu/grad/sites/default/files/mdragojevic_cv_9-2016.pdf

Meerangani, K. A. (2019). The Role of Zakat in Human Development. *SALAM: Jurnal Sosial Dan Budaya Syar-I*, 6(2), 141–154. 10.15408/sjsbs.v6i2.11037

Méndez, M. (2013). Autoethnography as a research method: Advantages, limitations and criticisms. *Colombian Applied Linguistics Journal*, 15(2), 279–287. 10.14483/udistrital.jour.calj.2013.2.a09

Merriam, S. B. (2009). *Qualitative research: A guide to design and implementation*. Jossey-Bass.

Messaoudi, L. (2002). Technolect and linguistic resources. The example of the highway code in Morocco. *Language in Society*, 2002(1), 53–75. 10.3917/ls.099.0053

Meyer, P. J. (1999). *An Essay in the Philosophy of Social Sciences.* https://www.academia.edu/27210801/An_Essay_in_the_Philosophy_of_Social_Science

Meyrick, J. (2006). What is good qualitative research? A first step towards a comprehensive approach to judging rigour/quality. *Journal of Health Psychology*, 11(5), 799–808. 10.1177/1359105306066643 16908474

Miles, M. B., & Huberman, A. M. (1994). *Qualitative Data Analysis: An Expanded Sourcebook*. Sage.

Miles, M. B., Huberman, A. M., & Saldana, J. (2013). *Qualitative data analysis: A methods sourcebook*. Sage publications.

Miller, R., Liu, K., & Ball, A. F. (2020). Critical counter-narrative as transformative methodology for educational equity. *Review of Research in Education*, 44(1), 269–300. 10.3102/0091732X20908501

Mingo, V., & Mistry, J. (2023). Home as the third place: Stories of movement among immigrant caregivers in an intercultural Chilean city. *Ethos (Berkeley, Calif.)*, 52(1), 68–88. 10.1111/etho.12415

Mishler, E. G. (1986). *Research interviewing: Context and narrative*. Harvard University Press. 10.4159/9780674041141

Mohajan, H. K. (2018). Qualitative research methodology in social sciences and related subjects. *Journal of Economic Development. Environment and People*, 7(1), 23–48. 10.26458/jedep.v7i1.571

Mohd, P., Fikri, F., Omar, A., Nur, M., & Hasbollah, H. (n.d.). *The Roles of Zakat Towards Maqasid Al-Shariah and Sustainable Development Goals (SDGs): A Case Study of Zakat Institutions in East Malaysia*. Academic Press.

Molm, L. D., Takahashi, N., & Peterson, G. (2000). Risk and trust in social exchange: An experimental test of a classical proposition. *American Journal of Sociology*, 105(5), 1396–1427. 10.1086/210434

Montalescot, L., Lamore, K., Flahault, C., & Untas, A. (2024). What is the place of interpretation in text analysis? An example using ALCESTE® software. *Qualitative Research in Psychology*, 21(2), 200–226. 10.1080/14780887.2024.2316624

Montañez-Serrano, M. (2010). *El grupo de discusión*. Cuadernos CIMAS-Observatorio Internacional de Ciudadanía y Medio Ambiente Sostenible.

Monteiro, L., de Melo, R., Braga, B., de Sá, J., Monteiro, L., Cunha, M., Gêda, T., & Canuto, A. (2021). ALCESTE X IRAMUTEQ: Comparative Analysis of the Use of CAQDAS in Qualitative Research. *Advances in Intelligent Systems and Computing*, 1345 AISC, 67–79. 10.1007/978-3-030-70187-1_6

Morgan, D. L. (2008). Snowball sampling. In Given, L. M. (Ed.), *The Sage encyclopedia of qualitative research methods* (pp. 816–817). SAGE Publications, Inc. 10.4135/9781412963909

Morgan, H. (2022). Conducting a Qualitative Document Analysis. *The Qualitative Report*, 27(1), 64–77. 10.46743/2160-3715/2022.5044

Morse, J. M. (1995). The significance of saturation. *Qualitative Health Research*, 5(2), 147–149. 10.1177/104973239500500201

Morse, J. M. (2010). How different is qualitative health research from qualitative research? Do we have a subdiscipline? *Qualitative Health Research*, 20(11), 1459–1464. 10.1177/1049732310379116 20693515

Morse, J. M., Barrett, M., Mayan, M., Olson, K., & Spiers, J. (2002). Verification strategies for establishing reliability and validity in qualitative research. *International Journal of Qualitative Methods*, 1(2), 13–22. 10.1177/160940690200100202

Morse, J. M., & Niehaus, L. (2009). *Mixed Method Design: Principles and Procedures*. Left Coast Press.

Motaung, L. B. (2024). Translanguaging pedagogical practice in a tutorial programme at a South African university. *International Journal of Language Studies*, 18(1), 81–104. 10.5281/zenodo.10468213

Muda, E., & Thalib, A. (2024). Innovative Approaches to Managing Zakat within the Context of Sustainable Development and Societal Well-Being in Indonesia. *European Journal of Studies in Management & Business*, 29, 74–89. Advance online publication. 10.32038/mbrq.2024.29.05

Mugenda, O. M., & Mugenda, A. G. (2003). *Research methods: Quantitative & Qualitative Approaches*. Acts press.

Munhall, P. (1988). Ethical considerations in qualitative research. *Western Journal of Nursing Research*, 10(3), 275–284.3394317

Munkejord, M. C. (2017). 'I work with my heart': Experiences of migrant care workers in a Northern, rural context. *Journal of Population Ageing*, 10(3), 229–246. 10.1007/s12062-016-9157-z

Murgado-Armenteros, E. M., Gutiérrez-Salcedo, M., Torres-Ruiz, F. J., & Cobo, M. J. (2015). Analysing the conceptual evolution of qualitative marketing research through science mapping analysis. *Scientometrics*, 102(1), 519–557. 10.1007/s11192-014-1443-z

Murphy, F. J., & Yielder, J. (2010). Establishing rigour in qualitative radiography research. *Radiography*, 16(1), 62–67. 10.1016/j.radi.2009.07.003

Murray, J. S. (1999). Methodological triangulation in a study of social support for siblings of children with cancer. *Journal of Pediatric Oncology Nursing*, 16(4), 194–200. 10.1177/104345429901600404 10565108

Muylaert, C. J., Sarubbi, V.Jr, Gallo, P. R., Neto, M. L. R., & Reis, A. O. A. (2014). Narrative interviews: An important resource in qualitative research. *Revista da Escola de Enfermagem da USP*, 48(2), 184–189. 10.1590/S0080-62342014 000080002725830754

Muzari, T., Shava, G. N., & Shonhiwa, S. (2022). Qualitative Research Paradigm, a Key Research Design for Educational Researchers, Processes and Procedures : A Theoretical Overview. *Indiana Journal of Humanities and Social Sciences*, 3(1), 14–20.

Naghdi, A. (2010). Iranian Diaspora: With focus on Iranian Immigrants in Sweden. *Asian Social Science*, 6(11), 197–208. 10.5539/ass.v6n11p197

Naidoo, L. (2012). *Ethnography: An Introduction to Definition and Method*. InTech. 10.5772/39248

Narcy-Combes, J.-P. (2005). *Language Teaching and ICT: towards responsible action research*. OPHRYS.

Natow, R. S. (2019). The use of triangulation in qualitative studies employing elite interviews. *Qualitative Research*, 20(2), 160–173. 10.1177/1468794119830077

Nayar, S., & StClair, V. W. (2020). Multiple cultures – one process: Undertaking a cross cultural grounded theory study. *American Journal of Qualitative Research*, 4(3), 131–145. 10.29333/ajqr/9310

Ndlangamandla, S. C., Chaka, C., Shange, T., & Shandu-Phetla, T. (2024). COVID-19 crosslinguistic and multimodal public health communication strategies: Social justice or emergency political strategy? *International Journal of Language Studies*, 18(2), 7–34. 10.5281/zenodo.10475208

Neergaard, H., & Leitch, C. M. (2015). *Handbook of qualitative research techniques and analysis in entrepreneurship*. Edward Elgar. 10.4337/9781849809870

Neergaard, M., Olesen, F., Andersen, R., & Søndergaard, J. (2009). Qualitative description – the poor cousin of health research? *BMC Medical Research Methodology*, 9(1), 52. Advance online publication. 10.1186/1471-2288-9-5219607668

Neuman, W. L. (2006). Social Research Methods: Qualitative and Quantitative Approaches. 6th Edition, Pearson International Edition.

Neuman, W. L. (2000). *Social Research Methods Qualitative and Quantitative Approaches* (4th ed.). Allyn & Bacon.

Nguyen, T. T., Criss, S., Michaels, E. K., Cross, R. I., Michaels, J. S., Dwivedi, P., Huang, D., Hsu, E., Mukhija, K., Nguyen, L. H., Yardi, I., Allen, A. M., Nguyen, Q. C., & Gee, G. C. (2021). Progress and push-back: How the killings of Ahmaud Arbery, Breonna Taylor, and George Floyd impacted public discourse on race and racism on Twitter. *SSM - Population Health*, 15, 1–9. 10.1016/j.ssmph.2021.10092234584933

Nicholls, D. (2009). Qualitative research: Part three: Methods. *International Journal of Therapy and Rehabilitation*, 16(12), 638–647. 10.12968/ijtr.2009.16.12.45433

Niedbalski, J., & Ślęzak, I. (2022). Encounters with CAQDAS: Advice for Beginner Users of Computer Software for Qualitative Research. *The Qualitative Report*, 27(4), 1114–1132. 10.46743/2160-3715/2022.4770

Noble, H., & Heale, R. (2019). Triangulation in research, with examples. *Evidence-Based Nursing*, 22(2), 67–68. 10.1136/ebnurs-2019-10314531201209

Noble, H., & Smith, J. (2015). Issues of validity and reliability in qualitative research. *Evidence-Based Nursing*, 18(2), 34–35. 10.1136/eb-2015-10205425653237

Novek, S. (2013). Filipino health care aides and the nursing home labour market in Winnipeg. *Canadian Journal on Aging*, 32(4), 405–416. 10.1017/S071498081300038X24063532

Nursalam, N., Chen, C. M., Efendi, F., Has, E. M. M., Hidayati, L., & Hadisuyatmana, S. (2020). The lived experiences of Indonesian nurses who worked as care workers in Taiwan. *The Journal of Nursing Research*, 28(2), 1–7. 10.1097/jnr.0000000000000035531714449

Nurul Izza, N. (2021). Review on Zakat Performance Studies using NVivo-12. *Islamic Social Finance*, 1(1). Advance online publication. 10.58968/isf.v1i1.109

Oizumi, M., Albantakis, L., & Tononi, G. (2014). From the phenomenology to the mechanisms of consciousness: Integrated information theory 3.0. *PLoS Computational Biology*, 10(5), e1003588. 10.1371/journal.pcbi.100358824811198

Okoko, J. M., Tunison, S., & Walker, K. D. (Eds.). (2023). *Varieties of Qualitative Research Methods: Selected Contextual Perspectives*. Springer Nature. 10.1007/978-3-031-04394-9

Oktay, J. S. (2012). *Grounded theory*. Pocket Guide to Social Work Re. 10.1093/acprof:oso/9780199753697.001.0001

Omusulu, R. (2013). The main features and constraints of social science's research methods. *International Journal of Development and Sustainability*, 2(3), 1907–1918.

Onwuegbuzie, A. J., & Leech, N. L. (2004). Enhancing the interpretation of "significant" findings: The role of mixed methods research. *The Qualitative Report*, 9(4), 770–792.

Onwuegbuzie, A. J., & Leech, N. L. (2005). The role of sampling in qualitative research. *Academic Exchange Quarterly*, 9(3), 280.

Orb, A., Eisenhauer, L., & Wynaden, D. (2001). Ethics in Qualitative Research. *Journal of Nursing Scholarship*, 33(1), 93–96. 10.1111/j.1547-5069.2001.00093.x11253591

Ortega, M. S. (2005). *El grupo de discusión: una herramienta para la investigación cualitativa*. Laertes.

Ortiz Fernández, F. (1999). *Contrapunteo cubano del tabaco y el azúcar*. EditoCubaEspaña.

Östlund, U., Kidd, L., Wengström, Y., & Rowa-Dewar, N. (2011). Combining qualitative and quantitative research within mixed method research designs: A methodological review. *International Journal of Nursing Studies*, 48(3), 369–383. 10.1016/j.ijnurstu.2010.10.00521084086

Oware, M. (2016). "We Stick Out Like a Sore Thumb..." Underground White Rappers' Hegemonic Masculinity and Racial Evasion. *Sociology of Race and Ethnicity (Thousand Oaks, Calif.)*, 2(3), 372–386. 10.1177/2332649215617781

Padgett, D. (2008). Qualitative Methods in Social Work Research (2nd ed.). Sage Publications.

Padley, R. H. (2022). Shame, discrimination and disability: Unveiling narratives of obesity. *International Journal of Language Studies*, 16(4), 43–64.

Paidós Hofstede, G. (1980). *Culture's consequences: International differences in work-related values*. SAGE Publications Ltd.

Palomares, N. A., Giles, H., Soliz, J., & Gallois, C. (2016). Intergroup accommodation, social categories, and identities. In Giles, H. (Ed.), *Communication accommodation theory. Negotiating personal relationships and social identities across contexts* (pp. 123–151). Cambridge University Press. 10.1017/CBO9781316226537.007

Papadopoulos, I. (2021). Translanguaging as a pedagogical practice in primary education: Approaching, managing and teaching diverse classrooms. In I. Papadopoulos. & M. Papadopoulos (Eds.), *Applied linguistics research and good practices for multilingual and multicultural classrooms.* (pp. 147-168). NOVA Science Publisher.

Papadopoulos, I. (2022). Translanguaging as a pedagogical practice for successful inclusion in linguistically and culturally diverse classrooms. In E, Meletiadou (Ed.), *Handbook of research on policies and practices for assessing inclusive teaching and learning* (pp. 422-448). IGI Global. 10.4018/978-1-7998-8579-5.ch019

Papadopoulos, I. (2020). *From translanguaging pedagogy to classroom pedagogy: Supporting literacy, communication and cooperative creativity*. Disigma Publications.

Papadopoulos, I., & Shin, J. K. (2021). Developing young foreign language learners' persuasive strategies through intercultural folktales. *Research Papers in Language Teaching and Learning*, 1(1), 185–202.

Parker, L., & Lynn, M. (2002). What's race got to do with it? Critical race theory's conflicts with and connections to qualitative research methodology and epistemology. *Qualitative Inquiry*, 8(1), 7–22. 10.1177/107780040200800102

Parkhe, A. (2004). Interviews: a key data source in international business research. In *Handbook of Qualitative Research Methods for International Business* (pp. 464-485). Edward Elgar Publishing. 10.4337/9781781954331.00010

Patnaik, E. (2013). Reflexivity: Situating the researcher in qualitative research. *Humanities and Social Science Studies*, 2(1), 98–106.

Patton, M. (2015). *Qualitative Research and Evaluation Methods* (4th ed.). Sage Publications.

Patton, M. Q. (1999). Enhancing the Quality and Credibility of Qualitative Analysis. *Health Services Research*, 34(5 Pt 2), 1189–1208. 10.1111/1475-6773.0013010591279

Patton, M. Q. (2002). Two decades of developments in qualitative inquiry: A personal, experiential perspective. *Qualitative Social Work: Research and Practice*, 1(3), 261–283. 10.1177/1473325002001003636

Patton, M. Q. (2023). *Qualitative Research & Evaluation Methods: Integrating Theory and Practice*. Sage Publications.

Paulus, M. T., & Lester, J. (2020). Using software to support qualitative data analysis. *Handbook of Qualitative Research in Education, 2*, 420–429. 10.4337/9781788977159.00048

Pauwels, P., & Matthyssens, P. (2004). The architecture of multiple case study research in international business. In *Handbook of Qualitative Research Methods for International Business* (pp. 464-485). Edward Elgar Publishing. 10.4337/9781781954331.00020

Payne, G., & Payne, J. (2004). *Key Concepts in Social Research*. SAGE Publications Ltd. 10.4135/9781849209397

Pelzang, R., & Hutchinson, A. M. (2017). Establishing cultural integrity in qualitative research: Reflections from a cross-cultural study. *International Journal of Qualitative Methods*, 17(1). Advance online publication. 10.1177/1609406917749702

Pérez-Milans, M. (2013). *Urban schools and English language education in late modern china: a critical sociolinguistic ethnography*. Routledge. 10.4324/9780203366189

Petrou, M., & Dragojevic, M. (2024). "Where are you from?" Language attitudes and (non)accommodation during native–nonnative speaker interactions in Germany. *Journal of Language and Social Psychology*, 43(3), 353–375. 10.1177/0261927X231222447

Phal, A. (1968). *Scientific Language and Linguistic Analysis*. CREDIF.

Pham, T., Kaiser, B., Koirala, R., Maharjan, S., Upadhaya, N., Franz, L., & Kohrt, B. (2020). Traditional healers and mental health in Nepal: A scoping review. *Culture, Medicine and Psychiatry*, 45(1), 97–140. 10.1007/s11013-020-09676-432444961

Phillippi, J., & Lauderdale, J. (2018). A guide to field notes for qualitative research: Context and conversation. *Qualitative Health Research*, 28(3), 381–388. 10.1177/104973231769710229298584

Pino Gavidia, L. A., & Adu, J. (2022). Critical narrative inquiry: An examination of a methodological approach. *International Journal of Qualitative Methods*, 21, 1–5. 10.1177/16094069221081594

Pitts, M. J., & Harwood, J. (2015). Communication accommodation competence: The nature and nurture of accommodative resources across the lifespan. *Language & Communication*, 41, 89–99. 10.1016/j.langcom.2014.10.002

Polit, D. F., & Beck, C. T. (2017). *Nursing research: Generating and assessing evidence for nursing practice*. Lippincott Williams & Wilkins.

Polit, D. F., & Hungler, B. D. (1999). *Nursing Research* (6th ed.). Lippicott.

Pomerantsev, A. L., & Rodionova, O. Y. (2021). New trends in qualitative analysis: Performance, optimization, and validation of multi-class and soft models. *Trends in Analytical Chemistry*, 143, 116372. 10.1016/j.trac.2021.116372

Ponterotto, J. G. (2010). Qualitative research in multicultural psychology: Philosophical underpinnings, popular approaches, and ethical considerations. *Cultural Diversity & Ethnic Minority Psychology*, 16(4), 581–589. 10.1037/a001205121058824

Popli, S. (2020). Phenomenology of vernacular environments: Wancho settlements in Arunachal Pradesh, in the north east of India. *Journal of Traditional Building Architecture and Urbanism*, (1), 539–550. 10.51303/jtbau.vi1.377

Porto Pedrosa, L., & Ruiz San Román, J. A. (2014). Los grupos de discusión. In Porto Pedrosa, L., & Ruiz San Román, J. A. (Eds.), *Métodos y técnicas cualitativas y cuantitativas aplicables a la investigación en ciencias sociales* (pp. 253–273). Tirant Humanidades México.

Poulos, C. N. (2021). *Essentials of autoethnography*. American Psychological Association. 10.1037/0000222-000

Prasitanarapun, R., & Kitreerawutiwong, N. (2023). The development of an instrument to measure interprofessional collaboration competency for primary care teams in the district health system of health region 2, Thailand. *BMC Primary Care*, 24(1), 55. Advance online publication. 10.1186/s12875-023-02013-936849902

Qadam, Z. S., Vafa, M. A., Hashemi, T., & Ali, A. P. (2023). Aging Enjoyment: A Grounded Theory Study. *Iranian Journal of Psychiatry*, 1–12.

Raffone, A. (2022). "Her leg didn't fully load in": A digitally-mediated social-semiotic critical discourse analysis of disability hate speech on TikTok. *International Journal of Language Studies*, 16(4), 17–42.

Rajasinghe, D., Aluthgama-Baduge, C., & Mulholland, G. (2021). Researching entrepreneurship: An approach to develop subjective understanding. *International Journal of Entrepreneurial Behaviour & Research*, 27(4), 866–883. 10.1108/IJEBR-10-2019-0601

Ramanujan, P., Bhattacharjea, S., & Alcott, B. (2022). A Multi-Stage Approach to Qualitative Sampling within a Mixed Methods Evaluation: Some Reflections on Purpose and Process. *The Canadian Journal of Program Evaluation*, 36(3), 355–364. 10.3138/cjpe.71237

Razali, R., Sundana, L., & Ramli, R. (2024). Curriculum Development in Higher Education in Light of Culture and Religiosity: A Case Study in Aceh of Indonesia. *International Journal of Society. Culture & Language*, 12(1), 39–55. 10.22034/ijscl.2023.2010108.3144

Reed-Danahay, D. (2009). Anthropologists, education, and autoethnography. *Revista de Antropologia*, 38(1), 28–47. 10.1080/00938150802672931

Reed-Danahay, D. (2017). Bourdieu and Critical Autoethnography: Implications for Research, Writing, and Teaching. *International Journal of Multicultural Education*, 19(1), 144–154. 10.18251/ijme.v19i1.1368

Reeves, S., Kuper, A., & Hodges, B. D. (2008). Qualitative research methodologies: Ethnography. *Clinical Research*, 337(aug07 3), a1020. Advance online publication. 10.1136/bmj.a102018687725

Reeves, S., Peller, J., Goldman, J., & Kitto, S. (2013). Ethnography in qualitative educational research. *Medical Teacher*, 80(8), 1365–1379. 10.3109/0142159X.2013.80497723808715

Reimsbach, D., & Hauschild, B. (2015). Testing vs. building accounting theory with experimental research: Insights from management research. *International Journal of Behavioural Accounting and Finance*, 5(1), 82. 10.1504/IJBAF.2015.071050

Remennick, L. I. (2001). 'All my life is one big nursing home': Russian immigrant women in Israel speak about double caregiver stress. *Women's Studies International Forum*, 24(6), 685–700. 10.1016/S0277-5395(01)00205-9

Renz, S., Carrington, J. M., & Badger, T. A. (2018). Two strategies for qualitative content analysis: An intramethod approach to triangulation. *Qualitative Health Research*, 28(5), 824–831. 10.1177/1049732317775358629424274

Richards, H. M., & Schwartz, L. J. (2002). Ethics of qualitative research: Are there special issues for health services research? *Family Practice*, 19(2), 135–139. 10.1093/fampra/19.2.13511906977

Riege, A. M. (2003). Validity and reliability tests in case study research: A literature review with "hands-on" applications for each research phase. *Qualitative Market Research*, 6(2), 75–86. 10.1108/13522750310470055

Roberts, P., Priest, H., & Traynor, M. (2006). Reliability and validity in research. *Nursing Standard*, 20(44), 41–46. 10.7748/ns.20.44.41.s5616872117

Roberts, P., & Woods, L. (2000). Alternative methods of gathering and handling data: Maximising the use of modern technology. *Nurse Researcher*, 8(2), 84–95. 10.7748/nr2001.01.8.2.84.c6152

Robinson, O. C. (2014). Sampling in interview-based qualitative research: A theoretical and practical guide. *Qualitative Research in Psychology*, 11(1), 25–41. 10.1080/14780887.2013.801543

Rodriguez, K. L., Schwartz, J. L., Lahman, M. K. E., & Geist, M. R. (2011). Culturally Responsive Focus Groups: Reframing the Research Experience to Focus on Participants. *International Journal of Qualitative Methods*, 10(4), 400–417. 10.1177/160940691101000407

Rolfe, G. (2006). Validity, trustworthiness and rigour: Quality and the idea of qualitative research. *Journal of Advanced Nursing*, 53(3), 304–310. 10.1111/j.1365-2648.2006.03727.x16441535

Roller, M. R. (2019). A quality approach to qualitative content analysis: Similarities and differences compared to other qualitative methods. *Forum Qualitative Social Research*, 20(3). Advance online publication. 10.17169/fqs-20.3.3385

Rose, J., & Johnson, C. W. (2020). Contextualizing reliability and validity in qualitative research: Toward more rigorous and trustworthy qualitative social science in leisure research. *Journal of Leisure Research*, 51(4), 432–451. 10.1080/00222216.2020.1722042

Roshan, A. (2023). *Trajectories of Iranian migrants in Madrid* [Unpublished Doctoral Dissertation]. Universidad Autónoma de Madrid.

Rostamalizadeh, V., & Noubakht, R. (2020). Sustainable development and migration in Iranian frontier counties. *European Online Journal of Natural and Social Sciences*, 9(1), 135–152.

Rowe, E. (2024). Network ethnography in education: A literature review of network ethnography as a methodology and how it has been applied in critical policy studies. In Stacey, M., & Mockler, N. (Eds.), *Analysing education policy: Theory and method* (pp. 136–156). Deakin University. 10.4324/9781003353379-13

Russo, K. E., & Grasso, A. (2022). Coping with dis/ableism in Twitter discourse: A corpus-based critical appraisal analysis of the Hidden Disabilities Sunflower Lanyard case. *International Journal of Language Studies*, 16(4), 65–94.

Sabar Ben-Yehoshua, N. (2016). *Traditions and Genres in Qualitative Research. Philosophies, Strategiesand Advanced Tools*. Mofet Institution.

Şafak-Ayvazoğlu, A., Kunuroglu, F., & Yağmur, K. (2021) Psychological and socio-cultural adaptation of Syrian refugees in Turkey. *International Journal of Intercultural Relations, 80,* 99–111. https://doi.org/.2020.11.00310.1016/j.ijintrel

Sahibzada, S., Kaur, S., & Khan, S. (2019). Triangulation in social science research: Concepts and methods. *International Journal of Advanced Research*, 7(2), 1200–1213.

Sakr, N., Son Hing, L. S., & González-Morales, M. G. (2023). Development and validation of the *marginalized*-group-focused diversity climate scale: Group differences and outcomes. *Journal of Business and Psychology*, 38(3), 689–722. 10.1007/s10869-022-09859-3

Saks, M. (2018). Methodological triangulation. *Nature Human Behaviour*, 2(11), 806–807. 10.1038/s41562-018-0458-531558816

Saldaña, J. (2021). *The Coding Manual for Qualitative Researchers* (4th ed.). Sage Publications.

Sale, J. (2008). How to assess rigour . . . or not in qualitative papers. *Journal of Evaluation in Clinical Practice*, 14(5), 912–913. 10.1111/j.1365-2753.2008.01093.x19018925

Salmani Nodoushan, M. A. (2021). Demanding versus asking in Persian: Requestives as acts of verbal harassment. *International Journal of Language Studies*, 15(1), 27–46. 10.5281/zenodo.7514622

Salmani Nodoushan, M. A. (2023). Native experts and reputable journals as points of reference: A study on research-article discussions. *Studies in English Language and Education*, 10(2), 562–574. 10.24815/siele.v10i2.29282

Sandelowski, M. (1995). Sample size in qualitative research. *Research in Nursing & Health*, 18(2), 179–183. 10.1002/nur.47701802117899572

Sandelowski, M. (1995). Triangles and crystals: On the geometry of qualitative research. *Research in Nursing & Health*, 18(6), 569–574. 10.1002/nur.47701806127480857

Sands, R. G., & Roer-Strier, D. (2006). Using Data Triangulation of Mother and Daughter Interviews to Enhance Research about Families. *Qualitative Social Work: Research and Practice*, 5(2), 237–260. 10.1177/1473325006064260

Sangasubana, N. (2011). How to Conduct Ethnographic Research. *The Qualitative Report*, 16(2), 567–573. 10.46743/2160-3715/2011.1071

Sanjari, M., Bahramnezhad, F., Fomani, F. K., Shoghi, M., & Cheraghi, M. A. (2014). Ethical challenges of researchers in qualitative studies: The necessity to develop a specific guideline. *Journal of Medical Ethics and History of Medicine*, 7.25512833

Sanjuán-Núñez, L. (2019). *El grupo de discusión, la investigación documental y otras técnicas cualitativas de investigación*. Operta UOC Publishing.

Santos, C., Abubakar, S., Barros, A., Mendonça, J., Dalmarco, G., & Godsell, J. (2019). Lessons for industrial development policies: Joining global aerospace value networks. *Space Policy*, 48, 30–40. 10.1016/j.spacepol.2019.01.006

Santos, K. D. S., Ribeiro, M. C., Queiroga, D. E. U. D., Silva, I. A. P. D., & Ferreira, S. M. S. (2020). The use of multiple triangulations as a validation strategy in a qualitative study. *Ciencia & Saude Coletiva*, 25, 655–664. 10.1590/1413-81232020252.1230201832022205

Santoso, S. W., Ma'ruf, A., & Zainuri, A. (2023). The Importance of Values and Culture in Public Administration: A Case Study of Indonesian Local Government. *Khazanah Sosial*, 2(2), 67–77.

Saraswati, L. A. (2017). The gender politics of human waste and human-as-waste: Indonesian migrant workers and elderly care in Japan. *Gender, Work and Organization*, 24(6), 594–609. 10.1111/gwao.12183

Sarif, S., Ali, N. A., & Kamri, N. (2024). Zakat for generating sustainable income: An emerging mechanism of productive distribution. *Cogent Business and Management*, 11(1), 2312598. Advance online publication. 10.1080/23311975.2024.2312598

Sarrica, M., Mingo, I., Mazzara, B. M., & Leone, G. (2016). *The effects of lemmatization on textual analysis conducted with IRaMuTeQ : results in comparison*. Academic Press.

Saunders, M. L., Lewis, P., & Thornhill, A. (2009). *Research methods for business students*. Prentice, Hall.

Saussure, F. (1916). *Course in General Linguistics*. Payot.

Scandura, T., & Williams, E. (2000). Research methodology in management: Current practices, trends, and implications for future research. *Academy of Management Journal*, 43(6), 1248–1264. 10.2307/1556348

Schatzki, T. R., Knorr-Cetina, K., & Von Savigny, E. (Eds.). (2001). *The practice turn in contemporary theory* (Vol. 44). Routledge.

Schultz, P. (2002). Environmental Attitudes and Behaviors Across Cultures. *Online Readings in Psychology and Culture*, 8(1). Advance online publication. 10.9707/2307-0919.1070

Shagrir, L. (2017). The Ethnographic Research. In *Journey to Ethnographic Research. SpringerBriefs in Education.* Springer. 10.1007/978-3-319-47112-9_2

Sharma, G. (2017). Pros and cons of different sampling techniques. *International Journal of Applied Research*, 3(7), 749–752.

Shih, F. (1998). Triangulation in nursing research: Issues of conceptual clarity and purpose. *Journal of Advanced Nursing*, 28(3), 631–641. 10.1046/j.1365-2648.1998.00716.x9756233

Shlasky, S., & Alpert, B. (2007). *Ways of writing qualitative research: From dismantling the reality to structuring the text*. Mofet Institute.

Shutes, I. (2012). The employment of migrant workers in long-term care: Dynamics of choice and control. *Journal of Social Policy*, 41(1), 43–59. 10.1017/S0047279411000596

Siddique, S. (2011). Being in-between: The relevance of ethnography and auto-ethnography for psychotherapy research. *Counselling & Psychotherapy Research*, 11(4), 310–316. 10.1080/14733145.2010.533779

Silverman, D. (2013). *Doing qualitative research* (4th ed.). SAGE.

Singh, N., Benmamoun, M., Meyr, E., & Arikan, R. H. (2021). Verifying rigor: Analyzing qualitative research in international marketing. *International Marketing Review*, 38(6), 1289–1307. 10.1108/IMR-03-2020-0040

Singleton, R. A.Jr, & Straits, B. C. (2005). *Approaches to Social Research* (4th ed.). Oxford University Press.

Sinkovics, R. R., Penz, E., & Ghauri, P. N. (2008). Enhancing the trustworthiness of qualitative research in international business. *MIR. Management International Review*, 48(6), 689–714. 10.1007/s11575-008-0103-z

Smith, B., Ehala, M., & Giles, H. (2018). Vitality theory. In H. Giles & J. Harwood (Eds.), *The Oxford encyclopedia of intergroup communication* (pp. 485-500). New York, NY: Oxford University Press.

Smith, D. E. (1987). The everyday world as problematic: a feminist sociology. Northeastern University Press.

Smith, C. W., & Mayorga-Gallo, S. (2017). The new principle-policy gap: How diversity ideology subverts diversity initiatives. *Sociological Perspectives*, 60(5), 889–911. 10.1177/0731121417719693

Sobh, R., & Perry, C. (2006). Research design and data analysis in realism research. *European Journal of Marketing*, 40(11/12), 1194–1209. 10.1108/03090560610702777

Solano, A. M. M. (2020). Triangulation and trustworthiness—Advancing research on public service interpreting through qualitative case study methodologies. *Fitispos-International Journal*, 4(1), 12–29.

Souza, L. G. S. (2020). Places from which We Speak: The Concepts of Consensual and Reified Universes and the Interpretation of the Outcomes Obtained with ALCESTE and IRAMUTEQ. *Papers on Social Representations*, 29(2), 11–25.

Spears, A. K. (1999). Race and ideology: An introduction. In *Race and ideology: Language, symbolism, and popular culture* (pp. 11–58). Wayne State University Press.

Starck, A., Gutermann, J., Schouler-Ocak, M., Jesuthasan, J., Bongard, S., & Stangier, U. (2020). The relationship of acculturation, traumatic events and depression in female refugees. *Frontiers in Psychology, 11*, 906.

Stratton, S. J. (2019). Data sampling strategies for disaster and emergency health research. *Prehospital and Disaster Medicine*, 34(3), 227–229. 10.1017/S1049023X1900441231204646

Streubert, H. J., & Carpenter, D. R. (2002). *Qualitative research in nursing: Advancing the humanistic imperative* (3rd ed.). Lippincott Williams & Wilkins.

Stupka, R. (2011). Communication accommodation in mixed gender dyads. *Oshkosh Scholar*, 6, 64–78.

Sun, G., & Zhao, L. (2024). The construction of competency training mechanism model for tourism undergraduates based on grounded theory. *PLoS One*, 19(2), e0296683. 10.1371/journal.pone.029668338422000

Suter, E., Deutschlander, S., Mickelson, G., Nurani, Z., Lait, J., Harrison, L., & Grymonpre, R. (2012). Can IPC provide health human resources solutions? A knowledge synthesis. *Journal of Interprofessional Care*, 26(4), 261–268. 10.3109/13561820.2012.66301422390728

Swavely, D., Vandenberg, R. J., & Mostov, K. E. (2022). The Use of Triangulation in Research. *Research in Organizational Behavior*, 4, 287–306. 10.1016/S0191-3085(82)80012-6

Tanggaard, L. (2014). Ethnographic Fieldwork in Psychology: Lost and Found? *Qualitative Inquiry*, 20(2), 167–174. 10.1177/1077800413510876

Tarman, C., & Sears, D. O. (2005). The conceptualization and measurement of symbolic racism. *The Journal of Politics*, 67(3), 731–761. 10.1111/j.1468-2508.2005.00337.x

Tashakkori, A., & Teddlie, C. (2003). *Handbook of Mixed Methods in Social and Behavioral Research*. Sage.

Teddlie, C., & Tashakkori, A. (2009). *Foundations of mixed methods research: Integrating quantitative and qualitative approaches in the social and behavioral sciences*. SAGE Publications.

Tessler, H., Choi, M., & Kao, G. (2020). The anxiety of being Asian American: Hate crimes and negative biases during the COVID-19 pandemic. *American Journal of Criminal Justice*, 45(4), 636–646. 10.1007/s12103-020-09541-532837158

Thurairajah, K. (2019). Uncloaking the researcher: Boundaries in qualitative research. *Qualitative Sociology Review*, 15(1), 132–147. 10.18778/1733-8077.15.1.06

Thurmond, V. (2001). The point of triangulation. *Journal of Nursing Scholarship*, 33(3), 253–258. 10.1111/j.1547-5069.2001.00253.x11552552

Timonen, V., Foley, G., & Conlon, C. (2018). Challenges when using grounded theory. *International Journal of Qualitative Methods*, 17(1). Advance online publication. 10.1177/1609406918758086

Ting-Toomey, S. (1988). Intercultural Conflict Styles: A Face-Negotiation Theory. In Kim, Y. Y., & Gudykunst, W. B. (Eds.), *Theories in Intercultural Communication* (pp. 213–235). Sage.

Ting-Toomey, S. (1999). *Communicating Across Cultures*. Guilford Press.

Ting-Toomey, S., & Chung, L. C. (2012). *Understanding Intercultural Communication*. Oxford University Press.

Tomaszewski, L. E., Zarestky, J., & Gonzalez, E. (2020). Planning Qualitative Research: Design and Decision Making for New Researchers. *International Journal of Qualitative Methods*, 19, 1–7. 10.1177/1609406920967174

Tuck, E., & Yang, K. W. (2014). Unbecoming claims: Pedagogies of refusal in qualitative research. *Qualitative Inquiry*, 20(6), 811–818. 10.1177/1077800414530265

Tuckett, A. (2005). Part ii. rigour in qualitative research: Complexities and solutions. *Nurse Researcher*, 13(1), 29–42. 10.7748/nr2005.07.13.1.29.c599816220839

Tümen-Akyıldız, S., & Ahmed, K. H. (2021). An overview of qualitative research and focus group discussion. *Journal of Academic Research in Education*, 7(1), 1–15. 10.17985/ijare.866762

Turner, D. W. (2016). Qualitative interview design: A practical guide for novice investigators. *The Qualitative Report*, 21(3), 572–586.

Valencia, M. (2022). Principles, scope, and limitations of the methodological triangulation. *Investigacion y Educacion en Enfermeria*, 40(2). Advance online publication. 10.17533/udea.iee.v40n2e03.36264691

Van Riemsdijk, M. (2010). Neoliberal reforms in elder care in Norway: Roles of the state, Norwegian employers, and polish nurses. *Geoforum*, 41(6), 930–939. 10.1016/j.geoforum.2010.06.008

Vasileiou, K., Barnett, J., Thorpe, S., & Young, T. (2018). Characterizing and justifying sample size sufficiency in interview-based studies: Systematic analysis of qualitative health research over a 15-year period. *BMC Medical Research Methodology*, 18(1), 1–18. 10.1186/s12874-018-0594-730463515

Verdonck, M., Chard, G., & Nolan, M. (2010). Electronic aids to daily living: Be able to do what you want. *Disability and Rehabilitation. Assistive Technology*, 6(3), 268–281. 10.3109/17483107.2010.52529120939677

Vigo, D., Jones, W., Dove, N., Maidana, D., Tallon, C., Small, W., & Samji, H. (2021). Estimating the prevalence of mental and substance use disorders: A systematic approach to triangulating available data to inform health systems planning. *Canadian Journal of Psychiatry*, 67(2), 107–116. 10.1177/07067437211006872338227278

Vivek, R. (2023). Theoretical foundations of triangulation in qualitative and multi-method research. *Qualitative Research Journal*, 17(2), 89–104.

Vliegenthart, R., & Van Zoonen, L. (2011). Power to the frame: Bringing sociology back to frame analysis. *European Journal of Communication*, 26(2), 101–115. 10.1177/0267323111404838

Wallerstein, N., Oetzel, J. G., Sanchez-Youngman, S., Boursaw, B., Dickson, E., Kastelic, S., Koegel, P., Lucero, J. E., Magarati, M., Ortiz, K., Parker, M., Peña, J., Richmond, A., & Duran, B. (2020). Engage for equity: A long-term study of community-based participatory research and community-engaged research practices and outcomes. *Health Education & Behavior*, 47(3), 380–390. 10.1177/1090198119989707532437293

Wall, S. (2006). An autoethnography on learning about autoethnography. *International Journal of Qualitative Methods*, 5(2), 146–160. 10.1177/160940690600500205

Wang, C., & Burris, M. A. (1997). Photovoice: Concept, methodology, and use for participatory needs assessment. *Health Education & Behavior*, 24(3), 369–387. 10.1177/109019819702400309158980

Wardina & Sudihartinih. (2019). Description of student's junior high school mathematical connection ability on the linear function topic. *Journal of Mathematics Science and Education, 4*(1), 53-60.

Warikoo, N. K., & De Novais, J. (2015). Colour-blindness and diversity: Race frames and their consequences for white undergraduates at elite US universities. *Ethnic and Racial Studies*, 38(6), 860–876. 10.1080/01419870.2014.964281

Weda, Z. L., & Lemmer, E. M. (2024). Managing status: A grounded theory of teacher migration from Zimbabwe to south Africa. *Mediterranean Journal of Social Sciences*, 5(7), 416–425. 10.5901/mjss.2014.v5n7p416

Welch, C., & Marschan-Piekkari, R. (2017). How should we (not) judge the 'quality' of qualitative research? A reassessment of current evaluative criteria in International Business. *Journal of World Business*, 52(5), 714–725. 10.1016/j.jwb.2017.05.007

Wickrama, K. A., Beiser, M., & Kaspar, V. (2002). Assessing the longitudinal course of depression and economic integration of South-East Asian refugees: An application of latent growth curve analysis. *International Journal of Methods in Psychiatric Research*, 11(4), 154–168. 10.1002/mpr.13312459819

Williams, A. M., & Irurita, V. F. (2005). Enhancing the therapeutic potential of hospital environments by increasing the personal control and emotional comfort of hospitalized patients. *Applied Nursing Research*, 18(1), 22–28. 10.1016/j.apnr.2004.11.00115812732

Willis, E., Xiao, L. D., Morey, W., Jeffers, L., Harrington, A., Gillham, D., & De Bellis, A. (2018). New migrants in residential aged care: Managing diversity in not-for- profit organizations. *Journal of International Migration and Integration*, 19(3), 683–700. 10.1007/s12134-018-0564-2

Wingfield, A. H., & Feagin, J. (2012). The racial dialectic: President Barack Obama and the white racial frame. *Qualitative Sociology*, 35(2), 143–162. 10.1007/s11133-012-9223-7

Wolcott, H., F. (1999). *Ethnography: A way of seeing*. A Division of Rowman & Littlefield Publisher, Inc.

Woodland, L., Blignault, I., O'Callaghan, C., & Harris-Roxas, B. (2021). A framework for preferred practices in conducting culturally competent health research in a multicultural society. *Health Research Policy and Systems*, 19(1), 1–11. 10.1186/s12961-020-00657-y33602261

Woods, M., Macklin, R., & Lewis, G. K. (2016). Researcher reflexivity: Exploring the impacts of CAQDAS use. *International Journal of Social Research Methodology*, 19(4), 385–403. 10.1080/13645579.2015.1023964

Wray, N., Marković, M., & Manderson, L. (2007). "Researcher saturation": The impact of data triangulation and intensive-research practices on the researcher and qualitative research process. *Qualitative Health Research*, 17(10), 1392–1402. 10.1177/104973230730830818000078

Xu, Y., & Fang, F. (2024). Promoting educational equity: The implementation of translanguaging pedagogy in English language education. *International Journal of Language Studies*, 18(1), 53–80. 10.5281/zenodo.10468187

Yin, R. K. (2015). *Qualitative Research from Start to Finish*. Guilford Publications.

Young, T. J. (2015). Questionnaires and surveys. *Research Methods in Intercultural Communication: A Practical Guide*, 163-180. .10.1002/9781119166283.ch11

Youngs, H. & Piggot-Irvine, E. (2011). The application of a multiphase triangulation approach to mixed methods. *Z*, 6(3), 184-198. 10.1177/1558689811420696

Zachrison, M. (2014). *Invisible voices: Understanding the Sociocultural Influences on Adult Migrants' Second Language Learning and Communicative Interaction* [Doctoral thesis, Linköpings University]. Retrieved from https://urn.kb.se/resolve?urn=urn:nbn:se:mau:diva-7388

Zheng-ying, L. (2021). An Empirical Study of Software Project Management Based on the Triangulation Method. *Frontiers in Psychology*, 12, 670153. 10.3389/fpsyg.2021.670153

Zwaan, L., Viljoen, R., & Aiken, D. (2019). The role of neuroleadership in work engagement. *SA Journal of Human Resource Management*, 17. Advance online publication. 10.4102/sajhrm.v17i0.1172

About the Contributors

Ali Elhami is a faculty member at the Unicaf university. He obtained his PhD from the univesridad autónoma de Madrid and has since been actively involved in conducting research and publishing his findings in reputable academic journals. His expertise lies in the fields of culture, migration, international students, acculturation, social adjustment, intergroup contact, identity, communication accommodation theory (CAT), and language learning. Additionally, he has a passion for working with diverse groups and enjoys the process of writing papers to disseminate his research findings. He is open to collaboration with fellow researchers and is particularly interested in interdisciplinary projects that can provide a comprehensive understanding of the subjects he investigates. He is also a board member of several international journals and regularly attends conferences and workshops to stay updated on the latest research in his field. Furthermore, he actively seeks opportunities to engage with community organizations and educational institutions to apply his expertise and contribute to the development of inclusive policies and programs.

Anita Roshan obtained her PhD with an international mention in philosophy and language science at the Universidad Autónoma de Madrid (UAM). Her research is situated in the field of sociolinguistics, with a special focus on language socialization, trajectories, language investment, social identity, ethnography, migration, diversity, and inclusion. Moreover, she is a reviewer in two peer-reviewed open-access journals, the MEXTESOL Journal and the International Journal of English and Comparative Literacy Studies. She is open to collaboration with fellow researchers and is particularly interested in interdisciplinary projects that can provide a comprehensive understanding of the subjects she investigates.

Harish Chandan retired as Professor of Business at Argosy University, Atlanta. He was interim chair of the business program in 2011. He received President's award for excellence in teaching in 2007, 2008 and 2009. His teaching philosophy is grounded in the learner needs and life-long learning. His research interests include research methods, leadership, marketing, and organizational behavior. He has published 20 peer-reviewed articles in business journals and five chapters in business reference books. Dr. Chandan has presented conference papers at Academy of Management, International Academy of Business and Management, Southeast Association of Information Systems, and Academy of International Business. Prior to joining Argosy, Dr. Chandan managed optical fiber and cable product qualification laboratories for Lucent Technologies, Bell Laboratories. During his career with Lucent, he had 40 technical publications, a chapter in a book and five patents.

* * *

Katherine Rose Adams is the Program Coordinator for and Assistant Professor in the Higher Education Leadership and Practice doctoral program at the University of North Georgia. Katherine teaches coursework on higher education leadership theory, qualitative research, student affairs administration, and law and ethics in higher education. Her research interests are in the areas of boundary spanning, higher education leadership, community engagement theory, university-community partnerships, student homelessness, and qualitative research communication. Katherine is an Associate Editor for the Journal of Community Engagement and Scholarship.

Handan Akkaş obtained her Ph.D by completing her doctoral education at Hacettepe University, Department of Business Administration, in 2020. Same year she joined the teaching staff of Ankara Bilim University, Department of Management Information Systems. She is currently working as a postdoc researcher in Social Psychology department at Tilburg University. Her academic interests include culture, acculturation, and research methods.

El Houssain Attak, Ph.D., is a Professor at the National School of Business and Management from Cadi Ayyad University, Marrakech, Morocco, affiliated with the Research Laboratory in Innovation, Responsibilities, and Sustainable Development (INREDD). He has published his research work in various indexed journals.

Casey Allison Esmeraldo, UNICAF University, Department of Law, is a second-year law student at UNICAF University in Zambia. She is currently building a solid foundation in legal studies with a focus on criminal and international law. Casey Esmeraldo has a keen interest in criminal law, international law and psychology. She is particularly fascinated by topics such as international criminal justice, transnational crime and human rights law. Additionally, she is exploring the intersection of multicultural studies and law. While focused on her studies, Casey Esmeraldo aims to contribute to the academic community through writings and her research in fields of interest. As a second-year student, Casey Esmeraldo is in the process of developing her academic writing and research skills. She plans to contribute to academic journals and conferences in the near future.

Howard Giles is a British-American social psychologist, a Distinguished Research Professor of Communication at the Department of Communication, University of California, Santa Barbara, and an honorary professor at the University of Queensland. He is Founding & Consulting Editor of both the Journal of Language & Social Psychology (1980-) and the Journal of Asian Pacific Communication (1990-). Past President of the International Communication Association (ICA: 2000-01), he is a Distinguished Research Professor of Communication at the University of California, Santa Barbara, and an Honorary Professor in the School of Psychology at the University of Queensland, Australia. He was also a former Reserve Detective Lieutenant at the Santa Barbara Police Department and was its Founding Director of Volunteers in Policing (2017-). He is an elected Fellow of eight learned societies (e.g., the Royal Society of Medicine) and recipient of numerous academic awards, including the inaugural Career Productivity Award from ICA in 2000. Giles has researched language and communication across a range of intergroup settings, including police-community and intergenerational ones, and published 30 books, 20 journal special issues, Handbooks, and an Encyclopedia, as well as many hundreds of academic articles and chapters.

Kelly Burmeister Long is an Assistant Professor in the Ed.D. program in Higher Education Leadership and Practice at the University of North Georgia (UNG). Prior to UNG, she served as the Assistant Vice President of Institutional Research at a private college and held a similar role at a community college. In these roles, she oversaw accreditation, assessment, business intelligence, and external reporting. She has also worked as a Survey Methodologist at Boston Children's Hospital and Mayo Clinic. She is a former editor and long-time peer reviewer for the Community College Journal of Research and Practice and is a peer reviewer for the Higher Learning Commission. Dr. Long holds a M.S. in Survey Methodology from the University of Michigan and a Ph.D. in Education Leadership from Oakland University.

Maha Mennani is a Researcher Ph.D. Candidate at the Research Laboratory in Innovation, Responsibilities, and Sustainable Development (INREDD), National School of Business and Management from Cadi Ayyad University, Marrakech, Morocco, whose research interests focus on analyzing zakat's compliance behavior in the Moroccan context.

Cem Harun Meydan is a professor of management at the Management Information Systems department. He has a diverse academic background, including Systems Engineering, an MBA, and a PhD in Defense Management. He is currently pursuing a second PhD in Aviation Management. Prof. Meydan specializes in management, strategic management, and organizational behavior. Additionally, he teaches research methods courses that include statistical analysis, information technologies, and statistical quality management. Prof. Meydan has a prolific research career and has authored numerous studies published in reputable journals and books, which have received over 4000 citations. Since 2020, Prof. Meydan has held important positions at Ankara Science University, serving as the Acting Dean of the Faculty of Humanities and Social Sciences, as well as Vice Rector, demonstrating a commitment to academic leadership and excellence.

Aissa Mosbah is an assistant professor of entrepreneurship and the Department of Marketing and Entrepreneurship, Dhofar University, Oman. He obtained a master's degree in international business and a PhD in Management from Malaysian universities. His PhD research dealt with the immigrant entrepreneurship phenomenon. Aissa is expert in both qualitative and quantitative research, and his research areas include entrepreneurship, family business, firm internationalization, and organizational behavior.

Isidro Miguel Martín Pérez has a Bachelor degree in Medicine from the Universidad de La Laguna (Spain) Expert University degree in Applied Statistics to Health Sciences from the Universidad de Valencia (Spain) Doctorate in Medical and Pharmaceutical Sciences, Development, and Quality of Life at the School of Doctoral and Postgraduate Studies at the Universidad de La Laguna (Spain) Researcher in Department of Pharmacology and Physical Medicine from the Universidad de La Laguna (Spain).

Sebastián Eustaquio Martín Pérez is a Professor in the Faculty of Health Sciences at the Universidad Europea de Canarias (Spain) Bachelor degree in Physiotherapy from the Universidad de La Laguna (Spain) Master's degree in Orthopedic Manual Therapy in the treatment of Pain from the Universidad Europea de Canarias (Spain) Expert University degree in Health Sciences Research from the Universidad de Alcalá de Henares (Spain) Expert University degree in Applied Statistics to Health Sciences from the Universidad de Valencia (Spain) Doctorate in Medical and Pharmaceutical Sciences, Development, and Quality of Life at the School of Doctoral and Postgraduate Studies at the Universidad de La Laguna (Spain) Researcher in Department of Pharmacology and Physical Medicine from the Universidad de La Laguna (Spain).

| **Mariam Sahraoui** obtained her PhD in French didactics at the Faculty of Letters and Human Sciences Mohammedia, Hassan 2 University. She is dedicated to qualitative research, interculturality, FSP (French for Specific Purposes) didactics, the study of innovative pedagogical practices, the integration of digital technologies in teaching, the analysis of classroom interactions and their impact on learning, intercultural approaches in French teaching, strategies for pedagogical differentiation to meet the diverse needs of learners, as well as teacher training, management of linguistic competencies in multilingual contexts, and the impact of educational policies on didactic practices. Between 2019 and 2024, she conducted a thesis titled "The Teaching and Learning of French for Specific Purposes: For Linguistic Integration of Second-Year Professional Baccalaureate Commerce Students in the Professional Field." She also obtained a Master's degree in Didactics of French as a Foreign Language from Abdelmalek Essaâdi University in 2019, a Bachelor's degree in French Studies and Education from Mohamed 5 University in 2014, and a Baccalaureate in Life and Earth Sciences from Imam Al Ghazali High School.

Index

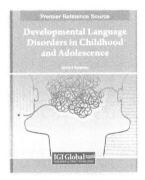

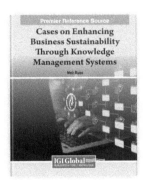

Ensure Quality Research is Introduced to the Academic Community

Become a Reviewer for IGI Global Authored Book Projects

Premier Reference Source

The Use of Artificial Intelligence in Digital Marketing

Competitive Strategies and Tactics

IGI Global

Premier Reference Source

Innovations in Materials Chemistry, Physics, and Engineering Research

Eugene de Silva and Pramudi Abeydeera

IGI Global

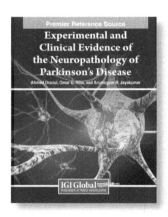

Premier Reference Source

Experimental and Clinical Evidence of the Neuropathology of Parkinson's Disease

Ahmed Draoui, Omar El Hiba, and Arunugam R. Jayakumar

IGI Global

Premier Reference Source

Balance and Boundaries in Creating Meaningful Relationships in Online Higher Education

Sarah H. Jarvie and Cara Metz

IGI Global

The overall success of an authored book project is dependent on quality and timely manuscript evaluations.

Applications and Inquiries may be sent to:
development@igi-global.com

Applicants must have a doctorate (or equivalent degree) as well as publishing, research, and reviewing experience. Authored Book Evaluators are appointed for one-year terms and are expected to complete at least three evaluations per term. Upon successful completion of this term, evaluators can be considered for an additional term.

If you have a colleague that may be interested in this opportunity, we encourage you to share this information with them.

www.igi-global.com

Milton Keynes UK
Ingram Content Group UK Ltd.
UKHW011626110824
446692UK00023B/60